SRK and Global Bollywood

SRK and Global Bollywood

Edited by
Rajinder Dudrah, Elke Mader, and
Bernhard Fuchs

OXFORD
UNIVERSITY PRESS

OXFORD
UNIVERSITY PRESS

Oxford University Press is a department of the University of Oxford.
It furthers the University's objective of excellence in research, scholarship,
and education by publishing worldwide. Oxford is a registered trademark of
Oxford University Press in the UK and in certain other countries

Published in India by
Oxford University Press
YMCA Library Building, 1 Jai Singh Road, New Delhi 110 001, India

ISBN-13: 978-0-19-946047-2
ISBN-10: 0-19-946047-7

Typeset in 10.5/13 Goudy Oldstyle Std
by Excellent Laser Typesetters, Pitampura, Delhi 110 034

Attempts made to inform Shah Rukh Khan's office about the inclusion of
'Message from Shah Rukh Khan' in this volume remain unsuccessful.

Contents

Acknowledgements

This book is based on the conference 'Shah Rukh Khan and Global Bollywood' that took place in Vienna in 2010. This three-day event brought together scholars from various subject disciplines in the arts, humanities, and social sciences to confer about a wide range of topics concerning the global cultural phenomenon of Shah Rukh Khan and Bollywood cinema. The editors wish to thank the funding institutions: the Austrian Ministry for Science and Research, the University of Vienna, the city of Vienna, the Austrian Research Association (ÖFG), the Weltmuseum (Museum of the World), and the Embassy of India in Vienna for their support. We want to thank all the participants of the conference for their contributions and discussions during the event and over many emails afterwards. We also note our gratitude to: Martin Gaenszle, Deana Heath, Meru Jaffer Hasnain, Christian Schicklgruber, and Claus Tieber for their activities on the committee and beyond; Nasreen Munni Kabir for her support and invaluable input during the conference; Satish Gandhi, Adelheid Herrmann-Pfandt, Maria-Stella Hinterndorfer, and Mira Lau for their special engagement with the conference and the exhibition of representations of Shah Rukh Khan in popular material and visual culture; Monika Hunjadi, Christian Rogler, Nat Satavet, Kerstin Tiefenbacher, and many others for managing the organizational tasks. Special thanks also go to Anna Ellmer for her work on the preparation of the manuscript of the book prior to its submission. We are grateful to colleagues at Oxford University Press and to the two anonymous readers for their insightful comments on an earlier draft of the manuscript. The editors are also thankful to all the individual contributors for working with us on this project from its conception to its publication and for adhering to our writing deadlines and our requests for editorial or peer review changes. The collaborative effort has been a real pleasure.

Message from Shah Rukh Khan[*]

I would like to begin by thanking the president of the Republic of Austria for his message, the vice chancellor of the University of Vienna, Arthur Mettinger, the deputy director of the Museum of Ethnology, Barbara Plankensteiner, His Excellency Dinkar Khullar, the Ambassador of India, and all the dignitaries, scholars, and friends who have come here today.

I would also like to thank Vice Dean Elke Mader and her team for initiating and organizing what I believe to be a most humbling event. I am truly overwhelmed to be the subject of a three-day seminar in this gorgeous country, Austria.

I am primarily an entertainer, everything else is rather incidental or accidental. I am blessed to have had the opportunity to touch hearts and bring smiles. The love, or at least the attention, of all you lovely people is my greatest remuneration and reward which drives me to go beyond my limitations and excel and, if I may add, the paycheck is not bad either.

The language of cinema erases boundaries of nationality, caste, creed, religion, and unites and enthrals the individual who submits himself to the darkness of a cinema hall and brings to him smiles, tears, and takes him on a journey away to a different world of

---

[*] This message was delivered at the opening of the conference 'Shah Rukh Khan and the Global Bollywood' on 30 September 2010 in Vienna, Austria.

enchantment for 90 minutes, or three hours if you are watching an Indian film. At times this journey is just enjoyable *and* at other times it leaves an indelible impression. This journey could be in the present, past, or future, or to a non-existent land but it always reflects a part of our society that is, has been, or could be. I am truly honoured and blessed to be one of the many presenters of this magical journey.

The various distinguished speakers at this forum I believe are not just mere spectators of cinema, instead they have dedicated time and effort to analyse *the impact of cinema* beyond the realms of the obvious and I salute their effort. Their efforts, this study, and interpretations will be noteworthy to say the least and teach us to understand the cinematic art and its impact around the world much better.

I am most proud, that my being discussed here today is evidence to the fact that Indian cinema has already made in-roads into the hearts of people in nearly every corner of the globe and am hopeful that this effort will contribute in creating close and emotional bonds between India and the rest of the world.

I wish I could have been here in person and participate in this conference, but my shooting schedule could not be changed. It would have been enriching to see my minuscule contribution to this art form being deconstructed. I believe deconstruction leads to a more creative and constructive teaching than any other form of discussion. It would have been my great pleasure to be in Vienna and share with you our thoughts on cinema, but I do assure you all that I am with you in spirit with all my love and best wishes.

P.S. *My kids believe I can fly, but they still don't believe that there is a conference being held with me as a subject. Thank you all for your interest.*

SHAH RUKH KHAN

Introduction

RAJINDER DUDRAH, ELKE MADER, AND
BERNHARD FUCHS

Stardom and Globalized Polysemy

A market stand in a small village in the Peruvian Andes sells Shah Rukh Khan (henceforth SRK) posters; a street vendor in Ghana offers DVDs of SRK films to passers-by. In Berlin, hundreds of German fans line the streets to catch a glimpse of the star when he presents one of his films at the Berlinale Film Festival; Russian or Austrian fan groups travel to Mumbai to see him wave to the crowd in front of his home on his birthday; at the Zee Carnival in London, the 'meet and greet' sessions with SRK draw thousands of fans from the South Asian diaspora as well as from diverse European countries to the fair. SRK presented the award-winning movie *Slumdog Millionaire* (Dir. Danny Boyle, 2008) at the Golden Globe in Los Angeles; together with Karan Johar and Kajol he toured the UK and the USA to promote *My Name Is Khan* (*MNIK*, Dir. Karan Johar, 2010) before attending its double premiere in Abu Dhabi and Berlin. SRK cheers his cricket team Kolkata Knight Riders along the international circuits of the Indian Premiere League (IPL); he performs on stage at diverse spectacular events worldwide; and endorses a wide range of consumer goods of local and global reach.

His film roles and his productions, his engagement with sports, art, and the commercial world as well as his daily life are the topic of myriads of TV interviews and press items that circulate in the global mediascape of the Internet. He interacts with millions of people worldwide on Twitter. Last but not least, his films are watched and admired by audiences dispersed widely around the globe.

During the past decade, the accelerated globalization of Bollywood has been strongly connected with SRK as a star, an entrepreneur of the cultural industry, and an icon for India and *Indianness*. In the case of SRK, Richard Dyer's (2003: 8) classic statement that 'stars articulate what it is to be a human being in contemporary society' is closely associated with the diverse aspects of globalization. This applies to his films and the characters he embodies, his activities as a star and producer, and his audiences.

The leading part that SRK has been playing in global Bollywood and the 'Bollywoodization of Indian cinema' (Rajadhyaksha 2003) goes hand in hand with changes in regard to production, circulation, and reception of Indian films as well as with transformations in cinematic styles and content. Virdi and Creekmur (2006: 133) argue that popular Hindi cinema is 'ingeniously reinventing itself' in accordance with its expanded circulation and consumption. Signs of globalization are invoked through stories, the use of a 'creative geography', and stars that represent the cosmopolitan India(n). Indian stars are 'national icons of beauty, desire, and utopian beings' (Dwyer 2000: 119) and SRK has been associated with several dimensions of Indianness throughout his career ranging from urban or cosmopolitan and diasporic identities (for example, cf. Dudrah 2006 and 2012; Dwyer 2000) to Indian secularism and changing modalities of national identity in a globalized world (Rao 2009). The significance of SRK as a global player is also closely connected with contemporary celebrity culture. As Nayar (2009: 3) states: 'the most unique feature of celebrity culture today, especially in metropolises after the advent and spread of mass media, is its global nature.' Stardom and celebrity culture cut across linguistic, regional, and national borders, and the circulation–reception of celebrities often moves through the scales of development and economy, as in the First World and Third World, upper class and lower class, and integrates diverse, often uneven, cultures into the fold of celebrity culture.

Accordingly, SRK's star image can be best designated as 'globalized polysemy'[1]: it comprises a wide range of meanings in regard to diverse fields of representation and agency that are interconnected with processes of globalization. This includes not only the polysemy of his movies for different fans around the world, but also allows him to become an ideal brand ambassador for multiple products ranging from everyday items such as washing powder and drinking chocolate to high-end material goods.

Stardom and SRK's Biography

SRK not only represents globalized polysemy in the characters he plays on-screen, but also in his entire 'celebrity ecology' that includes visual, material, textual, oral, commercial and non-commercial, personal and public components working in tandem (Nayar 2009: 22). Marshall (1997: xi) argues that stardom and celebrity, comprise an active construction of identity in the social world and can be understood as one form of resolution of the role and position of the individual and his or her potential in modern society. The blurring of boundaries between the private and public and the idea of an authentic individual behind the public persona make celebrity images particularly potent social symbols (Meyers 2009: 891).

SRK (born 2 November 1965) grew up in a Muslim middle-class family in New Delhi with wider ancestral roots in pre-Partition Peshawar and Afghanistan. He earned a degree in economics, studied mass communication, and gained acting experience in the Theatre Action Group while at college. In 1991 he married Gauri Chibber, a Punjabi Hindu, and since then his family life has become a vital element of his star persona. Several aspects of his biography such as the early death of his parents, his interreligious marriage, his life at his homes in Mumbai (Mannat) and in London with his wife, his children (Aryan, Suhana, and AbRam), and his sister (Shahnaz) are a continuous topic in innumerable interviews that constitute significant elements in the construction and reception of his personal affairs. His family life has also featured in various documentaries (most prominently in Nasreen Munni Kabir's *Inner and Outer World of Shah Rukh Khan*, 2005) and has become an important part of SRK's statements on Twitter during the past years and connects the 'inner world' of his personal life with the 'outer world' of globalized media practices (see Mader, this volume). This also applies to other fields of activities and their global reach, for example, as an entrepreneur in the film industry and beyond (Vajdovich, this volume), or as an owner of a cricket team, the Kolkata Knight Riders that plays—just like the star himself—on the interface of national and international spaces. Furthermore, SRK represents a liberal Islam; he is often seen in his private and public life as standing for religious tolerance and cosmopolitanism and is engaged in a wide range of humanitarian and ecological projects.

The close connection between Bollywood and SRK's super stardom which also flows outside the cinematic texts has been a topic of several biographies which constitute a connection between star studies and the film industry (Chopra 2007; Mehra 2006; Shiekh 2006 and 2009a). Furthermore, they have been received extensively by the international fan community and have partially also been published in German translation (for example, Chopra 2008; Shiekh 2009b). Anupama Chopra's book *King of Bollywood* (2007) is based on extensive interviews with the star and intertwines film studies and journalism. It contextualizes his life, his career, and his films within the larger framework of Indian cinema and society, and provides insights into the interconnections between his life story, the rise of his star status as the 'King of Bollywood', and the developments of the film industry during the past decades. A different approach is represented in Shiekh's book *Still Reading Khan* (2006) that combines biography (based once more on extensive interviews), aspects of popular cultural studies, and visual culture. It integrates a substantial collection of pictures of SRK with detailed excerpts from interviews about various stages of his career in connection with his work and his roles in the respective films. Furthermore, it includes analytical chapters, for example, on SRK, gender and the erotic gaze, or on endorsement and branding (Shiekh 2006). Whereas both authors have also written books on films starring SRK (Chopra 2003; Shiekh 2001 and 2008), furthermore, Mushtaq Shiekh has been engaged as a scriptwriter for *Om Shanti Om* (Dir. Farah Khan, 2007) and *Billu* (Dir. Priyadarshan, 2009). These films were produced by SRK's company Red Chillies

Entertainment (a joint venture undertaken with wife Gauri Khan) and comprise an overt star text that merges the protagonist with elements of SRK's star persona (for example, the use of popular photographs and endorsements).

Following on from Dyer (1998, 2003: ix), interconnections between SRK's stardom and his wide range of activities on- and off-screen also play a crucial role in bringing together the star, as he is seen as a set of media signs, with the various ways in which people feel about him as being able to communicate something for them. Such processes are, on the one hand, linked to the personal life of the star, and, on the other hand, to his representation of various roles on-screen (see also Dwyer, this volume). Both dimensions of this process are part of an overarching dynamic of the construction of meaning that arises from an interaction with the plurality of social, symbolic, and discursive spaces. As Mazumdar (2000) has demonstrated, in relation to Amitabh Bachchan in the 1970s as the 'angry young man' and SRK in the early 1990s as the 'psychotic' hero in the film *Darr* (Dir. Yash Chopra, 1993), star images are interconnected with multiple contexts on- and off-screen. These processes go hand in hand with a blurring of boundaries between the character and the actor, thus investing the body with a new mobility. The polymorphous body of the performer as well as complex processes of masking and de-masking—in the case of the early SRK films with regard to the image of the psychotic—reflect and transform the larger framework of society, and constitute the cultural politics of performance (Mazumdar 2000: 240). Thus, the globalized polysemy of SRK should be understood as a result of various transformative processes that embrace his private life, his performance as a public persona, his multiple activities in the film industry and related entertainment media, as well as his embodiment of diverse heroic and anti-heroic roles.

Phir Bhi Dil Hai NRI[2]

Another important dimension of SRK's globalized polysemy is linked to his on-screen star text connected with issues of migration, diaspora, and transnationalism and their significance for the relationship between the local and the global. A prevailing theme in this context has been his embodiment of Indianness in the transnational space. From *Dilwale Dulhania Le Jayenge* (*DDLJ*, Dir. Aditya Chopra, 1995) to *Jab Tak Hai Jaan* (Dir. Yash Chopra, 2012), SRK has been the most prominent hero of Bollywood's stories about the figure of the NRI who struggles with, and then mediates, the challenges of transnationalism. In Arjun Appadurai's (1996: 31) terms, such films underline the significance of the 'work of imagination' in regard to the reproduction of culture in global contexts as well as for the 'complex transnational construction of imaginary landscapes'. SRK's roles and film texts negotiate the aspirations of rising middle- and upper-middle-class Indian values and symbols around cultural and national identity. Often, when he is wooing the British-Asian heroine, in either aforementioned film, there is almost always a return to the homeland for renewal and sustenance in order to reset one's moral compass. In *Swades: We, the People* (Dir. Ashutosh Gowariker, 2004), SRK can be seen as an elite NRI, a scientist employed by NASA, who finally decides to return to India to improve the living conditions of the rural poor. The movie takes up issues of patriotism, diasporic philanthropy, and grass-roots politics. Different from other NRI movies, here the involvement with the homeland becomes de-glamourized, transformed from sentimental gestures of remembrance to material engagement and social work (Sinha 2012: 193). SRK's roles and films mediate and negotiate a transnational sense of being Indian and diasporic, most notably in Europe and the USA, through a cultural ideology which, more generally, has its moorings in India and South Asia. Part of the textual pleasures of his roles and films are to do with offering audiences these local and global imaginations through the fictional stories of popular Hindi cinema.

Rachel Dwyer (this volume) examines SRK and Karan Johar films to ask why they are set partially or wholly in an imaginary diaspora, usually in the UK or the USA, yet in which the lead character played by SRK has his lifestyle and language marked as Indian rather than as diasporic. She suggests reasons why these films are so popular at home and overseas, what SRK comes to represent in them, and why he can be called a diasporic star. She argues that his stardom is closely connected with his enactment of emotions; SRK represents a modern Indian emotionality which appeals to his audience as a gentle, suffering person; and it is perhaps a sign that emotions are valued differently by the new middle classes and the diaspora in their negotiation of new values in India and overseas.

SRK has also become a multidimensional icon for the social sensibilities of everyday life in transnational communities and 'world families' (Beck and Beck-Gernsheim 2014), as well as for processes of continuity and change of South Asian cultures and Indianness in postcolonial constellations. In *Kabhi Khushi Kabhie Gham...* (K3G, Dir. Karan Johar, 2001), for example, the topic of the transnational family is combined with motifs from the Ramayana and represents 'the repackage of traditions to suit this new modern world' (Dwyer 2006: 156). Furthermore, as Rahul in *K3G* or Aman in *Kal Ho Naa Ho* (*KHNH*, Dirs Nikhil Advani and Ron Reid Jr., 2003) SRK enacts, negotiates, and integrates multiple meanings in connection with diasporic cosmopolitanism.[3] In *KHNH* he dances—both with Preity Zinta and Saif Ali Khan—through a wide range of transnational scenarios ranging from a 'traditional' wedding to diverse cosmopolitan contexts and locations (most notably in *Pretty woman* or *It's the time to disco*)[4] and his star image becomes part of the negotiation of the possibilities and limitations of the 'bothness' of cultural or national selves and globalized values (cf. Glick Schiller, Darieva, and Gruner-Domic 2011).

Social sensibilities of everyday life are also discussed by Kamala Ganesh and Kanchana Mahadevan (this volume) who focus on the construction of new masculinities in SRK and Karan Johar films. They demonstrate that these movies are not simply reducible to exclusive endorsements of conservative family values, but also reveal subversive elements in the portrayal of SRK in a softer or 'non-hegemonic masculinity' (Connell 2005) that questions machismo, critiques traditional family, and advocates a post-national spirit, transcending the Indian diaspora towards a global audience. These films and SRK's star persona have had particular significance in transforming the Bollywood family-film formula and the representation of intimate relationships and masculinities. The collaboration between SRK and Karan Johar is also discussed by Jaspreet Gill (this volume) who emphasizes the significance of the film *MNIK* for the creation of a new (globalized as well as diasporic) Muslim hero. Gill's chapter explores the multiple interconnections between the film's focus on the family and interpersonal relationships between family members with questions of belonging to national and diasporic identities that concern Muslim Indians in the larger context of a globalized world. Gill argues that *MNIK* is a clear avowal of SRK's global star power as the film moves beyond the local to engage in larger, global concerns of the representation of Muslims and their societal status.

The Global Player

Globalized polysemy and cosmopolitanism in regard to the star text of SRK is not limited to his representation of the NRI, but comprises a large variety of elements related to global flows in and out of India. Films like *Chak De! India* (Dir. Shimit Amin, 2007), *Don: The Chase Begins Again* and *Don 2* (Dir. Farhan Akhtar, 2006 and 2011 respectively), or *Ra.One* (Dir. Anubhav Sinha, 2011) invoke signs of globalization in various contexts ranging from sports, gender, and nationhood, stylized material culture in relation to the world of organized crime, and emerging new intermedia contexts in India, where film interacts with videogames (see Ashish Rajadhyaksha, this volume). An analysis of *Chak De! India* (Villarejo, this volume) provides insights into the changing modalities of Indian national identity in a globalizing world and into the transformations certain forms of Indian culture have wrought globally. Through the genre of hockey, notions of gender and the nation are articulated to argue for India's prominence on the international sporting and cultural landscape as a team of young women take on conservative mores at home and cultural prejudices overseas. Symbols of globalization are also encoded in SRK movies in multiple ways: one example is the visual and material culture in the world of *Don: The Chase Begins Again* as Aradhana Seth—the production designer of this movie—explains in her contribution, co-authored with Bernhard Fuchs, locations, objects, and colours in the film that have been chosen to construct a notion of cosmopolitanism and globalization that distinguishes the 'old Don' and the 'old India' from a 'new Don' who is portrayed as a global player and incorporates parts of SRK's star persona. This comparison of the 'original' *Don* (Dir. Chandra Barot, 1978) with Amitabh Bachchan in the leading role and its remake with SRK highlights transformations in the Indian film industry resulting from economic liberalization and the spread of consumerist aspirations in society; mutual influences between production design, star texts, and different socio-political contexts are discussed. From this perspective, cinema is more than a reflection of social condition, it also gives expression to dominant values and thus contributes to the creation of the spirit of a time. In the set design of the 2006 remake, abstract notions of globalization, Indianness, Occidentalism, and Asianness become an aesthetic experience invested with specific meanings. Moreover, Ann R. David (this volume) examines how songs and their accompanying dance choreographies form a significant element in the analysis of SRK's global appeal. Song-and-dance sequences are effective on many levels within a specific film; they often create an imagined fantasy space, intensifying the emotional content of the story and offering suggestions of eroticism. She elaborates this aspect of SRK's global polysemy through an investigation of his appearances in the dance sequences of films such as *Dil Se..* (Dir. Mani Ratnam, 1998), *Asoka* (Dir. Santosh Sivan, 2001), and *Om Shanti Om*. Aesthetic engagement with the SRK-persona is far from restricted to the audio-visual-textual elements; intensive emotional involvements as well as bodily and haptic experiences produced by dance practices, and the consumption of star-related commodities or location tourism come together to form a 'corpothetic' mode of reception (Pinney 2008). This includes hybrid, semi-devotional fan-practices that are partially influenced by traditions of Indian aesthetics such as darshan,[5] where notions of the semi-divine and star-gazing coalesce. In his contribution to this volume, Bernhard Fuchs studies this field of transcultural exchange focusing on creative practices developed around a celebrity doll which represents SRK. This UK-based enterprise can exemplify how diverse ancillary industries are emerging as a corollary of the globalization of the Indian film industry. This commodity is circulated within international networks of fans as an object and also in digitized visuals. Again, polysemy can be found in the multiple meanings of the doll. Fuchs' contribution analyses a wide range of perceptions of this item: from the perspective of the entrepreneur to the discourses of fans, and what the doll means in SRK's own eyes.

Within this complex assemblage of meanings of local/global relations is, as Sudhanva Deshpande (2005: 197) puts it, SRK's image as the new 'consumable hero of globalized India' wherein he embodies new fantasies of consumer culture. Here, he usually does not dance with Indian peasants but rather with white girls, in front of McDonald's outlets, wearing GAP shirts and Nike sneakers. Shakuntala Rao describes such films as dreamworlds that have taken on new meanings and signifiers, and articulate the forces of globalization. This dreamworld is represented in terms of the material, spatial, and personal. The globalized Indian in Bollywood films is represented by the upper-class urban Indian who has enough material wealth to cross national or cultural borders fluidly, travel to exotic locales, and be a modern-day hyperconsumer (Rao 2007: 65, 69).

Besides his global image, SRK comes close to being a pan-Indian movie star. In India, the admiration for film stars is part of public culture, and active audiences combine popular or visual culture, ritual practices, politics, and civic engagement (for example, Nayar 2009: 146). These dimensions of fandom in India are expressed most visibly by the activities of fan clubs that have been studied almost exclusively in South India—above all in the states of Tamil Nadu and Andhra Pradesh (for example, cf. Dickey 1993 and 2001; Gerritsen 2009; Srinivas 2000). However, an SRK fan club in Kolkata indicates a high degree of congruence with examples from South India (Herrmann-Pfandt 2009 and 2010). Members of fan clubs form a special section of the social and active audience of Indian cinema. Fans and fan clubs engage in a wide range of activities that focus on 'their' star. As Srinivas (2000: 299) points out, their commitment to the star is unquestionable; fans stand solidly by his or her side when he or she needs them. This attitude finds expression in cinematic as well as political contexts and, in south India in particular, members of fan clubs are often involved in political affairs as movie stars have been frequently pursuing political careers. In such cases, fans campaign for and join political parties; some fan clubs have been transformed into party cadres upon their hero's entry into the political realm (Dickey 1993; Gerritsen 2009; Punathambekar 2008; Srinivas 2000). Fans' associations celebrate new film releases in the public space combing through visual, performative, and ritual culture. One of the most distinctive examples of the interface between admiration of a star and ritual as well as religious activities are the members of the All Bengal Amitabh Bachchan Fans' Association who have set up a temple in Kolkata in honour of their hero.

Active audiences are also 'repeat viewers' who go to see a movie in the cinema several times—in particular films featuring their favourite stars. Srivinas (2002: 168) describes this particular relationship of audiences with the characters and the plot that enables repeat viewers to talk back at the screen and sing along with the soundtrack. This type of interactive viewing counts among the liminal pleasures of going to the movies in India (Derné 2000) and, is at times, transferred to a globalized setting by Bollywood or SRK fans. In one instance, a group of German fans proudly reported their adventures in local cinemas, when they were applauding, whistling, and shouting during screenings of *Om Shanti Om*. They had a great time, but had to cope with harsh remarks from other members of the audience who considered this form of active viewing quite out of place.

In recent years, SRK has constructed an explicit affinity with South-Indian traditions of stardom and fandom that have become, time and again, part of his films (for example, in *Billu* or *Ra.One*). Furthermore, *Chennai Express* (Dir. Rohit Shetty, 2013) pays homage to the southern megastar Rajnikant. This new aspect of SRK might also be interpreted as a strategic step to reach out to the South-Indian market. Interestingly, this focus on the entire national market came only after 'Brand SRK' was confirmed as being successfully linked with the diaspora. 'It is hard to imagine an American or British actor referring openly to him or herself as a brand as Hindi film star Shah Rukh Khan does,' writes Wilkinson-Weber (2010: 15). In her analysis of the work of costume designers in contemporary Indian cinema and in the context of globalized commodity culture, she identifies practices of 'productive consumption'. In contemporary Bollywood, the integration of brands has become of central importance (while, for instance, the idea of creating new costumes has become obsolete).[6]

In the case of Brand SRK this interactive construction of the star image can be traced through his association with globalized material culture and consumption. Product placement in films often goes hand in hand with SRK's real-life endorsements, and with SRK using some of these items in his public—or better—publicized life.[7] His own ads in turn appear occasionally as signifiers of stardom in his films (for example, *Om Shanti Om* and *Billu*). His stardom endorses the aesthetics and meanings of material culture and at the same time, global luxury goods or his participation in prestigious commercial events form an essential part of his star image. Many TV commercials can be regarded as 'micro-movies' starring SRK; his roles in such spots often display an intertextual relationship with his films or broad issues concerning his life and work.[8] Movie texts and advertisements have become inseparable; deeply intermingled, both constitute a complex media assemblage. When Reebok launched a special collection for the movie *MNIK*, wherein this product is centrally placed, the ad for the shoes looked like a trailer of the movie. In India, Reebok outlets dedicated their shop windows to this SRK starrer. SRK ads form an intrinsic part of his reception as an actor and star; they are collected, watched, circulated, and commented on the Internet by fans worldwide. The reading of his branding is, again, marked by polysemy and controversial voices. While the advertisement for LUX soap—that depicts him bathing with rose petals surrounded by Bollywood divas—has acquired cult status among a large numbers of fans, other commercials have been the subject of exceedingly critical comments, in particular his endorsement of the Fair and Handsome cream.

This aspect of SRK illustrates that stardom can be understood as a genre of representation that provides us with a semiotically rich body of texts and discourses that fuel a dynamic culture of consumption (Turner 2010: 13). Furthermore, as Nayar (2009: 29) points out, celebrity culture influences the cultural economy in many ways, the star is situated at the intersection of, and is the effect of, the interaction between the financial and cultural economy. In the case of SRK, this intersection goes way beyond endorsement and branding—his varied economic sources and activities grant him power and agency in Bollywood and beyond, and are strongly related to his globalized star persona (cf. Dasgupta 2014). With regard to such questions, Vajdovich (this volume) provides insights into the manifold economic activities of one of the richest stars of Bollywood.

The mutual constitution of the local, national, and global with regard to cinema is marked by an interactive relationship between content and diverse contexts of production, distribution, and reception (Gray 2010). Such processes can be observed very well in and around SRK's home production *Ra.One*. 'I think I have done something for the industry ... created a new genre,' SRK remarked in an interview (Raghavendra 2011), referring to the new 'Indian superhero'. The characters Ra.One and G.One (like Krrish or Drona before them) are composed of motifs and material culture from Western superhero tales blended with narrative elements and heroes from Hindu mythology. They can be seen as representing at the same time a localization or Indianization of Western superheroes, and a new dimension of globalized popular culture in a hybrid 'third space' in the sense of Homi K. Bhabha's work on the subject (2006). The reference to Western superheroes echoes the origins of the Indian graphic novel series *Amar Chitra Katha*. In 1967, Anant Pai realized that children from Delhi were more familiar with Greek mythology than with the Ramayana, so he used the foreign medium of comic books to promote knowledge about Indian heroes and saints (Pritchett 1997: 76). The first scene of *Ra.One* also includes a reference to the Japanese genres of manga or anime, another global player in the world of pop-cosmopolitanism (Jenkins 2006). Furthermore, the figure of G.One can also be read as a fusion of the older star image of SRK as an NRI with the 'new' role as a superhero. The new Indian superhero (G.One) and the star image of himself as actor and producer have a lot in common—they are both heroes of a globalized India, cosmopolitans who demonstrate openness to diversity, to other cultural frameworks, and multiple worlds of consumption and interaction, but, at the same time, express a strong sense of belonging to India and Indian culture.

Creating a new genre with *Ra.One* goes beyond narrative and star text, and also refers to new forms of marketing and merchandise that were explored in connection with this film on a scale never done before in India. Toys, gaming, a graphic novel (story written by SRK), mobile games for smart phones, i-Pads, etc. accompanied the movie. 'Why should Indians be wearing only Batman T-shirts or collect toy merchandize from Hollywood movies?' SRK argued (Raghavendra 2011). The merchandize, the technical level of special effects in the film, its global distribution, marketing, and so on are interlinked with a wide range of global as well as local dynamics in regard to the relationship between Bollywood and Hollywood. The integration of cinematic technologies that mark superhero movies and other popular genres of American cinema (for example, diverse special effects or 3-D film) into Indian cinema challenges the global dominance of Western film industries in this field, and aims at attracting young audiences in the subcontinent and beyond to genres such as 'Made in India'.

Hypervisibility and Interactive Spaces

Stars are everywhere (Nayar 2009: 72). As demonstrated earlier, SRK can be regarded in many ways as an embodiment of the diversified dynamics and flows in the 'new global cultural economy' (Appadurai 1996). He acts in and on various levels as 'scapes' of this complex, overlapping, and disjunctive order of fluid, irregular, and often imaginary landscapes that characterize international capital as deeply as they do popular culture. According to Appadurai (1996: 35), the most prominent sphere in this context is the flowing world of global mediascapes, marked by image-centred, narrative-based accounts of strips of reality out of which scripts can be formed of imagined lives, of one's own as well as of those others living in different places. When we follow SRK, as he makes his way through the global mediascape, it is possible to distinguish two overlapping 'scapes' of his being *everywhere*—his presence in the media-assemblage of Bollywood and beyond and his reception by local audiences embedded in a variety of local and global configurations of cinematic and popular culture.

Within contemporary media and convergence culture, stars are always present. The Internet and its social networking sites constitute a globally shared space for communication and interaction that is used by cultural industries, stars, press, and audiences alike. Their respective products contribute to a constant media flow that is available immediately worldwide. As Nayar (2009: 69) and Baker (2013) point out, what makes SRK or other people of fame global celebrities is not only their skills in their respective professions, but the round-the-clock visibility of these skills for the consumer.

For Nayar, this hypervisibility is essential for stardom as a spectacle that includes its consumption by the audience. This dimension of SRK's globalized stardom is discussed in this volume in several chapters dedicated to media practices, in particular on the Internet. Amy Villarejo, for example, discusses the theoretical implications of 'intermediality' that unseats the long-standing opposition between tradition and modernity that has governed much of the study of South Asian cinema. Understood as a shift in emphasis from communication devices to the broader domain of media practices and materialities, intermedia describes a way of understanding Bollywood as a new form of global culture. As Mader (this volume) elaborates, SRK has a very high presence on the Internet—he is at the same time content and agent of media practices and takes centre stage in a complex interactive and co-creative digital environment. As an exceedingly mediated person, he generates and (or) is the source of a more or less continuous flow of texts, pictures, and videos.

New media constellations, in particular social networking sites, are shaping celebrity culture today. These media practices transform stardom as an element of representational culture and include new forms of performance of the self of a star (Marshall 2010). Furthermore, new modes of interaction with fans (for example, on facebook or Twitter) involve performed intimacy, authenticity, and access as well as the construction of a consumable persona (Marwick and Boyd 2011). Already in 2001, Ciecko discussed the implications of interconnectedness, availability, and interactive communication on the Internet for SRK's star persona. She refers to SRK as a 'cyber-friendly star' who has been discursively positioned as an important agent in the invention of online Bollywood, for example, in the creation of the entrepreneurial website 'SRK world' in the 1990s. By being cyber-present and vocal (and echoed by fan-sites), he is local and global at once (Ciecko 2001: 133).

Hypervisibility and constant virtual availability on the Internet—'e-SRK'—constitute an important part of SRK's star persona as well as of the cultural economy of fandom (Fiske 1992). Media practices by fans on the Internet constitute a specific form of fan productivity that shapes popular culture out of the products of cultural industries. Today, a large part of the audience uses the Internet as the primary medium for gathering information about stars and their work. Fans also engage in 'intertextual play' by 'weaving elements from the media they have consumed into new narratives and artefacts that can be displayed to construct particular forms of sociality' (Petersen 2005: 130). This process involves both personal and social constructions of meaning by active consumers who, in the process, shape and reshape mediascapes through their creativity and communicative behaviours (Petersen 2005: 130). Mader (this volume) investigates such media practices that take place on diverse Internet fan sites focusing on two dimensions: to share in the life and work of SRK and to participate in a globalized Bollywood media culture with diverse forms of co-creativity.

Media content that fosters extensive fan culture is often termed 'cult media' (Jenkins 2006) and frequently represents a complex system of stories, imaginary worlds, characters, heroes/heroines, and stars. In addition, Harris (1998) and Hills (2002) emphasize the emotional involvement of fans with various dimensions of media content and with each other. As Rajagopalan (2011) demonstrates in the context of online SRK fan groups in Russia, SRK's celebrity status is a discursive tool in the hands of these fans, and is constructed in the negotiated ties between fans and star as well as between fans and other fans. Monia Acciari and Petra Hirzer analyse such processes in different local settings. Acciari (this volume) investigates Italian Bollywood blogs and fan sites and their significance for the reception of SRK in this country. She demonstrates how personal approaches brought in by each follower and contributor form small, yet significant, pieces of a bigger global collage on SRK. The users' film-viewing practices, as suggested by some of their comments, are scanned by linguistic and regional milieu, or filtered by the knowledge or affiliation with India and Indian culture, providing a flavour to the engagement with this cinema, wherein SRK is at the core of their debates. In SRK's performances in Italy, Acciari identifies attempts to localize his work and strategies to penetrate a local market. Hirzer (this volume) emphasizes the significance of digital media for fan communities in Peru; they are marked by constant dynamics between online and offline spaces where SRK's star image is negotiated through processes of reading and re-reading, consuming and producing, coding and decoding, or decontextualizing and recontextualizing. This type of construction and negotiation of the star persona by fan communities take place in a highly emotive space marked by transformation, interactivity, and sociality (also cf. Mader 2011). SRK and his films are 'cult media' for active audiences dispersed around the globe; he is at the centre of a particular mediascape that encompasses the star and his audience or fans. This mediascape integrates the imaginary world of Bollywood into a space of virtual closeness and conviviality that transcends geographical, cultural, and/or religious boundaries.

Local Transformations and 'Pop Cosmopolitanism'

The globalized polysemy of SRK is constituted—last but not least—by his audience. Hindi cinema has been circulating outside of the Indian subcontinent for a long time and has attracted diasporic as well as non-South Asian spectators for several decades (for example, Russia, the Middle East, Africa, or South America).[9] Since the 1990s, the expansion and diversification of audiences has increased significantly (Desai et al., 2005; Kaur and Sinha 2005) and SRK and his films have mostly played the lead in acquiring new audiences or revitalizing older realms of reception of Indian cinema. Since the turn of the millennium, a variety of 'glocal' fan cultures, for Bollywood in general and SRK in particular, have emerged. Many non-South Asian fans have not only acquired profound knowledge about Indian cinema and established a strong affective relationship to films and stars, but also engage in a 'cineastic popular culture' (Fuchs 2007) including a variety of cultural practices connected to Indian fashion, food, music, and dance.

This form of transcultural reception of cinema and celebrity culture can be understood as 'pop cosmopolitanism' (Jenkins 2006: 152) and goes hand in hand with an increasing diversification of popular culture worldwide. In this context, SRK is part of a globalized mediascape that comprises cultural products such as Anglo-American movies and TV series, Bollywood films, Mexican and Brazilian telenovelas, and Japanese manga and anime. For many non-South Asian audiences, SRK can act as a cultural broker and gatekeeper for the cinematic world of Bollywood and other aspects of Indian popular culture.

As Eriksen (2007) points out, one aspect of globalization includes that people, wherever they are, can participate in a shared production of meaning, appropriate the same information, and yet interpret it into widely different lifeworlds. Accordingly, the reception of SRK is marked by multiple readings and has to be analysed in connection with the diversity of the cultural background of his audiences who integrate the star into their respective lifeworlds. In Germany, Austria, and Switzerland, for example, SRK fans are mostly local women from a wide range of professional, educational, and economic fields.[10] Furthermore, SRK fan communities in these countries include many people with a migratory background from eastern Europe, Turkey, the Middle East, and South Asia (also cf. Krauß 2012 on Bollywood audiences in Berlin). In France and Belgium, a large number of SRK fans have a (north) African background (Roudot 2008). Thus, European SRK audiences are interconnected in many ways with processes of postcolonialism, transnationalism, and cosmopolitanism. In general, the reception of SRK's films and star persona is marked by cultural flows and glocal transformations. In this respect, globalized polysemy represents a kaleidoscope of multiple realities, as an idea or image changes its context, depending on the spectator (Appadurai 1996).

Glocal transformations and pop cosmopolitanism take place in diverse settings and involve a wide range of cultural practices; some of these processes are connected with Bollywood dance (see Gopal and Moorti 2008) and theatrical performances of film plots. Hanna Klien (this volume) demonstrates how elements of SRK's star text have been incorporated into identity formations and performative practices in Trinidad's popular culture by using the concept of remix: the vibrant field of Trinidad's popular culture displaying long-standing traditions of remix such as musical forms of the African diaspora that can offer new insights into its role in Bollywood's globalized circuits. Moreover, she argues that SRK's position as a global star might be better understood in the light of the eligibility of his star text to remix practices. Petra Hirzer (this volume) describes comparable processes in Peru where almost every fan club has its own SRK, always taking the lead and performing certain parts of the star's choreographies; fans incorporate and transform the star's image and recreate images of their own selves within the star. The Peruvian 'roletaking' and 'rolemaking' of the SRK star persona takes place in events such as dance performances, SRK lookalike contests, or theatrical plays. Fans absorb elements of the star's persona and reinterpret them by adding their own personality and dancing skills into a specific type of hybridization. Acciari (this volume) looks at other processes of reception and hybridization. Through Homi K. Bhabha's (2006) concept of a 'third space' she investigates how the global appeal of SRK is constructed within the Italian panorama. This analysis of SRK across the Italian mediascape takes into account the proximity of the Bollywood icon with the distinctive personality of the Italian commedia dell'arte Harlequin. Case studies of localization of Bollywood can be supplemented by an analysis of trans-local practices that strengthen international ties in the fan communities via digital networks, material exchange, travel, and face-to-face communication (Mader, this volume; Fuchs, this volume).

SRK and Star Studies in India

This book also contributes to developments in the studies of stars and celebrities in the Indian film and media landscape. Even as information relating to this area of work has been around for some time now, not in the least through 'fanzines' and trade press magazines, where sections exist on popular Indian cinema, stars and celebrities from yesteryear to the present (see, for instance, the back copies of trade journals such as *Stardust*, *Filmfare*, and *Cineblitz*), this work exists sporadically and has not been brought together under any organizing rubric in existing scholarship. Studies of Indian film stars have covered the star texts and personas of leading men and women from 1930s onwards (for example, on Amitabh Bachchan see Dasgupta 2008; on Ashok Kumar see Ghosh 1995; on the Telugu film star Chiranjeevi see Srinivas 2009; on Helen see Pinto 2005; on Meena Kumari see Mehta 2013; on M.G. Ramachandran see Dickey 2008; on Raj Kapoor see Reuben 1996; on Rajnikant see Balasubramanian and Ramakrishan 2012). Our emphasis on SRK adds to this literature by locating our leading star text and his persona in the context of a globalizing Bollywood cinema, as part of a liberalized post-1990s urban Indian culture and economy. While Amitabh Bachchan (most famously dubbed as the 'angry young man of Indian cinema' in the

1970s and 1980s; cf. Sharma 1993) has perhaps been considered in media reports and the trade press as the most immediate predecessor in terms of contextualizing the fame of SRK (that is, as a precursor figure in terms of fame and wealth spanning the 1970s to the 1990s, pre-liberalization), the collection of essays here draws attention to the ways in which SRK's stardom signals more contemporary aspirations and acts as an emblem for diasporic and transnational desires in late modern India. SRK is also perhaps the most famous of all the 'Bollywood Khans' currently working in popular Hindi cinema and his stardom is often in conversation, or in public disagreement, with co-actors such as the A-listed Aamir Khan and Salman Khan. Arguably, he is the premier star of the globalized Bollywood moment whose instant recognition and star power is often used as a barometer for how well contemporary upper class and elite India is doing. One such case in point includes his appearance in the Annual Forbes India Celebrity 100 List since its inception in 2011, where he is regularly featured in the top three ahead of sports celebrities and other Bollywood stars.

The chapters brought together in this volume address in varying ways aspects of SRK as star text. For instance, Rajinder Dudrah undertakes a media assemblage analysis to consider the development of SRK's star persona in *Veer-Zaara* (Dir. Yash Chopra, 2003) and *Billu*, in part, examining SRK's persona vis-à-vis his articulation with Preity Zinta as Zaara, and in on- and off-screen dynamics as transported to *Billu* where references are made to his real-life public clashes with Salman Khan. Ashish Rajadhyaksha considers the interplay of new media, the state, and SRK's star and celebrity reach over a number of other entertainment mediums such as gaming, TV, and sports, alongside cinema. Amy Villarejo, in part, considers SRK's star text in *Chak De! India* where he acts alongside several relatively unknown and new actresses, where he is clearly not only the star of the film, but at times also offers himself on-screen in a supporting role to these newcomers. Rachel Dwyer's analysis of SRK's star text focuses on him as the figure who makes the transition between India and the West, as well as between the old and the new India. His role as the ultimate diasporic star is based on a variety of representations of Indianness, and can be attributed to many elements of his stardom beyond the film roles themselves. He is the figure who represents the modern Indian, at home in India and the world, the cosmopolitan, or the truly global citizen.

SRK and Global Bollywood—Come Fall in Love ...

In the middle of the year 2000 via the website www.planetsrk.com, SRK, in tandem with his media and public relations team, part knowingly, part jokingly, and part sincerely sent a message out to his fans and to visitors of this site.[11] In that message, a welcome note, SRK could be heard proclaiming—almost in the voice of an avatar—words to the effect of: 'If you are feeling down, if you are missing me, just say my name three times and I will appear in front of you. *Pyaar Se*/With Love, Shah Rukh Khan.' This collection of essays is presented to you in a related and different manner: part critical, part knowing (especially in not wanting to claim any avatar or quasi-religious connotations), and part, we hope, full of sincere scholarship that endeavour to engage with the phenomenon that is SRK and global Bollywood cinema. We contend that this is a necessary task in order to understand and to comment on the range of socio-cultural, cinematic, multimedia, and affective modes of operations that exist in this relationship of a star and his contemporary cinema. Still, concerning the emotional quality and invitation, our mode of address has something in common with SRK's web performance in his welcoming message. Then not only is this book a presentation of our intellectual labour, it is also, in related ways, the varying degrees of *pyaar*/love that we as different scholars share in SRK and global Bollywood.

Notes

1. Richard Dyer (1998: 3) coined the term 'structured polysemy' to analyse the star image and its functions as a polysemy, wherein it contains a 'multiplicity of meanings and affects', and is structured in such a way 'that some meanings and affects are foregrounded and others are masked or displaced.'

2. NRI (Non Resident Indian) is a term referring to Indians living abroad. Here, the patriotic formula *Phir Bhi Dil Hai Hindustani*—translated as 'The Heart Is Still Indian'—becomes ironically transformed. A scene in *Om Shanti Om* re-enacts a Filmfare Award show and draws on the star texts of many celebrities of the Indian film industry in

humorous ways. The event was hosted by Karan Johar and the protagonist O.K. (played by SRK) was nominated as the best actor for two films
that feature him as a hero called Rahul. Of these, one was titled *Phir Bhi
Dil Hai NRI*—referring to SRK's representation of the NRI in several of
his films—and the other was titled *Main Bhi Hoon Na*.

3. Cosmopolitanism refers to openness to diversity. It is sometimes connected with diasporic and transnational lifeworlds, and also forms part
   of general processes of interaction with 'others' in diverse settings. It
   can be applied to various contexts ranging from interreligious relations
   to global flows of consumer goods and global/local interconnections.
   For the concept of cosmopolitanism, for example, cf. Hannerz (1999)
   and Vertovec and Cohen (2002).

4. For an analysis of these kinds of song-and-dance sequences featuring
   SRK, cf. Dudrah (2006).

5. Darshan, here, referes to the practice of star-gazing explained by Ravi
   S. Vasudevan and M. Madhava Prasad where a two-way look endows
   the image or the star as well as the beholder with authority.

6. SRK is not alone in this respect. The branding strategy of South-
   Indian megastar Rajnikant is analysed as 'Grand Brand Rajini'
   (Balasubramanian and Ramakrishan 2012).

7. For a discussion of commercial ads as part of the star image of SRK,
   cf. Cayla (2008) and Shiekh (2006: 314).

8. Good examples of this kind of intertextuality are: an ad for ONN
   innerwear (2012, available at http://www.youtube.com/watch?v=AyJl-
   GHZp00) that refers to *Don 2*, a Pepsi ad with SRK and Kareena
   Kapoor that is staged in Venice and is constructed in the style of a
   romantic song-and-dance sequence (2003, available at http://www.
   youtube.com/watch?v=IpGc5YDbN3E), or SRK playing a double role
   in a Top Ramen Curry ad (1999, available at http://www.youtube.com/
   watch?v=6ZmYkks7WAg) in the style of *Duplicate* (Dir. Mahesh Bhatt,
   1998). For an overview of topics or plots of TV commercials with SRK,
   see http://www.afaqs.com/news/misc/shahrukh_ads.html (all Internet
   sources accessed on 1 October 2013).

9. For example, cf. Larkin (1997) on Nigeria or Rajagopalan (2008) on
   the Soviet Union.

10. Fans range from children and teenagers to senior citizens, the majority
    of fans active on the Internet are in their twenties and thirties.

11. This audio message was present on the website for at least a few years
    between 2006 and 2010. At the time of writing in 2013, the message
    was no longer available on the website.

References

Appadurai, Arjun. 1996. *Modernity at Large: Cultural Dimensions of Globalization*. Minneapolis: University of Minnesota Press.

Athique, Adrian. 2008. 'The "Crossover" Audience: Mediated Multiculturalism and the Indian Film', *Continuum: Journal of Media & Cultural Studies*, 22 (3): 299–311.

Baker, Steven. 2013. 'Virtual Darshan: Social Networking and Virtual Communities in the Hindi Film Context', in Moti Gokulsing and Wimal Dissanayake (eds), *Routledge Handbook of Indian Cinemas*, pp. 215–25. London and New York: Routledge.

Balasubramanian, P.C. and Ram Ramakrishan. 2012. *Grand Brand Rajini: Brand Management the Rajnikanth Way*. New Delhi: Rupa Publications.

Banaji, Shakuntala. 2006. *Reading 'Bollywood': The Young Audience and Hindi Films*. Basingstoke: Palgrave Macmillan.

Beck, Ulrich and Elisabeth Beck-Gernsheim. 2014. *Distant Love*. Cambridge: Polity Press.

Bhabha, Homi K. 2006. 'Cultural Diversity and Cultural Differences', in Bill Ashcroft, Gareth Griffiths, and Hellen Tiffin (eds), *The Post-Colonial Studies Reader*, pp. 155–7. New York: Routledge.

Cayla, Julien. 2008. 'Following the Endorser's Shadow: Shah Rukh Khan and the Creation of the Cosmopolitan Indian Male', *Advertising & Society Review*, 9 (2), available at http://muse.jhu.edu/journals/advertising_and_society_review/v009/9.2.cayla01.html (accessed on 15 May 2015).

Chopra, Anupama. 2003. *Dilwale Dulhania Le Jayenge ('The Brave-Hearted Will Take the Bride')*. London: British Film Institute Publishing.

———. 2007. *King of Bollywood: Shah Rukh Khan and the Seductive World of Indian Cinema*. New York and Boston: Warner Books.

———. 2008. *King of Bollywood: Shah Rukh Khan und die Welt des Indischen Kinos*. Köln: Rapid Eye Movies HE.

Ciecko, Anne. 2001. 'Superhit Hunk Heroes for Sale: Globalization and Bollywood's Gender Politics', *Asian Journal of Communication*, 11 (2): 121–43.

Connell, Raewyn W. 2005. *Masculinities*. Berkeley: University of California Press.

Dasgupta, Koral. 2014. *Power of a Common Man: Connecting with Consumers the SRK Way*. Chennai and New Delhi: Westland.

Dasgupta, Susmita. 2006. *Amitabh: The Making of a Superstar*. New Delhi: Penguin Books.

Derné, Steve. 2000. *Movies, Masculinity, and Modernity: An Ethnography of Men's Filmgoing in India*. Westport: Greenwood Press.

Desai, Jigna, Rajinder Dudrah, and Amit Rai. 2005. 'Bollywood Audiences Editorial', *South Asian Popular Culture*, 3 (2): 79–82.

Deshpande, Sudhanva. 2005. 'The Consumable Hero of Globalised India', in Raminder Kaur and Ajay J. Sinha (eds), *Bollyworld: Popular Indian Cinema through a Transnational Lens*, pp. 186–203. London: SAGE Publications.

Dickey, Sara. 1993. 'The Politics of Adulation: Cinema and the Production of Politicians in South India', *Journal of Asian Studies*, 52 (2): 340–72.

————. 2001. 'Opposing Faces: Film Star Fan Clubs and the Construction of Class Identity in South India', in Christopher Pinney and Rachel Dwyer (eds), *Pleasure and the Nation: The History, Politics and Consumption of Popular Culture in India*, pp. 559–99. New Delhi: Oxford University Press.

————. 2008. 'The Nurturing Hero: Changing Images of MGR', in Selvaraj Velayutham (ed.), *Tamil Cinema: The Cultural Politics of India's Other Film Industry*, pp. 77–94. London: Routledge.

Dudrah, Rajinder. 2006. *Bollywood: Sociology Goes to the Movies*. New Delhi: SAGE Publications.

————. 2012. *Bollywood Travels: Culture, Diaspora and Border Crossings in Popular Hindi Cinema*. London: Routledge.

Dwyer, Rachel. 2000. *All You Want Is Money, All You Need Is Love: Sexuality and Romance in Modern India*. London: Cassell.

————. 2006. *Filming the Gods: Religion and Indian Cinema*. London and New York: Routledge.

Dyer, Richard. 1998. *Stars*. London: British Film Institute Publishing.

————. 2003. *Heavenly Bodies: Film Stars and Society*. London and New York: Routledge.

Eriksen, Thomas H. 2007. *Globalization: The Key Concepts*. Oxford and New York: Berg Publishers.

Fiske, John. 1992. 'The Cultural Economy of Fandom', in Lisa Lewis (ed.), *The Adoring Audience: Fan Culture and Popular Media*, pp. 30–49. London and New York: Routledge.

Fuchs, Bernhard. 2007. 'Bollywood-Fans Meeting Online and Offline: Filmkultur im Internet, bei Stammtischen und auf Clubbings', *ZfK-Zeitschrift für Kulturwissenschaften*, 2: 69–84.

Gerritsen, Roos. 2009. 'Cine-Addictions: Image Trails Running from the Intimate Sphere to the Public Eye', *South Asian Visual Culture Series*, 2: 1–32.

Ghosh, Nabendu. 1995. *Ashok Kumar: His Life and Times*. New Delhi: Indus Publishing Company.

Glick Schiller, Nina, Tsypylma Darieva, and Sandra Gruner-Domic. 2011. 'Defining Cosmopolitan Sociability in a Transnational Age: An Introduction', *Ethnic and Racial Studies*, 34 (3): 399–418.

Gopal, Sangita and Sajata Moorti (eds). 2008. *Global Bollywood: Travels of Hindi Song and Dance*. Minneapolis: University of Minnesota Press.

Gray, Gordon. 2010. *Cinema: A Visual Anthropology*. London and New York: Berg Publishers.

Hannerz, Ulf. 1999. 'Cosmopolitans and Locals in World Culture', *Theory, Culture & Society*, 7 (2): 237–51.

Harris, Cheryl. 1998. 'Introduction', in Cheryl Harris and Alison Alexander (eds), *Theorizing Fandom: Fans, Subculture, and Identity*, pp. 3–8. Cresskill: Hampton Press.

Herrmann-Pfandt, Adelheid. 2009. '"Just Go Ahead and Achieve It!": Ein Besuch beim "Shah Rukh Khan Fans' Club" in Kolkata', in Naseem B. Khan (ed.), *Ishq: Bollywood und Lifestyle Magazin*, 5 (6): 76–79.

———. 2010. '"Der Gott, zu dem wir beten, versteht alle Sprachen": Religion und Interreligiosität im zeitgenössischen Hindi-Film', in Adelheid Herrmann-Pfandt (ed.), *Moderne Religionsgeschichte im Gespräch: Interreligiös, Interkulturell, Interdisziplinär*. Festschrift für Christoph Elsas zum 65. Geburtstag am 1. August 2010, dargebracht von Schülern, Freunden und Kollegen, pp. 414–35. Berlin: EB-Verlag.

Hills, Matt. 2002. *Fan Cultures*. London: Routledge.

Jenkins, Henry. 2006. *Fans, Bloggers, and Gamers: Exploring Participatory Culture*. New York: New York University Press.

Kaur, Raminder and Ajit J. Sinha (eds). 2005. *Bollyworld: Popular Indian Cinema through a Transactional Lens*. London: SAGE Publications.

Krauß, Florian. 2012. *Bollyworld Neukölln: MigrantInnen und Hindi-Filme in Deutschland*. Konstanz and München: UVK.

Larkin, Brian. 1997. 'Indian Films and Nigerian Lovers: Media and the Creation of Parallel Modernities', *Africa: Journal of the International African Institute*, 67 (3): 406–40.

Mader, Elke. 2011. 'Stars in Your Eyes: Ritual Encounters with Shah Rukh Khan in Europe', in Axel Michaels (ed.), *Ritual Dynamics and the Science of Ritual*, vol. IV, pp. 463–84. Wiesbaden: Harrassowitz Verlag.

Marshall, P. David. 1997. *Celebrity and Power: Fame in Contemporary Culture*. Minneapolis: University of Minnesota Press.

———. 2010. 'The Promotion and Presentation of the Self: Celebrity as Marker of Presentational Media', *Celebrity Studies*, 1 (1): 35–48.

Marwick, Alice and Danah Boyd. 2011. 'To See and Be Seen: Celebrity Practice on Twitter', *Convergence: The International Journal of Research into New Media Technologies*, 17 (2): 139–58.

Mazumdar, Ranjani. 2000. 'From Subjectification to Schizophrenia: The "Angry Man" and the "Psychotic" Hero of Bombay Cinema', in Ravi S. Vasudevan (ed.), *Making Meaning in Indian Cinema*, pp. 238–64. New Delhi: Oxford University Press.

Mehra, Sunil. 2006. *The Phenomenon: India's Most Successful Movie Star Shah Rukh Khan*. Mumbai: Magna House.

Mehta, Vinod. 2013 [1972]. *Meena Kumari: The Classic Biography*. New Delhi: HarperCollins.

Meyers, Erin. 2009. '"Can You Handle My Truth?": Authenticity and the Celebrity Star Image', *The Journal of Popular Culture*, 42 (5): 890–907.

Nayar, Pramod K. 2009. *Seeing Stars: Spectacle, Society and Celebrity Culture*. London: SAGE Publications.

Peterson, Mark Allen. 2005. 'Performing Media: Towards an Ethnography of Intertextuality', in Eric W. Rothenbuhler and Mihai Coman (eds), *Media Anthropology*, pp. 129–38. London: SAGE Publications.

Pinney, Christopher. 2008. *Photos of the Gods: The Printed Image and Political Struggle in India*. London: Reaktion Books.

Pinto, Jerry. 2005. *Helen: The Life and Times of an H-bomb*. New Delhi: Penguin Books.

Pritchett, Frances W. 1997. 'The World of Amar Chitra Katha', in Lawrence Babb and Susan Wadley (eds), *Media and the Transformation of Religion in South Asia*, pp. 76–106. New Delhi: Sri Jainendra Press.

Punathambekar, Aswin. 2008. 'We're Online, Not on the Streets: Indian Cinema, New Media, and Participatory Culture', in Anandam Kavoori and Aswin Punathambekar (eds), *Global Bollywood*, pp. 282–99. New York: New York University Press.

Raghavendra, Nandini. 2011. 'Indian Cinema Must Evolve; Ra.One Not Urban Centric: Shahrukh Khan', *Economic Times of India*, 13 September, available at http://articles.economictimes.indiatimes.com/2011-09-13/news/30149445_1_indian-cinema-raone-film (accessed on 15 November 2013).

Rajadhyaksha, Ashish. 2003. 'The "Bollywoodization" of the Indian Cinema: Cultural Nationalism in a Global Arena', *Inter-Asia Cultural Studies*, 4 (1): 25–39.

Rajagopalan, Sudha. 2008. *Indian Films in Soviet Cinemas: The Culture of Movie-going after Stalin*. Bloomington: Indiana University Press.

———. 2011. 'Shah Rukh Khan as Media Text: Celebrity, Identity and Emotive Engagement in a Russian Online Community', *Celebrity Studies*, 2 (3): 263–76.

Rao, Shakuntala. 2007. 'The Globalization of Bollywood: An Ethnography of Non-Elite Audiences in India', *The Communication Review*, 10: 57–76.

———. 2009. 'Shah Rukh Khan: Bollywood Superstar and Icon of the Postcolonial Nation', in Robert Clarke (ed.), *Celebrity Colonialism: Fame, Power and Representation in Colonial and Postcolonial Cultures*, pp. 173–88. Cambridge: Cambridge Scholars Publishing.

Reuben, Bunny. 1996. *Raj Kapoor: The Fabulous Showman*. New Delhi: South Asia Books.

Roudot, Segolene. 2008. 'Watching Bollywood: The French Audience for Hindi Movies' (bachelor's thesis, University of Oxford).

Sharma, Ashwani. 1993. 'Blood, Sweat and Tears: Amitabh Bachchan, Urban Demi-God', in Pat Kirkham and Janet Thumim (eds), *You Tarzan, Masculinities, Movies and Men*, pp. 167–80. London: Lawrence and Wishart.

Shiekh, Mushtaq. 2001. *The Making of Asoka*. New Delhi: HarperCollins.

———. 2006. *Still Reading Khan*. New Delhi: Om Books International.

———. 2008. *The Making of Om Shanti Om*. New Delhi: Om Books International.

———. 2009a. *Shah Rukh Can. The Life and Times of Shah Rukh Khan*. New Delhi: Om Books International.

———. 2009b. *Shah Rukh Can: Das Leben des Superstars Shah Rukh Khan*. Köln: Rapid Eye Movies HE.

Sinha, Suvadip. 2012. 'Return of the Native: Swades and the Re-thinking of Diaspora', *South Asian Popular Culture*, 10 (2): 185–96.

Srinivas, Lakshmi. 2002. 'The Active Audience: Spectatorship, Social Relations and the Experience of Cinema in India', *Media, Culture & Society*, 24 (2): 155–73.

Srinivas, S.V. 2000. 'Devotion and Deviance in Fan Activity', in Ravi S. Vasudevan (ed.), *Making Meaning in Indian Cinema*, pp. 297–317. New Delhi: Oxford University Press.

———. 2009. *Megastar: Chiranjeevi and Tamil Cinema after N.T. Rama Rao*. New Delhi: Oxford University Press.

Turner, Graeme. 2010. 'Approaching Celebrity Studies', *Celebrity Studies*, 1 (1): 11–20.

Vertovec, Steven and Robin Cohen (eds). 2002. *Conceiving Cosmopolitanism: Theory, Context and Practice*. Oxford: Oxford University Press.

Virdi, Jyotika and Corney K. Creekmur. 2006. 'India: Bollywood's Global Coming of Age', in Anne T. Ciecko (ed.), *Contemporary Asian Cinema: Popular Culture in a Global Frame*, pp. 133–43. Oxford and New York: Berg Publishers.

Wilkinson-Weber, Clare M. 2010. 'From Commodity to Costume: Productive Consumption in the Making of Bollywood Film Looks', *Journal of Material Culture*, 15 (10): 3–29.

Filmography

Asoka. Dir. Santosh Sivan. Arclightz and Films, 2001.

Billu. Dir. Priyadarshan. Red Chillies Entertainment, 2009.

Chak De! India. Dir. Shimit Amin. Yash Raj Films, 2007.

Chennai Express. Dir. Rohit Shetty. Red Chillies Entertainment, 2013.

Dil Se… Dir. Mani Ratnam. India Talkies and Madras Talkies, 1998.

Dilwale Dulhania Le Jayenge. Dir. Aditya Chopra. Yash Raj Films, 1995.

Don. Dir. Chandra Barot. Nariman Films, 1978.

Don. Dir. Farhan Akhtar. Excel Entertainment, 2006.

Don 2. Dir. Farhan Akhtar. Excel Entertainment, 2011.

Duplicate. Dir. Mahesh Bhatt. Dharma Productions, 1998.

Kabhi Khushi Kabhie Gham…. Dir. Karan Johar. Dharma Productions, 2001.

Kal Ho Naa Ho. Dirs Nikhil Advani and Ron Reid Jr. Dharma Productions, 2003.

Jab Tak Hai Jaan. Dir. Yash Chopra. Yash Raj Films, 2012.

My Name Is Khan. Dir. Karan Johar. Dharma Productions, 2010.

Om Shanti Om. Dir. Farah Khan. Red Chillies Entertainment, 2007.

Ra.One. Dir. Anubhav Sinha. Red Chillies Entertainment, 2011.

Slumdog Millionaire. Dir. Danny Boyle. Celador Films, Film4, and Pathé Pictures International, 2008.

Swades: We, the People. Dir. Ashutosh Gowariker. UTV Motion Pictures, 2004.

The Inner and Outer World of Shah Rukh Khan. Dir. Nasreen Munni Kabir. BBC Channel 4 and Red Chillies Entertainment, 2005.

Veer-Zaara. Dir. Yash Chopra. Yash Raj Films, 2004.

Stardom and Globalized India

Unthinking SRK and Global Bollywood

RAJINDER DUDRAH

The idea of 'unthinking Shah Rukh Khan and global Bollywood' owes a debt of gratitude to the pioneering work of Ella Shohat and Robert Stam (1994) in their critically acclaimed and groundbreaking book *Unthinking Eurocentrism*. In this publication, Shohat and Stam lay the foundation for a cultural-historical and analytical unthinking of a hegemonic position of how 'the West and the rest' are constructed and represented in relation to each other through the Western media and its global circulation in the late modern period. Unthinking European hegemony, especially how that hegemony seeks consent in and through representation since colonial times, allows us to think it critically and anew. Drawing on this critical aspect of their term of 'unthinking'—as in undoing, and in critically unravelling—and applied to our focus of study in this chapter, what might it mean to *unthink* SRK and global Bollywood?

Unthinking both SRK and global Bollywood is to undertake an analysis of what these two terms or referents mean to us, by us, and for us as scholars, teachers, and students in film, media, and cultural studies interested in the growing phenomenon that is Bollywood cinema. To unthink, then, is to start from a known position and to reconsider it anew due to existing frames of reference that appear as already stated, or always regularly circulated as taken for granted, or asserted as near truths. SRK, made up of the initials of his name, stands for not only the name of the actor, but more so for a brand of star appeal that arises from a certain constellation of aspects in contemporary global Bollywood cinema.[1] There exists a kind of truism, an almost taken for granted-ness about SRK and his stardom, whether in the Indian film trade press or in Western reportage about him as a given uber-star figure in contemporary popular Hindi cinema. While his global popularity and economic success as the '*Baadshah*/Emperor of Bollywood'—that he is also sometimes referred to in India—is undeniable, we need to take heed of what SRK's stardom might illuminate for us and how his star persona is constructed out of a particular moment in contemporary Bollywood. Let us begin by situating our star in an understanding of what global Bollywood might refer to.

Global Bollywood

Drawing on research undertaken in two previous monographs (Dudrah 2006 and 2012), two simultaneous purchases are being made on the use of the term 'Bollywood' in this chapter. Firstly, Bollywood is identified as cinematic entertainment and a cultural industry with its related cultural practices and key personnel (stars, directors, producers, wider film production teams, entertainment-*wallahs*, the state, and so on) that facilitate a field of action. In this field of action, as Bollywood cinema and popular culture are socio-culturally constituted, it is possible to witness the growing multimillion financial and international aspirations of the commercial Hindi film and related entertainment and cultural industries. This also usually entails an ideological story or at least a pitch, that is repeatedly used in the media and by some Bollywood film-wallahs themselves, about the global rise of commercial Hindi cinema (cf. Rajadhyaksha 2003). A focus on such claims made about Bollywood cinema alerts us to read these statements critically (Dudrah 2012: 6).

Secondly, and in an equally related sense, Bollywood is used to refer to a global cinematic phenomenon with a particular kind of audio-visual aesthetic in its films (Dudrah 2006), that works through certain kinds of ideologies; for example, of national identity, communalism, religion, diaspora, and so forth. These are ideologies that can be, and often are, contested by film-makers in the act of production, as well as in the act of media consumption by audiences themselves (Dudrah 2012: 7).

The 'global' in global Bollywood is also used critically as it acknowledges the rise of the profile of Bollywood cinema and popular culture on the international media landscape over the past 15 or more years, but equally locates Bollywood as part of a much wider trajectory of popular Hindi and Indian cinema long before this recent past. In this respect, a publication that uncovers part of this longer history includes the special issue of the journal *South Asian Popular Culture* titled 'Indian Cinema Abroad' (Iordonova and Eleftheriotis [eds] 2006). This consists of a range of essays by a number of authors that vary from scholarly work to personal testimonies and historiography, and offers an alternative film history and geography of Indian cinema beyond Indian diaspora audiences alone. It illustrates a mosaic of transnational exchanges from the 1930s through to the 1980s of Indian cinema, and Hindi cinema in particular, as it circulates in an unsystematic way and at different historical moments; for example, in the 1950s and 1960s in the USSR and Greece, and in the 1970s and 1980s in Egypt and Bosnia.[2]

As an actual and textual signifier, SRK is part of Bollywood's historical formation and global dissemination. He is also of key significance in terms of his acting roles and star persona that are part of the field of action in which Bollywood ideologies are socioculturally constructed and offered for pleasure, economic profit, and mediation by its producers and audiences. In unthinking SRK and global Bollywood is to then ask, how is a notion of global Bollywood achieved in and through the on- and off-screen possibilities that circulate around the star figure of SRK? How does SRK—who can be considered as one of, if not the current premier star of popular Hindi cinema—successfully articulate this notion of global Bollywood in the contemporary moment? As stated at the outset, in Shohat and Stam's (1994) use of 'unthinking' they do so in order to deconstruct a hegemonic notion of Eurocentrism. In what follows in my argument and film analysis of unthinking SRK and global Bollywood, there is also an attempt to illustrate and place emphasis on a critique of the hegemonic nature of how global Bollywood and the star signifier of SRK articulate, both textually and industrially.[3]

In order to answer these questions, aspects of SRK's recent on-screen performances are analysed here. In particular, I offer a reading of select sequences from two of his recent films *Veer-Zaara* (Dir. Yash Chopra, 2004) and *Billu* (Dir. Priyadarshan, 2009), and will breifly reference others. These two films have been selected for close readings as they include SRK dealing with issues that have helped secure him and global Bollywood as appealing to, and communicating across, local and global audience constituencies. In *Veer-Zaara* he plays a romantic lead, secularly crossing the Indo-Pak divide, and in *Billu* he plays a metropolitan Indian star-hero who is global, while also retaining his small town, rural appeal simultaneously. Methodologically, this chapter draws on elements of star studies (Dyer 1979; Ellis 1982; Mishra 2002: 126; Shingler 2012) to consider and analyse how the star is textually constituted on-screen. This is further coupled with a media assemblage analysis (Basu 2010; Dudrah 2006: 42; Rai 2009) that reveals the workings of the cinematic medium (and as shall be argued, it is sometimes deliberately uncovered within the filmic text itself) as an assembly of different filmic and pro-filmic events around the SRK star signifier. This combined effort of aspects of star studies and media assemblage critique might usefully give us access to particular kinds of effects and affects that come together around SRK in the contemporary moment of Bollywood cinema and popular culture amidst processes of globalization.

Veer-Zaara

This Indo-Pak love story, featuring SRK as Veer and Preity Zinta as Zaara, was the international blockbuster hit of 2004 being released in the latter part of the year during the religious festivals of Diwali and Eid. Veer is an Indian air force squadron leader who meets and falls in love with Zaara while she is on a visit to India to perform the final rites of bestowing the ashes of her Sikh nanny, Bebe (Zohra Sehgal) at the Gurdwara Patal Puri in Kiratpur. Zaara is betrothed to Razaa (Manoj Bajpai) and has to return to Pakistan for the wedding ceremony. However, due to a turn of fate, Veer arrives in Lahore after a telephone plea from Shabbo, Zaara's maid (Divya Dutta), to save Zaara from her arranged marriage of convenience as she claims Zaara is in love with Veer. Although Veer and Zaara have not formally declared their love to each other at this point in the film, Veer risks all and resigns from his job to cross the Indo-Pak border in order to pledge his love for Zaara and to ascertain whether Zaara is in love with him, or not.

The scenes leading up to their first meeting in Pakistan at a dargah (Sufi shrine) in Lahore are carefully crafted as a high moment of melodrama, wherein the couple are momentarily reunited. Moreover, these scenes, leading up to and part of one of the film's several highly popular songs, *Aaya tere dar par tera hee deewana* (Your lover has come to your door; sung by Ahmed and Mohammed Hussain), also insert SRK, quite literally, in between the space of India and Pakistan as the leading mediating man, whose star persona is simultaneously reconciling a number of socio-cultural, almost liminal Indo-Pak constituencies for us on-screen.

Veer stays overnight as a guest in Shabbo's house before being escorted to the dargah where he will meet Zaara the next day. The mise-en-scène of Veer's guest room is carefully staged mostly in green from floor to wall, with a few domestic objects coloured in brown and beige and a minor red-and-white bed sheet. Shabbo is dressed in a white and green salwar kameez, with a matching green cardigan. Veer is also dressed in green, wearing a green jacket and a T-shirt underneath in a lighter shade of green with blue jeans. By arranging the room in this way and encoding elements of the mise-en-scène as such, our main protagonist is allowed to blend in with the green of the décor and mise-en-scène of the room in Lahore. In one sense, Veer is almost camouflaged and blends in with his new surroundings in Pakistan, and, in another sense, the colour green signifies that we are now in the state of Pakistan. At this point, Veer is also wearing a pendant around his neck, a *khanda* hanging outside his T-shirt, which identifies him as Sikh. SRK's star persona as a real-life Indian Muslim playing a good North-Indian Sikh character, although through Bollywood's lens of a Hindu–Punjabi hegemony, is used to good effect. Aspects of SRK's on-screen and off-screen lives intersect here to produce an ideal mediating star machine—one that also navigates in-between his star character and real-life socio-cultural constituencies across India and Pakistan and the religious signifiers of Hindu, Sikh, and Muslim. The dialogue between Veer and Shabbo is telling in this respect too:

> Shabbo: I didn't think you'd come, but now after meeting you I'm sure you will take Zaara with you.
> Veer: How could I not come? My Babuji says, true love happens only once in a lifetime. And when it does no God (Bhagwan) or Allah (*Khuda*) can come in its way. Tomorrow we'll know how true my love is in Allah's eyes.

The use of both, the Hindu word 'Bhagwan' and the Muslim 'Khuda' in the same sentence about true love in Veer's speech unites liberal Hindu and Islamic interpretations of a shared understanding of divine love. The on-screen body that utters these words is of a young Sikh man, as identified through the symbol of the khanda that he wears and through his full name—Veer Pratap Singh; but here it is Bollywood's predominant use of the North-Indian Hindu referent that presides, as oddly, for a Sikh man. Veer does not use the word '*Waheguru*' from Sikh Gurmukhi to refer to God. SRK's ideal star persona then is not just depicted pictorially through aspects of the mise-en-scène but is also audio-visualized through the use of Hindu–Urdu dialogues and script of a melodramatic mediating star—one who is known both on- and off-screen for his arbitrating of these trials and possibilities across urban India and the diaspora (see Dudrah 2006).

As Veer finishes his lines, Shabbo and he exchange passing gestures of an *adaab* as she leaves the room, filmed through a medium long shot. The song beings with the lyrics: 'I have broken all the barriers of society. I have left the world and come to you' and from the medium long shot, the camera zooms in to a medium close-up of Veer's chest and face where he looks as a weary traveller, contemplating deep, almost sad, inner feelings. The spiritual registers of the song begin with him and are about Veer and Zaara. The next scene of this sequence cuts to the shrine with a rumbling of thunder over the soundtrack: the following day has a rainstorm brewing and the devotional spiritual-cum-love song develops, through its chorus refrain of: a besotted lover has come to your door. The song is picturized as diegetic music being sung by a duo of qawwali singers with their group at the shrine.

The two families of the engaged couple—Zaara and Razaa—visit the shrine to offer prayers and seek blessings for the newly-weds-to-be. Razaa's family arrives first, followed by Zaara's. Dressed in regal clothing, signalling their high status in Pakistani society, they all carry flowers as offerings. Shabbo walks with Zaara's family holding a large tray of flowers, indicating her servant class.

As Zaara and Razaa appear in the same frame together, Razaa looks at Zaara but their eyes do not meet. Zaara deliberately and nervously bows her head averting his gaze, and begins to pray with cupped hands. The lyrics of the song are emphasized over this action as Razaa attempts to assert an affectionate gaze at Zaara, hoping for her reciprocal approval. Razaa appears besotted by her and Zaara's refusal of returning his gaze confirms the lack of interest in this arranged relationship. For the confirmation of love, we have to wait for the arrival of Veer to find out whether or not Veer and Zaara are in love with each other.

Veer's arrival at the entrance of the shrine is signalled through the music and singing which gathers pace through the wailing ebbs and flows of the qawwali. The ecstatic and gleeful cries of the singers are syncopated over a crane movement of the camera which moves swiftly from the top of the screen to appear in line with a front-medium focus on Veer, standing mid-point in the entrance. SRK as Veer is audio-visually asserted as the lead male protagonist of the film and this accentuates his star presence on-screen. Such synchronizations occur innumerable times, not only in this song sequence but throughout the film.

Zaara experiences his presence, although she is unaware that he has actually arrived, since physically she is yet to see him. This moment is picturized as if Zaara is receiving a blessing from the shrine while she stands in prayer with her hands cupped. Zaara receives an *ehsaas* of sorts—a kind of spiritual and enlightening energy that appears to uplift her spirit—as Veer enters the building. This is fitting as it takes place in the dargah, a tactile place and space which is created to touch and move visitors through the orality of the singers, its aura and decoration that is endowed with Sufi mysticism which includes the scent of wafting incense and fresh flowers. All of this adds to an idea of spiritual energy as present in the shrine which can touch and enrapture any devotee, and through Zaara's ehsaas we see this played out. The dargah is also a multi-faith place of prayer and pilgrimage for visitors other than Muslims throughout India and the transcendental possibilities at this site are open for multiple viewing pleasures.

The lyrics of the qawwali at this point summon the need for a visible manifestation of the spirit, acting as a need for the love between Veer and Zaara to take on a human form in order to be seen and witnessed: 'Have mercy, cast just one glance upon me/Beloved, I'll hazard my heart, I'll lay down my life/Just like the moth who dies in the flame', chorus: 'Your maddened lover has come to your door.' The images that are edited and juxtaposed with the refrain of these lyrics are that of our hero and heroine moving closer to each other, with Veer aware of Zaara at the shrine, but as yet she has not seen him.

A force awakens Zaara, allowing her to acknowledge the predicament that her life is in—the marriage of convenience to Razaa—while her thoughts sway for Veer. She begins to walk backwards, away from the shrine; not in any disrespectful way to the dargah itself, but away from the social arrangement of the two families who have gathered for a mutually beneficial prayer and blessing. Here, the melodrama is heightened with the onset of the rain. A crescendo of thunder rumbles and the downpour of water starts immediately. The water is natural and also signifies Zaara's weeping and internal longing; it also appears to quench a thirst of some sort. Zaara is moved by nature, literally, to turn and see her beloved. Veer has arrived, as if sent by the saints in heaven; and through a series of quick facial close-ups and medium long shots of Veer and Zaara on different sides of the shrine, they exchange gazes and acknowledge their recognition of each other. The emotion is intense and is seen in their eyes; they communicate through a haptic touch of sight.

Zaara walks closer to Veer in the pouring rain. The two families look on; they are interpolated via the camerawork through a series of quick zooms towards each member responsible for this social gathering and anticipates what might happen next as a moment of tension begins to build. Zaara leaves their world, albeit temporarily, moving physically closer to Veer and reaching within a metre of him, she pauses. They are standing facing each other, filmed through a medium close up. The camera swirls around them revolving on a

360 degree axis, creating the effect of a Sufi dervish whirl along with the lyrics and music, a spiritual heaven, the natural elements and earth are articulated in their coming together. Zaara swiftly moves forward to embrace Veer to a celebration from the play of the harmonium's keys to a refrain from the qawwali: 'What a turn this story has taken.' Veer embraces Zaara and places his hand on her head as a comforting gesture and also as a reciprocal sign of his show of love towards her, just as she accepted him in a public setting. The *kara* (steel bangle) as one of the five Ks of Sikh religious symbols is clearly visible on Veer's wrist as he holds his hand over the back of her head. This marks a potential moment of danger and anger in a predominantly Muslim place in Pakistan, as Veer is clearly identified as an outsider, a Sikh at a Muslim shrine. Razaa with an expression of anger on his face attempts to move forward to intervene but he is stopped by his father. The song sequence comes to an end as a crane shot moves out from the action and towers above the characters in the mise-en-scène: Veer and Zaara embrace in the centre of the screen, the singers and their group are to the right, and the two families look on from the top centre of the frame.

What is also of interest in this sequence is how religion, or rather notions of faith are grounded in broad and liberal understandings that are used and mediated here (that is, faith as a belief system in a higher being, a metaphysical understanding of a wider spiritual universe, and of a belief in one's lover that sits somewhere in relation to the above two constructs). Representations of the major religions in South Asia can often be conveyed through dominant ideology in popular Hindi cinema leading to conservative social representations (Dwyer 2006). In the case of *Veer-Zaara*, dominant ideology around religious interpretations of faith are set up as well as interceded through our leading protagonists. Rather than simply using the dominant understandings of faith as prescribed by some religious authority; or, in another extreme, doing away with faith altogether, faith (as a belief in Allah and/or a Bhagwan and one's earthly love and spiritual love as existing in relation to that) is mediated and experientialized as affect, as emotion, as trial and tribulation, which has to be negotiated by our two main characters. With the arrival and meeting of our lovers at the dargah, the energetic qawwali with its chorus (a besotted lover has come to your door) is both a calling towards an imagined spiritual universe and a call towards an actual earthly one. The call takes on a spiritual and transcendental quality that is in keeping with the tradition of the mystic saints in both Sikhism and Sufi Islam that profess the oneness of mankind and the immeasurable sweet-pain and longing for a loved one that is akin to the yearning of the soul's quest for union with its divine source. The spiritual-cum-romantic lyrics used through the qawwali, as a call to the saint, to Allah, to God, become a narrative in the film for and about our hero and heroine as they make their way towards each other in love and life.

SRK as the star hero in *Veer-Zaara* can also be assessed in relation to his on-screen chemistry with actress Preity Zinta. The role of the star heroine, in this case Zinta as Zaara, is crucial to the development of our star actor's persona on-screen alongside his acting and performances and how these are executed through the further technical skills of directing, editing, and post-production, and how these two star actors embody the role of Veer and Zaara. Both Zinta and SRK have starred in two films together leading up to the release of *Veer-Zaara* and this film will have further helped to create understandings about their on-screen star coupling amongst film trade reviews, fan audiences as well as for academic analyses, as offered in this chapter.[4] Often the heroine is a counter-balance to the hero's qualities, and sometimes not though an attempt is made by the filmmaking team to cohere their on-screen chemistry as a perfect fit for maximum affect, pleasure, and profit. Arguably, this is certainly the case in this film.

SRK's star persona both on- and off-screen is also brought into play through the implicit and explicit references to SRK's ideal Indian Muslim-ness where he often plays a North-Indian Hindu or Sikh character on-screen, enshrined by his actual real-life secular and anti-sectarian religious views in South Asia. SRK is an effective and affective mediator across these differences, and this effective/affective mediation can also be witnessed in the box office success that his films achieve as they are watched by millions of Hindus, Sikhs, Muslims, and other religious groups as well as by people of no faith from around the world. A focus here on his on-screen star persona allows us to un-think and mediate SRK in *Veer-Zaara* through some of the textual and analytical tools of film studies and to draw attention to how SRK can be considered as part of, and as constructing himself through, the notion of a media assemblage. In doing so, textual, affective, and material properties of the cinematic machine, and its articulations as popular culture, are also brought into focus. This working of the media assemblage can be seen to be further articulated in the next film under examination, *Billu*.

Billu Barber/Billu

Billu Barber or *Billu*, as it came to be renamed, is a charming and simple story of two childhood friends who get separated.[5] Billu (Irrfan Khan) from a background of a family of struggling haircutters goes on to become a poor haircutter himself, supporting his wife Bindiya (Lara Dutta) and two children; and his friend, Sahir Khan (SRK) goes on to become the country's biggest star actor in commercial Hindi cinema. Through a process of life imitating art, Sahir Khan's next big film is about two young brothers who get separated and then are reunited by the film's resolve. Sahir Khan instructs his production team to shoot parts of the film in the fictitious village of BudhBuddha, as he has learnt that this is possibly where his childhood friend Billu may have settled. When news reaches the village of Sahir Khan's production, excitement and comic mayhem ensues and Billu makes a number of unsuccessful attempts to contact Sahir Khan, while Sahir Khan also secretly hopes that he will meet his lost friend. Billu's lowly status and self-pride hold him back in coming forward to his now superstar friend. The film's happy ending sees them both reunited.

The film went on to be classed as a commercial flop according to its box office takings in India but it received mixed to favourable reviews for its tale about ordinary, small-town India meeting larger than life Bollywood through the emotional comedy drama of the two friends.[6] Made by SRK's production company, Red Chillies Entertainment, the film, both in its production aspects and its on-screen textual formation, deliberately takes on and plays with SRK's star status. The creative team included director Priyadarshan who was directing SRK for the first time and friends and family, who by 2009, had worked with SRK on various other projects. The screenplay was co-written by SRK's long-time friend and director,

Mushtaq Sheikh and was co-produced by his wife Gauri Khan and co-produced and distributed by SRK's own production company. Red Chillies Entertainment developed out of an earlier production company, Dreamz Unlimited, which itself was formed together by SRK, co-star and friend Juhi Chawla, and their friend and film-maker Aziz Mirza. Red Chillies went on to diversify into five areas of multi-media and, more widely, sports and entertainment, including film production and distribution (Red Chillies Entertainment), visual effects (Red Chillies VFX), TV commercials (Red Chillies TVC), TV programmes, and media equipment leasing (Red Chillies Idiot Box), and owning a 50 per cent stake in the Indian Premier League cricket team Kolkata Knight Riders. The visual effects for *Billu* were also handled by Red Chillies VFX.[7] The media assemblage of SRK's creative personnel and of Red Chillies Entertainment working together can be seen from the outset of his introduction in this film to promote him as the star vehicle in interesting ways.

Daamchand (Om Puri), a conniving moneylender who always travels with his hired goons, is seen as urging Billu to take a loan from him at extortionate rates but Billu wisely refuses. Daamchand is quick to take offence and retorts '... you have not a penny in your pocket, and you dream colourful dreams' and orders one of his men to push Billu away. As he makes this command, his voice echoes his last few spoken words '*aur sapne rangeen*' (and colourful dreams) and we are transported from the village location into outer space in the next shot as part of the continuing sequence of action and narrative.

The shift to outer space, a Computer Generated Imagery (CGI) of special effects crafted by the team at Red Chillies VFX, marks the formal entry of SRK on-screen as a small spaceship races across the universe through an asteroid belt to make its way to a space station. As the ship moves to dock into its landing position, orchestral music mixed with electro-acoustic sounds marks another worldly atmosphere and the colour palette of the mise-en-scène changes from the starry black of outer space to a mysterious emerald green hue. The spacecraft's door opens with a whoosh of opaque smoke which conceals SRK as he takes off his helmet to the introduction of the electronically synthesized sounds and the beats of the song *Love mera hit hit* (My love is a hit). His reason for being at this station is revealed in the next cut as we see a futuristic costume-clad Deepika Padukone, who twirls around to look at and exchange a welcoming gaze with SRK; she is with an entourage of female dancers who all walk stylishly in sync towards our leading man. The song, sung by Neeraj Shridhar and Tulsi Kumar to the music composition of Pritam, gets into full swing. Once the spectacle factor of this song settles in—its science-fiction setting, its green *Matrix-* and *Don-*like colours, films both SRK has gone on record in trade press and interviews as being amongst his favourites and in fact stars in the 2006 remake of *Don*—as spectators, we do begin to wonder what links this futuristic detour with the rural setting of the film. As the song draws to a close, all is revealed. As SRK hugs and then blows a kiss to Deepika Padukone's character, we see in the same frame a close-up of her hand waving goodbye to SRK. The camera pans back to reveal a film within a film as the song is being watched on a private cinema screen and is being applauded towards its end by Sahir Khan and the members of his production team.

This opening sequence to the introduction of SRK as our hero Sahir Khan deliberately plays with SRK's star persona, not just as the loveable romantic hero, romancing his leading ladies on-screen, but also as a latter-day star in Bollywood film industry where his role is central to the economics of film production. The song sequence also plays with the idea of itself as a spectacle of textual pleasure, and also as a spectacle that is an important part of the production process of commercial, popular Indian filmmaking. In and of itself it is important as it lavishly marks the entry of our star actor SRK as our hero Sahir Khan in the film alongside appearing with a special appearance from actress Deepika Padukone—one of the three actresses who make special appearances with SRK in three different songs as spectacular item numbers. Furthermore, as it ends we are witness to a private screening of this song where we see Sahir Khan being narrated the wider film plot which is yet to be written and filmed. An interesting scene for a film made in the latter part of the first decade of 2000s when older models of film-making—including filming the songs and showing them to financiers for more money with which to shoot the rest of the film—would have perhaps been succeeded by more studio models with fuller scripts in place. This sequence pays homage to that older school of film-making, but it is not simply a producer who is calling the shots but the star actor himself in tandem with his production team. SRK as Sahir Khan is placed centrally, literally in the middle of the frame of this sequence as demanding attention and from which he speaks and communicates with his team about the next stages of the film's production. The star is hailed as a co-producer and key component of the film-making process as he talks with the screenplay writer, which includes tongue-in-cheek jokes about lost and found narrative arcs from commercial Hindi cinema, mostly from the 1970s and 1980s. In *Billu*, the film-making process and the star's role within it is part and parcel of the film. Not only then does Red Chillies Entertainment produce this film, across at least a few of its production arms, it also reveals in the film the way in which the production company makes films with SRK as an integral part of its creative output.

As the film moves to its location shooting in the village of BudhBuddha, Sahir Khan's stardom and the pleasures and challenges that it entails across India are depicted as a stand-in for the recent experiences of SRK's own stardom. An analysis of the following film sequences helps to bring into focus how this is achieved.

Sahir Khan's pictures are present throughout the villagers' homes as posters and, in some cases, as enclosed in a wooden frame in the living room's mantelpiece. This seeks to promote the idea that Sahir Khan is considered as one of the villagers through their shared imaginings about him as part of their rural community, and as part of a wider extended family of fans throughout India.

In the *Khudaya khair* (Lord's grace) song, a romantic ballad in which Bindiya (Lara Dutta) dreams of Sahir Khan being nearby her in the village. In this sequence, he is cycling, enjoying a ride on a rope swing from a tree (almost Krishna-esque), and is dressed in cosmopolitan light pastel colours, whereas she and the other village women around her are in everyday attire. The everyday woman of the rural village shares dreams and fantasies of Sahir Khan, as wanting to be near him, as he sings and acts for them and to them.

Sahir Khan is cherished by the villagers and we see this love being lavished on him through an *aarti* (ritual) of his framed photograph by an elderly lady, as a sign of a protective blessing being bestowed on him. In the photograph, Sahir Khan is seen with a red tilak placed on his forehead. Sahir Khan is adopted as one of their own through a predominantly Hindu ceremony. Like SRK, Sahir Khan too is an Indian Muslim who regularly plays the idealized Indian Hindu on-screen, and Sahir Khan stands in as the representation of SRK's liberal cosmopolitanism both on- and off-screen; being married to an Indian Hindu, Gauri Khan, who has retained her Hindu religious identity after their marriage, both SRK and Gauri Khan participate in Muslim and Hindu religious festivities at home.

Sahir Khan is also a trendsetter and his looks are being emulated by his fans. Young men and boys of the village get their hair styled like SRK's from Billu's haircutting shop, with a mopped fringe and a left-side parting. As a line of young men leave the shop, they look straight into the camera and then laugh self-consciously: SRK's fans partake in the adoration of him through active, lived cultures.

The scene in the song shifts to Billu and his family watching a film at the cinema, starring none other than Sahir Khan. The motif of a film within a film sets into motion again, as the *Khudaya khair* song lifts from its rural lilt to a remixed mellow urban version of the same track, featuring actress Priyanka Chopra dancing with Sahir Khan to an MTV style video. The song ends with a fade out to black on the cinema screen, and the next scene takes us back to the village with a medium long shot of the home at night, with the tempo and rhythm of the rural lilting version of the song reinstated. In this way, SRK's all-India appeal across villages and small towns, urban India, and overseas is represented audibly and visually.

The second sequence is the *Marjani marjani* (Murderous heartbreaker) song, another popular track from the film. It was widely used in the film's promotion and publicity ahead of its official release and was played extensively over the radio and 24X7 Bollywood satellite channels as a bouncy floor-filler. The sequence features as a song that is being shot for Sahir Khan's film on location in the village of BudhBuddha and serves the role of a lavish item number full of spectacle and colour. Singing and dancing alongside Sahir Khan is the actress Kareena Kapoor as the item girl; we never get to know her character's name as she appears in the film in a special appearance for this item number alone. Arabesque disco music pulsates and gives meaning to the constructed on-location Eastern outdoor set, with large pillars and archways—it is traditional yet modern, full of energy and a titillating sexual call and response between the two protagonists.

The mise-en-scène of the song is further made picturesque with sky blue-and-white costumes which the leading pair and their ensemble of male and female background dancers wear.

The song is filmed in mostly three ways. In the first instance, the camerawork focuses on the leading couple and their entourage as they sing and perform with each other. In the second instance, the camerawork shifts during the interlude, in between the lyrics, to focus on the set of the fictional film being shot. Here, we see a reel-to-reel audio cassette player which gives sound to the song and music that the actors and performers lip synch and dance to; a camera on a crane hovering overhead captures a number of different perspectives; props including a box full of wedges, several spot boys uniformed in red T-shirts; a white Western crew alongside the Indian director and his team; on location sound amplifiers; hundreds of villagers as onlookers, and some holding large SRK posters. The third example of filmmaking is deep focus camerawork and shots which bring into relief the three layers of spectacle for the audience-spectators in the cinema or at home; this includes the village audience/onlookers in the foreground, the camera crew in mid-ground, and Sahir Khan and the heroine with dancers in the background.

Amidst this, we also get a sense of professionalism of the filmmaking process during the excitement and challenges of trying to picturize a song sequence on location with a live crowd in attendance. The police are on standby in large numbers and undertake lathi charges with their batons in order to control the crowd, keeping them a good distance away from the shooting that is taking place. A crane shot also pans over the villagers watching the filming in front of them: crowds are cheering, waving, and shouting; some males even climb a tree to get a better view.

Scenes within the song sequence also move to shots of a laptop screen on site, where the director and camera crew are viewing the action unfolding in front of them with a live rolling time code of the shot functioning as an electronic metre of the recorded performance. Next to the laptop a can of Pepsi sits strategically in the frame. This can be seen as a quick reference to SRK's relationship with the consumer product as co-sponsor of some of his films and also as SRK as the brand ambassador for the beverage being clearly endorsed in this segment.

The *Marjani marjani* sequence, then, acts as song as spectacle through its placement and use in the film as an item number and is primarily there for the repeat-viewing value of the film, or at least its songs, which the film-makers hope will click with the paying audience. More than this, the sequence adds further layers of meaning, which are depicted on-screen for us as implicit messages about co-production, on-location shooting, and the collaborative and international nature of Bollywood productions and these processes of filmmaking in contemporary Hindi cinema are displayed and conveyed as a media assemblage, together with the audio and visual style of the song per se.

Alongside *Billu* revealing some of the mechanics of its own construction as a piece of cinema and media assortment, it is also deliberately a confessional film in places. SRK as Sahir Khan enacts moments from his reported real life in the wider trade press, news media, and in Bollywood gossip columns. Fragments of SRK's star-self are articulated through the film in an open and, at times, explicit way. In one telling scene, a group of school teachers approach Sahir Khan on the set of his film to visit their school and to inspire the students through a speech by the actor. One of the teachers Damodar Dubey (Manoj Joshi) is arrogant and borders on the offensive with a disrespectful tone at Sahir Khan. Dubey even brings up personal information from the star's life, to which Sahir Khan firmly responds:

> Dubey: I have read about you too in *Film City* (magazine). I have heard you have quite a few problems. That you have an enmity with another Khan, I have read that.
> SRK: Excuse me, what did you say your name was?
> Dubey: Dubey ji.
> SRK: Yes, Dubey ji. You are going on as if you know all the heroes of the film industry personally.
> [Dubey chuckles, self-congratulatory, as if claiming to know other film stars.]
> SRK: Our film industry is a family. We have a sense of brotherhood amongst us.
> Dubey: I see.
> SRK: And as happens in a family we have a lot of love for each other and sometimes we even quarrel. But these are very personal matters. You do understand the meaning of personal? So you should leave this matter alone.

Sahir Khan's firm rebuttal at Dubey's intrusion into a personal matter via reports in the wider film press is filmed in medium close-up, though not exclusively as a shot-reverse-shot where he is simply replying to Dubey. The angle of the frame is slightly canted and, through the camerawork and visual style of this scene, Sahir Khan blurs the line between SRK as a real-life actor using the character of Sahir Khan in the film to address Dubey, but also to communicate with the audience writ large, beyond the screen. The incident that Dubey refers to is the widely reported verbal and almost physical altercation that SRK had with actor Salman Khan at a birthday gathering. Since then, the media has been keen to report SRK's alleged rivalry and the love-and-hate relationship between the two, often making celebrity news headlines not least around the time of the release of each star's latest release.[8] SRK in this instance is clear and firm about that relationship and the alleged incident as off limits, and uses his star status, quite literally, in order to make a statement on the matter.

The film *Billu*, then, is a tale in part as much about SRK's stardom and how it is achieved and constructed, as much as it is about a small villager being able to dream and reconnect with his lost best friend-cum-brother from before. In the closing moments of the film as it moves towards its climax, SRK's stardom and its affinity with his fans as everyday people, and not just in urban India or the diasporic centres of the West, is reaffirmed yet again. Sahir Khan gives a speech at the local school where Billu's children also attend and Sahir Khan goes on record praising his lost friend and the reasons for his coming to the village in search of him—much to the surprise of the villagers. Billu's family leave the speech early and gather back at their house, as the revelation of the speech and in turn the sacrifices that Billu made along the way as a child for his best friend are emotionally too much for the family to come to terms with in public.

Billu's house is of wooden construction and bears the frayed hallmarks of a struggling man and a young family trying to make their way. Tears flow and Billu, Bindiya, along with their son (Duggoo/ Ronak) and daughter (Gunja) bond and reunite as a family. In the preceding scenes they had bickered and fought over whether a relationship actually existed between Billu and Sahir Khan; or, whether Billu had made the whole story up. Overhearing their emotional union is SRK off-screen who appears in the doorway of the house through a medium shot. He is wearing a white jacket and an aqua-coloured T-shirt, which sets him up as bright and lighter in an otherwise dark mise-en-scène; this, together with the lighting highlights his appearance in the frame accentuating an almost aura-like appearance around him. Left of the screen is the brown doorway and darkness from the surrounding night. This creates the impression as if the star has appeared from the silver screen as it were, and into the everyday of the household to re-establish his relationship with Billu in real life as part of the diegesis. Melodramatic strings and an orchestral score accompany this reunion sequence as we move towards our happy ending.

Taken side by side and through film and media assemblage analyses, these two films reveal how SRK's star persona is produced and represented on-screen for local and global audiences simultaneously, while always with an eye and ear on the star's actual relationships on- and off-screen. In *Billu* we are especially treated to the depiction and uncovering of the workings of SRK's stardom in explicit ways and how that stardom is central to the cinematic viewing experience, not least in the case of latter-day SRK films. *Billu* follows on from SRK's 2007 international hit *Om Shanti Om* directed by Farah Khan and produced by wife Gauri Khan, with the special effects handled by Red Chillies VFX and distributed by Red Chillies Entertainment. This earlier film also deals with aspects of the film set as part of the spectacle and directly engages with the cinematic apparatus and media assemblage within the filmic text as well.

In both *Veer-Zaara* and *Billu* we see SRK's ideal Indian-Muslim identity invoked and ideologically used for particular kinds of effects and affects. This trope of SRK's star biography as a Khan and/or a liberal and secular Muslim on-screen, even at times when he is not directly playing a Muslim character, can be traced back to at least SRK's more prominent roles in *Dil Se..* (Dir. Mani Ratnam, 1998), in his Sufi-esque singing and dancing numbers and in *Hey Ram* (Dir. Kamal Hassan, 2000) where he plays the supporting role of Amjad Ali Khan. It is by the early–mid 2000s onwards that we are able to witness his star biography as an Indian Muslim being more explicitly developed on-screen, in tandem with the rise of his star power and Bollywood's increasing global ascendancy in the international arena in his other films such as *Chak De! India* (Dir. Shimit Amin, 2007) and *My Name Is Khan* (Dir. Karan Johar, 2010).

To unthink SRK and global Bollywood, then, is to continue to explore critically even when only some of the key questions have been asked and perhaps only partially answered. In this respect, what makes SRK so endearing for us and by us as film, media, and cultural studies scholars and students? And what kinds of pleasures, possibilities, and problems does the study of SRK and global Bollywood pose? To unravel some of the issues at stake in SRK, as a particular moment in global Bollywood, is not only to try and decipher what it means when, for instance, SRK and Karan Johar in collaboration have us believe that his name is 'Khan' and that he is not a terrorist,[9] but also to ask questions and attempt to answer them about SRK as text, as star, as a media assemblage with its effects, affects, and performative possibilities that might assist us in grasping and making useful critical commentaries on this international phenomenon.

Notes

1. The actor's name in numerous film credits and on official websites has been listed as either 'Shah Rukh Khan' or 'Shahrukh Khan'. I have used the former spelling in this chapter and all subsequent references have been given as SRK.
2. On the global circulation of Hindi cinema, see also for instance the collection of essays edited by Raminder Kaur and Ajay Sinha on 'Bollyworld' (2005) and essays edited by Aswin Punathambekar and Anandam Kavoori (2008) on 'Global Bollywood'.
3. A word of thanks to Bernhard Fuchs for helping me to clarify this signpost here.
4. Preity Zinta made her screen debut with SRK in the film *Dil Se..* where she played the role of the supporting actor, Preeti Nair, a potential love interest for SRK's character, Amar. However, Amar is romantically interested in and pursues Meghna, played by Manisha Koirala. Nonetheless, Zinta's role as Preeti was acknowledged widely by fans and in film trade reviews as creating a new on-screen pairing with SRK. Zinta and SRK then appeared together in *Kal Ho Naa Ho* (Dirs Nikhil Advani and Ron Reid Jr., 2003) as a potential romantic couple that is

unable to be together due to SRK's character's seriously deteriorating heart condition. This love story is set in New York City where they both play urban Indian and diasporic leads.

5. The original title of the film, and in particular the word 'barber', was deemed to be offensive by The Salon and Beauty Parlours Association in India. SRK, after discussions with them, agreed to change the title of the film for its India release to *Billu*, for more see, Zeenews, 'Shah Rukh Khan Assures to Change "Billu Barber" to "Billu"', available at http://zeenews. india.com/entertainment/movies/shah-rukh-assures-to-change-billu-barber-to-billu_22687.htm (accessed on 8 December 2014). However, in the USA the film was released under its original title of *Billu Barber*. See Film Journal, 'Film Review: Billu Barber', available at http://www.filmjournal.com/filmjournal/content_display/reviews/ specialty-releases/e3i83b3be812614cf9914f15c8b1f8ec0c9 (accessed on 8 December 2014).

6. For more, see Box Office India, 'All India 2009', available at http:// www.boxofficeindia.com/Movies/movie_detail/billu#.VIV9LmdA2sM (accessed on 8 December 2014).

7. See the Red Chillies Entertainment website at http://www.redchillies. com/aboutus/profile.aspx (accessed on 8 December 2014). Interestingly, as part of a critical unthinking of global Bollywood in which a field of action can be found as being produced by its media makers, on the 'About Us' hyperlink on the company's website, as part of its corporate discourse and global aspirations, it states: 'Red Chillies Entertainment headed by Shah Rukh Khan and Gauri Khan is a company that is surging ahead in the global entertainment industry. With global entertainment conglomerates evincing keen interest, Red Chillies Entertainment is all set to blitzkrieg the world of entertainment.'

8. For examples of such film trade reports relating to the SRK and Salman Khan relationship see, for instance, 'Salman Has the Support of the Actors and Shah Rukh of the Directors', Masala, 'Sallu–SRK Fight Divides Bollywood', available at http://www.masala.com/4788-sallu-srk-fight-divides-supporters (accessed on 30 October 2012), and IBN Live. com Videos, 'SRK, Salman Picks Up Fight at Katrina's B'day Bash' available at http://www.youtube.com/watch?v=S28YDqBZ_tM (accessed on 8 December 2014).

9. 'My name is Khan and I am not a terrorist', a dialogue uttered by SRK's character Rizvan Khan in the 2010 film *MNIK*, became one of the popular taglines of the film as a particular response to post-9/11 media in which Muslims were considered to be dealt with pejoratively.

References

Basu, Anustup. 2010. *Bollywood in the Age of New Media: The Geo-televisual Aesthetic*. Edinburgh: Edinburgh University Press.

Dudrah, Rajinder. 2006. *Bollywood: Sociology Goes to the Movies*. London and New Delhi: SAGE Publications.

————. 2012. *Bollywood Travels: Culture, Diaspora and Border Crossings in Popular Hindi Cinema*. London: Routledge.

Dwyer, Rachel. 2006. *Filming the Gods: Religion and Indian Cinema*. London: Routledge.

Dyer, Richard. 1979. *Stars*. London: British Film Institute Publishing.

Ellis, John. 1982. *Visible Fictions: Cinema, Television, Video*. London: Routledge and Kegan Paul.

Iordanova, Dina and Dimitris Eleftheriotis (eds). 2006. 'Indian Cinema Abroad: Historiography of Transnational Cinematic Exchanges', *South Asian Popular Culture* (special issue), 4 (2): pp. 79–183.

Kaur, Raminder and Ajay Sinha (eds). 2005. *Bollyworld: Popular Indian Cinema through a Transnational Lens*. London: SAGE Publications.

Mishra, Vijay. 2002. *Bollywood Cinema: Temples of Desire*. London: Routledge.

Punathambekar, Aswin and Anandam Kavoori (eds). 2008. *Global Bollywood*. New York and London: New York University Press.

Rai, Amit. 2009. *Untimely Bollywood: Globalization and India's New Media Assemblage*. North Carolina: Duke University Press.

Rajadhyaksha, Ashish. 2003. 'The "Bollywoodization" of the Indian Cinema: Cultural Nationalism in a Global Arena', *Inter-Asia Cultural Studies*, 4 (1): 25–39.

Shingler, Martin. 2012. *Star Studies: A Critical Guide*. London: British Film Institute Publishing.

Shohat, Ella and Robert Stam. 1994. *Unthinking Eurocentrism: Multiculturalism and the Media*. London and New York: Routledge.

Filmography

Billu. Dir. Priyadarshan. Red Chillies Entertainment, 2009.

Chak De! India. Dir. Shimit Amin. Yash Raj Films, 2007.

Dil Se… Dir. Mani Ratnam. India Talkies and Madras Talkies, 1998.

Hey Ram. Dir. Kamal Hassan. Raajkamal Films International, 2000.

Kal Ho Naa Ho. Dirs Nikhil Advani and Ron Reid Jr. Dharma Productions, 2003.

My Name Is Khan. Dir. Karan Johar. Dharma Productions, 2010.

Om Shanti Om. Dir. Farah Khan. Red Chillies Entertainment, 2007.

Veer-Zaara. Dir. Yash Chopra. Yash Raj Films, 2004.

SRK, Cinema, and the Citizen

Perils of a Digital Superhero

ASHISH RAJADHYAKSHA

Batman, Not Hanuman: We Need the Acceptance

'It is high time we stopped saying it's good enough for a Hindi film,' says Shah Rukh Khan (henceforth SRK). This *Front Row* discussion on Star World[1] with his usual television interlocutor and biographer Anupama Chopra is slightly more serious than usual, for he has a point to make. They are talking about the 'art of being a superhero', and Khan is desperately concerned to show that, firstly, we can create one without condescension; secondly, we have the technology to make superhero films as good as they can in the USA; and thirdly, it is most important that we must do it now to keep the Hindi cinema alive. Don't do it and you sink.

'We have the bucks: I have the bucks, I have the infrastructure, Karan Johar has it, Mr Yash Chopra has it—it's ten times cheaper to make a film like this in this country. We just don't have the acceptance.' For SRK, superherodom had to be the next thing, it had to be done so our cinema could survive and could bring back an Indian audience growing up on the English Premier League, the National Basketball Association (NBA), the National Football League (NFL), and on American superheroes. 'And sad as it may sound, they like Batman more than Hanuman.'

For SRK, technology is all. VFX or visual effects is where the action is, since that relates to fantasy untrammelled, and thence to freedom. Technology gives the film-maker the big canvas, the capacity to experiment.

> I think all of us are still not fantastic enough in our beliefs: the greatest achievement an Indian can have is hope for a Ferrari, not hope for flying to the moon or saving the earth. We are more seeped in reality in India, we have smaller issues, we need to have to deal with having a house, a little car, so this fantasia, so to say, or this leap of faith where the superhero is going to save you against Krypton, fly down and save a thousand people, is still too fantastic for us. It's like, roti, *kapda aur makaan* (food, clothes, shelter), once we have taken care of that in films, then come sports, and so you have a few sports films that have started doing well, and then—finally, it will be just fantasia, just go mad with the fantasy, even in terms of characters. For example, Heath Ledger: he's the greatest superhero we have, I'm not talking about a villain and a good guy and a bad guy, but look at the way he's played it, it's dizzying, it's anarchic, it's dark, it's brooding, it's edgy, it's free. We are somehow not being able to marry this fantastic form that exists which should actually give you freedom of flight or fantasy. (SRK on *Front Row* discussion)

And so, what he is now doing, as he tries to give back to the industry something in return for what he has got from it, is nothing less than an art film about superheroes: *Ra.One* (Dir. Anubhav Sinha, 2011) is, he says, 'an art film in the commercial sphere.'

This chapter tries to make something of the desperate anxiety that can be read in the lines of SRK's quotes, mentioned above. I shall propose that his definition of superherodom relates to a curious situation that SRK is trying to define for himself in India, a situation with some admitted similarities to a superhero but more like the character of Trishanku in the Ramayana, trapped between heaven and earth, between what the cinema in India used to be and has been, and what SRK thinks Indian cinema wants to be and can be. What it used to be is a combination of sheer rubbish—'I was watching a film the other day, I won't name it, and everyone said, "arre yaar kya effects hain"—(but) they're rubbish, and not because we can't do better, but because we accept this, *arre theek hai baki* picture *achhi thi* (it's okay, at least the rest of the film was all right)—and fear—of straying out of our familiar zones.' For example, in India, whatever you do, you have to have a song.

If SRK is right, he has the 'bucks', even though he admits that it's expensive. The main reason to make the flight of fantasy is *not* financial, he is at pains to say that it *has to be done*, if we are to keep Indian cinema alive, to keep it somehow *relevant*.

Why, it is interesting to ask in this great relevance debate, does he pick on *Batman* as the model to follow? On the particular instance of *Batman*, vis-à-vis *Ra.One*, there is of course the specific practical fact of the role of the video game to both films. The *Ra.One* game was formally released in October 2011 on the Sony PlayStation 2 (PS2) platform. As in the tradition of film games after *Matrix*, and as the Arkham games especially show, we are meant to get some additional background information here about the kind of weaponry that the good–bad guys bring to bear, but also on devices, like (in *Ra.One*) the 'item spawn point', a tool for 'delivering weapons to armies across the globe.' 'This mini-teleportation device is designed for small objects and its mobility helped *Ra.One*'s armed forces recuperate much faster allowing them to win almost every battle,' says the kit accompanying the PS3 version.

It is certainly true that the very idea of a Hindi film narrative working with a console in the hand of the movie-going fan opens up possibilities that take us back into the very history of Hindi cinema, the reason for why it exists. The pact between fan and star, the role of fans who did more than merely watch, the possibilities of a spec-tatorial call to action, all gets enlivened the moment we speak of a technologically enabled fan-audience. As *Batman* resonates through 50 years and more of the fanzine, SRK hopes that *Ra.One* will create, in its console-enabled fan, a similar historical resonance.

But there is potentially still more to the parallel. Arguably the real meat in the argument is the fact that all superhero movies, and the *Batman* series especially, have been required to work within a social memory: of oppression, tyranny, corrupt states, citizen helplessness— all the structures of everyday life, realist representation, and physical and mental incapacity that gives birth and power to the fantasy.[2] This leads us to the question: What kind of memory of oppression could determine Khan-style superherodom? Can we, importantly, bring into its ambit figures as apparently dissimilar as his G.One and

Rizwan Khan—the Alzheimer's-afflicted protagonist of *My Name Is Khan* (*MNIK*, Dir. Karan Johar, 2010)? Is SRK's superhero then trapped, at one level, in individual incapacity, but, at another, also within a technologized audience incapable of navigating two of Indian cinema's basic contradictions? This chapter proposes that both characters are a literal embodiment of the conflict between a Hindi cinema unable to shed its moorings, trapped, as it were, in cultural memory, and a future that we find almost imcomprehensible because these moorings are such that the fantasy is unable to take on free rein. SRK's 'crisis of acceptance' is thus, not necessarily a crisis from the outside. It is not a problem of mundane things such as finances or distribution; it is a crisis from *within the cinema itself*. The chapter attempts to explore, with admittedly initial evidence, what such a conflict could mean to the actual experience of the gamer within this environment.

My Name Is Khan (and I'm a Star)

When *MNIK* was released in 2010 with a major eye on the US market, there was little doubt as to who the Khan referred to was. SRK, himself, as perhaps the leading member of the fabled Khan trio (Shah Rukh Khan, Salman Khan, and Aamir Khan), had by then already taken hyperstardom to such heights as it is unlikely to have ever seen in its cinematic history. In the year 2012, the already very exclusive 100-crore club gives way to the super-exclusive 200-crore club with *Jab Tak Hai Jaan* (Dir. Yash Chopra, 2012) and *Dabangg 2* (Dir. Arbaaz Khan, 2012) comprising only these three and no other, not Akshay Kumar, not Ajay Devgan, no one else.[3] And yet it is another Khan who is being referred to, the Khan who also asserts that this is his name and that he is 'not a terrorist.' This is clearly a darker Khan, one who takes us back to a quite different attribution to one with such a name.

The story in *MNIK* is well known: San Francisco-based autistic Rizwan Khan travels to meet the president of America so that he can convey to him that though his name is Khan, he is not a terrorist. Khan recalls his life, initially with his Bombay-based (now Mumbai) father Dilawar Amanullah Khan, his mother Razia, and his brother Zakir. Dilawar works for the State Transport workshop in Borivali, and Rizwan accompanies him, learns the trade, and can repair virtually anything. This bit of anchoring in Mumbai realism is important to the story as we will see later in the chapter. Years later, when Zakir relocates to the USA, sponsors Rizwan, and hires him as a door-to-door salesman for his Mehnaz Herbal Beauty Products, Rizwan meets and marries single mother Mandira Rathod. The two relocate to Banville with Mandira's son Sameer, encounter racial profiling after the 9/11 terrorist attacks, are blacklisted, suffer losses, and Sameer gets killed. Mandira blames Rizwan for her plight and asks him to leave, while she decides to pursue Sameer's death. Rizwan sets out on his journey to meet the president. On the way, he has numerous encounters that require us to recall various kinds of cultural oppression, mainly located in the USA: Hurricane Katrina, black politics, and the nature of domestic migration attached to the genre of road movies.

This cultural undertow—the reference to a cultural memory of oppression, victimhood, and terrorization, in a cinema that at the same time yearns to break free—continues to be an extraordinary aspect of Indian popular culture. The failure of freedom, so to say, forces the popular to reveal uncomfortable and disconcerting truths that popular culture is usually meant to cover in its fantasy. It forces the popular to turn political, to even take on radical responsibilities unbeknownst to itself. As the subaltern spectator of this kind of cinema is driven increasingly underground in globalized spaces, the knowledge *you* need to have to be able to understand a Hindi film has become both cinematic and political. To know a film like *Kites* (Dir. Anurag Basu, 2010), to take a random example, you need to know *Bonnie and Clyde* (Dir. Arthur Penn, 1967), *Easy Rider* (Dir. Dennis Hopper, 1969), *Gun Crazy* (Dir. Josef H. Lewis, 1950) and telenovela conventions. Just to understand *MNIK*, or say for Kabir Khan's *Kabul Express* (2006) and *New York* (2009), you need to have known 9/11 from the inside. This is knowledge that defines the name Khan; or, what it means to have such a name in the world today.

On the other hand, at the other extreme, the name 'Khan' signals another, very Bollywood, anxiety—one of sustainability of the cinematic hyperstar. What next for Khan after the cinema? Has a star of such magnitude outlived his usefulness? Or rather, has the figure become so large that it has become larger than the cinema itself?

Although the cinema has been the par excellence vehicle for creating the movie star/superstar/hyperstar, does this overbloated star now need newer vehicles, new technologies to survive in this stage of his career?

There is good reason to ask this question at a time in the cinema's global career when people are asking serious questions about the true worth of a star. Anita Elberse (2007), doing a report for the Harvard Business School, points to a similar exclusive club in Hollywood who can command a fee of millions of dollars per movie in salaries, perks, and profit participation deals, and can have a powerful influence on movie development and trigger the 'green light' by generating commitments from investors, producers, distributors, and exhibitors. But, as things change, she asks exactly how important are such stars to the success of films? Elberse quotes a 2004 *Forbes* article titled 'The Myth of Brad Pitt', which did a comparison across more than 200 recent films, revealing that fewer than half of the highest-grossing hits featured an actor who had top billing in at least one hit movie previously. The top three movies of all time—*Star Wars*, *E.T. the Extra-Terrestrial*, and *Titanic*—had no stars. This leads her to endorse a well-established belief in the industry that 'it is the movie itself—not the star—that makes the hit.'

Such studies have been threatening for a while now to reverse a mantra of stardom, originally coined by Abraham Ravid's classic 1999 study 'Information, Blockbusters, and Stars: A Study of the Film Industry', that 'stars capture their rent', or that the minimum guarantee that stars offer a film is a box office draw at least equalling the extra cost of hiring them. Ravid claims that although this has been historically true, it has also forced major shifts in the industry wherein the contract system—where the stars were owned by the studios who then charged rental—gave way to a more diversified structure in which the stars exercised control over the intellectual property of the commodity. This system allowed the stars to mazimize their rental worth by developing sequels and a range of outcomes that considerably exceeded the single film thereby emphasizing a de-risking strategy through which dependency on box office returns could be minimized. SRK perhaps has been the only Indian hyperstar to make this kind of transition with some degree of planning. There seem to be no reliable indicators of what he is financially worth, but a *Times of India* report dated, 21 October 2009 estimated that his assets were worth Rs 2,500 crore, or almost 10 per cent of the total annual revenues of the Indian cinema as a whole.[4] However, only a small part of this comes from the cinema itself in the orthodox sense. His production outfit Red Chillies Entertainment is majorly invested in VFX (this aspect was especially showcased in *Ra.One*) and, of course, into both market spinoffs and sports (the Kolkata Knight Riders). *MNIK* had tied up with the market the core values of the film, its '*honge kamyaab*' (*We shall overcome*) line, with Century Ply and Samsonite luggage.

What *MNIK* itself directly shows then, and which I think *Ra.One* can also show, is a particular moment in the contradiction of the career of the star that I think SRK is talking about when he speaks of being conflicted within a cinema of the past and the future. To me, the past is the political undertow of memory that popular culture is condemned to always carry in India, and the future, that of a post-cinematic hyperstar, both leveraging this memory into diverse outlets but also freeing it from its suffocating narrative bindings in the cinema.

Rajni Power, Or, To Keep Browsing, Switch Off Your Internet

Rajni's email: gmail@rajnikant.com
When Rajni logs onto facebook, facebook updates its status message.

Let me take a detour to explore an ever larger star than SRK, with an even bigger problem with the cinema. If it is indeed the case that the twentieth century has seen cinema becoming the par excellence producer of stardom, are we now in a situation where cinema is impeding the growth of the twenty-first century star? Are we seeing a star who is, so to say, trying to be bigger than the cinema itself? Who is, like the proverbial Kal-el/Superman's glass ice, trapped in the cinema...

Am I the only person to see something curiously tragic in the famous Rajnikant jokes? 'When the Koodankulam nuclear reactor is to be relocated outside his house, since he does not switch on the light but turns the dark off', do we not also, perhaps, see what this humour is actually saying?

The website, www.desimartini.com/allaboutrajni.htm runs, it claims, on Rajni Power. You are welcomed with much fanfare—'*Aye Macha! Vanakkam Ayyappam*' (Welcome, Welcome! Pick one, read on, Macha). You are asked to 'Pick one' from the man, the star, the legend. The man gives you a curiously unvarnished story of an extraordinarily humble life. He was born as the youngest son of Jijabai and Ramoji Rao Gaikwad who lost his mother aged five and worked as a coolie and bus conductor. The legend, on the other hand, comprises almost entirely of the jokes.

Long before I get to any of this, however, something happens that I consider devastating for star power. As soon as you enter the site, it requires you to first cut off all your external supplies: your LAN and your wifi. If you don't do it, the site will. Only then does the fanfare begin. I do not have to describe to you, dear reader, what a self-lacerating experience it can be to switch off one's web supplies. Not least when, having enjoyed—if enjoyed is the word—this website, I am instantly brought back to reality, fighting the ultimate fear that some nifty programmer may have changed my settings, as I fight to get the juice back. Gurbaksh Singh of Webchutney (who made this site) calls it an 'unbelievable spectacle of running a website without the Internet.' The complex algorithm that runs in the back end, which kicks in as soon as the Internet speed is down to zero—the basic premise on which the site and the concept have been constructed—is, he claims, a direct tribute to Rajinikant's larger-than-life image. Unfortunately, when I do reconnect when the site is up, I get a decidedly un-Rajni line, '*Aiyyo!* This was unexpected. To keep browsing, switch off your Internet.'

Aiyyo! Rajni Power, capable of replacing Koodankulam, must therefore be precisely not what it says it is. It is so evidently a statement about inability, maybe tragic failure, if anything, of a hyperstar trapped inside the cinema, now inside my hard disk, deluding himself interminably with the number of guns, flying kicks, and bullets he can handle, only pygmified, provincialized by the Internet, by atomic energy, by globalization itself. It is so evidently a statement about the limits of the cinema—the one medium that, through the twentieth century, constituted the par excellence production machine for stardom now seizing up.

Arming the Spectator

I want to stay on this for just a little bit longer because I am propos-
ing that something dramatic is going on here. At one level, this business of switching off the Internet is relatively easily interpreted as
cinema, the pioneer of everything grander and larger than life, being
dethroned, dwarfed by an even larger technology. But what precisely,
is 'larger' about the Internet? Do we return this to Ra.One-type
horror, of a gigantic neural construction run amuck, and which
neither Rajni nor Khan can battle anymore because the genie has
now been well and truly bottled? (This precise situation, in fact,
obtains in the Ra.One game, where in Zone 5 all that G.One has to
do is to run for his life for 30 seconds.) Or is there something else of
even greater significance? Can it be that the real act of a spillover
of cinematic fiction beyond its frames and into the streets has been
handed over by cinema into a radically new vision of narrative? Such
a vision, perhaps most directly evidenced in military video games,
moves into actual reality too, as Eyal Weizman's much-quoted
2006 essay on Israeli military manoeuvres in Frieze magazine shows.
Apparently, in their attack on the city of Nablus in April 2002,
Israeli Defence Forces attempted something new that they called
'inverse geometry'. Described in the essay as the 'the reorganization
of the urban syntax by means of a series of micro-tactical actions',
they worked on the theory that when soldiers defined urban spaces
as 'overground tunnels', they could so 'saturate' the urban fabric that
very few would have been visible from the air. Such overground tunnels allowed them to move horizontally through walls and vertically
through holes blasted in ceilings and floors; a movement named
'infestation' that redefined inside as outside, and domestic interiors
as thoroughfares. At stake in all this, says Weizman, was a great deal
of theory on urbanism, psychology, cybernetics, and postcolonial and
post-structuralist theory, now taught in military schools.

Of course, both SRK and Rajni can walk through walls. We know
that. But if we do take seriously the prior need to switch off the
juice, should we also see this bar on the Internet as a threat to that
spillover? Can this be linked to a further transference of agency
that the cinema has already seen, and is now being re-enacted on
different platforms? Here, on the Internet, and in contrast to an ever

larger and more grandiose screen action incarnating the self-image of spectatorial action, we see action at the other end, direct spectatorial intervention into the action itself—the possibilities of inverse geometry and infestation and the rest of it most directly evidenced by a once-upon-a-time film spectator now fully armed, first with the zapper and now with a full-scale gaming console with two trigger fingers, the capacity for physical movement and an extraordinary arsenal of weapons to choose from. Today, the Indian superhero's ability to walk through walls fundamentally depends on the skill of the *spectator* to manoeuvre the star hero through them. If the fan fails, the hero must too.

This must have significance for cinema, if the political link between cinema and everyday life—the signature achievement of Indian film studies—has any salience. If India has provided one basic, foundational, iconic formulation about cinema, it is surely this: Cinema stands at the cusp of narrative, apparatus, and citizenship. It is able to provide a uniquely interpellative device in its ability to first, incarnate the democratic rights of a citizen-spectator as constitutive of the very act of buying a movie ticket, to walk in, sit down, and see a movie with full democratic rights, and second, for the film itself—in response to the spectator's gaze—to narratively reaffirm an identificatory/interpellative pact through conventions of editing, sound mixing, and performance. The spectator watched, the apparatus did the work for him. No apparatus did this better than that which surrounded the Indian megastar.

Taking this forward, I want to make the following suggestion. I believe it is foundational. We see all around us the process of the Indian citizen going digital with at least, if not a gaming console, a computer mouse to navigate through his rights and act upon his benefits. The best example for this continues to be social networking, which has provoked its own brand of citizen action and direct politics and includes, at once, various candle-light protests, the Arab Spring, and Indian anti-corruption activist Anna Hazare. On the other hand, the larger, if more silent, revolution would be transmogrification of states into e-states, requiring all citizens (and sometimes residents) to become digital natives in order to qualify for e-citizen benefits—from PAN cards to gas connections, to homeless shelters in Delhi, to direct cash transfers, to digital land records, to insurance to health, and of all the bill payments at Common Service Centres and State Date Centres, all linked through Statewide Area Networks. This half, the aggressive enrolment of India's entire population into a digital ecosystem of governance further splits into two parts—one, that is market-driven, includes those seeking to link credit information with bank accounts, in turn with the Public Distribution System, major government schemes including those of employment guarantee, housing, and health; and two, potentially draconian plans of surveillance like the proposed National Counter-Terrorism Centre (NCTC) and the National Intelligence Grid (NATGRID) that the Government of India is bent on putting together despite stiff civil-society opposition.[5]

So let me now propose this: What we are seeing now, the opening up of a digital ecosystem of governance, is fully as epochal a development as the original invention of the public sphere, that theories of citizenship are likely to survive and indeed take their multi-form identities in the digital ecosystem almost as much as, and perhaps even more than, they do in the 'real world'. If this is right, and if we expect to have a digital structure as fully laid out as the original public sphere was, it must follow that the process of navigating this space—including knowing where you can be spotted, where you can hide, what you can do, and how you can represent yourself—indeed, all the functions that the denizens of the public domain do today, would find themselves translated en masse into the digital ecosystem. If land ownership and credit data—the twin pillars of any self-identity in India—are to be virtualized, as has already happened in astonishingly large parts of the country, it must also follow that digital denizens of this space, including cyber-citizens along with cyber-tricksters, cyber-touts, cyber-beggars, and cyber-victims, would fully occupy the new cyber-highways, neighbourhoods, and alleys, as their originary spaces in the real-life public domain do.

Let me now assume that, for good or ill, we are increasingly part of a digital state. If so, this space must have properties that make it inhabitable, however such a habitus may be defined. If this is right, then digital space must have a realism of its own and perhaps this realism, coming out of the excesses of cinema, may have very different navigable properties than its now-staid ancestor. I am suggesting, therefore, that a digital citizen directly links to the idea of new, post-celluloid fictions in which the armed spectator plays the key role and the star, with all his power, mainly works like a puppet at the other end of a long wireless string, one end of which carries the properties of a gaming console.

The Back Story: Mumbai

If what we are seeing is a new realism emerging, what would be its memory? Let me now present the denizen of such a digital space, its citizen-navigator in his profoundly lonely, existential glory, his own private island on *Second Life*, as having one possible ancestry in an equally bombed-out moonscape; in the Hindi cinema, it is the byways and slums of the city of Mumbai. We have repeatedly encountered the mandatory Mumbai back story of such a hero—once Amitabh Bachchan as Vijay who buys a gigantic multistorey building in Mumbai to gift to his mother, because she once worked there as a construction labourer,[6] and today Rizwan Khan, whose father works in the Borivili suburb, in the State Transport workshop. We encounter it again in *Ra.One*, in the family's return and the problems they have the moment they step out of the airport.

Personally, I have long been fascinated with the presence within global Bollywood of a particular brand of Mumbai realism that always somehow grounds it, makes it the grim past that can never be forgotten, however, globalizes the glamorous present and thereby, prototypes a remarkable link between cinematic realism in Hindi cinema and what I have elsewhere (Rajadhyaksha 2009) tried to dub uniquely as Mumbai *territorial realism*. This is not only obvious in Mumbai films like *Shootout at Lokhandwala* (Dir. Apoorva Lakhia, 2007) or *Mumbai Meri Jaan* (Dir. Nishikanth Kamath, 2008); the memory of Mumbai, its locality, local knowledges, even local politics that both attract and repel, are apparently an essential component of the globalized fantasy.

I now further propose that such a Mumbai back story typically includes a local denizen, even an all-seeing spectator-stalker who is very close to his gaming counterpart, as the city produces through local knowledges a bounded realism of the insider, the denizen, the man who walked through his neighbourhood like he owned it, and in that act also claimed for himself the right to describe it as a once-upon-a-time-in-the-past gritty realism that becomes essential for producing cultural memory in practically all major globalized Bollywood films.

There has, historically, been a great deal of work done in the spillover of cinema into spaces outside. In a longue durée ancestor to some of the concerns of gaming theory today, as far back as the early 1920s debates raged on whether movies about bank heists were not, in the final analysis, how-to manuals on the correct way to rob a bank, and whether were we all not learning unsafe sexual habits in addition to losing our eyesight? Since then we have of course had several more sophisticated specific theorizations on the spillover—on how, say, diegetic space can replicate into street architecture or determine, the other way round, the role of horror in capturing certain kinds of urban experience in a way that no other form could. Elsewhere (Rajadhyaksha 2009: 84), I have proposed the significance in Indian cinema of the 'cinema-effect', the performance of a specifically symbolic gesture prototyped on celluloid but now capable of being replicated everywhere else—to the extent that, for the first time, both technologies (such as gaming) and cultural industries (such as fashion) could 'do' cinema better than cinema itself could.

Such a denizen of that Mumbai is, for instance, the real-life figure of Marathi-Dalit poet Namdeo Dhasal, who walked Virgil-like through 'Central Bombay's Inferno' (as Dilip Chitre describes him), who knew the city, defined himself by the city, but literally owned it—or rather her, as though she were his 'whore'—by the possession of this knowledge. Dhasal's famous poem 'Bombay' has him saying goodbye to 'her': 'But not before/I will take you/in multiple ways/Not before/I will pin you down/here and now/thus and thus.'[7] Dhasal's use of territorial realism, though spectacular, is by no means unique, and indeed access to such insider realism in the city of Mumbai has become increasingly available to the artist and film-maker (an early example of this is Saeed Mirza, but now, via actors like Nana Patekar in Vinod Chopra's *Parinda* (1989) also an entire 1990s generation of Bombay regionalism originating in N. Chandra, Govind Nihalani, and even Jabbar Patel films, are later commodified into a larger market in films like Ramgopal Varma's *Satya* (1998).

This was a very particular realism, unique in India, and it alluded to a specific period, a determinate set of political histories and to a given set of spaces. The period was the 1970s and early 1980s, the political movements referred to the decade leading up to the landmark 1982 textile strike, the first of two defining political moments that have commonly been seen as having transformed contemporary Bombay (the other being the post-Ayodhya 1992–3 riots), and the space in which it happened was Girangaon (where the city's former textile mills once stood). While the 1982 strike has commonly been seen as Girangaon's 'last stand', since the collapse of the strike also effectively saw the dismantling of the industry itself, both the forms of industrial capital and the histories of state formation and radical-symbolic opposition characteristic of that era continued to be evoked in numerous art practices, particularly in music, poetry, and theatre.

'A striker in the 1928 textile strike, parachuted into Girangaon in 1982,' writes Chandavarkar (2004: 67), 'would have recognized the same massive, enthusiastic groundswell that drove the leadership forward.' This realism was therefore cast, directly or indirectly, over the time span of the popular cultures that the working class of Girangaon spawned, as did the larger context within which the 1982 strike mounted its historical significance as it hit at the city's financial elite. The realism that emerged, found itself engaging with foundational questions about the city, its reasons for being (or not being) a part of India—questions that often ran along the lines of capital and class, rather than region, leading to distinct local variations in India's national imaginary as well as the role of realism in constructing such an imaginary.

Hypervisible Action

A crucial aspect of the politics was a symbolic representation of this imaginary, and the most favoured representation was that of spectacular political action as a particular variant of exceptional spectator activity. Hypervisible action—the expressive political gesture to which the influential Bombay-based visual artist Sudhir Patwardhan constantly refers—here goes beyond its usual function of verisimilitude. It reprises, I propose, the characteristics of a state rationality over a different, expressly political arena, even going so far as to reconstruct state realism's capacity to embody and to disburse specific rights into an instrument for the exclusive use of an independent citizen/protagonist/author.

If I am right on all the above, I want finally to suggest that it may now be possible to excavate explicit rights-bearing properties within the symbolic gesture, whose content, I suggest, reveals shades of social power with startling resemblances to the symbolic domain of seemingly 'rational' state operation. The political-symbolic gesture derived its formal energy not so much from the radical-ecstatic self-description of the clenched fist, but, rather, from a somewhat specific history of spectatorial imbalance and anxiety arising—I argue—from a particularly 1980s Bombay legitimation crisis. Hypervisible political action in numerous texts in the cinema and the visual arts, functions as a distinct species of the cinema-effect in direct tension with realist textuality, encroaching upon the template of the state's own production of symbolic action.

Here I mean 'encroach upon' literally, since the political underpinnings often had to do with space. Bombay's political articulations of territory (and the bounded realism policing that territory) have been strident in drawing attention to the hypervisible ambitions of realism as *reclaiming space*, often the very spaces that Article 15 of the Indian Constitution names in its prohibition of 'discrimination on grounds of religion, race, caste, sex, or place of birth' with regard to access to 'shops, public restaurants, hotels and places of public entertainment; or the use of wells, tanks, bathing ghats, roads and places of public resort ... dedicated to the use of the general public' (Constitution of India, Part III, Fundamental Rights: The Right to Equality, 15/2). If the ambitions of such territorial realism were any indication (and we may now no longer limit the instance to Bombay alone), it would appear that political realism would also test every step of the way the rights that such territory embodied for the postcolonial citizen. Its effort to usurp urban realism away from state authentication and into a strategy of survival-through-description sharply draws attention to the fact that illegitimate realism often means the illegitimacy of citizenship. A primary right that this particular variant of Bombay realism underpinned was the pragmatic and concretely cognizable right to shelter, further equated with the fundamental right to livelihood. For a number of political art practices working on the plane of symbolic realism, the effort is to recast the state's declared 'authenticity-effect' into a new register, to render that effect as an objective urban manifestation, as such realism develops an expressivity via its proven ability to slice through mechanisms that would otherwise render such representations both impossible and illegitimate.

Digital Mediations

If all this is so, and if it is this citizen who is now being digitized, there is surely a role for post-celluloid cinema in this new terror-spooked cyberspace, a role similar to the one it had in the era of celluloid. Including the not-so-quaint revisiting of the debate on whether a movie about a bank heist is or is not a how-to manual on the essential facets of successful bank robbery. It is in this sense that Rajnikant's seeming inability to move his persona into the new virtual domain, the entrapment that I read into Rajni jokes, becomes so tragically significant.

I move to a specific exercise. Digital mediations are increasingly becoming part of everyday life, as actually existing people incarnate their cyborg variants as they both strap on howitzers and drive choppers through dizzying heights, or swipe their credit cards and give their biometrics to an enrolment officer of India's much-discussed Unique Identification Project. As we recognize this fact, what if we take the concept of mediation seriously as also having to do with a mediator? This could be the local delivery person who brings the digital universe actually to your door—once the hoary character of the postman who also read out letters to their illiterate recipients, and now the 'street bureaucrat' in today's developmental language, the man you actually encounter in an otherwise faceless state. In the cinema he once was the *benshi*, a species of film-instructor who physically stood between spectator and screen, explaining what the film was about. In the cinema the mediator has a long history; one that Gunning (1991) called the film-instructor, later inducted into the storytelling idiom of cinema, and, we may propose in India, a somewhat diverse and devolved narratorial authority reproduced by many kinds of social mediation.

Such a mediator has resurfaced to radically new meaning in post-celluloid narrative structures. S/he is not only the bodily consequence of actual individuals putting on various prosthetic or orthotic devices. The category also arises as an entity seemingly capable of mediating a larger problem that digital technologies are presenting across the board to various kinds of meaning-making authority. Traditionally, the main carrier of what has come to be dubbed as the 'last mile problem' in India,[8] inappropriate intermediation has often been held as a primary cause for why state benefit does not reach its intended beneficiaries but gets diverted, usually by some middle-man. The concept of the 'last mile problem' is derived from communications theory, in addressing the basic question of why a signal does not reach its intended recipient or when distortions come into play. Often viewed as a principal consequence of corruption, such misdirection is usually sought to be overcome by making an unmediated link between the state as source for delivery of benefit and the recipient, the best examples being in the phenomenon of direct cash transfers now attached to employment-guarantee schemes, when a state-recognized digital identity is attached to a no-frills bank account and the money goes straight into that account.[9] Such a formulation assumes the middleman as basically the cause of distortion, at worst personally corrupt, at best the cause of the distortion through his incomprehension of the message he is meant to deliver.

Recent modifications proposed to the Information Technology Act of 2000, which many see as a direct attack on social networking sites, brings matters full circle. A critical rule concerns the kind of 'due diligence' that is to be observed by the mediator of data. This mediation agency now has to notify users of the computer resource that they are not to do any of the many things that 'decent' people should not be doing. Among the things users should not do is to display, upload, modify, publish, transmit, update, share, or store any information that belongs to another person. The intermediate agency becomes responsible when the user accesses data that is harmful, threatening, abusive, harassing, blasphemous, objectionable, defamatory, vulgar, obscene, pornographic, paedophilic, libellous, invasive of another's privacy, hateful, or racially, ethnically, or otherwise objectionable, disparaging, relating or encouraging money laundering or gambling, or otherwise unlawful in any manner whatsoever, or which harms minors in any way, infringes any patent, trademark, copyright, or other proprietary rights, contains software viruses or any other computer code, files, or programmes designed to interrupt, destroy, or limit the functionality of any computer resource, and so on.

It is one thing to agree or disagree as to whether some of these acts are illegal, and quite another to make the mediating agency legally responsible for the data that he is processing; this also has significant political consequences for the entire history of the very concept of mediation. Is a postman legally responsible for the content of the letter that he reads out? Prashant Iyengar (2011) of the Centre for Internet and Society has argued that a mediation agency that houses user-generated content, such as Wikipedia, would need different terms of use from an intermediary such as an email provider like Hotmail. Similarly, the liability that a newspaper accrues is different from that accrued by the post office. But what if the intermediary is of a very different generation? What if he is no longer merely our local cable guy, or our Internet Service Provider (ISP), but is a part Google or facebook? In short, what if the user is an unintended mediator? Or even an ordinary man who is secretly a heavily armed urban guerilla?

The rules further make it necessary that if intermediaries are informed of any violation, which includes even an email with an electronic signature, they should remove access to such information that is claimed to be infringing or to be the subject of infringing activity, and within 90 days inform the police about such information. This is of course staggering, and Iyengar clearly shows that it is fundamentally unconstitutional. If any person is aggrieved by information posted online, they may seek their remedies—including the relief of injunction—from courts of law, under generally applicable civil and criminal law. Inserting a rule such as this one would take away the powers of the judiciary in India to define the line dividing permissible and impermissible speech, and vest it instead in the whims of each intermediary. This, he says, can only have a chilling effect on debates in the public domain (of which the Internet is a part), which is the foundation of any democracy.

Reconsidering Hypervisible Action

The problem of hypervisible action is, it seems, a serious one, meriting serious action from our armed spectator. If, as we agree, the video gamer is almost certainly a direct descendant of the urban guerilla of Mumbai's 1980s realism, how can we imagine today's Dhasal? What would hypervisible political action mean today? Galloway (2006) points out that crucial to any video game is the expressive act, where you select, pick, get, rotate, unlock, open, talk, examine, use, fire, attack, cast, apply, type, or emote. What is important is the coupling of acting agent (the player character) and the actionable object, which can come in the form of buttons, blocks, keys, obstacles, doors, words, non-player characters, and so on. Non-actionable objects are inert scenery, and indeed certain objects are deliberately created as inert masses whereas others are linked to specific functions that can produce action responses.

Imagine a Dhasal-like-figure walking through Mumbai's metropolis, amid explosions, explaining to his readers which spaces, in his moonscape of a *Golpitha*, are 'inert scenery' and which related to functions can produce 'actionable objects'. In those days, the realistic representation of everyday life in Mumbai would commonly be seen as covering up for dark misdeeds where the more ordinary the view, the more likely that, far from inert, it only hid deeper secrets. It is fascinating to imagine the politicized fan-spectator of a celluloid film entering this domain, and perhaps salutary to imagine its reverse—a curious limit, or ceiling, or glass box into which SRK appears trapped within the cinema. We may need to track closely how, say, conventions of editing, sound mixing, and shot-taking, the entire cinematic grammar that was associated with spectatorial action, now translates into gaming language.

A curious and significant means by which the hyperstar cuts through the fiction and seemingly addresses the spectator directly is through a hypervisible act, most famously perhaps, Rajnikant's cigarette-throwing gesture or the many gags associated with SRK's *Don* series (Dir. Farhan Akhtar, 2006 and 2011). If the hypervisible gesture can be seen to find its ancestry in the symbolic political act, can it also show its ability to cut through the maze of civil society to address its beneficiary with the directness that only digital technology can allow? Back in 2002, a furious debate had taken place, in which Lawrence Liang, S.V. Srinivas, and I, along with several friends, had virtually fallen out over the famed Rajnikant gesture.[10] The problem was that Rajni had sought to copyright his gesture from the film *Baba* (Dir. Suresh Krishna, 2002), and the question was whether he, as a movie star with a movie-audience, 'owned' this gesture or not. Was such a copyrighting process—to which adherents of copyleft furiously objected, correctly perhaps, but which they were unable to see as being any different from other forms of corporate copyrighting—not integral to the kind of narrative contract that the movie star established with his audience? Would the radical position, that of attacking the star's effort to copyright his gesture, not threaten to crack open the very edifice of both the political and then the populist gesture, even as these moved into their purely commodified phase? The crucial problem in this was what the gesture implied. It was a kind of contract that bound spectator and star together. The question now was whether a naïve copyleft position had adequately accounted for the transformation, the *political* transformation, of this gesture from such a contract into a commodity.

Let me take this to a specific example of the only narrative crisis for an Indian game that I have come across. *Ra.One* is an SRK movie that is also a top-down 3D arcade action game available online, on PlayStation 2, and on all Apple platforms. You are the mighty superhero G.One who has to defend the world against the wrath of a surreal creation codenamed Ra.One. G.One not only switches on the dark, he can solidify electricity. The gamer's mission is to survive, and then to destroy Ra.One and his commanders. The publicity claims that the encounter will include 'epic boss battles, tons of character customization and purchasable weapons, armor and upgrades', and you can also track your unlocked achievements over Game Centre or publish them on your facebook wall.

It does not take more than a few minutes to see that the *Ra.One* game, even if you haven't encountered Batman's Arkham series, is—to use SRK's own language—'rubbish'. The characters have no depth at all; neither is the arena worked out, nor, importantly, the enhancement of power capacity. That the Indian gaming market has fumbled with how to arm an Indian spectator with this kind of armoury—the hyper-technologization, almost overnight, of what used to be no more than the plain act of looking, or at most whistling, or maybe dancing in the dark, the fact that such multidimensional functions are not easily technologized is perhaps understandable. And so a reviewer complains that in the *Ra.One* game you start off with:

... a tutorial, where you'd want to keep track or note down what each button does on paper because there's no explanation of the controls via the option menus. Yes. This is a video game in 2011 that decides it's cool to let you fumble your way through it. I think that's the way you're meant to play it because even though each button has a specific function, such as ranged and melee attacks or block, the camera doesn't zoom in to the action so you'd rarely know what you're doing without sitting less than a foot away from the screen. (Alwani 2011)

But the Indian spectator can never be taken for granted and quickly this very review decides that there appears to be a curious and very 'Bollywood' method in the madness, since this confusion involves hammering down on your melee and ranged attacks long enough to fill up your, yes, power meter.

Doing so allows you to unleash a special attack that does an effective job of clearing a room full of baddies. There are power-ups that allow you to regain health or enhance your speed, among other things. Certain levels have you trying to survive a rather timid onslaught before the timer runs out. Before you know it, the game devolves into a race to tap your controller long enough to get to a super attack. (Alwani 2011)

These 'powermetres', by which the good guys can recoup, are startlingly similar to the kinds of covert knowledges that I had pointed out in the Mumbai instances: streets that you cannot take or ones where there is shelter, spaces where you can hide, or where you can top-up. I am less interested in these aspects than in returning to the crisis that Rajni narratively finds himself in; in having to switch off his own power to generate Rajni Power.

————

Once upon a time the famous Rajni and SRK gestures were par excellence acts of slicing through cinematic fiction to directly address real-life situations. Can we now have arrived at a situation where, as symbolic modes of meaning production prototyped on celluloid film move into the treacherous domain of the digital, cinema's famed capacity to spill out into spaces beyond the unstable film-frame has itself been trapped? At the same time as we see post-celluloid action marching towards a new brand of citizen empowerment, we also see citizen action being boxed in, their biometric data safely ensconced in a state repository, even as they play out their apparent freedoms with howitzers and machine guns.

In this chapter, I have tried to address a particular new turn to the concept of cinematic excess, translated into a specific techno-performative crisis that SRK chooses to embody in his new superhero avatar, an avatar that I think has the same salience to the very un-superheroic Rizwan Khan as it does to the actual superhero, G.One. Khan is correct, I propose in conclusion to speak of both technology and freedom, even as he works out his own economic model for his hyperstardom, both beyond the cinema and within it. The march of cinematic action is, in Khan's work, being virtually driven by a need for narrative exegesis that the traditional apparatus of celluloid simply finds insufficient.

Notes

1. Quotes have been taken from the *Front Row* discussion titled 'SRK Talks about His Favourite Superheroes', available at http://www.youtube.com/watch?feature= player_detailpage&v= tk5sIpwIJv4#t=937s (accessed on 9 November 2013).

2. See especially the work of psychiatric experts H. Eric Bender, Vasilis K. Pozios, and Praveen R. Kambam on the mental health conditions of 'Batman, The Hulk and Spiderman' (Moye 2010).

3. Released on 19 December 2014, *PK*, directed by Rajkumar Hirani, has reportedly made more than Rs 600 crore.

4. In an article in the *Times of India*, 'Shah Rukh Khan's Net Worth Is 2500 Crore', available at http://timesofindia.indiatimes.com/videos/celebs/Shah-Rukh-Khans-net-worth-is-2500-crore/videoshow/5146155.cms (accessed on 9 November 2013).

5. Both the NCTC and NATGRID have been pet projects of the Government of India, usually attributed to former Home Minister P. Chidambaram. Both have been branded as sequel instruments for state-intelligence gathering and have had trouble getting implemented following major political resistance.

6. In *Deewar* (Dir. Yash Chopra, 1975) when Vijay buys the building, we see it glinting on his glares as he utters the immortal Salim–Javed dialogue: '*Aaj se bees saal pehle meri maa ne yahan ite uthayin thi. Aaj mai use yeh building tohfa dene jaa raha hoon.*' (Twenty years ago my mother lifted bricks here as a labourer. Today I am going to gift this building to her.)

7. Namdeo Dhasal (1949–2014) is one of the best-known Marathi Dalit poets and has written extensively on the city of Bombay in his poetry. This iconic poem on Bombay is translated as 'Mumbai, Mumbai, My Dear Slut', and discussed in Vidyut Bhagwat and Sharmila Rege's 1995 essay.

8. The 'last mile problem' is a concept drawn from communication studies describing signal decay and has been widely adopted by Indian developmental discourse as the key problem for the Indian state: how to ensure that benefit actually reaches its beneficiary. See Rajadhyaksha (2009).

9. This refers to the controversial 'Direct Cash Transfers' scheme implemented by the Government of India in 2012–13, where the government directly pays out employment guarantee benefit into people's bank accounts.

10. This was a discussion thread on the Sarai site, the thread does not exist any longer. For a reference to the debate, see Liang (2003).

References

Alwani, Rishi. 2011. 'Review: Ra.One: The Game', *Indian Video Gamer*, 30 October, available at: http://www.indianvideogamer.com/reviews/review-ra-one-the-game (accessed on 9 November 2013).

Bhagwat, Vidyut and Sharmila Rege. 1995. 'Bombay in Dalit Literature', in Sujata Patel and Alice Thorner (eds), *Bombay: Mosaic of Modern Culture*, pp. 113–25. New Delhi: Oxford University Press.

Chandavarkar, Rajnarayan. 2004. 'From Neighbourhood to Nation: The Rise and Fall of the Left in Bombay's Girangaon in the Twentieth Century', in Meena Menon and Neera Adarkar (eds), *One Hundred Years, One Hundred Voices: The Mill Workers of Girangaon: An Oral History*, pp. 7–80. Calcutta: Seagull Books.

Chitre, Dilip. 2005. 'The City of My First and Last Love', *Tehelka*, New Delhi, 2 July, available at http://archive.tehelka.com/story_main13.asp?filename=hub070205The_city_of.asp (accessed on 15 May 2015).

Elberse, Anita. 2007. 'The Power of Stars: Do Star Actors Drive the Success of Movies?', *Journal of Marketing*, 71 (4): 102–20, available at http://www.people.hbs.edu/aelberse/publications/Elberse_2007.pdf (accessed on 15 May 2015).

Galloway, Alexander R. 2006. *Gaming: Essays on Algorithmic Culture*. Minneapolis: University of Minnesota Press.

Gunning, Tom. 1991. *D.W. Griffith and the Origins of American Narrative Film: The Early Years at Biograph*. Urbana: University of Illinois Press.

Iyengar, Prashant. 2011. *Privacy and the Information Technology Act: Do We Have the Safeguards for Electronic Privacy?* Bangalore: Centre for Internet & Society, available at http://cis-india.org/internet-governance/blog/privacy/safeguards-for-electronic-privacy (accessed on 9 November 2013).

Liang, Lawrence. 2003. 'Conceptualizing Law and Culture', *Seminar*, p. 525, available at http://www.india-seminar.com/2003/ 525/525%20 lawrence%20liang.htm (accessed on 9 November 2013).

Moye, David. 2010. 'Super Shrinks Psychoanalyze Superheroes', *AOL News*, 22 July, available at http://www.aolnews.com/2010/07/22/super-shrinks-psychoanalyze-superheroes/ (accessed on 9 November 2013).

Rajadhyaksha, Ashish. 2009. *Indian Cinema in the Time of Celluloid: From Bollywood to the Emergency.* Bloomington: Indiana University Press.

————. 2010. *The Last Cultural Mile: An Inquiry into Technology and Governance in India.* Bangalore: Centre for Internet & Society, available at http://cis-india.org/raw/histories-of-the-internet/last-cultural-mile.pdf (accessed on 15 May 2015).

Ravid, S. Abraham. 1999. 'Information, Blockbusters, and Stars: A Study of the Film Industry', *The Journal of Business*, 72 (4): 463–92.

Weizman, Eyal. 2006. 'The Art of War', *Frieze*, p. 99, available at http://www.frieze.com/issue/article/the_art_of_war/ (accessed on 9 November 2013).

Filmography

Baba. Dir. Suresh Krishna. Lotus International, 2002.
Bonnie and Clyde. Dir. Arthur Penn. Warner Brothers and Seven Arts, 1967.
Dabangg 2. Dir. Arbaaz Khan. Arbaaz Khan Productions, 2012.
Deewar. Dir. Yash Chopra. Trimurti Films, 1975.
Don. Dir. Farhan Akhtar. Excel Entertainment, 2006.
Don 2. Dir. Farhan Akhtar. Excel Entertainment, 2011.
Easy Rider. Dir. Dennis Hopper. Columbia Pictures, 1969.
Gun Crazy. Dir. Josef H. Lewis. King Brothers Productions, 1950.
Jab Tak Hai Jaan. Dir. Yash Chopra. Yash Raj Films, 2012.
Kabul Express. Dir. Kabir Khan. Yash Raj Films, 2006.
Kites. Dir. Anurag Basu. Bollywood Hollywood Production, 2010.
Mumbai Meri Jaan. Dir. Nishikanth Kamath. UTV Motion Pictures, 2008.
My Name Is Khan. Dir. Karan Johar. Dharma Productions, 2010.
New York. Dir. Kabir Khan. Yash Raj Films, 2009.
Ra.One. Dir. Anubhav Sinha. Red Chillies Entertainment, 2011.
Shootout at Lokhandwala. Dir. Apoorva Lakhia. Balaji Motion Pictures, 2007.

Innocent Abroad

SRK, Karan Johar, and the Indian Diasporic Romance

RACHEL DWYER

Shah Rukh Khan (henceforth SRK) is one of the biggest stars of Hindi cinema since the mid-1990s, both at home and abroad. However, in the overseas market he is the biggest star, starring in 11 of the top 25 overseas grossers of all time,[1] whereas in the worldwide market (including India), he stars in five of the 25.[2] The statistics of box office returns are not only unreliable but also open to multiple interpretations. For example, Aamir Khan is clearly a strong rival as his *3 Idiots* (Dir. Rajkumar Hirani, 2009) is considered to be one of the biggest hits of all time, and Salman Khan and Hrithik Roshan have massive popularity. However, SRK's overseas popularity seems uncontested.

Among these 11 hits of SRK, five big-budget family romances are closely associated with Karan Johar's (KJo) Dharma Productions. The following shows their ranking: 2. *My Name Is Khan* (*MNIK*, Dir. Karan Johar, 2010); 4. *Kabhi Alvida Na Kehna* (*KANK*, Dir. Karan Johar, 2006); 11. *Kabhi Khushi Kabhie Gham...* (*K3G*, Dir. Karan Johar, 2001); 20. *Kuch Kuch Hota Hai* (*K2H2*, Dir. Karan Johar, 1998); and 23. *Kal Ho Na Ho* (*KHNH*, Dirs Nikhil Advani and Ron Reid Jr., 2001).

This chapter examines some of these SRK–KJo films to ask why they are set partially or wholly in an imaginary diaspora, usually in the UK or the USA, yet in which the lead character played by SRK has his lifestyle and language marked as Indian rather than as diasporic. It suggests reasons why these films are so popular at home and overseas, and what SRK comes to represent in them and why he can be called a diasporic star.[3]

SRK the Star

SRK's star text can be said to be a mix of the real person, the image in the films, and the image created elsewhere in the media (Dyer 1998). Ashish Rajadhyaksha (this volume) argues that SRK is a hyperstar, wherein the twenty-first century notion of stardom is moving from film to new technologies, such as gaming, where the star text exceeds his star image. SRK's *Ra.One* (Dir. Anubhav Sinha, 2011) seems to reinforce this suggestion. However, this chapter argues that with SRK, the image in the films has by far eclipsed the other elements of his star text. SRK's interviews reveal little about the real person and indeed seem to reinforce his film image as the young, international, emotional, and desirable hero.

Relatively less, is known about the private person despite his seeming willingness to talk and even allow filming of himself at home in Nasreen Munni Kabir's documentaries *The Inner and Outer World of Shah Rukh Khan* or to be interviewed for Anupama Chopra's 2007 book, even though these are two of the most astute interviewers of Indian film stars. Their work is the major source on SRK the person. Indian, Delhi-born, and after some success in television, SRK joined the film industry and settled in Bombay (now Mumbai). He is a Muslim, who practises to at least some degree, is married to a Hindu, and has three children. He is fond of gadgets, cars, and technology. SRK is very wealthy indeed, with his film work supplying him with just a portion of his massive income, the rest of which is from his end-less hard work in advertising endorsements, his property in Dubai and London, and the Indian Premier League (IPL) cricket team he owns.

SRK's paternal family is originally from Peshawar, where they lived in the same area as Dilip Kumar's family and several generations of the Kapoors, before migrating to Delhi. Peshawar has a special status in India, where there is a certain nostalgia for this city whose major freedom fighter, Khan Abdul Ghaffar Khan (1890–1988), the *Sarhaddi Gandhi*, 'Frontier Gandhi', and his Khudai Khidmatgar Party, that opposed the Muslim League and its demands for a separate homeland, and who, despite being a Pakistani, was given a Bharat Ratna in 1987. What SRK's status as a Pathan means for his fans, both Hindu and Muslim, in India as well as overseas and for Pakistanis is not clear but seems likely to reinforce a stereotypical image of the 'good Muslim' who is loyal to India and is modern and secular.

There is an obsession about SRK's sexuality, which actually says more about the desire of his fans, which enables discourse about alternative sexualities, although homosexual acts are illegal under Section 377 of the Indian Penal Code. Bollywood is a key part of the gay imaginary of the diasporic Indian (see discussion below). This fantasy sits alongside frenzied discussion of SRK's relationships with his female co-stars, but is of interest to this chapter only in that this reinforces the enigma of SRK.

Beyond his numerous interviews and plugs for his new releases, SRK has a substantial media presence in India. He appears in many advertisements, ranging from his appearance in the Pepsi commercials to being 'brand ambassador' for watches, cars, banks, and mobile phone networks. He is seen on chat shows, he owns an IPL cricket team, and runs his own production company, Red Chillies Entertainment, and in his recent film *Ra.One* shows that he is developing an interest in gaming.

While SRK's private life remains just that, his star text has been built up by his roles in more than 77 films, in which he often stars as characters whose intertextual references are made clear by his name—Rahul, Raj—and his surnames which mark him as an upper-caste Punjabi—Khanna, Malhotra—many of which have him living in, or at least travelling to, the diaspora. While there is a long history in Hindi cinema of stories where Indians have returned from abroad, from *Bilat Pherat* (Dir. N.C. Lahiri, 1921) in the silent era till today, overseas locations, mostly used to show the glamour of travel (Dwyer and Patel 2002), became popular with colour film in the 1960s. However, the earliest films to show Indians living overseas, that is the Indian diaspora, were mostly from the late 1960s but were usually about bringing the family home, to escape the material

West and to return to the spiritual East shown in films such as *Purab aur Pacchim* (Dir. Manoj Kumar, 1970). It was only in the 1990s that films began to show Indians as permanently settled overseas, thereby marking the rise of the diasporic romance.[4]

The Formation of 'Bollywood'

Hindi film underwent changes almost as drastic as the country itself in the 1990s after the economy underwent liberalization resulting in the emergence of the new middle classes and explosion of media (Dwyer 2011b), leading to the formation of what is now known as Bollywood (Rajadhyaksha 2003; Vasudevan 2011). The diasporic romance is important to the Bollywood formations not only in the representation of the Indian diaspora, or at least the diaspora in the UK and the USA, but also in the increasing importance of the overseas market to the economics of the film industry (Dwyer 2006; Washbrook and Chatterjee 2013).

Vasudevan (2011) argues that the new type of Hindi cinema known as Bollywood begins with *Dilwale Dulhania Le Jayenge* (*DDLJ*, Dir. Aditya Chopra) in 1995 (Chopra 2003; Uberoi 1999). After this, the diaspora moves into playing a key role in Indian cinema, both as audiences and as characters within the films where they are no longer Hindi-speaking exiles waiting to return to the motherland, but second-generation immigrants born and brought up in the West. The father dreams of a return to homeland but he seems to be alone in this wish. In fact, when the daughter is taken to India for her wedding, the local intended groom is shown in a very negative light compared to her British-Asian lover. Yet these films do not present the characters as realistically diasporic; these are Hindi-speaking Indians whose fantasies, styling, and interiors are those of Indians or, at most, recent migrants even if they now dream of a 'return'. This means that the parents may be convincing as first-generation migrants, the children are not. However, this goes along with the lack of realism in other parts of the film, notably in the geography of London.

SRK plays Raj, a British Asian, but he does not attempt a British accent. Yet when he follows Simran to Punjab where her extended family lives, he does not seem to have any family there and seems to be totally separated from India. However, in the film, he knows what his duty is as an Indian and is equally aware of the ritual of *kanyadaan*, wherein the bride is given in marriage by the father.

So while this lack of realism is not surprising in Bollywood melodrama, the success of the diasporic family genre suggests that there is some underlying resonance that these films have with the audiences in India as well as overseas which may allow the exploration of the relationship between the diaspora, Indians, and the notion of Indianness. These films also mark SRK's emergence as the dominant hero of Bollywood and the most popular star in the diaspora.

SRK's Films

SRK began his career in television and then in slightly offbeat art films (for example, *Ahmek*, Dir. Mani Kaul, 1991) before becoming an anti-hero (*Baazigar*, Dir. Abbas Mastan, 1993; *Anjaam*, Dir. Rahul Rawail, 1994; *Darr*, Dir. Yash Chopra, 1993), and then, finally, a major Bollywood star (*Karan Arjun*, Dir. Rakesh Roshan, 1995). After *DDLJ*, he acted in many non-diaporic films, but his most memorable roles are mostly where he is in the diaspora. He plays a diasporic hero in *Pardes* (Dir. Subhash Ghai, 1997), as he saves Ganga, the pure Indian woman, from her violent fiancé, takes her back to her family in India and wins them over by showing that he is the one who really understands Indian values.

One of SRK's more realistic films was *Swades: We, the People* (Dir. Ashutosh Gowarikar, 2004), a Gandhian film which specifically refers to activist Rajni Bakshi's 1998 book on neo-Gandhianism, *Bapa Kuti* (Dwyer 2011a). In this film, SRK plays a character called Mohan (cf. Mohandas Gandhi) who returns to India, leaving behind his work for NASA. He has no family in the USA but finds himself a place in India by locating himself within a family and a community in the village as he reunites with his adoptive mother and falls in love with a teacher, tellingly named Gita. Mohan becomes involved in promoting education for all and various anti-caste activities. Although he needs to be in India to find himself as an Indian, he uses his overseas experience just as Gandhi formed his ideas of Indian nationalism in South Africa but experimented with them in India.

SRK plays the Indian everyman rather than a diasporic Indian in a group of films that were very popular in the diaspora. Among these, it is notable that the production company Yash Raj Films (YRF), whose *DDLJ* began the trend, had him in these roles: a modern theatre producer in *Dil to Pagal Hai* (Dir. Yash Chopra, 1997); a school teacher in *Mohabbatein* (Dir. Aditya Chopra, 2000); an Indian Air Force officer in *Veer-Zaara* (Dir. Yash Chopra, 2004); the women's national hockey coach in *Chak De! India* (Dir. Shimit Amin, 2007); and as a clerk at the Electricity Board in *Rab Ne Bana Di Jodi* (*RNBDJ*, Dir. Aditya Chopra, 2008). Although these films may involve travel, it is mostly there as a backdrop—a work trip or a holiday rather than an encounter with the diaspora. Yash Chopra's last film, *Jab Tak Hai Jaan* (*JTHJ*, Dir. Yash Chopra, 2012), locates Samar Anand (SRK) in two places: a diasporic Indian in London who moves around well-known landmarks, old and new—the O2 Centre, the London Eye, Canary Wharf, Billingsgate Market, St Pancras Station—as well as showing him as an Indian Army sapper in Kashmir and Ladakh. When in London, the character is lively and falls in love with a diasporic Indian; in India, he is silent and withdrawn, oblivious to the love of an Indian journalist.

Many of SRK's other major films are not set in the diaspora, such as *Devdas* (Dir. Sanjay Leela Bhansali, 2002) and *Om Shanti Om* (Dir. Farah Khan, 2008), although these were popular in the diaspora. SRK's other major hits overseas were *Don: The Chase Begins Again* (Dir. Farhan Akhtar, 2006) and *Don 2* (Dir. Farhan Akhtar, 2011), where he plays the role of the Bombay Don played by Amitabh Bachchan (*Don*, Dir. Chandra Barot, 1978), who has now become an international criminal, moving in a very different overseas world from that of the diasporic hero.

Yet despite these other roles, SRK's status as the leading diasporic star is unique. While earlier stars, such as Amitabh Bachchan (AB), had a sophisticated cosmopolitan nature, it was from the 1990s that a new generation of major stars (Aamir Khan, Salman Khan, Hrithik Roshan, Saif Ali Khan) took roles as diasporic figures but they are less closely associated with them than SRK is. Akshay Kumar, an action hero but most loved for his comic roles, has been successful in playing an innocent who travels overseas, presenting the comedy of other cultures and Indians who travel in them. Other important roles have been played by Rishi Kapoor, who plays a parental figure in films such as *Love Aaj*

Kal (Dir. Imtiaz Ali, 2009). The film shows that an Indian can live overseas and still cherish 'the old ways' and how love and romance come first for a younger generation of Indians.

Nonetheless, the diasporic films form a significant body of SRK's work, his roles with the biggest banners or production houses, and includes some of the all-time greatest hits of Hindi cinema at home and overseas. I now turn to look more closely at the diasporic hero in KJo's big budget, hugely successful, family romances which have reshaped and defined the Bollywood genre.

SRK's Films with Karan Johar

Karan Johar, son of producer Yash Johar, protégé of Yash Chopra, and close friend of Aditya Chopra, for whose *DDLJ* he was an assistant director and even made a brief appearance, is very closely associated with SRK, and says he will never make a film without him. KJo is a major celebrity in India, as host of popular star chat show *Koffee with Karan* and is the most media-friendly—and media-savvy—of his group of close friends, now regarded as a major industry spokesperson. All of KJo's film titles begin with letter 'K' for numerological reasons; their long titles are all abbreviated, perhaps to sound cool but also perhaps to benefit non-Hindi speakers as they are difficult to remember.[5]

In Kjo's debut film, *K2H2* (1998), Rahul (SRK) does not even go overseas but overseas locations are used to stand in for India as well as for romantic songs and for the location of the college. The film strongly has an American feel with its summer camps for children and its world of fun and colour. The film raises questions about the family, which are often raised in the diasporic film, notably about remarriage, duties of parents to children, and children's love for their parents.

KJo's next film *K3G* (2001) is a great family drama and is perhaps regarded as the film that defines the Bollywood style. It is inspired by Yash Chopra's 1976 intergenerational family romance, *Kabhi Kabhie*, which is partly located in a diasporic setting, with the emphasis in the film on the parent–child relationship as reflected in its slogan: 'It's all about loving your parents.'

The first half of the film is set in Delhi—though the Raichand house and the school in 'Mussoorie' are clearly in Europe—with the only specific location in India being a studio set which recreates Delhi's famous Chandni Chowk where the poorer characters live. Locations are used as decorative settings for songs, such as the pyramids for *Suraj hua maddham*, which establishes the romance between Rahul and Anjali, when the family migrates to the UK where well-known public buildings, such as Blenheim Palace, are used as a college setting and a wealthy family reunion happens in a bland mall.

Overseas locations are used in part for the spectacle of wealth and glamour and a location for romance, placing consumerism and lifestyle at the heart of romance. London is a location for education and work, but it is also a place for the new India to win admiration for its style, dancing, and being cool. It is also a place to feel a specific Indian nationalism and have a nostalgic view of India. However, it is also the place where the broken family begins to reunite. The exiled family adds a nanny as a mother figure and a brother pretending to be a lodger lives under a massive photograph of the parents. The death of a grandmother reunites the family in the sacred city of Haridwar as the three men hold the torch to light her pyre. Overseas is a place of exile, a temporary place, and the brother's quest to bring his older brother home has clear reference to the Ramayana, reminding us of the images of Rama, Sita, and Lakshmana in the first song, while the reunion is marked by the Gayatri Mantra and the image of Radha–Krishna. This image overrides resonances of the adopted child as Karna in the Mahabharata, whose birth condemns him to exile from his family, turning the film's focus to love across generations of the family and a demand for new values of understanding and forgiveness. Although the film's slogan is 'It's all about loving your parents', this is the one element that is never in doubt in the film; whereas, the father's love for his family is subordinated to duty. Amitabh reprises his role of the angry and unforgiving patriarch that he played in Yash Chopra's *Kabhi Kabhie* (1976) and Aditya Chopra's *Mohabbatein* (2000). His word is final in the family ('*Maine keh diya*'/'I said so') and his wife has to obey and serve him. His values are based on tradition (*parampara*), honour (*izzat*), and the notion that their wealth makes them more important than ordinary (*mamuli*) people. His break with his adopted son (although it seems unlikely someone so obsessed with tradition would have adopted a stranger) appears as outright unpleasant and the audience would lose sympathy if it were not for AB.

The other great theme is forgiveness (*maafi*). From the beginning of the film, the younger generation is forever apologizing: Rahul for calling the young Rohan 'Fatty'; Rohan for calling Pooja a 'vern' and lower class; Anjali for breaking vases at the Raichand house; Rahul for not loving Naina. The father is the one who has to apologize at the end after his wife points out he is not a *pati parameshwar* (husband-god) but one who makes mistakes (*galat*).

The film's plot is the construction of the complete family, mentioned at the beginning as having two children. The film begins with the last meeting of the family before the break up at Diwali which leads to the exile (Diwali marking the end of Rama's exile), through a fantasy reunion in the major song *Bole kangana* to end with the two younger couples being brought into the joint family—the final reunion at a Hindu wedding. India is a sacred space, where the family has its *khushi* (happiness), while overseas marks the years in the wilderness, the *gham* (sorrow).

Although KJo was only the producer of *KHNH* (2001), directed by Nikhil Advani—his former assistant—the style and content mark it as a KJo film. An unhappy, fractured Indian family in New York City prays for an angel and SRK arrives to mend their broken hearts and teach them how to live again through talking, understanding, forgiveness, and coming to terms with the failure of the father who committed suicide. Once the angel has united the diasporic family and has created a new family for his beloved by getting her to marry her best friend, he dies.

In this film SRK is not diasporic but he brings his magic from India to mend broken hearts, while he himself has a heart condition and comes to seek medical treatment. The diasporic family tread the paths of other diasporas by taking over a restaurant in New York City that was run by an earlier generation of migrants.

KHNH has a comedy track where a Gujarati servant walks in on situations where SRK and Saif seem to be in a homosexual relationship. This track was extended by Saif and SRK when presenting the 49th Filmfare awards, 2004, where they created a 'new ending' with them falling in love with each other. This picks up on star gossip, or rather fantasy, and SRK's gay-friendliness (Henniker 2010). However, this is good marketing as it is well known that a number of the diaspora bond and enjoy Bollywood as an outlet for camp and gayness (Dudrah 2006; Gehlawat 2010; Gopinath 2005; Waugh 2003). Gay audiences create their own readings of this and other films, often imagining the heroines changing gender or that the strict fathers reject the sons when they come out, before finally forgiving them.

In *KANK* (2006) the families are settled in New York City, although it is unclear how long they have lived there; why is it that they all speak Hindi; and why SRK is a soccer star. Dev (SRK) is angry with his wife for not giving him and their son time and he is angry with his son for not being a sportsman like him. The first time he meets Maya (Rani Mukerji) who is on the way to her wedding, he falls in love with her, not for any obvious reason other than she is very beautiful.

Maya does not love Rishi but married him out of duty. Rishi does not mind that she is infertile but says she has to treat him like a baby, which seems a strange relationship. Rishi's father, 'Sexy' Sam, and Dev's mother, Kamaljit, love each other as friends but know he is still in love with his dead first wife. But Sam has kept his son close, and also Maya. The parents are family makers but they cannot hold their children's families together and it is Sam who encourages Maya to leave Rishi.

Popular opinion has it that while the film did very well with the overseas audiences, it had only moderate success in India because divorce is not so widely acceptable in India. However, its reworking of *Silsila* (Dir. Yash Chopra, 1981) gives attention to mixed feelings, confused loyalties, not knowing what to do when living in a society that emphasizes romance and easy divorce without the networks of jobs, friends, and community that would be available in India. In the film, the couple suffer and are forgiven by their former partners and it seems that the case for divorce the film makes, may, like *Silsila*, give it later success.

In KJo's *MNIK* (2010), SRK plays Rizwan Khan, who is autistic but with special talents to repair machines and even people's lives. He migrates to live with his brother in the USA as communal (Hindu–Muslim) troubles kill his mother. However, there too Muslims face problems. Rizwan's brother throws him out because he marries a Hindu, then he has to face the wider issues of being a Muslim in the post-9/11 world. His stepson, who is Hindu, is killed by Islamophobes and his wife leaves him as she doesn't want to be associated with Islam. Rizwan's goal is to tell the US president, 'My name is Khan and I'm not a terrorist', encountering racism and helping flood victims in Georgia on his way. He finally meets the President who understands Muslims are not all terrorists before reuniting with his wife and his brother.

Overseas Locations

In India, it is often thought that films are deliberately seeking foreign audiences and will do this by shooting in those locations. When *DDLJ* appeared, the UK audiences loved the shots of Trafalgar Square at the beginning which made it 'their' film, but now overseas locations are becoming more frequent and it is not clear why the use of a much-seen city, such as London or New York City, would make the film appeal more to the diaspora. Film-makers draw attention to a more practical reason, namely, that while they use studios in India for many indoor locations, they want the outdoors for romantic scenes as well as street life. For example, many of KJo's films feature train stations for chance encounters and departures. While the American train stations are particularly cinematic, some of the Indian ones are spectacular, but it would be very difficult to shoot at a station with SRK in India (Gopal 2011: 80). In fact, it would be unlikely that permission would ever be granted. Other shots for romantic couples to meet are those framed at coffee shops, malls, and restaurants as well as luxurious homes (which could be shot in India). However, locations popular with tourists such as the Brooklyn Bridge and the London Eye are indeed spectacular. It is striking when *K3G* moves to London, the camera swoops through the streets to the refrain of 'Vande mataram' which looks as though perhaps London is the *maata* (mother) or that London has been totally Indianized.

Hindi films are shot overseas for business and production reasons. Yash Chopra has long said that it makes it easier for the producer to have the stars and personnel in a place for blocked dates, while also creating team spirit and keeping everyone focused. Now many countries, aware of the spending power of Indian tourists, want to encourage units to shoot in their locations, so offer tax breaks, subsidies, and assistance.[6] In recent years, many key figures, including SRK, have bought homes in London so they are keen to stay there, while others have children studying at schools and universities in Switzerland, the UK, and the USA, and many undergo regular medical treatment in these places. The level of comfort is helped by key hotels, notably the Washington Hotel in London, whose owners, the Sanger family, are personally known to most people in the industry, and they specialize in catering to Indian tastes and expectations.

Moreover, the overseas markets remain important, less for foreign exchange nowadays than the fact that the cost of a seat remains much higher. Although Indian films still dream of having the international market of Hollywood (USD 60 billion Hollywood and USD 2–2.5 billion Bollywood),[7] and there has been no film which has succeeded with mainstream audiences in the UK, USA, and India, SRK's box office power overseas is guaranteed and his films do exceptionally well (as stated above). SRK is not just a star but a canny businessman and has opened a production office in the USA in the hope of at least capturing the South Asian market there, if not the mainstream.[8]

There may be another possible reason for overseas locations for SRK's films, which is that they may engage with issues that cannot be tackled in India. While *KANK* could have been set in India, *MNIK* probably could not. It is part of a small group of big budget films including *Kurbaan* (Dir. Rensil d'Silva, 2009) and *New York* (Dir. Kabir Khan, 2009) that deal with issues of Islamist terrorism, in particular with the impact of post-9/11 Islamophobia on South Asians in the USA. *MNIK* was attacked in India, where SRK's complaint about Pakistanis not being allowed to play in the IPL led to a conflation of issues concerning the film with issues of Muslims in India. (It is not entirely clear if SRK was actually stopped by US Homeland Security allegedly because of being a Muslim or not.) It may well be that the problems faced by African Americans in the film may be loosely compared to the situation of India's Muslims. This is very different from *Chak De! India*, where SRK—as Kabir Khan—is accused of pro-Pakistan sentiments and has to establish his support for India, an issue that faces the Muslim community when India plays Pakistan in cricket.

Another determining factor is that although the new India that wants to take its place as a global power is emerging from the old socialism, it is still home to one of the largest populations of the poor in the world. Depicting India's poor is seen as almost an anti-national act, as the debates around *Slumdog Millionaire* (Dir. Danny Boyle, 2008) highlighted (Banaji 2010). India's new middle classes (NMCs, around 200m; Dwyer 2011b: 185–6), who form much of the cinema audience, want to see images of this new India (Dwyer 2011b). Until recently in India, it was usual for the media and the anglophone middle classes to dismiss the Hindi film as rubbish, whereas the NMCs celebrate its form and values. They do not share the postcolonial angst about India being marginalized and peripheral under the state-controlled socialism of the Permit Raj when there was little or no access to consumer goods and foreign travel for anyone other than the elite. This new group has benefited from the new opportunities created by liberalization in 1991, and enjoys their new wealth and embraces a consumerist style, wanting to get away from the poverty of India and sees any mention of it as an attack on their status. Many Indians are weary, after decades of negative views of India as a modern country, from images of poverty (poverty porn), and now are tired of hearing about poverty, many of them feeling that the poor are spoiling India, that they disfigure it, and that modern India is rising and shining (Pinney 2005). They want to see the image of a richer, more glamorous, more consumerist India, and reject images of the things they feel are holding back modernity—poverty, caste, corruption, and wider social problems—which they often blame on the poor themselves. They want to keep old India out of the films. Rural India and the poor are rarely seen in Bollywood films where even servants have mostly disappeared, perhaps seen as bringing an intrusion of the street into the house. It is in this context that the diasporic films have become popular as they show Indians, not diasporic Indians, living in London, New York City, or San Francisco, where poverty need not be shown and consumerism can be celebrated. This new space is imagined as Indian and is what India itself is poised to become.

The use of overseas locations to stand in for an India that is yet to emerge, shows a familiar feature in other narratives about India, namely, that Indian modernity is something which is shaped overseas and then imported to India. For example, Indian nationalism was shaped by leaders in (mostly) British universities and courts of law. Gandhi's ideas about the freedom struggle were shaped in London and in South Africa and he was truly a diasporic Indian by the time he finally returned to India. In the films we see the shaping of modern romance and indeed of the modern Indian family in the diaspora, which is the central concern of these films.

The Meaning of SRK in These Family Romance Films

All these films examine the problems of the Indian family, a narrative that has been explored throughout the history of Indian narrative from the great epics, the Mahabharata and the Ramayana, to the television soaps. In KJo's films, the family problems are often associated with change, largely brought about by modernity and westernization. So the diasporic Indian, who has been most exposed to these threats, seems an unlikely figure to save the Indian family. Yet, he is also removed from the pressures that affect the modern Indian elite—including urban squalor, traffic congestion, dreary work, inefficiency—by living a life of privilege which is hard to have in India without the old, poor India seeping through. In the West, wealth can be shown to be ubiquitous, shabbiness absent, and the different set of social problems largely does not impact these South Asians, at least until *MNIK* raises post-9/11 issues. The characters in these situations focus on the family and romance, yet they can still suffer as they seek to negotiate these relationships. Public life overseas is meaningless beyond garnering recognition for the self and for India.

These films show the life of the super-rich Indian overseas, but create an aspirational lifestyle for Indians who increasingly want to have an Americanized lifestyle, supplemented by servants and Indian food. Although Hindi films have long avoided issues of caste, these films—at least post *K3G*—also move away from representing class as the lead actors are all super-rich belonging to the business group, minimally interested in culture and education.

SRK is the figure who makes the transition between India and the West, as well as between the old and the new India. This is seen most closely in *KHNH*, where he is the Indian who comes to New York

City, seeking treatment but really to die. Self-sacrificing, loving, and more than a little divine, this Indian angel unites broken families and couples and even unites fractured American communities on 4th of July. He is the figure who represents the modern Indian, at home in India and the world, the cosmopolitan, or truly the global citizen.

SRK's success in this role as the ultimate diasporic star can be attributed to many elements of his stardom beyond the film roles themselves, although he is such a consummate actor that it is hard to distinguish the two. This includes his physical appearance, where his good looks, noted for his unruly hair, dimples, and his quizzical eyebrow, fit an international standard of wiry energy. His striking resemblance to Dilip Kumar and his undeniable charm have marked him as an urban, indeed urbane role model for Indian men. While looking more 'Indian' than some of the fairer stars, SRK could easily pass for a wide range of nationalities and has a very international image. His heroines—Rani, Kajol, Preity—are fair, sophisticated, modern women who can pass as Western or Indian, but like him, none of them could pass for a villager or even a non-metro Indian.

SRK's dressing style, often selected by KJo, is Western and modern but, although he sometimes wears designer clothing, he is not seen as a fashion icon which adds to his non-threatening masculinity. SRK is redefining what being middle-aged means in India as he has kept his youthful appearance. SRK is the star who can appear in the West as the new, cool Indian backed by his association with Western celebrities such as Lady Gaga and Akon.

SRK's high level of articulacy in English as well as Hindi and Urdu is striking. As a modern Muslim, he may use Urdu and Islamic vocabulary, but this serves only to mark his cultural background. To sum up, he appears classless, ageless, international, and has extraordinary charm. Creating a new image of the wealthy new Indian, he is admired for his uncompromising Indianness as well as being comfortable with non-Indians, he appears as something of a chameleon. He is the one character who can promote himself, and, by extension, the whole Hindi film industry as simultaneously Indian and global.

SRK represents the new post-1991 India with his rockstar chic, and is yet able to perform Bollywood melodrama and dance with great aplomb, albeit with a knowing irony. He expresses emotions and romance in a way few Hollywood stars ever have to or could do and creates a role model/object of desire. SRK prefers other roles, but it is as the emotional diasporic hero that he has been most popular.

It may well be that the charisma of a star is the ability of that person to embody and communicate emotions (Dwyer 2009), and it is undeniable that SRK has a unique ability to communicate and charm. SRK represents the modern hero, an emotional man, who, especially in the family melodramas with KJo, expresses every nuance of his feelings throughout the film and, in particular, in the song-and-dance sequences. These films foreground the tender sentiments and pain which are not usually aired in public in the West, and certainly not by men, but they link the audience to Indian sentiments and emotional worlds where these are not only expressed but admired.

SRK's songs usually have a particular emotionality from their plangent music to their picturization. SRK is often shown feeling the emotionality by reacting to the music with his full body, stretching his hands in the air and gesturing expansively. These are songs of pain and love as well as some fun, dance songs.

It is striking that in all these films SRK suffers from some form of disability or disadvantage, which means that although he remains good looking, he does not play a powerful male but a victim—widowed, rejected, ill, injured, or disabled—where it is never his fault. Although many may read this as having gay references (Henniker 2010), it certainly presents him as a more 'feminized' male, emotional and not seeking—indeed, even having lost—alpha status. Rather, this suffering and pain show him weeping, melancholic, suffering with threatened loss of status and respect. This pain is beyond his control but he adds to his pain through his own self-sacrifice as he aims to redeem himself through suffering. SRK's characters do not display the noble sentiments of Amitabh's star roles (Dwyer 2009) but are inclined towards the more 'feminine' tender sentiments and quest for romance. These characters give meaning to pain and suffering and may lead to the 'pleasure of tears' in his audiences, whether through empathy or identification. SRK represents a modern Indian emotionality which appeals to his audience as a gentle, suffering person who responds with tears and only occasionally with anger and, indeed, in many films his emotions are opposed to those of Amitabh's whose emotions are driven by anger which is based on reason rather than emotion. It is perhaps a sign that emotions are valued differently by the new middle classes and the diaspora in their negotiation of new values in India and overseas.

———

SRK produced and financed a sci-fi film, *Ra.One* (Dir. Anubhav Sinha, 2011) which is about characters from a game escaping into the real world. With a budget of USD 27.5 million, this is one of the most expensive Hindi films made. The first part of the film is set in London, although SRK's character Shekhar Subramaniam, a South-Indian software engineer, would be more likely to live in Silicone Valley or even in India. Perhaps it is filmed in London to allow the dramatic use of outdoor sequences, although one of the highlights of the film is the demolition of CST, a Bombay railway station, and the film *Slumdog Millionaire* has showed that chases through Bombay's streets may be difficult, but not impossible. Although his widow takes their son back to India and action in the second half unfolds in Bombay, the family ultimately returns to London. Narrative reasons for the overseas section seem rather thin beyond the use of landmark buildings and streets.

Perhaps, this is partly SRK's image as the diasporic hero. Even when he plays a localized hero in *RNBDJ*, he brings his stardom with him and once again; it is pain and hurt that make the movie so gripping for the audience. SRK may want to act in a wider variety of films but his massive audience love him for the diasporic films. In *JTHJ*, he romances Katrina, a real-life diasporic Indian, and Anushka Sharma, who are both approximately twenty years younger than him. Just as the authenticity of the Indian connection is irrelevant, so is the age difference. SRK remains the youthful star who represents the Indian and the diasporic Indian, his star image being more powerful than reality. SRK the star is not his performance in any one film but an amalgam of all his previous performances, which he further develops in his skilful performance in interviews. When I asked him half-jokingly, 'What does SRK mean?' he talked of the way that disabled people, particularly autistic and paralysed people, even those he meets outside India who are unaware of his star status, seem to feel some special link to him. It seems that the quality that has made him such a star, namely, his ability to convey emotion, is part of who SRK really is and his emotionality speaks to people in India and overseas. Of course, there is the other factor which he told me with a big grin—'I am sex on toast.'[9]

Notes

1. Refer to the article on Boxofficeindia.com, 'Top Overseas Grossers All Time: Three Idiots Number One', available at http://www.boxofficeindia.com/arounddetail.php?page=shownews&articleid=3946&nCat (accessed on 15 March 2012).
2. Refer to the article on Boxofficeindia.com, 'Top Worldwide Grossers All Time: 37 Films Hit 100 Crore', available at http://www.boxofficeindia.com/arounddetail.php?page=shownews&articleid=3997&nCat (accessed on 15 March 2012).
3. Among key works on Hindi cinema in the diaspora are: Dudrah (2006), Gopal and Moorti (2008), Kaur and Sinha (2005), Kavoori and Punathambekar (2008), Punathambekar (2005), and Therwath (2007).
4. This chapter concentrates on mainstream Hindi films set in the diaspora rather than diasporic films in the sense of films that are produced or made in the diaspora, such as those of Gurinder Chadha, Mira Nair, and Deepa Mehta. See Desai (2003).
5. For more on KJo, see Gopal (2011: 76).
6. For more details, refer to Indian Summer Films, available at http://www.indiansummerfilms.com/Film_services.html (accessed on 22 March 2012) and Jivraj Burman (2008).
7. Refer to Amy Kazmin (2011).
8. Refer to Aarti Virani (2012).
9. From a personal interview, dated 18 March 2012.

References

Banaji, Shakuntala. 2010. '"Seduced Outsiders" versus "Skeptical Insiders"?: *Slumdog Millionaire* through Its Re/Viewers', *Participations: Journal of Audience and Reception Studies*, 7 (1): 1–30, available at http://www.participations.org/Volume%207/Issue%201/banaji.htm (accessed on 10 December 2011).

Burman, Jivraj. 2008. 'West Wooing Bollywood Like Never Before', *Hindustan Times*, available at http://www.hindustantimes.com/

News-Feed/Business/West-wooing-Bollywood-like-never-before/ Article1-282988.aspx (accessed on 20 March 2012).

Chopra, Anupama. 2003. *Dilwale Dulhania Le Jayenge* ('*The Brave-hearted Will Take the Bride*'). London: British Film Institute Publishing.

—————. 2007. *King of Bollywood: Shah Rukh Khan and the Seductive World of Indian Cinema*. New York: Warner Books.

Derné, Stephen. 2008. *Globalization on the Ground: Media and the Transformation of Culture, Class, and Gender in India*. New Delhi: SAGE Publications.

Desai, Jigna. 2003. *Beyond Bollywood: The Cultural Politics of South Asian Diasporic Film*. London: Routledge.

Dudrah, Rajinder. 2006. *Bollywood: Sociology Goes to the Movies*. New Delhi: SAGE Publications.

Dwyer, Rachel. 2006. 'Planet Bollywood: Hindi Film in the UK', in Nasreen Ali, Virinder Kalra, and Salman Sayyid (eds), *Postcolonial People: South Asians in Britain*, pp. 366–75. London: C. Hurst & Co.

—————. 2009. 'Ich mag es, wenn du zornig wirst: Amitabh Bachchan, Emotionen und Stars im Hindi-film', in Claus Tieber (ed.), *Fokus Bollywood: Das Indische Kino in Wissenschaftlichen Diskursen*, pp. 99–115. Münster: Lit. Verlag.

—————. 2011a. 'The Case of the Missing Mahatma: Gandhi and the Hindi Cinema', *Public Culture*, 23 (2): 349–76.

—————. 2011b. '*Zara Hatke!*: The New Middle Classes and the Segmentation of Hindi Cinema', in Henrike Donner (ed.), *A Way of Life: Being Middle-class in Contemporary India*, pp. 184–208. London: Routledge.

—————. 2013. 'Bollywood's Empire: Indian Cinema and the Diaspora' in Joya Chatterjee and David Washbook (eds), *Routledge Handbook of South Asian Diaspora*, pp. 407–16. London: Routledge.

Dwyer, Rachel and Divia Patel. 2002. *Cinema India: The Visual Culture of Hindi Film*. London: Reaktion Books and the Victoria and Albert Museum.

Dyer, Richard. 1998. *Stars*. London: British Film Institute Publishing.

Gehlawat, Ajay. 2010. *Reframing Bollywood: Theories of Popular Hindi Cinema*. New Delhi: SAGE Publications.

Ghosh, Shohini. 2001. 'Queer Pleasures for Queer People: Film, Television and Queer Sexuality in India', in Ruth Vanita (ed.), *Queering India: Same Sex Love and Eroticism in Indian Culture and Society*, pp. 207–21. London: Routledge.

Gopal, Sangita. 2011. *Conjugations: Marriage and Forming New Bollywood Cinema*. Chicago: University of Chicago Press.

Gopal, Sangita and Sujata Moorti (eds). 2008. *Global Bollywood: Travels of Hindi Song and Dance*. Minneapolis: University of Minnesota Press.

Gopinath, Gayatri. 2005. *Impossible Desires: Queer Diasporas and South Asian Public Cultures*. Durham, North Carolina: Duke University Press.

Henniker, Charlie. 2010. 'Pink Rupees or Gay Icons? Accounting for the Camp Appropriation of Male Bollywood Stars', *South Asia Research*, 30 (1): 25–41.

Kaur, Raminder and Ajay J. Sinha. 2005. *Bollyworld: Popular Indian Cinema through a Transnational Lens*. New Delhi: SAGE Publications.

Kavoori, Anandam and Aswin Punathambekar (eds). 2008. *Global Bollywood*. New York: New York University Press.

Kazmin, Amy. 2011. 'Bollywood to the Next Level', *Financial Times*, 28 October, available at http://www.ft.com/cms/s/0/735cc752-00c4-11e1-8590-00144feabdc0.html#axzz1pqYxC9HS (accessed on 28 October 2011).

Pinney, Christopher. 2005. 'The Political Economy of Gloss', *Bidoun*, available at http://www.christopherpinney.com/Text_in_pdf/Political_gloss (accessed on 22 April 2013).

Punathambekar, Aswin. 2005. 'Bollywood in the Indian-American Diaspora: Mediating a Transitive Logic of Cultural Citizenship', *International Journal of Cultural Studies*, 8 (2): 151–73.

Rajadhyaksha, Ashish. 2003. 'The "Bollywoodization" of the Indian Cinema: Cultural Nationalism in a Global Arena', *Inter-Asia Cultural Studies*, 4 (1): 25–39.

Therwath, Ingrid. 2007. 'L'état en face à la diaspora: strategies et trajectories indiennes' (PhD thesis, IEP de Paris, France).

Uberoi, Patricia. 1998. 'The Diaspora Comes Home: Disciplining Desire in *DDLJ*', *Contributions to Indian Sociology*, 32 (2): 305–36.

Vasudevan, Ravi S. 2011. 'The Meanings of Bollywood', in Rachel Dwyer and Jerry Pinto (eds), *Beyond the Boundaries of Bollywood: The Many Forms of Hindi Cinema*, pp. 3–29. New Delhi: Oxford University Press.

Virani, Aarti. 2012. 'SRK Targets NRIs with New Production House', *The Wall Street Journal*, 9 March, available at http://blogs.wsj.com/indiarealtime/2012/03/09/srk-targets-nris-with-new-production-house/tab/print/ (accessed on 10 March 2012).

Waugh, Thomas. 2003. 'Queer Bollywood, or "I'm the Player, You're the Naive One": Patterns of Sexual Subversion in Recent Indian Popular Cinema', in Matthew Tinkcom and Amy Villarejo (eds), *Keyframes: Popular Cinema and Cultural Studies*, pp. 280–98. London: Taylor & Francis.

Filmography

3 Idiots. Dir. Rajkumar Hirani. Vinod Chopra Films, 2009.

Ahmek. Dir. Mani Kaul, 1991.

Anjaam. Dir. Rahul Rawail. 1994.

Baazigar. Dir. Abbas Mastan. United Seven Combines, 1993.

Bilat Pherat. Dir. N.C. Lahiri. Indo-British Film, 1921.

Chak De! India. Dir. Shimit Amin. Yash Raj Films, 2007.

Darr. Dir. Yash Chopra. Yash Raj Films, 1993.

Devdas. Dir. Sanjay Leela Bhansali. Mega Bollywood, 2002.

Dil To Pagal Hai. Dir. Yash Chopra. Yash Raj Films, 1997.

Dilwale Dulhania Le Jayenge. Dir. Aditya Chopra. Yash Raj Films, 1995.

Don. Dir. Chandra Barot. Nariman Films, 1978.

Don. Dir. Farhan Akhtar. Excel Entertainment, 2006.

Don 2. Dir. Farhan Akhtar. Excel Entertainment, 2011.

Jab Tak Hai Jaan. Dir. Yash Chopra. Yash Raj Films, 2012.

Kabhi Kabhie. Dir. Yash Chopra. Yash Raj Films, 1976.

Kabhi Khushi Kabhie Gham.... Dir. Karan Johar. Dharma Productions, 2001.

Kal Ho Naa Ho. Dirs Nikhil Advani and Ron Reid Jr. Dharma Productions, 2003.

Kabhi Alvida Naa Kehna. Dir. Karan Johar. Dharma Productions, 2006.

Karan Arjun. Dir. Rakesh Roshan. Film Kraft, 1995.

Kuch Kuch Hota Hai. Dir. Karan Johar. Dharma Productions, 1998.

Kurbaan. Dir. Rensil d'Silva. Dharma Productions and UTV Motion Pictures, 2009.

New York. Dir. Kabir Khan, Yash Raj Films, 2009.

Love Aaj Kal. Dir. Imtiaz Ali. Illuminati Films and Eros International, 2009.

Mohabbatein. Dir. Aditya Chopra. Yash Raj Films, 2000.

My Name Is Khan. Dir. Karan Johar. Dharma Productions, 2010.

The Inner and Outer World of Shah Rukh Khan. Dir. Nasreen Munni Kabir. BBC Channel 4 and Red Chillies Entertainment, 2005.

Om Shanti Om. Dir. Farah Khan. Red Chillies Entertainment, 2007.

Pardes. Dir. Subhash Ghai. Mukta Arts, 1997.

Purab aur Paschim. Dir. Manoj Kumar. V.I.P. Films, 2007.

Ra.One. Dir. Anubhav Sinha. Red Chillies Entertainment, 2011.

Rab Ne Bana Di Jodi. Dir. Aditya Chopra. Yash Raj Films, 2008.

Silsila. Dir. Yash Chopra. Yash Raj Films, 1981.

Slumdog Millionaire. Dir. Danny Boyle. Celador Films, Film4, and Pathé Pictures International, 2008.

Swades: We, the People. Dir. Ashutosh Gowariker. Ashutosh Gowariker Productions, 2004.

Veer-Zaara. Dir. Yash Chopra. Yash Raj Films, 2004.

The Don's World

Designing the Milieu of Shah Rukh Khan

ARADHANA SETH AND BERNHARD FUCHS[1]

Design should not be seen. What's not seen should be designed.[2]
—Farhan Akhtar, film director

Art direction is creating. Without uttering a single line of dialogue, you start conveying the character right from the beginning.[3]
—Sharmishtha Roy, art director

The work of a production designer is rooted in the observation of everyday objects, translating material things to visual representations on the screen. In this profession, life and work are closely interrelated as sensitivity for banal habits is essential. For a production designer the pressure cooker has memory and form, a history, a shape. Even dirty plates in a household are piled up in a certain way that characterizes the personality of the inhabitants.[4]

Production design is the art of envisioning and manifesting the context in which characters come to life on the silver screen. Expected to simultaneously build the persona, the style, and the characters that inhabit the design, as well as literally fade into the background so that the story, action, and stars can occupy the foreground, production design is an art that has morphed over time in Indian cinema.

Using the marker of the film *Don* (Dir. Chandra Barot, 1978), first produced in the 1970s with India's then superstar, Amitabh Bachchan, and then remade post-2000 with India's current reigning superstar, Shah Rukh Khan (henceforth SRK), changes in stage architecture from the old *Don* to the new *Don* (Dir. Farhan Akhtar, 2006) can be explored. The director of the remake, Farhan Akhtar, is the son of the original scriptwriter, Javed Akhtar.[5] Aradhana Seth is the production designer of the SRK *Don*.[6]

This chapter is centred on the creation of the world that surrounds SRK's contemporary *Don*. The blueprint of the Don's headquarters, his home, and the design choices that inhabit his world will be discussed, as will the choices that were made to contrast the good, working class Vijay's character, and a discerning Don, who is as conversant with the value of stolen world art as he is with guns. Although the old Don was said to be sought by the police in 11 countries, the movie did not include any foreign locations.

Of particular interest is the interplay between SRK's global superstar image and the design of the Don character in the 2006 film which presents a globalized, slickly produced twenty-first century India. Don of the 1970s tacks between the streets of Churchgate and the Filmistan sets of Bombay (now Mumbai), generating a character rooted in the visual life of the city. The present-day Don exhibits an ease in moving between the Champs Elysees in Paris, the Cable Car in Langkawi, the Petronas Towers in Kuala Lumpur, as well as returning to the streets of Mumbai and singing on the sets of Film City. The film in a sense becomes a microcosm of global Bollywood and the increasingly far-flung reaches of SRK's cosmopolitan, globe-trotting existence, and popularity.

In this movie, production design included: a) the selection of locations; b) the decision of a colour palette and materials; c) the redressing of locations; d) creating and building studios in and on locations. Often one scene is a combination of an outdoor location and a shot in a studio (in some instances even in a different country). Many small details have to be considered to ensure continuity. For example, for the Malaysian police headquarter shots inside a building in Kuala Lumpur, where a completely barren floor could be transformed into a huge modern office, have been combined with a studio set in Mumbai. In this case, a picture with the Malaysian king and queen and mineral water from a Malaysian label had to be at hand in Mumbai. In the production designer's work, the semiotic act of encoding is embedded in a cinematic context. This permanently necessitates considerations of technical and logistic aspects (camera positions, lighting, etc.). Already with the selection of locations the Don's globalism is emphasized. The colour palette and the high-tech environment highlight modernity and luxury. Production design is communication based on things.[7]

The Times they Are a-Changin

In a talk show, SRK explained what he considered as the risk of the *Don* remake:[8]

> If you make a remake of an old film which is not really so relevant in terms of time—it's not 15, 20 years ago—then it's not such a big chance to take; maybe *Devdas* is an okay film to remake. I think none of you who are born in the same year as I would have seen *Devdas*. So it was an interesting thing to do for a film person. But *Don* was a little bit scary because it's in the minds and heart of everybody—and the wonderful television channels showing it every day .... What I like about the film was the fact the guys who are making it, Farhan Akhtar and Ritesh (Sidhwani), and the whole team, they loved *Don* as much as I do. And they have very clearly changed it a lot. I didn't say this earlier because then all the tabloid would start talking about the changes and stuff .... What I liked about the film [...], this *Don*, is the new change, and what I liked about the old *Don* is what everybody likes: *Khaike paan banares walah* and Helen auntie and everyone. So on that front it is little scary, but I think once you see the film—I've seen it yesterday—I think there won't be comparisons. It does make you forget that you're watching something that you've seen before and creates its own identity.

Obviously, it was scary but a considered decision by SRK to invite discussion with Amitabh Bachchan by starring in this remake. Entering direct competition, he established himself as the 'heir' of this megastar (Dasgupta 2014).

The remake is based on the minute study of the original and highlights the changes in Indian society and cinematic culture since the 1970s. A multitude of references to the original is given not just in dialogues but also in costume design, music, and production design. The funky music of the 1970s is transformed into a contemporary sound. Designs and colours are intentionally cited and interpreted in a new way and is a transfer to modern times, which includes translation and variation. In some aspects, the movie is a very close remake, but fundamental alterations, conscious changes in the plot, the milieu, and the style add to the movie's value. It is fascinating to compare both films and observe continuities and discontinuities. The remake has added comparison as a special viewing pleasure to both movies in making audiences see these two as paired together in a fascinating *jugalbandi* (fusion) giving each one its own right and appreciating the art of both the original and the remake. SRK also stated that he particularly liked *the new changes*, which can only be fully enjoyed while keeping the original in mind.

One cautionary remark should be made here: we suppose that our readers would be familiar with both movies and know the alterations in the plot. If not, it is highly recommended to watch the films before reading; otherwise, the surprise value would be spoilt.

Let us summarize in order to discuss some major differences in the plot and style (especially for readers who do not plan to watch these two movies). The Don is the head of a gang of smugglers and drug dealers that is part of an international syndicate. In the original, his headquarters are in Bombay, India; in the remake in Langkawi, Malaysia. And then there is Vijay, a Don lookalike who is a simple musician living in Bombay.

The old movie is much more straightforward presenting a secure world with a clear moral order. It contains no riddles. The dangerous Don is already dead and buried before the interval. This fact is kept secret by one police inspector who persuades Vijay, who is essentially good and noble, to impose as the mafia-boss in order to help the police pursue organized crime. But in the uncertain modern world of the new *Don* the good guy, Vijay, has no chance to turn into a hero. There are several instances which make the audiences suspicious that the original story is not simply repeated; only at the end of the thriller is it revealed that Vijay has been killed by the Don who uncovers the attempt of the police to replace him. Stylistic differences become especially clear in the fight scenes; the new movie has extremely fast and 'realistic' martial art scenes and stunts, while in the old *Don*, circus-like acrobatics with repetitious somersaults and comic relief is accompanied by Mickey Mousing sounds.

Essentially, the original employs a patriotic rhetoric of nationalism while the remake celebrates globalization. Although in a critical reading, the new *Don* might even be understood as a metaphor for the destructive nature of globalized modernity, such an interpretation is discouraged by the fact that the victorious Don is not vilified. On the contrary, he is presented as an 'achiever' enjoying a luxurious lifestyle that is only endangered by the multitude of his enemies. The worrying fact, that the expected moral order is completely lost and that the Don—who is a criminal forever ready to kill traitors—embodies middle-class aspirations, produces a fascinating tension.

From Scarcity to Consumerist High-tech Hypermodernity

A comparison of these two movies can be found in a passage of a book by Valentina Vitali (2008: 239) who stated that 'the original Don featured a reasonable number of luxury items, but the film was not built around them. Cars, fashionable clothes, and fancy women in Don were part of the Bachchan persona and of his character.' In her opinion, the SRK movie is 'a very close remake except for the goods on display and their function within the narrative' (Vitali 2008: 239).

When the old movie cannot hide signs of economic scarcity, the new one proudly displays the spirit of consumerism.[9] Vitali summarizes differences between the original and remake as effects of modernization and commodification:

While in the 1978 version the Don has a meeting in a public sauna, in the remake Shah Rukh Khan's Don is seen in an oversized jacuzzi (the Don's own) doing business over the phone; Bachchan's 1978 hero's idea of leisure is to indulge in a glass of imported brew; in the new version, Shah Rukh Khan plays golf. Modern technology has a prominent place in the remake. When a mole inside the Don's gang is found to be passing on information to the police, in the original version he is exposed by a message written on a piece of paper that is hidden inside the heel of his shoe; in the remake, the item hidden inside the shoe is a small microphone. In the 1978 version, the Don forces an acrobat to help in a bank robbery,[10] in the later version, the same character is transformed into a software engineer. In the new *Don* cars, motorbikes, motorboats, airplanes, helicopters, and a long list of other fashionable items hold the narrative together. Technology here is not treated as a means of transport or production, as it was in earlier Hindi films, but as something to display, a luxury item. (Vitali 2008: 239)

Of course, a red Ford Mustang in the old *Don* is also more than just 'a means of transport'. But the perception that technology is a central element of the new *Don* is absolutely right. The red diary (with essential information about the syndicate) as a central object of the original is replaced by a uniquely designed and sized disc (combined with a special decoder) symbolic of the era of digitization. The new production design emphasizes an impressive high-tech-chic full with computers, surveillance cameras, palm scanners, and remote-controlled bombs as signs of modernity. Even the microphone for the interrogation room in the police headquarters should look 'cool' (as penned by Aradhana Seth in her notes). These signifiers of modernity characterize not only the Don's world but also the technolust environment today. Vitali's list of 'fashionable items' is slightly incorrect: SRK's Don does use a motorboat in the sequel (Dir. Farhan Akhtar, 2011), but not in the remake. And the only plane shown in the new movie is a prisoner-transporter, which is not really 'fashionable'. The fact that 'fashionable items hold the narrative together' should be stated without a culture-pessimistic and pejorative tone. Material culture and a homogenous look are fundamental for filmmaking, generally.

The remake displays rhetoric of augmentation. Compared to the old *Don* everything is increased in scale and value, the local Indian context becomes global, modernity and super-luxury items and lifestyle are displayed. A circus-like rope-walking stunt is replaced by a stunt on the sky bridge of the Petronas Towers in Kuala Lumpur, the escape from a jail truck is turned into a dangerous sky-diving stunt.

The 'rescue' of the Don in an ambulance is turned into a spectacular action scene shot on the highway, where the crane lifts the entire vehicle. The comparison with the hospital scenes shows, most clearly, this tendency to exaggerate. In contrast to the simplicity of the original, for the remake, a futuristic high-tech operation theatre had been designed with 12 digital screens to observe the patient's health—a totally secluded private space with the implication of luxury. In that scene, the production design necessitated VFX technology to equip SRK to appear in his double role in the same frame. In the old movie, simple door latches block the entrance; in the remake, a technical device with number codes (like in the hospital) or palm scanners (in the headquarters of the Don) can be seen in the corresponding scenes.

Visual-material Symbols of Economic Transformation

Reflections on the lack of purchasing power and Indian citizens' urge to sacrifice consumption dreams are a typical issue of old Hindi cinema. In *Sangam* (Dir. Raj Kapoor, 1964), a couple on honeymoon in Paris (Raj Kapoor and Vyjayanthimala) is attracted to window-shop but cannot afford to buy the aspired commodities. In the 1970s' *Don*, scarcity is symbolized by the foreign wristwatch of a police officer. This luxury item immediately becomes the target of cynical comments of the Interpol's Officer Malik, 'Inspector Verma, you have a beautiful watch, once I've seen such a watch in Geneva, but I could not afford it.' Thus, he suspects corruption.[11] This scene impressively mirrors the economic limitations of the era of centrally planned economy.[12] The Amitabh-Don tried to bribe a police officer, 'This is more money than you have ever seen in your life.' In the 1978 version, the Don's world reflected only a few signs of luxury such as fashion, extravagant telephones, imported cars, alcoholic drinks, and his leisure activity of playing poker. Whereas in contemporary Bollywood many Indian stars (for example, SRK, Aishwarya Rai, Deepika Padukone, Farhan Akhtar) have become brand ambassadors for Swiss watches. Consumerism is the ethos of modern Bollywood, where audiences are regaled with the visual pleasures of a shiny world of global brands. Movie-makers embrace advertisement aesthetics. Art has become inseparable from commercials; advertising videos as an art form intermingle with star texts and cinematic narration. While in former times Indian citizens often felt humbled in foreign contexts, nowadays conspicuous consumption in a globalized world becomes a major sign of national pride. Cinema confirms the image of 'India shining' that has turned into a prominent global player.

SRK endorses the Swiss brand TAG Heuer and for the sequel, this company even produced a limited edition of Don watches. At the launch of this product SRK joked that, like in the movie, it could be even used to detonate a bomb.

Dealing with cocaine and the use of foreign currency, both are different symbols of the new Don's globalism. Foreign currency symbolizes the modern Don's global identity. Contrary to the original movie, that is centred in Bombay, the new one is more concentrated on the global characterized by cocaine, crime, international artwork, the dollar and euro. In the old Don it is all rupees, and comparatively small amounts such as lakhs and not crores. The movie is constantly echoing the globalization that is going on in society. Even when they are in India, Don does not transact with the rupee. This was a very conscious design decision.

Aradhana Seth had many bundles of dollar bills with her including the band that binds them together. She took an original hundred dollar bill to the printer to print a room full. It was important to get a special permission letter from the Film Production Company because committing such an act falls under counterfeit. The printer could get into trouble. It had to be destroyed afterwards and only one side was printed. Basically, they printed a few thousand notes both sides and everything else on just one side.

The on-screen financial culture in both films seems to mirror the real economy, which is also responsible for fundamental changes in cinematic culture. A major shift in filmmaking results from economic transformations effected by the liberalization of the Indian market since the 1990s (Punathambekar 2013). Comparing the budgets for both movies, the increased turnover becomes obvious. The new Don did cost INR 35 crore (USD 5.4 million) and cashed at the Box Office INR 105 crore (USD 16 million). In comparison, the financial figures for the old Don are INR 85 lakh (USD 130,000) and its Box Office returns, INR 7 crore (USD 1.1 million).[13] Koral Dasgupta (2014: 76) observes the absence of marketing strategies in the old Don:

The film was released without any promotion on 12th May 1978 and was declared a flop post the collections of the first week. Within a week however, the song 'Khaike paan banaraswala' became a hit in some music programmes [...] and word spread. By the second week, the film was declared a hit. The fact that there were no marketing strategies for *Don* in 1978 is quite evident. The energies of the producer were focused on just the product and all the other variables or levers of marketing were left to the audience and the distributors.

While the sets of the old *Don* give a rather unsophisticated and shabby impression, the modern version, in contrast, appears ultra-glossy, thereby indicating the advancements that have taken place in the Indian economy. Consumerism and brand consciousness are not only typical for contemporary Indian cinema, but also signs of economic and cultural change in Indian society in general.

Production Design: An Art That Has Morphed over Time

When we look at the designing of SRK's cinematic worlds, it is essential to mention Art Director Sharmishtha Roy. The first movie she independently worked on as an art director was *Dilwale Dulhania Le Jayenge* (*DDLJ*, Dir. Aditya Chopra, 1995). She was art director of 10 SRK films[14] and has won three Filmfare awards for SRK movies.[15]

Her parents worked for the original *Don*: father Sudhendu Roy worked as art director and her mother Krishna Roy was set decorator. Stemming from a 'film-industry family', Sharmishtha Roy has first-hand experience of the development in film production from her practice as an assistant on the sets of her father to the time when her own style became paradigmatic for globalized Bollywood, especially with the Karan Johar movies that she came to be identified with. She herself characterizes this style as very European or American, and also as unrealistic. Several interviews have been published where she explains the fundamental changes in production design:

> As an assistant to my father—Sudhendu Roy, I had observed producers/directors narrating to him scenes that had only recently been developed. Often, this was the basis for a set to be designed and constructed within a few days. While it was amazing what great work my father and other art-directors of his time were able to achieve, those were certainly not the ideal conditions to work in. Today, we work off bound scripts and have ample time for pre-production—which entails

research, drawings, and budgets. It allows for better communication and clarity between departments. Time is not a luxury anymore. And I'm glad this is so. Even up to the 1990s, it took almost three years to complete a film. Most art directors worked on several films simultaneously to ensure that their teams were constantly employed. Today, with more actors and technicians committed to a single project, it is possible to wrap up a film within a considerably shorter time frame.[16]

Increased budgets for production and decoration are in the context of modern commodity culture:

> According to [Sharmishtha] Roy, art directors in the past were only asked to prepare the set with certain props brought in from specific rental companies that the film industry patronized. Today, Roy insists on a decoration budget, which many of the new art directors see as necessary to create a designer aesthetic that will counter what they perceive to be the flashy aesthetic of the 1960s and 1970s. Roy now rents furniture and other accessories, including small decoration items from well-known home furnishing shops. (Mazumdar 2007)

Consumption should be understood as an element of film production (cf. Wilkinson-Weber 2010). The look of movies reflect the economic context of their times. Wilkinson-Weber analyses changes in the costume design of Indian cinema and highlights that the new style is based on consumerism and the integration of global brands; whereas, the work of old designers is described as conditioned by scarcity:

> Not only are they distanced from personal participation in commodity clothes markets, but the context for their professional work was a theatrical, craft-heavy production, and retail environment in which commodities were relatively scarce. [...] For old designers, this manipulation and transformation of meagre resources was the source of their professional satisfaction in the industry. (Wilkinson-Weber 2010: 22)

In discourses of the persons working in the film industry, brand consciousness is identified as cultural capital and a symbol of social distinction:[17]

> Old designers in essence articulate a critique of the brand, for far from accepting that mass-manufactured goods can be 'original' because

they are created under the auspices of the label, they focus only on their status as undifferentiated copies. To the new designers, this is a kind of brand illiteracy, but to old designers, it is resistance to brand persuasions. (Wilkinson-Weber 2010: 24)

Brand-conscious audiences also read brand placement as a form of realism, but on the other hand emotional engagement with the story impedes brand recognition (Nelson and Devanathan 2006). Special collections 'inspired by the confidence and flamboyance of the character Don' have been launched.[18] Product placement creates semiotic surplus for labels, which capitalize spill-over effects through special collections dedicated to movies. Cinematic characterization is supported by the integration of 'a premier lifestyle brand'[19] and a 'global luxury brand'.[20] To new designers 'assembling costume from label clothing is not [...] abandonment of original design, but fulfils the brief of the dress designer to embed the character in the midst of a very real, global commodity economy' (Nelson and Devanathan 2006: 24).

The economic conditions of old Bombay cinema are in sharp contrast to global Bollywood. Generally speaking, product placement is not a new trend in cinema but can be observed right from the beginning of filmmaking, in earlier times described as 'tie-up' (Newell, Salmon, and Chang 2006). Product placement is more than sponsoring and advertisement:

An understanding of the long-term development of product placement as essentially a barter system is beneficial in navigating the confused landscape of current brand integration practices, where in a single programme one product's on-screen appearance can be the result of cash payment, other products receive airtime in return for reciprocal advertising, whereas other products are included to save money on the purchase of props. (Newell, Salmon, and Chang 2006: 591)

The luxurious lifestyle of the SRK-Don required expensive high-end designer commodities that could only be obtained through barter-credit.[21] There was little expectation of brand recognition in this context. The quality of these things symbolizes that Don is not just an ordinary buyer but a consumer of luxury goods and services.

Transformations in film-production culture correspond with social and economic change and highlight the aspirational lifestyle of contemporary Indian middle- and upper-classes (cf. Chakravorty 2009).

> Where the limited resources of a more insulated, parochial Bombay used to be manipulated to populate and define the fantastic spaces of film, now the seemingly boundless resources of global space are redirected, via film's new cultural producers, into film visuals that attempt to capture the 'reality' of affluent, localized lifestyles. (Wilkinson-Weber 2010: 25)

Comparative analysis of the *Don* movies and their production design supports this insight. Amitabh's *Don* and SRK's *Don* can be seen as paradigmatic for the contrast between the scarcity and limitations of India in the 1970s and contemporary globalized Bollywood in a time when India has become a major global player. Through his NRI roles and endorsements, SRK is seen as a symbol for globalized India. Intertextual references between movies and commercials are salient aspects of his work (Cayla 2008).

The bathtub scene in the new *Don* can be seen as a reference to an advertisement for the LUX soap (Cayla 2008).[23] Interestingly, two different styles of maleness are combined in the movie (emphasizing the polysemy of SRK). The bathtub scene indicates a soft kind of masculinity that boldly integrates aspects of femininity (SRK was the first man to advertise LUX, previously only Bollywood heroines were seen in these soap commercials). In other sequences of the movie—for example in the Wushu martial art scenes full of violent eroticism with sporty Priyanka Chopra—SRK displays an aggressive form of maleness.

On the reconnaissance when a hotel like the Four Seasons in Langkawi is chosen as a part of Don's headquarters, it needs to be morphed keeping in mind a certain heightened luxury. Furniture is taken from one place to another, some furniture is added, and some furniture is subtracted. All the bed sheets were made in silk with 'D' for Don monogrammed. In his luxurious bathtub, Don is drinking champagne and watching cartoons. Here as well, towels with a big 'D' on it can be seen. This use of towels decorated with the letter 'D' attributes a style of self-branding to the Don, who lives in a glamorous home like a superstar, thus echoing the brand SRK.[23]

Interiors and Exteriors

Production design is both technical and visual. The production designer recreates the place in the script. It will convey that a person walked into a room. But what kind of room does that person have? Where do they live? How do they think? Do they read? What all do they put in their room? So, as a production designer you are constantly thinking of what sort of environment that person likes.[24]

Fashionable interior design and spectacular global locations are two aspects of the aspirational spirit of contemporary Bollywood which can also be identified in SRK's professional activities both as a movie actor and a brand ambassador.[25]

Ranjani Mazumdar (2007) analysed a turn to the interior as a recent development in Indian film-making. This tendency corresponds with the longing of the middle and upper classes for ordered and sanitized consumer landscapes. As the postcolonial metropolis Mumbai cannot fulfil capitalist dreams of aesthetic commodification, cinema serves as a substitute for the ideal window shopping experience.[26] On the other hand, movies about the underworld present the chaotic and unmanageable cityscape of Mumbai as a dangerous gangland. The middle-class utopia of an erasure of chaos, dirt and poverty can only be visualized in cinematic dreamworlds by a combined strategy of chic interiors and stunning global locations. Previously Hindi cinema preferred class-specific spaces populated by several people, as typically seen in the staircase sequences.

Comparison of the *Don* movies confirms this thesis. The environment of the Bachchan-Don is dominated by spaces that are more public in character while the new Don enjoys greater privacy, as exemplified by the old Don in a hotel sauna among other guests (pistol hidden under the towel) versus the new Don in his private Jacuzzi. SRK's Don finds more seclusion in his designer headquarters among beaches and mangroves: 'A home away from home for those who know and appreciate the best' (as the homepage of the real hotel advertises). These exclusive tourist locations in Malaysia are described with the words 'icon of luxury', 'seclusion', and 'privacy'.[27] Also, in this context, the qualities of brands define the personality of the Don.

While global locations and impressive interiors produce the image of a clean modernity, India is presented as chaotic in the *Don* remake. But in small-town India where Don loses control, Vijay is completely at home. His character represents the poverty, simplicity, and honesty of traditional India. In Vijay's world, locality is celebrated as spectacular, colourful, and spiritual where he is introduced with the Ganesh Chaturthi festival scene. The Don does not fit into this Indian world. Here he suffers his only defeat. But on the contrary, it is the local guy Vijay who cannot survive the exposure to the modern world of globalized crime. As he states, he cannot even ride a bicycle; it would be completely incredible for him to transform into the Don, as Amitabh Bachchan's Vijay does quite easily. (But in the original, Vijay just confesses his inability to handle a gun and does not mention bicycles.) The differences between social classes, the global and the local, tradition and modernity have certainly increased since the 1970s.

The Don's Headquarter and the Vault

The innermost part of Don's headquarters, a highly protected circular vault, gives the strongest signification of his personality. In the 1970s the corresponding object was a simple safe filled with gold, jewellery, some papers, and the quintessential red diary. Compared to the grandiose vault of the new Don, the impression in the 1970s, version is shabby and chaotic. The modern vault is protected by high-tech facilities. The strict order of things is almost museum-like. The Don's distinguished taste is performed through an exquisite ensemble of things such as stolen art from all over the world, of which the most famous piece is *The Scream* by Edvard Munch[28] (which was indeed missing during the production of the movie but was discovered before the premiere). Asian art, Buddha statues, and vases symbolize the locality of Malaysia and counter the impression of Eurocentrism, which might have been produced by a restriction to European paintings. Together with cocaine packets (marked with a scorpion symbol), these objects confirm the Don's globalism (he does not collect art stolen from Indian temples). The reflecting materials—chrome, glass, the greenish light, and the pedantic order—give the impression of a modern, cold, and controlling character. The collection of weapons symbolizes his fetishistic addiction to violence. The vault is remniscient of the renaissance rulers' collections ('Wunderkammer'), where things have been turned into significant objects, 'semiophores' as Krzysztof Pomian (1988) has termed these carriers of meaning.

A small circular motif can already be identified in the old *Don* on the safe and also with a round table as a social centre of his headquarter. In the new *Don*, the whole architecture of the vault is circular, thereby stressing the character of centredness and producing the association of a womb.[29]

Don's Colour Palette

The selection of a typical colour palette, which produces the coherent style of a movie, is characteristic for star-driven mainstream cinema. The makers of the new *Don* worked in an extremely colour-conscious way.[30]

The designer also proposes the look of the film and then, of course, the decision is taken together with the director; so in this case for instance, it was a combination of the director, the cinematographer, K.U. Mohanan, and the production designer. So you decide: This is the look you want to make for the film. Costumes usually have to take the cue. During the preparation of this film we carried out various look-tests that not everybody does. We[31] took 15 different shades of greens and greys, and we did colour tests on the skin tones to decide the final palette. So basically we made walls where we painted one half in different greens. Then we put it behind SRK and Priyanka Chopra and filmed them to get a sense of the tone. This combination of colours had not really been used in Indian films. Probably there is no other film that had so much metal, green, and grey emphasizing a cold look. It has been used in Western films, but not in Bollywood.[32]

Already the original movie shows a very defined—but wider—colour palette,[33] blue and grey, black and white can be discerned as the dominant colours. The costumes of members of the Don's gang constantly repeat the broad range of colours: blue, red, light-yellow, black, and white. Objects of particular importance (like the diary, a suitcase with money, or a Ford Mustang) are marked with red. The interiors in the Don's headquarter (especially in more relaxed situations when he is playing poker) are characterized by warm red-brown tones. During songs in festive occasions the colour palette of brown, red, and blue is widened; the image becomes even more colourful, sometimes red is combined with fuchsia.

In the vault scene SRK's dress matches the colours of the dollar-bundles and cocaine packets. He is the personification of wealth. The same pink-beige colours appear even in the landscape in an outdoor scene connected to the dollars. The pink-beige combination can already be detected in the costumes of Amitabh Bachchan and Zeenat Aman in the old *Don*. In the *Khaike paan* scene, Zeenat Aman wears a soft-pink blouse and in the remake the pattern on SRK's shirt is reminiscent of the waistcoat of Amitabh Bachchan in the same scene.

Interestingly, the colour structures become inverted in the seduction scene with Helen, later played by Kareena Kapoor: here Amitabh wears a green shirt while SRK sports the most colourful shirt in the movie. The red-blue paisley pattern symbolizes the eroticism of the situation. Contrary to the character of Amitabh's Don, who states that he was only still alive because he wouldn't care for girls, SRK's Don is open to sexual attraction. The set decoration of the old movie operates with a typical form of Hindi film iconography:[34] the coldness of Amitabh's Don is symbolized by pictures from Himalayan landscapes on the wall, suggesting an ascetic character. Later (when he warms up a little bit and has a drink), different pictures are displayed on the walls: the then pin-up girls are visible.[35]

According to the classic *Navarasa* concept, green would be the colour of *sringara rasa* (like the bright green of the female dancers in the *Ganapati* scene), but in the hybrid aesthetics of Bollywood red symbolizes the erotic mood. Later in the remake Priyanka Chopra wears a red swimsuit reminiscent of this paisley shirt (when she seductively passes the Don whose erotic gaze is recognized by his jealous girlfriend).[36]

Although colour patterns are probably perceived more on a subliminal level, they contribute to the coherence of the movie.

Sometimes consecutive scenes are integrated into a sequence by homogenous colours. In other instances, even scenarios divided by great temporal distance become united by chromatic similarity. Thus in the remake, the colours gold, black, and blue produce a balance between the two familiar song sequences from the old *Don*—the things SRK loved most about the old movie, 'Helen auntie' in the seduction scene and much later just before the *Khaike paan* scene. Here the Petronas Towers, the architectural stars of the movie, are presented from different angles: first in an elite view from a first-class hotel and later they can be seen from below, from the 'Little India' of Kuala Lumpur. The window wall in the hotel indicates harmony with the outer world in the ideal context where the celebration of the interior does not necessitate erasure of the exterior (cf. Mazumdar 2007). In the second scene the Don is on the run. Displaced from his modern world and hiding from the police in 'Little India' he has to adopt the desi lifestyle of Vijay, chewing betel, drinking bhang (a drink made from Cannabis), and talking, singing, and dancing in a rural style. This *Khaike paan* song is the least satisfying scene in the remake as this sudden transformation of the Don to the character of Vijay lacks credibility, while in the original, Vijay, who poses as the Don, can easily take pleasure in a return to his rural roots, when he suddenly enters a religious gathering of the displaced Biharis in Bombay.

The Petronas Towers

Concentrating the gaze on landmark buildings is a common strategy of cinematic landscaping in Bollywood.[37] The diffused urban space, which is difficult to represent as a whole, is substituted by famous buildings (cf. Bunnell 2004; King 1996). Kuala Lumpur has been selected not at least for these triumphant symbols of the rising East. Through the choice of locations the opposition of old Europe with Paris in the initial scene and Kuala Lumpur is constructed—both easily identifiable by the Eiffel Tower[38] and the Petronas Towers— the old Occident signified by an already aged icon of future versus contemporary rising Asian modernity.

For Malaysia, the Petronas Towers are a strong symbol of wealth, progress, and modernity. Accordingly, the Hollywood movie

Entrapment (Dir. Jon Amiel, 1999) has been eagerly awaited as the first international film production that would present Kuala Lumpur's landmark buildings to the world. But a split scene that combined the modern skyscraper with impressions from a slum-like colony offended Malaysian audiences, and especially enraged politicians of this nation (Bunnell 2004). Malaysian and Indian developmental ideas not only share similar modernist fantasies but also the same frights—the uncontrollable chaos and poverty. In India the political failures of attempts to erase the ugly signs of the poor masses lead to cinematic dreams of clean consumer landscapes (Mazumdar 2007). From an Indian position, the impressive symbols of a successful Tiger-nation are especially attractive as India also seeks recognition as a global player. In Malaysia the successful construction of a clean and modern centre has been ignored by the neo-oriental gaze of Western film-makers, who created their stereotypical Asia on-screen. Out of a convergence of social imagination between India and Malaysia, Bollywood (a globalized culture industry often imagined as surpassing the influence of Hollywood) offered an attractive alternative. Kuala Lumpur and Langkawi are employed to produce the clean image of a high-tech modernity with green parks, rain forests and beaches, and environmental beauty without slums.

Malaysia: An SRK-friendly Nation

Bollywood cinema is extremely popular in Malaysia—it goes beyond the large Indian diaspora (2.6 million, 8 per cent of the Malaysian population). Cooperation with India is sought in order to develop the Malaysian film industry and Indian tourism to Malaysia as well. Recently, even a Malaysian princess produced an album of old Hindi film duets together with Kumar Sanu in order to express the friendship between both countries. Malaysia attempts to become the top destination for Indian tourists.[39] Kuala Lumpur is a very SRK-friendly city—he has already shot scenes of *One 2 Ka 4* (Dir. Shashilal K. Nahir, 2001) in Malaysia. The *Don* remake has been supported by the premier's office and by the Malaysian Tourism Board.[40] In the year 2008, SRK has been conferred the title of Malaysian knighthood 'Datuk'[41] and he has an excellent relation-ship with the former Prime Minister Mahathir Mohamed.[42] In the year 2013 he toured Malaysia with his show *Temptations Reloaded*. He has been featured together with his wife Gauri on the cover of a prestigious Malayan woman's lifestyle magazine,[43] and his Malaysian fanclub reports every SRK news on facebook.[44]

The Paris Scene

The remake movie starts with the Eiffel Tower as a landmark building of Paris. Cafés and a ballet school that reminds us of paintings by Edgar Degas are staged as icons of Frenchness. The colours combine a blue, classically European in hue, from the production designers living room in Vienna with the new *Don*'s green. The walls are adorned by photographs by Henry Cartier-Bresson. For the production design, the etched glass windows deserved special attention as the scene shot in Paris had to be combined with the interior scene shot in a studio in Mumbai where they were custom-made to scale in order to match the café doors in Paris through photographs of the location. These windows are even reflected in the mirror in the background and although they can only be seen for a split second, they are essential for the continuity. The diligent work of production design has to remain in the background (probably unnoticed by the audience) behind the fast action scene.

Construction of Indianness

When the movie reaches India, a bullock cart that is overtaken by fast limousines symbolizes the speed of modernity versus ancient Indian tradition. The ritual context of the song *Bappa moriya* includes a documentary approach as the first day of the movie's shoot was the real day of the Ganesh Chaturthi festival. The festival has been documented on several locations in Mumbai.

Ganesh Chaturthi was documented with five cameras all over Mumbai. This can be compared with shooting on Christmas Eve or New Year all over a European city. This ritual is something that one cannot really create like it is, and from that documentary footage the decision was taken to create that big scene. The director and the the production designer looked at all the footage and selected a particular situation that had the best emotion and emersion; and from choosing the statue that had been documented on the real day, they went back and created the statue exclusively for the song sequence. So, confounding the norm, in this case reality preceded fiction.

In this instance we[45] took the Ganesh statue, we chose, and we recreated it. In the filming of *Don* every song took five days to film. The Ganesh Chaturthi song was split into two locations, three days in one area and two days in the other. One shot was inside a chawl[46] which was quite tight and had been entirely dressed up. There was a gate which blocked the passage for the huge statue. The other location was by the Arabian Sea. We cut from the chawl to the final immersion. But interestingly now, post the movie, this particular song is performed every year at this place during the ritual; cinema influenced the tradition.[47]

This introduction of the new Vijay brings to the fore the Hindu identity of modern Mumbai (in contrast to the secular context of the original). But with the symbolic participation of Sikhs and Muslims it represents a typical form of Hindu inclusivism.[48] Interestingly, in his fashion even the local guy Vijay shows signs of globalization, unlike the lungi-wearing Amitabh Bachchan who is presented as a rustic new to the city. SRK wears jeans and a shirt also in contrast to the bright 'Indian' costumes of the other dancers (often the best dancer is marked by the brightest colours).

SRK's double role of two opposite characters produces maximum polysemy, especially as both characters are presented as highly attractive. It remains unclear for most of the time whether SRK is acting as the Don, or as Vijay who poses as the Don thereby making it difficult to favour or despise either. The old movie is free of such ambiguity.

The world of Vijay stands for the displaced locals in the urban space of Bombay. In the old movie, this simple character is introduced by a song about the city that can be read as a critique of urban lifestyle from a rural perspective. Here—in the old *Don*—Bombay is staged as a fascinating icon of urbanity and modernity that is seen as rather ambivalent.

———

Is it the time that makes the movies; or is it the movies that make the time? Is it what is going on today that is heavily influencing cinema of this kind; or, is this cinema making the template for contemporary culture? Actually it is both. This means that global Bollywood not only mirrors globalization and modernity but also simultaneously produces images and meanings of globalization and modernity—breathing life into abstract terms. The movie *Don* capitalizes on the global image of SRK while at the same time it contributes to the aura of the globalized star via the mise-en-scène, international locations, and the iconicity of globalization in the production design. Production design is based on references to existing semiotic codes from everyday life and the commercial world that become integrated in a cinematic narrative; but it also produces new meanings by creative combinations of signs, an environment in which a story and its characters are embedded. In this particular instance, a transfer to modern times enhanced the reflexive expression of social and temporal consciousness. Cinema has the ability to produce new popular symbols and imaginary repertoires like a 'Donish' habitus that is coded not only by a typical style of speech, but also by a specific colour palette. The film industry produces not only images of modernity and globalization, but also simultaneously nostalgic dreams; it reiterates national stereotypes and even contributes to religious tradition. This comparison of movies has also demonstrated how the economic basis of cultural industries and the political-economic context of society becomes visible in products.

Notes

1. This chapter originated from Aradhana Seth's—the production designer of *Don* (2006)—presentation at the Vienna conference. She later showed all her files of the making of *Don* to Bernhard Fuchs and Elke Mader, spending a Sunday together, watching both movies and discussing at length her experience of the production process. Some quotes from this exchange as well as from other interviews are integrated in this chapter in order to highlight Aradhana Seth's perspective of an insider in the film industry. Starting with this material and contributing additional research, Bernhard Fuchs and Aradhana Seth developed this essay. Originally, it was a visual essay which was not convenient for the book format and the reduced text-only version should be understood as an invitation to (re-)watch the movies

discussed. We wish to thank Elke Mader for her inspiration, support, and hospitality.

2. Spoken by Farhan Akhtar in a TV commercial from the year 2012 for Xylys—a Swiss brand watch—produced by Titan, available at http://www.youtube.com/watch?v=Tt1FjZ5r7K0 (accessed on 2 December 2013).

3. Sharmishtha Roy in an interview, available at http://www.rediff.com/entertai/1999/mar/23sha1.htm (accessed on 2 December 2013).

4. Aradhana Seth in an interview, available at http://www.thefuschiatree.com/310/fullview (accessed on 2 December 2013).

5. Javed Akhtar worked in a team with Salim Khan.

6. Before this she had worked with the young SRK when she co-directed the TV play *In Which Annie Gives It Those Ones* (Dir. Pradip Krishen, 1989), script written by Arundhati Roy.

7. In an interview with Aasheesh Sharma, Aradhana Seth expressed her sadness caused by the usual destruction of sets after a film has been finished (2013) for *Hindustan Times*. With her exhibition Everybody Carries a Room about Inside (in Mumbai 2011), she took the innovative step to carefully remove the art of set design from the cinematic context; for more, see an article in *Time Out Mumbai*, available at http://www.timeoutmumbai.net/art/featurespreviews/housing-policy (accessed on 2 December 2013) and an interview of Aradhana Seth by Himali Singh Soin (2013).

8. This has been taken from NDTV in 2006 from a show titled. 'India Questions SRK on Smoking & *Don*', available at http://www.youtube.com/watch?v=dm-ih8LCIBE (accessed on 2 December 2013).

9. The attitude towards consumption has changed only concerning cigarettes. In the old *Don*, almost all the characters can be constantly seen smoking, while in the contemporary version, smoking has become a guilty pleasure. When the new Don lights his cigarette, he confesses that he wants to stop this habit 'because it kills'. Certainly, media is shaped by the legal requirements of our time; but in this respect, the real life of the star gets integrated with the movie.

10. It is not the Don who forces Jasjeet to commit the crime, but one of his men.

11. In the end it is discovered that Malik is an imposter who in reality is the criminal, Vardhan. The brave Indian police officer D'Silva in the old movie is beyond doubt; while in the new movie, a fake D'Silva turns out to be Vardhan.

12. In the old *Don*, scarcity is presented in a positive light. Material culture also becomes verbally expressed. The children of the imprisoned J.J.

(Jasjeet) for whom Vijay takes care are not only fond of their (visible) new school uniforms, but also highlight the aspect of nutrition. In their boarding school they do not get 'chana' (chickpeas, that can be seen in the scene) but only 'poori' (fried bread). Chickpeas are a symbol of simplicity and poverty that has become famous by the movie *Jay Santoshi Ma* (Dir. Vijay Sharma, 1975) and the corresponding cult.

13. For further details, refer to the following website http://en.wikipedia.org/wiki/Don_(2006_Hindi_film) and http://en.wikipedia.org/wiki/Don_(1978_film) (accessed on 15 May 2015).

14. The 10 SRK films for which Sharmishtha Roy was the art director are as follows: *Kabhi Alvida Naa Kehna* (2006, Dir. Karan Johar); *Veer-Zaara* (2004, Dir. Yash Chopra); *Kal Ho Naa Ho* (2003, Dirs Nikhil Advani and Ron Reid Jr.); *Kabhi Khushi Kabhie Gham...* (2001, Dir. Karan Johar); *Mohabbatein* (2000, Dir. Aditya Chopra); *Phir Bhi Dil Hai Hindustani* (2000, Dir. Aziz Mirza); *Kuch Kuch Hota Hai* (1998, Dir. Karan Johar); *Duplicate* (1998, Dir. Mahesh Bhatt); *Dil To Pagal Hai* (1997, Dir. Yash Chopra); *Dilwale Dulhania Le Jayenge* (1995, Dir. Aditya Chopra).

15. Some of these movies are *Dil To Pagal Hai*, *Kuch Kuch Hota Hai*, and *Kabhi Khushi Kabhie Gham....*

16. Sharmishtha Roy quoted by *mid-day.com* in the article 'Venue Think of Movies...' available at http://www.mid-day.com/anniversary/bollywood/article.php?id=144 (accessed on 2 December 2013).

17. In the creative practice of the set design, often the dichotomy between the old style and the new style has to be bridged. For example, Sharmishtha Roy collaborates with the same people who have already worked for her father. 'I had a fabulous team that was a legacy from my father. They worked just as hard as I did. It must have been hard for them to move from my father's style to mine. [...] I find it amazing that they could translate all my designs into reality. They could grasp what the new generation needs. They just keep on working,' says Roy in an interview, available at http://www.rediff.com/entertai/1999/mar/23sha1.htm (accessed on 2 December 2013).

18. Aditya Birla Nuvo (2006).

19. Louis Philippe.

20. The Four Seasons Hotel.

21. For example, the living room design was taken from Good Earth available at http://www.goodearth.in/ (accessed on 1 December 2014); furniture from La-z-boy, available at http://www.la-z-boy.com/ (accessed on 1 December 2014), or sound systems by Bang & Olufsen, available at http://blog.bang-olufsen.com/ (all Internet accessed on 1 December 2014).

22. The LUX commercial is available at http://www.youtube.com/watch?v=_lf7_AcsIqI (accessed on 2 December 2013).

23. In this context, a commercial for the *Times of India* is of particular interest, where SRK presents the letters 'DO' explaining that domination starts with 'DO', thus propagating an active and aggressive Indian identity opposed to Gandhian ideals (Cayla 2008). This commercial can also be seen as a reference to the SRK-Don.

24. Aradhana Seth interviewed by Jennifer Chong, available at http://www.asiaarts.ucla.edu/article.asp?parentid=15190 (accessed on 2 December 2013).

25. Together with his wife Gauri Khan, he is also brand ambassador for the global interior designer brand, D'decor. See http://www.ddecor.com/about/about.aspx; for TV commercials, see http://www.ddecor.com/mediacenter/televisionad.aspx (both accessed on 2 December 2013).

26. Shopping malls are typical sites of Bollywood movies and in reality multiplexes produce a convergence of cinema and malls.

27. Four Seasons Hotels and Resorts, 'Four Seasons Resort Langkawi', available at http://www.fourseasons.com/langkawi/landing_3/?source=gaw11lngS05&kw="four+seasons+langkawi"&creative=14023597822&KW_ID=sldBQltXq_dc | pcrid | 14023597822&gclid=CN6N9vfb9boCFfMctAodimIAYg; see also http://www.thedatai-langkawi.com/ppc/?gclid=CI63pN7a9boCFesSwwodLToA_A (both accessed on 2 December 2013).

28. Interestingly, the Jackie Chan print on Vijay's sweatshirt in the hospital scene repeats the image of *The Scream*.

29. Circular forms are repeated in the remake: the vault, platforms of the Petronas Towers, the dance floors, and finally the cable car of Langkawi.

30. In different film projects, an impression of a documentary style is created by the avoidance of strict colour palettes. For more, see the interview by Esha Verma with K.U. Mohanan (2013).

31. Of course, here the 'we' does not include co-author Bernhard Fuchs, but refers only to the film-makers.

32. The cinematographer K.U. Mohanan is highly conscious of colour palettes as can be seen from his interviews. For more see the one mentioned in a previous note as well as an interview from Pandolin titled 'The Style-Bender', see http://pandolin.com/the-style-bender/; another article from *Time Out Bengaluru*, available at http://www.timeoutbengaluru.net/search%3Fkeyword%3Dku-mohanan; and one from rediff.com, available at http://www.rediff.com/movies/report/mohan/20071130.htm (all Internet sources accessed on 2 December

2013). Regarding *Don*, Mohanan stresses that the movie was very stylish with dramatic angles and was always focused on SRK.

33. Achyut Y. Gupte was the colour consultant in the original.

34. It is very common in Hindi movies to integrate popular iconography, especially from political or religious contexts.

35. A poster of actress Tina Munim—in her first movie *Des Pardes* (Dir. Dev Anand) appeared in the same year, 1978.

36. In the corresponding scene, Zeenat Aman also wears a red swimsuit indicating that the character of Vijay—who is posing as Don—is also frolicking in the swimming pool (a change of character that makes the Don's girlfriend suspicious).

37. The sight of the international landmark buildings from the windows of a luxury hotel is also emblematic of globalization in SRK's commercial for the ICICI Bank.

38. Tips Records published a special edition of *Don* equipped with a comic book based on screenshots. Here, in the initial Paris scene, the Don mouths the ironic idea that he might even include the Eiffel Tower into his collection. The comic remark hints at his collection of international art.

39. This album *Tum Mile* is part of a tourist campaign for the year 2014. 'India is Malaysia's second largest tourism source market, with a total of 7,80,000 Indian tourist arrivals this year, and an expected 8,00,000 Indian arrivals next year.' For more, see 'Malaysia Tourism Targets Indian Tourists, Launches Bollywood Music Album with Kumar Sanu', *International Business Times*, 2013, available at http://www.ibtimes.co.in/articles/487277/20130707/malaysia-tourism-music-album-kumar-sanu.htm (accessed on 2 December 2013).

40. A poster of Malaysia Tourism appeared in the movie in a morbid scene, where Kamini's (Kareena Kapoor) corpse blocks the door of the lift.

41. 'SRK Is Now Datuk Shahrukh Khan', *Times of India*, 2008, available at http://articles.timesofindia.indiatimes.com/2008-12-06/rest-of-world/27908308_1_bollywood-actor-malacca-british-knighthood (accessed on 2 December 2013).

42. 'Dr Mahathir Mohamad Is My Favourite Person in the World: Shahrukh Khan', available at http://www.aajkikhabar, *Aaj Ki Khabar*, 2010, com/en/News/Entertainment/Dr-Mahathir-Mohamad-is-my-favourite-person-in-the-world-Shahrukh-Khan/672895.html (accessed on 2 December 2013).

43. Datuk Shah Rukh Khan and Datin Gauri Khan featured on the Malaysian Magazine *Nona*.

44. The following facebook page is available at Shah Rukh Khan Malaysia Fan Club, https://www.facebook.com/SRKMalaysiaFC.
45. Again, 'we' refers to the film-makers.
46. Chawls are buildings typical in Bombay built in the early 1900s where people from several communities live under one roof.
47. Four different choreographers worked for this movie. Most films have only one choreographer. For the song *Bappa Moriya*, Rajeev Surti was selected, who is known to be a very 'folk' kind of a choreographer.
48. In the movie *ABCD: Anybody Can Dance* (Dir. Remo D'Souza, 2013), there is also a *Bappa Moriya* dance and constitutes a big scene of this festival. In this sequence, a Muslim butcher, who forbids his son to dance, accepts this activity only because of the traditional dance for Lord Ganesh.

References

Bunnell, Tim. 2004. 'Re-viewing the *Entrapment* Controversy: Megaprojection, (Mis)Representation and Postcolonial Performance', *Geo Journal*, 59: 297–305.

Cayla, Julien. 2008. 'Following the Endorser's Shadow: Shah Rukh Khan and the Creation of the Cosmopolitan Indian Male', *Advertising & Society Review*, 9 (2), available at http://muse.jhu.edu/journals/advertising_and_society_review/v009/9.2.cayla01.html (accessed on 2 December 2013).

Chakravorty, Pallabi. 2009. 'Moved to Dance: Remix, Rasa, and a New India', *Visual Anthropology*, 22 (2–3): 211–28.

Dasgupta, Koral. 2014. *Power of a Common Man: Connecting with Consumers the SRK Way*. Chennai and New Delhi: Westland.

King, Anthony D. 1996. 'Worlds in the City: Manhattan Transfer and the Ascendance of Spectacular Space', *Planning Perspectives*, 11: 97–114.

Mazumdar, Ranjani. 2007. *Bombay Cinema: An Archive of the City*. Minneapolis and London: University of Minnesota Press.

Mohanan, K.U. 2012. 'We Have Done a Lot of "Jugaad" In this Film', available at http://pandolin.com/makingof-fukrey/ (accessed on 2 December 2013).

Nelson, Michelle R. and Narayan Devanathan. 2006. 'Brand Placements Bollywood Style', *Journal of Consumer Behaviour*, 5: 211–21.

Newell, Jay, Charles T. Salmon, and Susan Chang. 2006. 'The Hidden History of Product Placement', *Journal of Broadcasting & Electronic Media*, 50 (4): 575–94.

Nuovo, Aditya Birla. 2006. The Don Collection from Louis Philippe, available at http://www.adityabirlanuvo.com/media/features/features.aspx?ID=1WG6KD86Wz0= (accessed on 2 December 2013).

Pomian, Krzysztof. 1988. *Der Ursprung des Museums: Vom Sammeln*, translated by Gustav Roßler. Berlin: Klaus Wagenbach.

Prasad, Harshita. 2013. 'LUX', available at http://www.digitalimpulse.in/insights/lux-marketing-strategy/#.Uo8u5ZgrmUk (accessed on 2 December 2013).

Punathambekar, Aswin. 2013. *From Bombay to Bollywood: The Making of a Global Media Industry*. New York: New York University Press.

Robinson, Andrew. 2004. *Satyajit Ray: The Inner Eye—The Biography of a Master Film-Maker*. London and New York: Palgrave Macmillan.

Sharma, Aasheesh. 2013. 'You Want to Cry When a Film Set Is Destroyed: Aradhana Seth', *Hindustan Times*, 22 February, available at http://www.hindustantimes.com/brunch/brunch-stories/you-want-to-cry-when-a-film-set-is-destroyed-aradhana-seth/article1-1015591.aspx (accessed on 2 December 2013).

Singh Soin, Himali. 2013. 'Aradhana Seth: On Rearranging the World Around Her', interview, *The Fuscia Tree*, available at http://www.thefuschiatree.com/310/fullview (accessed on 2 December 2013).

Vitali, Valentina. 2008. *Hindi Action Cinema: Industries, Narrative, Bodies*. New Delhi: Oxford University Press.

Wilkinson-Weber, Clare M. 2010. 'From Commodity to Costume: Productive Consumption in the Making of Bollywood Film Looks', *Journal of Material Culture*, 15 (3): 3–29.

Filmography

ABCD: Anybody Can Dance. Dir. Remo D'Souza. UTV Spotboy, 2013.

Des Pardes. Dir. Dev Anand. Navketan, 1978.

Dil Chahta Hai. Dir. Farhan Akhtar. Excel Entertainment, 2001.

Dil To Pagal Hai. Dir. Yash Chopra. Yash Raj Films, 1997.

Dilwale Dulhania Le Jayenge. Dir. Aditya Chopra. Yash Raj Films, 1995.

Don. Dir. Chandra Barot. Nariman Films, 1978.

Don. Dir. Farhan Akhtar. Excel Entertainment, 2006.

Don 2. Dir. Farhan Akhtar. Excel Entertainment, 2011.

Duplicate. Dir. Mahesh Bhatt. Dharma Productions, 1998.

Entrapment. Dir. Jon Amiel. Fountainbridge Films, 1999.

In Which Annie Gives It to Those Ones. Dir. Pradip Krishen. Kaleidoscope Entertainment, 1989.

Jay Santoshi Ma. Dir. Vijay Sharma. Bhagyalakshmi Chitra Mandir, 1975.

Kabhi Kabhie. Dir. Yash Chopra. Yash Raj Films, 1976.

Kabhi Khushi Kabhie Gham…. Dir. Karan Johar. Dharma Productions, 2001.

Kal Ho Naa Ho. Dirs Nikhil Advani and Ron Reid Jr. Dharma Productions, 2003.

Kuch Kuch Hota Hai. Dir. Karan Johar. Dharma Productions, 1998.

Mohabbatein. Dir. Aditya Chopra. Yash Raj Films, 2000.

One 2 Ka 4. Dir. Shashilal K. Nahir. Glamour Films, 2001.

Phir Bhi Dil Hai Hindustani. Dir. Aziz Mirza. Dreamz Unlimited, 2000.

Sangam. Dir. Raj Kapoor. R.K. Films, 1964.

Veer-Zaara. Dir. Yash Chopra. Yash Raj Films, 2004.

Beyond Diasporic Boundaries

New Masculinities in Global Bollywood

KAMALA GANESH AND
KANCHANA MAHADEVAN[1]

I like it that people have started to love Bollywood.

—Christina Wininger[2]

Invocations of family and nation have been staple in the history of popular Hindi cinema. 'Family films' by Aditya Chopra, Yash Chopra, Subhash Ghai, and Karan Johar (KJo) have given this formula new life with glamorous packaging in a global context contributing to the heterogeneous Bollywood genre. Yet these films pose provocative questions regarding the changing nature of masculinity in the context of the family and the nation-state, perhaps the very features that explain their transnational popularity. In contrast to the views of Brosius (2005), Rajadhyaksha (2008), and Uberoi (1998), these films are not reducible to exclusive endorsements of conservative family values. A scrutiny of KJo's films, for instance, also reveals subversive elements in his portrayal of Shah Rukh Khan (henceforth SRK) in a softer image of masculinity that questions machismo, critiques traditional family, and advocates a post-national spirit, transcending the Indian diaspora towards a global audience.

KJo's collaboration with SRK and its implications for transforming the Bollywood family-film formula is the theme of this chapter which begins with a discussion of Bollywood as national cinema. It explores the evolution of intimate relationships and softer masculinities in KJo's films through content analysis to finally examine the post-national consequences of their reception in German-speaking countries (Brosius 2005; Mader 2011; NDTV 2010).

Bollywood and National Cinema

Despite its elusiveness, complexity, and heterogeneity, 'Bollywood' can be used to refer to export-oriented commercial Hindi films since the 1990s. With music, melodrama, elaborate costumes, and the feel-good factor, these films evoke the nation through cultural practices of the diasporic Indian family. They structure these practices with a certain attitude of nostalgia and sentiment towards the 'family film' that was a prominent part of the history of Indian cinema. Aditya Chopra's *Dilwale Dulhania Le Jayenge* (*DDLJ*) inaugurated this genre in 1995 at the global box office, riding on Suraj Barjatya's national mega-hit, *Hum Aapke Hain Koun..!* (*HAHK*, 1994). Bollywood received a boost through the Indian government conferring industry status to filmmaking in the year 1998 in the context of its larger pro-diaspora policy since the early 1990s, to become what KJo termed as 'big business' (Johar and Ruhani 2007).[3] Projecting India as a soft power,[4] Bollywood films also have an elite connotation as they are made and watched by the well-heeled and educated sections of society. As KJo notes, 'People who are educated with proper degrees are considering Bollywood today' (Johar and Ruhani 2007).[5]

During the 1990s, films such as *DDLJ*, Subhash Ghai's *Pardes* (1997) and KJo's *Kuch Kuch Hota Hai* (*KKHH*, 1998) and *Kabhi Khushi Kabhie Gham...* (*K3G*, 2001) among several others revived the family drama genre of popular Hindi cinema which had fallen into obscurity.[6] Indeed, in keeping with their chosen genre and the tradition of commercial Hindi film finance, several Bollywood film production houses are family businesses, such as Yash Raj Films and Dharma Productions. As is well-rehearsed in Bollywood literature, these export films fulfil the diasporic Indian's nostalgia for home as a hearth against alienation in host countries. Yet, the home which has a dual meaning as nation and family is 'de-territorialized' (Uberoi 1998: 333) and subsequently re-territorialized in a diasporic location. Deepa Mehta's film *Bollywood/Hollywood* (2002) summarizes this with a character that ironically proclaims that anyone who knows about Bollywood qualifies as an honorary Indian. The film shows Hindi melodramatic films mediating the everyday lives of Indians living in Canada who consume it through videos. It also parodies the conflict between individual desire and duties to the family. Unlike earlier films that presented living abroad as moral decay,[7] Bollywood presents the non-resident Indian (NRI) as rooted in Indian culture despite living abroad, overcoming the binary between the moral East and the material West.

Yet Bollywood's indigenous identity is not novel because since their inception with Dada Saheb Phalke, Indian films established a distinct identity for themselves as indigenous national products.[8] Though they evoked what Rajadhyaksha (2008) terms as 'cultural nationalism', there were also strong tones of territorial nationalism. Moreover, as with Indian cinema, the Indian state did open up the possibility for the creation of an indigenous identity soon after Independence. Film-makers saw a constant need to move away from Hollywood and invent an Indian idiom located in traditional art and craft. Satyajit Ray (1976) argued that Indian cinema cannot simply copy American cinema because of the distinctiveness of the Indian way of life and the absence of Hollywood's technological sophistication. Thus, 'What Indian cinema needs today is not more gloss, but more imagination, more integrity, and a more intelligent appreciation of the limitations of the medium' (Ray 1976: 22). The family film with doses of melodrama was one such response. Paradoxically Bollywood has integrated—albeit unintentionally—Ray's insight to give an indigenous cultural product that connects with the nation in a re-territorial way via the conduit of family and romance. It circulates the nation '… as brand … a global nation in its identity, triumphs and struggles, and earning substantial profits' (Vasudevan 2008). The Indian state which started the process of disinvestment in the 1990s negotiated its identity through Bollywood as a commodity for economic gain; it perceived the diaspora as having the capacity to help India through investments. As KJo's proclamation above reveals, film-makers themselves saw the prospect of an enriching global market. Nationalism underwent a transition from the boundaries of the nation-state to a cultural avatar in the contemporary diasporic context.

However, unlike post-Independence cinema, Bollywood articulates its localism in a global canvas through hybrid constituency and global distribution to diverse audiences (Kaur and Sinha 2005). Yet in this process, it acquires the stature of national cinema in the relational context of Hollywood. Mehta's *Bollywood/Hollywood* aims at reminding Canadians that Bollywood and Indianness contribute to their multiculturalism. As Fung (2005) observes, by depicting Bollywood dance against the Toronto skyline, Mehta challenges the notion of Toronto as North Hollywood. Rather than play a subordinate role to Hollywood or any other global force, despite its nomenclature, Bollywood constitutes itself as national cinema in global contexts.[9] National cinema can be understood from territorial, functional, and relational perspectives (Choi 2006). Unlike its post-Independence predecessor, Bollywood is not territorially national either in location or spirit, given its diasporic global context, but it has elements of being functionally national, for it reinforces the nation through cultural practices. Moreover, Bollywood is also relationally national, since it affirms its own identity by distinguishing itself from Hollywood.[10] Thus, Bollywood opens 'alternative cultural and social representations away from dominant white ethnocentric audio-visual possibilities' (Dudrah 2002: 23). As Choi (2006: 314) argues, the relational concept of national cinema goes beyond the binary of financing and distributing the national in the domestic domain and the transnational in the international domain.

However, the relation between Hollywood and Bollywood is not unidirectional in the sense of reversing the translation of Hollywood to an Indian idiom as Gopal (2010: 19) suggests in the context of KJo films. Rather, although a film-maker like KJo does structured Hindi cinema through the grammar of Hollywood in terms of glossy appearance and technological prowess, he also Indianizes Hollywood films. The difference is that unlike earlier Hindi films that plagiarized Hollywood, he openly acknowledges his sources by purchasing copyright for films and music. The song *Pretty woman* in the film scripted by him *Kal Ho Naa Ho* (*KHNH*, 2003) produced by Yash Johar, his father, and directed by his former assistant Nikhil Advani is a rap–bhangra remix of Roy Orbison's *Pretty woman*, while *We Are Family* (WAF, 2010), which KJo produced and scripted, is an Indian version of Chris Columbus's *Stepmom* (1998). Besides being upfront about acknowledging its foreign influences,[11] there are both Hindi cinema and Hollywood moments in KJo films. Hindi cinema indicates commercial Hindi films prior to the advent of Bollywood in the 1990s. His *Kabhi Alvida Naa Kehna* (*KANK*, 2006), set against the Manhattan skyline, tackles the theme of adultery in a manner that is reminiscent of not only Woody Allen's *Crimes and Misdemeanors* (1989) or *Husbands and Wives* (1992),[12] but also of his uncle Yash Chopra's *Silsila* (1981). The film follows the destiny of two couples and depicts adultery like *Silsila*. But the couple in *KANK* does not break into song and dance in the tulip gardens of Holland like *Silsila*, rather they converse with each other in the crowded streets of New York like Allen's characters. Thus, the relational approach to national cinema allows it to 'weave in and out of these two sets of industrial modes' (Choi 2006: 314).[13]

Two critical features mark Bollywood as a genre. Thematically, it shifts from macho violence and revenge to romance and family relationships with a hero embodying soft masculinity who does not have a clearly identifiable villain to fight. In terms of style, it uses song, dance, and copious melodrama from popular Hindi cinema in a lavish and technically slick mode, imbuing it with the character of nostalgic homage. This new genre, which invokes the nation through evoking the family, was honed for export—to appeal to the diaspora and the newly emerging global Indian, both in the Indian metropolis and abroad. Bollywood's national identity in relation to Hollywood and its context of the Indian diaspora in the West also serves as a facilitator in subtly transforming the concepts of family, relationships, and masculinity in the 'family film'.

A turn to the collaborative films of KJo and SRK is instructive at this juncture given their definitive contribution to this transformational moment, right from *DDLJ* where KJo was assistant director to his cousin Aditya Chopra.[14] *DDLJ* itself can be seen as a transitional film between the performatives of the earlier macho and the later soft masculinity in Hindi films. Although its protagonist advocates the position of persuasive compromise in winning his fiancée from her father, the film still has a fight sequence towards the end. It is with the family films, such as *KKHH*, *K3G*, *KHNH*, *KANK*, and *My Name Is Khan* (*MNIK*, 2010), that are independently directed by KJo that soft masculinity comes of age. All these films are collaborations between SRK as an actor and KJo as director. *KKHH*, *K3G*, *KHNH*, and *KANK* are films in which SRK and KJo have worked together and are at the iconic heart of the genre with romance, love, and family. Although *KHNH* was directed by KJo's former assistant Nikhil Advani, as its scriptwriter and producer KJo was closely associated with all aspects of its making and has left his imprint in theme and treatment. This makes *KHNH* in effect a KJo film. Yet KJo has not necessarily conveyed his image of the non-violent sensitive man solely within the intimate domain of the family. *MNIK* deals with both tender and harsh family relationships, but it marks a transition for KJo from his trademark canvas of the family into one with a broader scope and a more explicit political agenda. While it has features common to the KJo family film genre, its scope and complexity are of a different order. Its protagonist Rizwan Khan (SRK) enters the domains of civil society and politics through the compulsions of his family life. He cannot continue his simple family life in the US because his being a Muslim comes in the way, resulting in the murder of his Hindu step-child. His wife, Mandira (Kajol) accuses him of being personally responsible for the murder because of his Islamic background. As a result, he is forced to prove his innocence to his wife by addressing Islamophobia in the US. Thus, in *MNIK*, KJo inextricably links the private domain of the family to the public one of politics.

The works of both SRK and KJo can be understood independently of each other, since SRK's repute precedes KJo's and several of KJo's scripted films have actors other than SRK. Besides KJo's directorial venture *Student of the Year* (2012) also does not feature SRK. Yet, an analysis of the four films mentioned earlier suggests that SRK and KJo have jointly pioneered a new masculinity in Bollywood.

The family location in a diasporic context portrays the male protagonist of these films as a sensitive urban man constituted by intimate relationships. This is indeed a transformation from the macho, violent, and angry young man of the preceding genre of Hindi films. Studies have shown how diasporic men find themselves 'disempowered in the wider society due to competitive antagonisms and wide-spread paranoia about non-white masculinity' (Kalra et al. 2005: 52). Further, in recent years, the figure of the non-white male has been viewed as a violent force in a world that is besieged by unipolarity of the West and its perceptions of terrorist threats. The following discussion shows that KJo and SRK's collaborative masculinity present a counterfoil to these stereotypes—the disempowered and threatening non-white male in the West.

The KJo Film: Reconstructing Family and Masculinity

The presentation of the 'family' in a KJo film, simultaneously conservative and radical, is a many-layered puzzle. At first glance, it is all about nostalgia for the traditional Indian joint family, located in a wealthy, upper-class Hindu (mostly Punjabi) milieu, mounted lavishly with emotion-drenched dialogue. The important moments of family life are celebrated with laughter and tears during festivals. As Sangita Gopal (2010: 29) argues, through the revival of the family film in exaggerated scale and colour, KJo establishes a relationship to the history of Hindi cinema. It is an aesthetic memorializing of the older figuration of family and conjugality from the 1950s to the 1970s.[15] The family in KJo's film is not a law unto itself, which takes the place of the state (which the older family film such as *Khandan* was), but becomes a transmitter of sentiment, in the domain of affect. His 'romance with patriarchy' is actually a sentimental stance towards the modes and affects of another time (Gopal 2010: 27), for KJo also makes some radical departures from the conventional notion of the Indian family by examining themes such as remarriage (*KKHH*), biological kinship (*K3G*), and adultery (*KANK*).

Beneath the external glitter and show of sex, Hindi films have traditionally adhered to a strict and narrow notion of family, upholding the normative Indian heterosexual, patriarchal, and extended family ethos with an image of the ideal Indian woman at its core who is self-sacrificing for the good of the family. The cinematic family model only reflected and endorsed other popular discourses prevalent about family that originated in colonial times and were echoed in the nationalist period and several decades of the newly independent nation. It is only recently that the sociological scholarship on family and kinship in India has recognized that the common sense view of the harmonious Indian joint family is actually a spin-off from colonial interpretations of India, buttressed by Indology (see, for instance, Ganesh 1994; Uberoi 2003). This normative, and thus selective, view in which three or more generations purportedly lived together under one roof, cooking at a single hearth, worshipping at one shrine, and economically and emotionally fused, was a product of Hindu religio-legal texts with its context of inheritance of property linked to the performance of mortuary rituals. The acceptance and perpetuation of such a construct by British scholar-administrators had other practical benefits. The picture of an eternal unchanging Indian society with its pillars of caste, village, and joint family also served to justify and consolidate the colonial rule since it implied that an external regime alone would help to bring in change and dynamism. The conventional, popular view still prevalent does not distinguish between household, which is a residential unit, and family, which is a diffused ideological concept. Even in the past, sociologists like A.M. Shah (1973 and I.P. Desai (1981 [1955]: 97)) argued that actual households were small and often nuclear, within an overall ethos of interdependence and mutual obligations within the extended kinship group. Class, community, and region influenced the form and composition of households. The purported harmony was based on patriarchal and authoritarian assumptions and concealed the dissents and negotiations within.[16] The Indian joint family, however, acquired the status of a trope. It became a prism through which 'modern Indians' came to regard their past. Even though originating in colonial (mis)interpretations, it developed other functions. It evoked nostalgia which helped to come to terms with the alienation and loneliness triggered by modernity.

KJo questions this harmonious façade of the Indian family and exposes its biases, hypocrisies, and conflicts without identifying them as part of structural patriarchy. He does so by interrogating Hindi commercial film's 'vigilante' masculinity (Gabriel 2010: 180) in the public domain and positing its antithesis of soft masculinity entangled in family relations. The former was characteristic of films starring Amitabh Bachchan, such as Prakash Mehra's *Zanjeer*

(1975), Ramesh Sippy's *Sholay* (1975), Yash Chopra's *Deewar* (1975), Manmohan Desai's *Mard* (1985), and several others from the mid-1970s to 1980s. The film *Mard* makes this point explicitly when the protagonist Raju states, '*Mard ko dard nahin hota*' (Men don't feel pain). This masculinity represented resentment against social injustice in the persona of the 'angry young man' in a way that was 'violent, redemptive, and capable of resolution' (Gabriel 2010: 181). The discontentment against the injustices of the Indian social political system is not relevant to KJo as the Indians who are his point of reference are part of the diaspora. Their expectations from the state are minimal, but they have a cultural bond to the nation. Hence, in his films the ideal men affirm their relation to India through the domain of intimate relationships and cultural nostalgia, where masculinity is transformed from Gabriel's 'vigilance' to a softness that is non-violent, sensitive, and vulnerable. The latter features are significant given that the characters in KJo films inhabit multiple locations of home and host in a diasporic context.

A turn to some of KJo's films will illustrate the transitional masculinity in his films. In *K3G*, there is a struggle between two masculinities, namely, the old that is represented by the hardline patriarch Yash (Amitabh Bachchan) and the adopted son Raj (SRK) whose flexibility is evidenced in the multiple locations he occupies with ease such as London and Delhi. The film questions patriarchal obsession with purity and authenticity of the bloodline. The patriarch Yash's castigation of his son is that he is after all adopted, not connected to the family by blood ties, and, therefore, capable of betraying the family lineage and legacy through his act of marrying the woman of his choice against the father's wishes. Ultimately, it is Raj's close bond with his mother that triggers a change of perception in Yash.

In *KHNH*, Aman (SRK) critiques the matriarch who is obsessed with biological lineage and who, thus, reproduces patriarchy. She rejects her daughter-in-law Jennifer's adopted child as biologically alien till she learns that the child is in fact her son's through an extramarital affair. Jennifer condones her husband's affair out of her motherly instinct which is not restricted to biological motherhood. Yet this aspect is brought out by Aman who makes the mother-in-law appreciate Jenny and the child. *K3G*'s patriarch and *KHNH*'s matriarch who think of the family in homogeneous ways meet with opposition by the characters played by SRK till they accept 'otherness' as a part of changing family life. In these films, SRK plays the outsider who enters families and brings them close through negotiation, understanding, and affection. These struggles differ from the 1970s' Hindi film *Deewar* which too projects the tussle between two masculinities—the lawful and the outlaw—as the conflict is between two brothers who are biologically related and equally macho; it is their relation to the state that varies. SRK changes the very nature of this struggle by redefining manhood as an identity that is acquired through personal relationships rather than in the public domain.

The most critical component of SRK's soft masculinity is that he demonstrates his emotions without any inhibitions by crying and making others cry. Thus, tears in KJo films are not representative of weakness, but of sensitivity and empathy. They also reveal that the protagonist who is close to his mother has imbibed her feminine qualities of empathy and nurture. This in turn empowers the soft man to handle complex relationships deftly and with care for the other's feelings. The relationship between Raj and his mother in *K3G* is the very opposite of that between Vijay (Amitabh Bachchan) and his mother (Nirupa Roy) in *Deewar*. Vijay is his mother's saviour and does not imbibe her femininity; his relationship to her is primarily one of protector who uses his brawn in a violent world. For Vijay, the domain of intimate relationships is necessary but not sufficient to his masculinity. In contrast, Raj in *K3G* depends upon intimate relations for his very existence; indeed, much of life is played out in the family context rather than the public sphere. It is in this spirit that KJo's portrayal of SRK in his films openly exhibits him as a hero with weaknesses and flaws, be it as an adopted son (*K3G*), as physically challenged (*KANK*), a fatally ill patient (*KHNH*), or an autistic man (*MNIK*). In these films, SRK as the protagonist is an imperfect vulnerable man who is nevertheless a role model because of the ideal way in which he builds human relationships.

There is a reference to the history of cinema in this gesture as well, for as Asit Sen's *Safar* (1970) and Hrishikesh Mukherji's *Anand* (1971) testify, Rajesh Khanna in the early 1970s played the romantic hero who was flawed by a fatal disease and who had to die. Yet as his character, Avinash, from Shakti Samanta's *Amar Prem* (1972), reveals in the famous line: he 'hated tears'.[17]

But a deeper look shows that despite radical positions on some issues, KJo does not develop a cohesive critique of the family, nor does he interrogate its structural parameters. His barbs at the family appear random and contradictory until one looks elsewhere for the motivation; the unifying theme across his films is his exploration of the nature of love across categories. The wellspring of his quest is to put romantic love, conjugal love, filial love, as well as love between friends as constituted by the same substance. He does not compartmentalize love. Friendship can turn into romantic love, yet romantic love can be sacrificed for friendship. Tender relationships can exist between male friends and also between mother and child, alongside sweethearts. He does not prioritize or foreground romantic love. If anything, the presence of the tender, loving mother (or sometimes more than one mother in the same film) is prioritized. His films are also meditations on the finitude of love. Unlike typical Hindi films, KJo's films convey that love is not forever, it can die, one can fall out of love, and one can fall in love for the second time with another person. This is borne out in several films. In *KKHH* Rahul's (SRK) initial insensitivity to Anjali's (Kajol) love for him, his marriage to Tina (Rani Mukerji), and subsequently, after her death, his love for Anjali are denials of Rahul's initial declaration that 'love happens only once'. Further, Naina's love for Aman and subsequent love for and marriage to Rohit in *KHNH* is not different from *KANK* where Dev and Maya, both married, embark on an adulterous relationship. Such explorations can perhaps also be interpreted as a reflection of KJo's sympathy for the world of alternate sexuality, in a decade when the LGBT movement has taken off in India.[18] The codes of this world, where what Gopal (2010: 25) terms as 'serial monogamy' is endorsed, and where a tender relationship with the mother is central, are unmistakable motifs.

The question arises as to how KJo manages to get away with these unorthodox themes that are acceptable to the box office. For one, he anchors his films away from India (UK in *K3G* and USA in the others), which he claims allows him the space and freedom to experiment (Gopal 2010: 27). The issues he addresses are commonplace in the Indian diaspora in the West. However, the contemporary urban Indian family too is beset with broadly similar dilemmas, but conventional Hindi cinema has not faced squarely except on rare moments.[19] Whatever his intentions may have been in choosing a diasporic setting, KJo's films appeal to the diaspora by reflecting their reality. They appeal to the elite sections of the Indian market by vicariously passing on the load of the emerging Indian reality to diasporic shoulders. Additionally, KJo has couched these issues in the language of nationalism and cultural nostalgia that is central to diasporic anxieties and identity.

The last two decades have seen an unprecedented overwhelming of several spheres of economy, civil society, and public life by Bollywood. Apart from export revenue generation, the everyday world of globalizing India is inundated with Bollywood. The 'Page Three' celebrity phenomenon, the world of fashion, advertising endorsements, film gossip in the print and electronic media, and the scale and style of wedding celebrations and other festivities in middle classes are some prominent examples where the films, personalities, and lifestyles of Bollywood stars intermingle and leave their imprint. The ease with which media-created monickers like SRK and KJo have passed into popular vocabulary is another example. This in fact is another key feature of this genre: the blurring of boundaries between actors' professional and private persona, its spillover into various other professional and private arenas and its dominant effect in shaping lifestyles of the new middle classes. A 'Bollyworld', by which I mean the real world of infrastructure and other paraphernalia of people, materials, and organizations that sustain Bollywood, exists in tandem with Bollywood in which SRK's role is obvious, but KJo too is not the typical low-key director. His popular chat show *Koffee with Karan*, his modelling in fashion shows and featuring in advertisements, his niche position in the celebrity circuit and his strong media presence, have all given him a profile that is comparable to SRK's in quality though not in scale (Chopra 2011).

But it is not just Bollywood characters that have 'crossed over', but the whole 'Bollyworld' phenomenon as well. The sensitive, negotiating, and peace-loving man created by the partnership between KJo and SRK has won fans across nationalities and ethnicities in Europe. The following section explores the contribution of such masculinity with all its accoutrements in creating a post-national culture.

Bollywood and Post-nation

Theoretical analyses of Bollywood's appeal tend to confine its reception to an Indian diasporic audience who play out their 'cultural insiderism' within the safe confines of 'homing' strategies and cultural citizenship in diasporic locations (Brosius 2005; Rajadhyaksha 2008: 38; Uberoi 1998). However, there is a need to rethink such accounts because Bollywood's appeal is not confined to the boundaries of the Indian diaspora in terms of viewership any more. A new trend reveals that it is appreciated by German-speaking people of multiple ethnic groups in Austria and Germany (Brosius (2005); NDTV (2010); Mader (2011)). SRK, in particular, has become very popular, primarily through the KJo films, among a transnational audience that includes Europeans, Africans, and people from the Middle East, apart from South Asians. One cannot translate this appeal to 'neo-orientalism'[20] or Indology[21] for KJo–SRK films do not merely portray normative 'Indian culture'. Though the community of filmgoers established by these films that are shown in public screenings[22] in Austria and Germany did begin with South Asians, they have now expanded to other ethnic groups and nationalities as well.[23] This transition to public viewing from watching DVDs with friends and family, within the confines of the home, opens up the possibility of a public display of alternative cultures of consumption.

Such popular interest in Bollywood cinema in Europe marks a dramatic shift in audience. For decades, Satyajit Ray's films were universally acclaimed in Western film festival circuits. They formed a part of a niche culture in the West that distinguished itself from mass audiences of commercial cinema. Ray's neo-realistic narratives of transition from tradition to modernity in a mostly postcolonial world appealed to connoisseurs of good cinema. They won him the Silver Bear at the Berlinale film festival for two consecutive years— in 1964 for *Mahanagar* and in 1965 for *Charulata*. However, 44 years later, in 2008, the Berlinale witnessed *Om Shanti Om* (Dir. Farah Khan, 2007) opening to a mass audience; followed through with an overwhelming response to *MNIK* at the non-competitive section of the Berlinale in 2010. Rather than Indian cinema, 'Bollywood' caught on with its fans taking up theme parties, music, toys, and clothing, creating a lifestyle 'Bollyworld', in the neologism coined by Raminder Kaur and Ajay Sinha (2005). At the same time, the global circulation of Bollywood has also triggered academic courses and research. Indeed, SRK, like several other Bollywood actors and film-makers, is periodically invited to speak at prestigious universities in the West. Thus, one could argue that the Ray film has been replaced by the KJo film in garnering appreciation in the Western world, flattening out the distinction.[24]

The heterogeneous reception of Bollywood family films has extended KJo and SRK's sensitive masculinity into a public domain that is inhabited by strangers who come from diverse nationalities. Bollywood reveals that diasporic cultural life is 'not as a one-off event with one-way consequences, but rather as an ongoing process of building links and relationships at the material and cultural levels' (Kalra et al., 2005: 15). The reciprocity between Bollywood and Hollywood, as discussed earlier, typifies these link between home and host reflecting the transnational character of diasporic communities with allegiances to multiple nations and ethnic groups. However, the term transnational (rather than diasporic) refers to corporations whose activities transcend that of the nation-states in economics and politics or 'the contemporary state of international capitalist relations' (Kalra et al., 2005: 35). Diaspora in contrast signifies cultural formations that have crossed the frontiers of the nation-state. 'If there is any single theme that emerges from a study of diaspora, it is that of multi-locational qualities, or the interaction between homes and abroads which cannot be reduced to one place or another' (Kalra et al., 2005: 17). Thus, the Bollywood film's entry into the diasporic context enables it to open up cultural identities that are transnational. It does not remain confined to one social group, namely, Indians, despite having strands of continuity with the Hindi commercial film genre in India. Moreover, instead of simply avowing the status quo of ready-made cultural possibilities such as Hollywood or Hindi commercial film, it creates a transnational cinematic form that lies between them. This transnational form also critiques—albeit indirectly—packaged cultural commodities, such as Hollywood, that assume human beings to be easily situated in a specific geography. Bollywood, thus, questions the notion of being comfortably located at one place, since location itself entails negotiating cultures from diverse geographies.

Hence, Bollywood demonstrates that the process of negotiating cultural identities in diasporic contexts is one of continuity as well as rupture, critique, and reconstruction. It accommodates multi-ethnicity by not being at home or at one place.

The alternative masculinity of KJo and SRK comprises conflicting images and is articulated in a diasporic cultural space that is between nation-states. Claus Tieber from the University of Vienna upholds that SRK's appeal 'is not just for Austria, it's for everyone. He combines opposites and he has something for everyone. He is very male in his body but he acts very female in a number of scenes. He is a Muslim playing Hindu, he is clothed in very Western clothes and still comes from India' (NDTV 2010).[25] Ironically, such a soft masculinity acquires its transnational space because of transnational corporations that distribute and market in complicit with global capital. The latter makes SRK–KJo films (and Bollywood in general) available to a non-diasporic, Western audience, despite them not being the initial target audience. In the German context, the catalyst was K3G's dubbed version, which was telecast on the German channel RTL II in 2004.[26] It opened the film to the German-speaking audience who surfed the Internet for more information and learnt about Indian DVD rentals. The 'Shahrukhis' or the German-speaking fans of SRK from Europe are, for the most part, women who appreciate his family orientation and 'emotionalism' constitutive of his alternate masculinity which includes the feminine as Tieber acknowledges. For instance, Marlene a 26-year-old Shahrukhi from Vienna claims that, 'He is a great human being. He is not only a brilliant actor, he is always there for his family, his wife, and kids. He takes out so much time for his fans and his friends' (NDTV 2010). Besides forming an association of SRK fans, she has travelled to Berlin, London, and even India to meet SRK, who, in her perception, idealizes the sensitive man. The profile of the German-speaking fan of SRK is astonishingly close to his popular constituency in urban India and the Indian diaspora. In Mumbai, a professional woman who is a pedagogical leader appreciates SRK for his portrayal of romance and security.[27] A survey done in the slums of Mumbai for the purpose of this chapter[28] suggests that his popularity and that of KJo's films in the working-class segment is not as high as it is among upper-class urban females of all ages in India. The small extent to which SRK is appreciated in the slums is for his acting, dances, and costumes, rather than emotional connect through romance.

All of this goes to show that the international aspect of the KJo–SRK collaborative films is not just about the economics of brand endorsements or production values as Rajadhyaksha (2008: 38) maintains. SRK's fan reception in Europe also belies his gloomy prognostication that the independence of Bollywood from the government is also its death knell. Further, Bollywood, with is elite audience profile, has led to the rising popularity of Bhojpuri[29] cinema among the non-elite Bihari migrants in Mumbai.[30] Thus, Bollywood has—unintentionally—multiplied rather than restricted the choices available for film audiences all over the world.

Against being reduced to mere nostalgia as Rajadhyaksha laments, Bollywood is thriving in a cinematic sense in the European context, where it exerts an integrating force on foreigners from diverse origins.[31] Thus, '[t]he Shahrukh cult is bringing in a multicultural influence' (NDTV 2010). Such a hybrid cultural flow has occurred because of changes in Europe. The weakening of national borders within Europe with the formation of the European Union as an alternative to the US is the outcome of 'a transnational economy in the wake of the globalization of markets' (Habermas 1999: 48). But then despite the defeat of an organized working class, it is leading to a new form of solidarity between people, or a 'post-national constellation' (Habermas 2001) between people of diverse ethnic and national origins, where 'Swedes and Portuguese will be ready to stand by one another' (Habermas 1999: 57).[32] However, SRK as a cult figure in Europe goes beyond Habermas's restricted account of interaction between Europeans to open the space for a social solidarity that brings both Europeans and non-Europeans together to fissure the cultural purism of what Habermas (2006) has called 'fortress Europe'.

Against Rajadhyaksha's (2008: 36) claim that Bollywood restricts itself to the citizen as family member, the films partnered by KJo and SRK open the family to the non-citizen. They do so by portraying a masculinity that is sensitive, vulnerable, and non-violent. By inhabiting multiple locations, the male protagonist in their films does not attempt at final resolution to conflict, but instead negotiates it through dialogue. Their films reveal that such negotiation is made possible not through a biological relation to the family (or the nation), but through a figure such as Raj, the adopted son in K3G, or Aman in KHNH. Such a figure is an outsider and insider position that empowers him to build new emotional bonds. Such an account of masculinity is a challenge (though unintentional) to the very notion of citizenship as fenced within the nation-state; instead of citizens with their easy sense of belonging, the male characters played by SRK in KJo's films essay the struggle to belong, through sensitivity, to the other. This resonates with people from diverse nations who inhabit contemporary Europe. Bollywood, consequently, returns to its post-Independence role of integrating diverse communities together with its 'suturing agency' (Rajadhyaksha 2008: 33), yet plays this role at a transnational level to address displacement and create new public spaces. One of SRK's Viennese fans, Christina Wininger, says that what appeals to her about him is his disavowal of hatred between ethnic groups (NDTV 2010). The soft masculinity of SRK and KJo makes meaning in the context of a unipolar, xenophobic, post–Cold War world.

The alternate cultural and normative openings of the collaborative films by SRK and KJo have become possible in a transnational space of diverse intersecting cultures and people catalysed by South Asian diasporas. These films do not have ready-made coded messages which determine that they are read in a linear stereotypical way as conservative family films or culturally nationalist films. To return to Choi's (2006) notion of national cinema invoked at the start of this discussion, Bollywood films are not always territorially national, but then they endeavour towards a functional nationalism through nostalgia for India or integration of diverse communities. In the course of performing the latter function, they belie their own intentions by bringing together unexpected audiences in unpredictable locations in a post-national direction. These films are also relationally national in offering an alternative to the hegemony of Hollywood; but in the course of this relationality, they have also assimilated aspects of the Hollywood film. All of this goes to show that Bollywood films in transnational contexts are a 'complex field of meaning and practices' (Mader 2011: 463), which lend themselves to varied communities that respond to them in multiple ways. Consequently, Bollywood has, in its own way, contributed to a progressive diversification and democratization of European culture through both the citizen and the migrant.

Notes

1. Many thanks to Sonja Majumdar for the detailed insights on Bollywood's reception in German-speaking countries. Thanks to Rajinder Dudrah, Bernhard Fuchs, and Elke Mader for helpful suggestions, and to Markar Melkonian and Biraj Mehta for their comments. However, all limitations in this chapter are entirely ours.
2. See Prasad (1998a, 2008), Kaur and Sinha (2005), Rajadhyaksha (2008), and Vasudevan (2008). As Rajadhyaksha (2008) cautions against the Western press (and one might add the Indian press), one cannot equate the Indian film industry with Bollywood.
3. This was accompanied by the collapse of non-commercial films that were earlier funded by the state.
4. See Vasudevan (2008).
5. KJo thought of himself as too westernized for Hindi films till he got involved with Aditya Chopra's *DDLJ* (2011).
6. The early 1970s, labour orientation was replaced by the action genre which continued into the 1980s to metamorphose into gangster films.
7. Besides Manoj Kumar's *Purab aur Paschim* (1970), mentioned as a case in point by Mehta (2010: 7), one can add Dev Anand's *Hare Rama Hare Krishna* (1971). Prior to Bollywood, the good heroes in Hindi films always returned to India after an education abroad.
8. As Prasad (1998b: 123) observes for Phalke's swadeshi location, 'the screen was a political space'.
9. Prasad (2008: 41) has pointed out that nomenclature of film production locations in India after Hollywood dates back to erstwhile Calcutta in 1932 with Tollywood.
10. Choi (2006: 312) distinguishes national cinema from the functional point of view and the relational point of view. Against the functional account, not all French films, for instance, are about reinforcing the state ideology. This chapter does not claim that all Indian cinema has the functionalist perspective. Bollywood does have a strong streak of such functionalism in a rather banal sense. But this is not all; they are also national in Choi's deeper relational sense.
11. Though KJo too does not acknowledge *Forrest Gump* (D. Robert Zemeckis, 1994) as an inspiration for his *MNIK* despite the obvious similarity between the two!

12. Though there are important differences in the way Allen tackles matrimony and adultery.
13. At the domestic level, Bollywood films can be distinguished from what is termed as the *Hatke* or 'off-the-centre' genre of film (Gopal 2010: 15). The latter types of films are made by corporate houses such as UTV and Pritish Nandy Communications for cosmopolitan domestic audience with offbeat themes, strong scripts, and actors who are not megastars. Bollywood and Hatke have some parallels to the distinction between commercial Hindi cinema and art films that emerged in the 1970s.
14. Yash Chopra's son.
15. The Bhim Singh film *Khandan* (1965) projects westernization as immoral, and sacrifice is posited as the basis for entry into the family. See Prasad (1998b: 65) for a discussion of this film in the context of Indian nation-building. Production houses, such as Gemini and Prasad, specialized in joint-family sagas which were imported to Hindi films from the south.
16. For a critique of the normative view of the Indian family, see Ganesh (1998), Shah (1973), and Uberoi (1993).
17. In a recent interview, Khanna claims, 'I hate tears…. I have always played characters that are strong' (Sharma and Shah 2011).
18. This section of the Indian Constitution, dating back to the British, criminalized same-sex relations.
19. Anurag Basu's *Life in a… Metro* (2007) is one such moment in the Hatke genre.
20. This possibility has been derived from the discussion with Dagmar Brunow.
21. This term is restricted to the study of classical Indian culture and language with a largely Sanskrit focus and an emphasis on philology rather than South Asian studies.
22. These include both official releases in theatres and informal ones. The former are not quite frequent and are confined to one or maybe two in a year, reaching a few months after their Indian release. There is a larger ethnic German audience for these films, unlike the significant South Asian audience for informal screenings. Since 2002 or so, informal screenings often coincide with Indian release dates; they publicize their screenings through word of mouth. Bollywood has reached audiences in Austria and Germany through DVD releases. Information received from Majumdar via email communication. See Mader (2011) for an account of the ritualized experience and behaviour of SRK fan culture

that is mediated through the Internet and digitalized photography in German-speaking countries.

23. Such an entry of Hindi commercial films into Germany and Austria differs from Eastern Europe and England. Hindi commercial films were available in Eastern Europe during the Soviet years due to film-trade treaty between Soviet Union and India. The presence of a large South Asian diaspora in England opened up Hindi films and programmes (by, for example, Nasreen Munni Kabir) on TV (in Channel 4 for instance). The reception of Hindi films in Austria and Germany is unique because they do not have a large South Asian diaspora. A word of thanks is extended to Majumdar for this insight.

24. Gopal (2010: 15) takes Rajadhyaksha's dichotomy between the Ray film and Bombay cinema as the basis of her analysis of KJo films as family-oriented. However, there is a difference between the kind of audience that sees these films. As Dagmar Brunow notes, in a personal communication the German audience for a KJo film is the reality-show viewer, while the Ray film appeals to an elite audience. Significantly, the academic study of Indian film in the West became visible with Bollywood.

25. This is from a documentary on SRK's Viennese fans in the Indian national news channel NDTV India.

26. This point was derived from a discussion with Sonja Majumdar. Also see Mader (2011: 468).

27. From a personal telephonic conversation on 30 April 2012. SRK's fan base in Mumbai is mostly from the upper-class sections encompassing women of diverse age groups ranging from pre-teen schoolgirls to the elderly.

28. A questionnaire regarding the films of KJo and SRK was circulated among 90 persons in the year 2010, out of which 60 lived in slums and the others belonged to lower-income groups residing in Palghar and Kalyan that lie in the vicinity of Mumbai. Only 43 out of those surveyed appreciated SRK and that too for his acting and comic roles. The rest categorically stated that they are not fans of SRK.

29. Bhojpuri is a Hindi dialect that is spoken in the Bhojpur district of the state of Bihar in India and also in Nepal.

30. See Ghosh (2010) for an account of Bhojpuri cinema.

31. One should not overstate this diversity though.

32. However, Habermas' account of the 'post-nation' tends to be Eurocentric, see Mahadevan (2013) for a critique. The intervention of Bollywood culture has the potential to remedy a post-nation that is West-oriented.

References

Brosius, Christiane. 2005. 'The Scattered Homelands of the Migrant: Bollywood through the Diasporic Lens', in Raminder Kaur and Ajay J. Sinha (eds), *Bollyworld: Popular Indian Cinema through a Transnational Lens*, pp. 207–17. New Delhi: SAGE Publications.

Brunow, Dagmar. 2010. '"Thank You Shah Rukh Khah!" Reconsidering Audience Studies: The Reception of Bollywood in Germany' (paper presented at the international conference 'Shah Rukh Khan and Global Bollywood', organized by the Department of Social and Cultural Anthropology, University of Vienna, 30 September–1 October).

Choi, Jinhee. 2006. 'National Cinema, the Very Idea', in Noel Carroll and Jinhee Choi (eds), *Philosophy of Film and Motion Pictures*, pp. 310–19. Malden: Blackwell Publishing Books.

Chopra, Anupama. 2011. 'Shah Rukh Khan: A Global Icon', in Jerry Pinto (ed.), *The Greatest Show on Earth: Writings on Bollywood*, pp. 25–34. New Delhi: Penguin Books.

Desai, Ishwarlal P. 1981 [1955]. *The Craft of Sociology and Other Essays*. Delhi: Ajanta Publications.

Dudrah, Rajinder. 2002. 'Vilayati Bollywood: Popular Hindi Cinema-Going and Diasporic South Asian Identity in Birmingham', *The Public*, 9 (1): 19–36.

Fung, Amy. 2005. 'Deepa Mehta's Canadian, American, Indian Bollywood Musical: Showing Canadians Their Country in *Bollywood/Hollywood*', *London Journal of Cultural Studies*, 21: 71–82.

Gabriel, Karen. 2010. *Melodrama and the Nation: Sexual Economies of Bombay Cinema 1970–2000*. New Delhi: Women Unlimited.

Ganesh, Kamala. 1994. 'Crossing the Threshold of Numbers: The Hierarchy of Gender in the Family in India', *Indian Journal of Social Science*, 7 (3–4): 355–62.

—————. 1998. 'Gender and Kinship Studies: Indian Material and Context', in Carla Risseeuw and Kamala Ganesh (eds), *Negotiation and Social Space: A Gendered Analysis of Changing Kin and Security Networks in South Asia and Sub-Saharan Africa*, pp. 113–36. New Delhi: SAGE Publications.

Ghosh, Avijit. 2010. *Cinema Bhojpuri*. New Delhi: Penguin Books.

Gopal, Sangita. 2010. 'Sentimental Symptoms: The Films of Karan Johar and Bombay Cinema', in Rinki Bhattacharya Mehta and Rajeshwari V. Pandharipande (eds), *Bollywood and Globalization: Indian Popular Cinema, Nation, and Diaspora*, pp. 15–34. London: Anthem Press.

Habermas, Jürgen. 1999. 'The European Nation-State and the Pressures of Globalization', *New Left Review*, 235: 46–59.

———. 2001. *Postnational Constellation: Political Essays*. Cambridge: MIT Press.

———. 2006. 'Opening Up Fortress Europe', *Sight and Sound*, 16 November available at http://www.signandsight.com/features/1048. html. (accessed on 10 November 2013).

Johar, Karan and Farheem Ruhani. 2007. 'We'll Be a Film Superpower', *DNA*, 1 January, available at http://www.dnaindia.com/entertainment/report-well-be-a-film-super-power-says-filmmaker-karan-johar-1072246 (accessed on 10 November 2013).

Kalra, S. Virinder, Raminder Kaur, and John Hutnyk. 2005. *Diaspora and Hybridity*. London: SAGE Publications.

Kaur, Raminder and Ajay Sinha. 2005. *Bollyworld: Popular Indian Cinema through a Transnational Lens*. New Delhi: SAGE Publications.

Mader, Elke. 2011. 'Stars in Your Eyes: Ritual Encounters with Shah Rukh Khan in Europe', in Axel Michaels, Udo Simon, Christiane Brosius, Karin Polit, Petra H. Rösch, Corinna Wessels-Mevissen, and Ahn Gregor. (eds), *Ritual Dynamics and the Science of Ritual*, vol. 4, pp. 463–84. Wiesbaden: Harrassowitz Verlag.

Mahadevan, Kanchana. 2013. 'Feminist Solidarity in India: Communitarian Challenges and Postnational Prospects', in Tom Bailey (ed.), *Deprovincializing Habermas: Global Perspectives*, pp. 71–95. New Delhi: Routledge.

Mehta, Rinki Bhattacharya. 2010. 'Bollywood, Nation, Globalization: An Incomplete Introduction', in Rinki Bhattacharya Mehta and Rajeshwari V. Pandharipande (eds), *Bollywood and Globalization: Indian Popular Cinema, Nation, and Diaspora*, pp. 1–14. London: Anthem Press.

NDTV. 2010. 'The Shahrukhis of Vienna', 22 August available at http://www.ndtv.com/article/world/the-shahrukhis-of-vienna-full-transcript-46441?cp (accessed on 23 August 2010).

Prasad, Madhava M. 1998a. 'The State in/of Cinema', in Partha Chatterjee (ed.), *Wages of Freedom: Fifty Years of the Indian-Nation State*, pp. 123–46. New Delhi: Oxford University Press.

———. 1998b. *Ideology of the Hindi Film: A Historical Construction*. New Delhi: Oxford University Press.

———. 2008. 'Surviving Bollywood', in Anandam P. Kavoori and Aswin Punathambekar (eds), *Global Bollywood*, pp. 41–51. New Delhi: Oxford University Press.

Rajadhyaksha, Ashish. 2008. 'The "Bollywoodization" of the Indian Cinema: Cultural Nationalism in a Global Arena', in Anandam P. Kavoori and Aswin Punathambekar (eds), *Global Bollywood*, pp. 17–40. New Delhi: Oxford University Press.

Ray, Satyajit. 1976. *Our Films, Their Films*. Hyderabad: Orient Longman.

Shah, A.M. 1973. *The Household Dimension of the Family in India*. New Delhi: Orient Longman.

Sharma, Amrapali and Kunal Shah. 2011. 'I'm the Original Superstar: Rajesh Khanna', *Mumbai Mirror*, 28 December, available at http://articles.timesofindia.indiatimes.com/2011-12-28/news-interviews/30564882_1_rajesh-khanna-big-bash-three-films (accessed on 10 November 2013).

Uberoi, Patricia (ed.). 1993. *Family, Kinship and Marriage in India*. New Delhi: Oxford University Press.

——————. 1998. 'The Diaspora Comes Home: Disciplining Desire in DDLJ', *Contributions to Indian Sociology*, 32 (2): 305–36.

——————. 2003. 'The Family in India: Beyond the Joint versus Nuclear Debate', in Veena Das (ed.), *Oxford India Companion to Sociology and Social Anthropology*, vol. 2, pp. 1061–103. New Delhi: Oxford University Press.

Vasudevan, Ravi S. 2008. 'The Meanings of "Bollywood"', *Journal of the Moving Image*, no. 7, available at 222/jmionline.org/jmi7_8.htm (accessed on 10 November 2013).

Filmography

Anand. Dir. Hrishikesh Mukherji. Rupam Chitra, 1971.

Amar Prem. Dir. Shakti Samanta. Shakti Films, 1972.

Bollywood/Hollywood. Dir. Deepa Mehta. Different Tree Same Wood, 2002.

Charulata. Dir. Satyajit Ray. R.D. Banshal & Co., 1965.

Crimes and Misdemeanors. Dir. Woody Allen. Jack Rollins and Charles H. Joffe Production, 1989.

Deewar. Dir. Yash Chopra. Trimurti Films, 1975.

Dilwale Dulhania Le Jayenge. Dir. Aditya Chopra. Yash Raj Films, 1995.

Forrest Gump. Dir. Robert Zemeckis. Paramount Pictures, 1994.

Hare Rama Hare Krishna. Dir. Dev Anand. Navketan, 1971.

Hum Aapke Hain Koun..! Dir. Suraj Barjatya. Rajshri Productions, 1994.

Husbands and Wives. Dir. Woody Allen. TriStar Pictures, 1992.

Kabhi Khushi Kabhie Gham…. Dir. Karan Johar. Dharma Productions, 2001.

Kabhi Alvida Naa Kehna. Dir. Karan Johar. Dharma Productions, 2006.

Kal Ho Naa Ho. Dirs Nikhil Advani and Ron Reid Jr. Dharma Productions, 2003.

Khandan. Dir. Bhim Singh. Vasu Films, 1965.

Kuch Kuch Hota Hai. Dir. Karan Johar. Dharma Productions, 1998.

Life in a… Metro. Dir. Anurag Basu. UTV Motion Pictures, 2007.

Mahanagar. Dir. Satyajit Ray. R.D. Banshal & Co., 1964.

Mard. Dir. Manmohan Desai. TNT, 1985.

My Name Is Khan. Dir. Karan Johar. Dharma Productions, 2010.

Om Shanti Om. Dir. Farah Khan. Red Chillies Entertainment, 2007.

Pardes. Dir. Subhash Ghai. Mukta Arts, 1997.

Purab aur Paschim. Dir. Manoj Kumar. Vishal International Productions, 1970.

Safar. Dir. Asit Sen. TNT, 1970.

Sholay. Dir. Ramesh Sippy. United Producers, 1975.

Silsila. Dir. Yash Chopra. Yash Raj Films, 1981.

Stepmom. Dir. Chris Columbus. TriStar Pictures, 1998.

Student of the Year. Dir. Karan Johar. Dharma Productions, 2012.

We Are Family. Dir. Siddharth Malhotra. Columbia, 2010.

Zanjeer. Dir. Prakash Mehra. Prakash Mehra Productions, 1975.

My Name Is Khan

Reinventing the Muslim Hero on the Global Stage

JASPREET GILL

Shah Rukh Khan's (henceforth SRK) *My Name Is Khan* (MNIK, Dir. Karan Johar, 2010) is number five in the top-grossers of 2010 in India (Box Office India), falling below films such as *Golmaal 3* (Dir. Rohit Shetty, 2010) and *Housefull* (Dir. Sajid Khan, 2010). *MNIK* set a new opening record in the UK, grossing GBP 936,000 (Mahmood 2010); the previous record was held by the SRK film *Kabhi Alvida Naa Kehna* (*KANK*, Dir. Karan Johar, 2006). In the US, where the film is set, *MNIK* had the largest opening weekend for a Bollywood film, grossing USD 1.94 million, eclipsing the previous record holder, *Om Shanti Om* (Dir. Farah Khan, 2007) which grossed USD 1.76 (DNA India 2010b). In Karachi, Pakistan, *MNIK* ran to 'packed houses' for all the shows; *MNIK* is the first major SRK-starrer in Pakistan since the Pakistan government allowed the screening of Indian films in 2008 (DNA India 2010a). These records serve to emphasize the extent of SRK's star power. It is his box office draw that resulted in Fox Star acquiring the distribution rights to *MNIK*.

It is interesting to note that with SRK's portrayal of a practicing, deeply faithful Muslim protagonist, Samar Khan, CEO of

Red Chillies Entertainment—a production company owned by SRK and his wife—directed a documentary, *Living with a Superstar: Shah Rukh Khan* which aired on 26 February on Discovery Travel and Living, two weeks after the release of *MNIK*. The documentary was Samar's idea and in an interview in *The Week*, he explains his motivation:

> I want the world to know the man I've known for 15 years. He is amazing! He is so many people in one person—an actor as much as a star, a businessman as much as a fantastic friend, a great father as much as a devoted husband, and a genuinely down-to-earth person for whom the sanctity of his craft is first and foremost. (Samar Khan, in Ghosal 2010: 42)

The release of this documentary on the heels of the release of the film is not a coincidence—the documentary casts a spotlight on the actor and functions as additional hype for the star and his newly released film. It also serves to emphasize SRK's superstar status while providing an inside look into the man and his life. It is another vehicle for fan consumption and demonstrates the global nature of his fandom.

MNIK is Karan Johar's fourth directed film; the previous films—*Kuch Kuch Hota Hai* (*KKHH*, 1998), *Kabhi Khushi Kabhie Gham...* (*K3G*, 2001), and *Kabhi Alvida Naa Kehna* (*KANK*, 2006)—were large-scale spectacles full of song-and-dance celebrations and family and relationship melodrama. *MNIK* both differs from and retains the hallmarks of Johar's cinematic style. The melodrama of human emotions remains as does the importance of songs depicted in the celebration of the marriage of the lead characters. Unlike his previous films, in *MNIK* Johar takes on a pertinent political issue; his treatment of the political realities of the post-9/11 world is to have it disrupt the harmony of the family. Front and centre of the film is the family and the relationship shared by the lead romantic pair. In all four of his films, Johar focuses on the family and the interpersonal relationships between family members. Through the focus on the family, Johar is able to explore the idea of love and belonging. The question of belonging is one that plagues the Muslim American and Muslim Indian in the larger context of the world.

MNIK is a clear avowal of SRK's global star power. The film moves beyond the local to engage in larger, global concerns of the representation of Muslims and their societal status. Bollywood cinema has become a means to engage in dialogue with the concerns of the day which is what Johar's *MNIK* directly does with the issue of a Muslim's place in the global world. This is Johar's first Muslim hero; the previous three films had Hindu heroes. This undertaking would not have been possible if Johar did not have SRK to cast as Rizwan Khan. The reality is that the 'Muslim hero' is a rare depiction in Bollywood. SRK has played a Muslim lead character in only one other film: *Chak De! India* (Dir. Shimit Amin, 2007) as Kabir Khan, the field hockey player whose patriotism is called into question when the Indian team loses to the Pakistani team because of his mistake. In *MNIK*, the character of Rizwan Khan has Asperger's syndrome, a form of autism that affects one's ability to communicate and engage in social situations, but he still manages to 'change his world'. In both these films, the patriotism of Islamic characters is questioned at a national and international level. In these particular roles, SRK recuperates the figure of the Muslim male from historical and contemporary stereotypical depictions, endowing him with characteristics of nobility, integrity, loyalty, and compassion. In *MNIK*, the character of Rizwan Khan embodies essential Islamic qualities—embodied by the Five Pillars of Islam—that are lost in the predominant representations of the aggressive Muslim who embodies the popularized negative aspects of Islam. The Muslim male body is marked as 'special'—Asperger's syndrome—that provides SRK with the licence to state what would normally remain unspoken; thus, actively working against a meta-narrative of the Muslim terrorist that pervades the global media.

The impact of seeing SRK in the role of a practicing Muslim in a post-9/11 world cannot be underestimated. The conference on SRK and global Bollywood in Vienna in 2010 highlighted his global star power and the importance of his films for young Muslim men even in remote parts of the world. It is ironic that a little more than two years after the release of *MNIK*, SRK experienced profiling as a result of his name. Invited to deliver a lecture at Yale University as a Chubb Fellow in 2012,[1] he arrived on Mukesh Ambani's private jet with Nita Ambani and a few others at Westchester

County Airport, New York on April 12. While Nita Ambani and the others swept through immigration, SRK was questioned for an hour and a half. Yale University officials called Homeland Security when word reached them of SRK's detainment.[2] This was the second time that SRK was questioned and detained; in August of 2009 he was questioned at Newark Airport. This recent detainment caused a bit of a furore in the media and on social networking sites. In a TV interview, film director Mahesh Bhatt voiced his discontent, referring to SRK as a 'national treasure'. The fact that this has happened a second time and that SRK was singled out from the small group of Indians on the flight seems to support the idea that his name is on a list; or at the very least the name 'Khan' is infused with negative suspicions. If anything, this occurrence highlights the relevance and pertinence of *MNIK*. In addition, originally Aamir Bashir was cast in the role of Rizwan Khan's brother, Zakir; as a result of his not being able to get a visa for the US, he was replaced by Jimmy Shergill. Despite the 'romance' structure of the film that dictates the resolution of all issues, the film is an important addition to a conversation that needs to take place in regard to the place of Muslims in the global world.

This chapter will examine the representation of the Muslim male on both the national and global stage. *MNIK* connects sectarian tension in the national space of India—as indicated by the flashback sequence—to the international space in the form of the prejudice and negative bias experienced by Islamic Americans in post-9/11 America and their global vilification. Ideologies of difference have rocked the nation-state and are also present in the diasporic communities. The titular character, Rizwan Khan, bore witness to communal violence in India and experienced a repetition of violence based on religion in America. *MNIK* focuses on the insidious nature of divisiveness along religious lines and its specific impact on family, both nuclear and national. The question of belonging no longer affects Muslims just in India—it is a concern that crosses national boundaries. In both the familial and political spaces, Rizwan's place as a Muslim American, as a family member, is questioned. The focus of the film is Rizwan's regaining of his lost place in the family which ultimately leads to the recovery of his place in the nation. The character and film are departures from SRK's cinematic work and speak to the global relevance of tolerance and understanding of the other. In *MNIK*, SRK provides an interiority to his portrayal that is generally lacking in Bollywood cinematic representations as Muslims are usually stock characters. This reconfiguring of the Muslim male in *MNIK* not only speaks to Bollywood representations, but to the pervasive global construction of Muslims, orthodox Muslims in particular. By 'orthodox Muslims' I refer to the common perception of Muslims who pray five times a day, abstain from alcohol, and so on, those who essentially follow the tenets of Islam. The general trend for the portrayal of 'secular Muslims' is to not highlight their praying or abstention from alcohol; the point of difference between them and Hindu characters resides in their names. *MNIK* is remarkable for its positive portrayal of orthodox Muslims as the Bollywood trend has been to portray heroic secular Muslims. This positive imaging has led to the film's playing to packed theatres in Pakistan which bodes well for an emerging solidarity between India and Pakistan as the ideologies of difference have historically wreaked havoc on the subcontinent.

There is a long tradition of Islamic othering, hearkening back to the Turko-Afghan invaders. Islam actually arrived on the Indian subcontinent in the seventh century, but it is with the Turko-Afghan invasions that began with Mahmud of Ghazni from 997 to 1030 (Bose and Jalal 2004: 20) that the dichotomy between Hindu and Muslim became more pronounced. This division between both communities was exacerbated by the British a few centuries later. With the popular belief that Muslims were foreigners to India, arriving as conquerors, the twentieth century saw the advancement of the two-nation theory and the expression of an essential Hindu-ness. The two-nation theory was first articulated by the founder of Aligarh Anglo-Muhammadan Oriental College (later Aligarh Muslim University), Syed Ahmad Khan, in the 1880s when he urged Muslims to distance themselves from the Indian National Congress (Jalal 1994: 52); it is the idea that Hindus and Muslims represented two distinct cultures and traditions (nations) within India, that resulted in the need for a separate nation for Muslims.

Muslims have been cast as demonic others since the twelfth century. There have been shifts in their construction as the 'Other', specifically the transition from being foreign invader to enemy of the dominant faith, but for the most part the polarity between Hindu and Muslim has been maintained by some factions. Bombay cinema has not provided an adequate space for Muslim representation outside of an underprivileged casting. It 'continues to position the Muslim as Other, making it unclear how the Muslim can be a citizen of modern India' (Dwyer 2006: 122). Past exceptions have been the grand historical films like Mehboob Khan's *Humayun* (1945) and K. Asif's *Mughal-e-Azam* (1960) as well as the Muslim social like *Mere Mehboob* (Dir. Harnam Singh Rawail, 1963) and the courtesan films. Vijay Mishra (2002: 217) clarifies that this may be a result of a 'Hindu reading of the Muslim establishment in India even before independence'. The All India League of Censorship—a self-proclaimed Hindu culture police force created in 1937—espoused inflammatory rhetoric aimed at 'cleansing the film industry of all its non-Hindu elements' (Mishra 2002: 217). Their mandate did not just include matters of representation of the Hindu body or Hindu thought, but 'extended to the question of who should control the means of representation' (Mishra 2002: 217). They highlighted what they perceived to be the contamination of the Indian film industry (in this instance Mumbai) by Muslims and Parsis—both groups were believed to hold anti-Hindu agendas. The goal of the All India League was to fan out non-Hindu functionaries by pointing to manufactured connections between on-screen ideology with the assumed general ideology of Muslims (Mishra 2002: 217). One of the realities of this was that many Muslim actors changed their names—Dilip Kumar, Meena Kumari, Madhubala, and Ajit are some of the more famous examples. At the same time, there were some artists who did not: Waheeda Rehman, Nargis, Noorjehan (she eventually left India to move to Pakistan), Mohammad Rafi, and Shamshad Begum.

There are some uneasy deductions to be made by the limited space occupied by Muslim culture and history in popular film. It should be noted, however, that the 'perception that the industry has a disproportionate number of Muslim stars, producers, directors, stunts, in fact at all levels, is only true of the Indian cinema after [post-1931]' (Dwyer 2006: 99). The marginalization of Muslims indicates their lack of legitimate status in the realm of the popular; when they do appear on-screen, their representation is stereotypical and provides limited parameters for emotional engagement; there is a lack of complexity with emotional or physical conflict with Hindus. Because Muslim history and culture have not been viable cinematic subjects, their lifestyle is shrouded in mystery. Full portraits of Muslim families are rare, but one example is Khalid Mohamed's *Fiza* (2000), a film which proposes that the 'rebelliousness of the Muslim youth is directly linked to a growing Muslim sense of exclusion in recent years from the central issues of the nation-state' (Mishra 2002: 218). The norm is the absence or silence of Muslims in cinema, a deliberate exclusion that heightens their peripheral status in India. Dwyer (2006: 130) has commented that 'Islam is not seen as a problem in Indian cinema provided it is within the Islamicate context rather than the world of politicized or globalized Islam'. This is indeed what makes *MNIK* remarkable: as a commercial film that is a commodity, a vehicle to generate money, it engages with the issue of the Muslim terrorist and pervasive stereotypes affecting Muslims in the global world by presenting a Muslim hero who retains the signifiers of his religious identity. SRK's casting as a Muslim protagonist who has a Hindu love interest—unlike his character in *Chak De! India* where it is only implicitly suggested—reconstructs the politics around the portrayal of Muslims in Hindi cinema.

While the attempt to unify the nation under the category of 'Indian' was made in the early years after Independence, this effort was repeatedly torpedoed by a variety of conflicts about ethnic, linguistic, and caste differences.

> The truncated colonial territories inherited by the Indian state after 1947 still left it in control of a population of incomparable differences: a multitude of Hindu castes and outcastes, Muslims, Sikhs, Christians, Buddhists, Jains and tribes; speakers of more than a dozen major languages (and thousands of dialects); myriad ethnic and cultural communities. This discordant material was not the stuff of which nation states are made; it suggested no common identity or basis of unity that could be reconciled within a modern state. (Khilnani 1997: 51)

In postcolonial India, minorities are caught in the fissures of a fragmenting secular state as the Hindutva philosophy has taken a strong hold. The most significant has been the violence from communal conflicts between Hindus and Muslims. The National Integration

Council in 2005 issued a report indicating that the frequency of instances of tension generated between majority and minority communities has increased; in other words, there is a decline in tolerance between them (Kavoori and Chadha 2008: 132). The unfortunate reality is that between 2000–5 India had an average of 800 annual communal incidents of varying intensity (Kavoori and Chadha 2008: 132), ranging from small-scale, local clashes to large-scale riots and mass killing of the type that occurred in Delhi in 1984, Mumbai 1992–3, or Gujarat in 2002.

The othering of Muslims in film has relied on representations that are consistently reducing, marginalizing, or demonizing them. There was a trajectory to their representation which has been discussed by Kavoori and Chadha (2008: 132). They inform that

> while representations of Muslims in terms of their exoticism dominated the early post-independence period of the 1950s and 1960s, these were followed in the 1970s and 1980s by films in which Muslim characters were increasingly marginalized, only to be succeeded by a series of ultranationalistic films dating from the early 2000s, in which they are demonized, typically through a conflating of Islam with terrorism and Muslims with Pakistan. (Kavoori and Chadha 2008: 135)

Kavoori and Chadha (2008: 135) argue that 'the representation of the Muslim as Other has in fact been a long-term trend within the discourse of popular Hindi cinema.' Early representations of Muslims were exoticized, romantic visions focused on the idea of Muslim kings or elites who lived in a world that was remarkably distinct from the one lived by the audience. K. Asif's *Mughal-e-Azam* and Mehboob Khan's *Humayun* are examples of this type of representation. While these films portrayed the ideal of Hindu–Muslim unity, they nevertheless underscored the differences between the two communities. The cinema of the 1970s saw the near disappearance of significant Muslim characters (Kavoori and Chadha 2008: 135). Muslim characters were relegated to the periphery in limited roles; cast in minor supporting roles, they were traditionally coded. They were positioned within stereotypical 'Muslim' occupations and they were distinguished by idiosyncrasies in language, clothing, and behaviour (Kavoori and Chadha 2008: 139). It is important to note that shifts in representational types were not indicative of a redefinition of 'Muslims' in mainstream Hindi cinema.

Muslim identity was—and is—articulated through specific external signifiers: names, appearance, mannerisms, and religious practices. Religious practices were usually demonstrated through the performance of namaz (daily prayer) and visits to dargahs (Muslim shrines), or masjids (mosques) (Kavoori and Chadha 2008: 139). Within the context of Hindi films, this was how 'Muslim' identity was constructed. They were token representatives of a secular ideal but not active participants in articulating 'Indianness' or essential to the film's narrative. But in the 1990s and 2000s Muslim characters can be seen more frequently and in roles of more significance; the caveat being that these more substantive roles generally had negative spins (Kavoori and Chadha 2008: 140). While the previous decades were remarkable for the consistent marginalization of Muslim characters, these last two decades saw the emergence of more villainous characters—whether small-time crooks, power-mongering politicians, corrupt policemen, or militant aggressors—highlighting the tension between India and Pakistan (Kavoori and Chadha 2008: 140). This developing demonization of Muslims found a key outlet in the depiction of Muslim terrorists whose acts of terrorism are against India. One such famous portayal was by one of the big Khans—Aamir in Kunal Kohli's *Fanaa* (2006). His character, Rehaan, has been inducted into this way of life by a terrorist grandfather—a disturbingly familial occupation. As mentioned earlier, SRK has played a Muslim protagonist once before as Kabir Khan, a field hockey player whose Indian national team loses to Pakistan.[3] As a result of his miss on the field, his patriotism is questioned and his religious identity is placed at the forefront. His redemption lies in coaching the female hockey team to international victory in the tournament in Australia. The minorities in India—especially Muslims and Sikhs—must constantly deal with their patriotism being questioned. On the twentieth anniversary of the 1984 massacre of Sikhs, Khushwant Singh in 2008 commented that 'in secular India there is one law for the Hindu majority, another for Muslims, Christians, and Sikhs who are in minority.' Singh subsequently stated that during the Delhi massacre, he felt like a refugee in his own land and understood how the Jews must have felt. Singh has questioned why a Sikh cannot be both Indian and Sikh and why a Hindu's allegiance is not questioned.

In Johar's cinematic world, love overcomes all obstacles. The interreligious marriage between Rizwan and Mandira occurs despite Rizwan's brother's disapproval. Johar presents some wonderful scenes of religious harmony: in one corner of the screen Rizwan does namaz while in the other corner, Mandira does puja. Interestingly, the female lead is divorced with a child. This is an uncommon portrayal for a Bollywood heroine that has not met with much success; Madhuri Dixit played a similar role in *Aaja Nachle* (Dir. Anil Mehta, 2007). It is beautifully picturized to a melodic song in typical Johar fashion with gorgeous sets and costumes. The song, *Sajda*, which means worship, neatly ties together the divine nature of love and its ability to cross all boundaries to unify people while highlighting the nature of the love shared by Rizwan and Mandira. The idyllic family life of Rizwan, Mandira, and Sam is interrupted by violent ripples from the aftermath of 9/11. Rizwan's life changes when Sam dies after being beaten by school bullies. In response to her son's death, Mandira lashes out at Rizwan, blaming his name for her son's death, stating that if Sam's last name had been 'Rathod' he would not have died. It is a melodramatic scene between husband and wife that occurs on the soccer field where Sam was beaten. In her anger, Mandira tells Rizwan to go and tell the US president: 'My name is Khan and I am not a terrorist.' Rizwan understands this and Mandira's demand that he leave literally and thus embarks on his quest to meet the president of the United States, beginning a cross-country journey that ends up changing people's lives and perceptions. The film opens with Rizwan's preparation for this cross-country journey soon revealing the motif of the quest that underpins the movie. Rizwan's narrating voice presents a one-sided conversation with Mandira; his goal is to fulfil his lady's desire and return home to her love. His quest is reminiscent of one of the oldest journeys to get back home: Odysseus desires nothing but to return home to his wife, Penelope. But, before he can do so, he must overcome various trials and tribulations. Similarly, Rizwan must overcome obstacles in order to fulfil his quest which is not politically motivated, but born of a desire to regain the love and harmony of the family, namely, Mandira. In *MNIK*, the political disrupts the happiness of the family; but the film does not privilege the political—it is secondary to the needs of the family. SRK (Ghosal 2010: 46) has described MNIK as a 'romance but it is very different from your usual commercial film. It is a love story, but with a difference that will hopefully open up the non-traditional international market for Bollywood. I want Bollywood to be everywhere.' The film is not a traditional love story in the vein of *Dilwale Dulhania Le Jayenge* (*DDLJ*, Dir. Aditya Chopra, 1995), but it positions at the heart of the film the importance of love and the concomitant sense of belonging that drives Rizwan to fulfil Mandira's mandate. While the film is a challenge to the stereotype of the Islamic terrorist and questions the status of Muslims in America and the world, it does not privilege the political sphere over the familial one.

The film's sense and presentation of history does not extend past 1983. The flashback sequence in the film locates this year as affected by communal violence and constructs it as a historical frame key to Rizwan Khan and his generation. The Partition of 1947—the usual locus of the legacy of communal violence—is replaced by 'modern' examples of violence, contemporizing the prejudice experienced by Muslims. The boundary between the national and international have become more porous. About six months after the tragic events of 11 September, 2,500 Muslims were brutally killed in Gujarat in March 2002, after a relatively quiet interlude since the 1992–3 riots in Bombay. The rhetoric of hatred on the subcontinent has continued to intensify since 2001. This is not to claim a direct co-relation between the events of 9/11 and the communal tensions in India, but to instead suggest that the aftermath of 9/11 has fuelled pre-existing tensions.

The opening sequence of the film—which takes place in November 2007—intentionally plays on the Muslim terrorist stereotype: a brown man searches online for Bush's itinerary; the music is ominous as the man arrives at the airport and lines up. He is praying in Arabic when he is pulled out of the security line-up to endure a humiliating examination of his person and his luggage. After the examination, the security guards ask whether Rizwan Khan is on the watch list. What the viewer absorbs is the profiling affecting Muslims and the important fact that Rizwan is autistic. Rizwan's autism becomes a signifying characteristic along with his religious identity. Unlike the representations in previous films, in MNIK, Rizwan's religious identity is not sublimated into a more palatable depiction. The powerful image of SRK as a devout Muslim who prays, re-appropriates the figure of the Muslim male whose religiosity has become coded in violence and intolerance. Rizwan on his quest somewhere in Georgia,[4] visually 'othered' but not shying away from performing his prayers five times a day, is among the most impressive images of the movie. The visual effect of a Muslim praying in the heart of America is a powerful rejection of Muslim stereotypes within national and international discourses.

The Muslim hero has a special gift: his ability to 'fix' things—the water pump in his Masterji's living complex—which foreshadows his ability to repair the Muslim terrorist stereotype (Rizwan carries a sign to this effect: 'Repair almost anything'). Rizwan is a practicing, deeply faithful Muslim and his values have been shaped by his mother, Razia Khan (portrayed by the talented Zarina Wahab). In the flashback sequence to 1983 in the wake of Hindu–Muslim riots, Rizwan overhears some Muslim rhetoric of hate—shoot Hindus for what they have done to our women—when he repeats some choice curse words in his mother's presence, she turns it into a teaching moment. She draws stick figures: one of Rizwan, one with a gun, and another who has a lollipop; she asks him to identify who is Hindu and who is Muslim. He is unable to tell the difference and his mother informs him that there are two types of people in the world: good people who do good things and bad people who do bad things. This is an oversimplified attempt to erase difference and within the context of the film it proves successful. The world of MNIK is relatively unshaded by grey—it is a world of clear contrasts where the good characters are good and the bad are indeed bad. By avoiding the grey areas, Johar's film forces the audience to work within these parameters.

A pivotal scene in the film occurs in the space of the masjid. Masjids have become misconstrued as spaces of recruitment and hotbeds of violent ideologies. This scene reclaims the masjid and it becomes a powerful example of the proper practice of Islam. Dr Faisal Rehman of St Benedict's Hospital gives an inflammatory speech to a small audience of 15 Muslim men. His issue is that Muslims are not given the same human grace as other communities receive. He presents a story with his interpretative spin: Allah asked Ibrahim to sacrifice his son and Ibrahim without asking any questions agreed to this; the doctor then points to the lesson that Islam demands they shed their blood for the sake of the religion. Rizwan is unable to remain silent and, in a very moving scene, contradicts the doctor's interpretation. He provides the alternate—what is supposed to be the tolerant and accepting reading of the story: he tells us that Allah did not ask for Ismail's sacrifice; he refers to his mother's retelling of the story—Ibrahim did not doubt Allah's compassion. The story is an example of Ibrahim's faith and belief and Rizwan's interpretation of the story demonstrates the principles of tolerance and acceptance that are the foundation of his interactions with diverse people. This is why, despite being repeatedly incited by a stranger, Ibrahim did not stray from the path of righteousness—he did not listen to the stranger. Ibrahim knew Allah would never let his son's blood be spilled and he was right. Rizwan's mother highlighted that the 'path of Allah is that of love not of hatred and war' and the varying interpretations of Allah's path lead to myriad Islamic practices and beliefs. When asked who the stranger was who tried to influence Ibrahim, Rizwan responds that he was a '*shaitan*'—devil—and he throws his stones at Dr Rehman—illustrating the parallel between the story and the doctor's sermon. The film demonizes the Muslims who perpetuate ideologies of hatred and intolerance; who misinterpret the teachings of Islam. It corrects the indiscriminate demonization of Muslims, redirecting along specific ideologies and values. The film glorifies the noble heroism of its Muslim hero who enacts the teachings of Islam as taught to him by his mother: he imparts love and kindness, coming to help Mama Jenny (played by Jennifer Echols) and her flooded town and thus inspiring others—Muslim and non-Muslim alike—to help the community in need. The Muslim hero comes to stand for a shared humanity with the lines of division based on practicing ideologies of love and hate that encompass all religious traditions. It is ironic that while breaking the Muslim figure away from negative stereotypes, the film is guilty of stereotypical slippage in its depiction of African Americans as impoverished, backwater people who are nevertheless warm and caring—reminiscent of earlier twentieth-century depictions of African Americans of the deep South, that is, *Gone with the Wind* (Dir. Victor Fleming, 1939).

Within Bollywood cinema, issues that have been presented must be resolved. This unwritten mandate informs Karan Johar's films and *MNIK* in particular; while the film problematizes the position of the Muslim Americans in a post-9/11 world, it also resolves this issue within the allotted time. Rizwan's fulfilment of his quest reunites him with Mandira; his return to the family also signals a hopeful, positive American nation (highlighted by the new leadership under President Barack Obama) that embraces the heroic Rizwan. This Muslim hero has positively impacted his society and serves as a new archetype of the Muslim, emancipating Muslims from the negative stereotypes that previously informed the nation and the world. Rizwan represents Islam and the Muslim man—he highlights the qualities of love, compassion, and humanity—qualities that describe Islam but are submerged by overpowering stereotypes of Islamic militancy and violence. Rizwan also emancipated Muslims to reclaim their identities; his sister-in-law, Hasina (portrayed by Sonya Jehan), is empowered to put her hijab on again. The resolution of the film presents an America that includes its Muslim citizens and replaces the figure of the Muslim terrorist with that of the compassionate, caring Muslim male.

SRK's status as a Bollywood star of global proportions allows *MNIK* to come to the rescue, to present a mode of articulation to the question of the place of Muslims in the world. Within and outside the film, SRK recuperates the figure of the Muslim to spotlight qualities that are neglected in an atmosphere of fear and hate. With his portrayal of Rizwan Khan, SRK has depicted a memorable Muslim hero on the big screen and into a new age of belonging in cinema.

Notes

1. The Yale Chubb Fellowship has included distinguished figures such as Chinua Achebe, Elie Wiesel, and Maya Angelou.
2. In his Chubb lecture, SRK, with his incisive wit, poked fun at his questioning and detainment. He commented that when he becomes too arrogant, he comes to America, where the officials kick the star out of stardom.
3. SRK had a supporting role as a Muslim archaeologist, Amjad Ali Khan, in Kamal Hassan's *Hey Ram* (2000).

4. The movie *MNIK* is available at www.filmicafe.com (accessed on 22 April 2012).

References

Bose, Sugata and Ayesha Jalal. 2004. *Modern South Asia: History, Culture, Political Economy*. New York: Routledge.

BoxOfficeIndia.com. 'Top Lifetime Grossers 2010–2019 (Figure in Ind Rs)', available at http://www.boxofficeindia.com/showProd.php?itemCat=3 17&catName=MjAxMC0yMDE5 (accessed on 30 November 2013).

DNA India. 2010a. '"My Name Is Khan" Runs to Packed Houses in Karachi', 14 February, available at http://www.dnaindia.com/entertainment/ report_my-name-is-khan-runs-to-packed-houses-in-karachi_1347774 (accessed on 11 November 2013).

——————. 2010b. '"My Name Is Khan Smashes" Box-Office Record in the US', 16 February, available at http://www.dnaindia.com/entertain- ment/report_my-name-is-khan-smashes-box-office-record-in-the- us_1348815 (accessed on 11 November 2013).

Dwyer, Rachel. 2006. *Filming the Gods: Religion and Indian Cinema*. New York: Routledge.

Ghosal, Bidisha. 2010. 'The Man behind the Superstar', *The Week*, 24 January, pp. 38–46.

Jalal, Ayesha. 1994. *The Sole Spokesman: Jinnah, the Muslim League and the Demand for Pakistan*. Cambridge: Cambridge University Press.

Kavoori, Anandam P. and Kalyani Chadha. 2008. 'Exoticized, Marginalized, Demonized: The Muslim "Other" in Indian Cinema', in Anandam P. Kavoori and Aswin Punathambekar (eds), *Global Bollywood*, pp. 131– 45. New York: New York University.

Khilnani, Sunil. 1997. *The Idea of India*. London: Hamish Hamilton.

Mahmood, Shabnam. 2010. 'My Name Is Khan Sets UK Box Office Record', *BBC News*, 16 February, available at http://news.bbc.co.uk/2/ hi/entertainment/8518194.stm (accessed on 11 November 2013).

Mishra, Vijay. 2002. *Bollywood Cinema: Temples of Desire*. New York: Routledge.

Singh, Khushwant. 2004. 'Oh That Other Hindu Riot of Passage', *Outlook Magazine*, 7 November, available at http://www.countercurrents.org/ comm-khushwantsing071104.htm (accessed on 30 November 2013).

Filmography

Aaja Nachle. Dir. Anil Mehta. Yash Raj Films, 2007.
Chak De! India. Dir. Shimit Amin. Yash Raj Films, 2007.

Dilwale Dulhania Le Jayenge. Dir. Aditya Chopra. Yash Raj Films, 1995.

Fanaa. Dir. Kunal Kohli. Yash Raj Films, 2006.

Fiza. Dir. Khalid Mohamed. The Culture Company, 2000.

Golmaal 3. Dir. Rohit Shetty. Shree Ashtavinayak Cine Vision Ltd., 2010.

Gone with the Wind. Dir. Victor Fleming. Selznick International Pictures, 1939.

Hey Ram. Dir. Kamal Hassan. Raajkamal Films International, 2000.

Housefull. Dir. Sajid Khan. Eros International, 2010.

Humayun. Dir. Mehboob Khan. Mehboob Productions, 1945.

Kabhi Alvida Naa Kehna. Dir. Karan Johar. Dharma Productions, 2006.

Kabhi Khushi Kabhie Gham.... Dir. Karan Johar. Dharma Productions, 2001.

Kuch Kuch Hota Hai. Dir. Karan Johar. Dharma Productions, 1998.

Mere Mehboob. Dir. Harnam Singh Rawail. Rahul Theatre, 1963.

Mughal-e-Azam. Dir. K. Asif. Sterling Investment Corp., 1960.

My Name Is Khan. Dir. Karan Johar. Dharma Productions, 2010.

Om Shanti Om. Dir. Farah Khan. Red Chillies Entertainment, 2007.

Intermedia, Assemblage, SRK

AMY VILLAREJO

Prologemena

It may be helpful to try to situate briefly the context of this chapter. Unlike many of the distinguished contributors who have been publishing work on Indian film that has in fact defined the field, I am a relative latecomer, not to cinema and media but to India. Let me share, then, my stakes. The first is postcolonial theory, derived particularly through the work of Gayatri Spivak and her penchant for comparative and deconstructive analysis (since Shah Rukh Khan, henceforth SRK, has used the term himself in his note to the participants in the conference from which this volume derives, I will use it freely here), that is, a rigorous exploration of contradictions in postcolonial cultures. The second, also from my training in film studies and perhaps most visible in this chapter, is a sense of regard for the variegated histories of form. Cinemas, and I use the plural to emphasize their own diversity, feed and are fed by other media streams, platforms, aesthetics, and industries, and if SRK belongs primarily to a cinema or even a domain of post-cinema we could describe as dominant and commercial, he emerges (in terms of his training and background) from theatre and then television, and his image and personae sustain other circuits that I would want to explore in this chapter alongside or beside his image. Finally, by happenstance, someone with whom I have watched Indian cinema on DVD at home is the granddaughter of Ardeshir Irani, a pioneer of the Indian cinema who worked in the late silent and early sound period. What is of course interesting about Irani is that it was for him that the American engineer Wilford E. Deming was working when he coined the term 'Tollywood' to refer to the Calcutta film industry that was, in 1932, giving rise to the emerging sound cinema in India. And it was through the mediation of Calcutta, the changing of that 'T' to a 'B', that Bollywood as a term was born, as both Bhaskar Sarkar (2008: 34) and M. Madhava Prasad (2003) have separately noted. All of which is simply to say that I emerge out of this jumble of Bengali intellectuals, Calcutta Marxism, poststructuralist film theory, and Parsi movie moguls and their Mumbai to present the very preliminary beginnings of some *conceptual* work on Indian cinema.

I also played field hockey competitively for eight years. I hope that this will go some way towards explaining why I am drawn to *Chak De! India* (Dir. Shimit Amin, 2007) in the latter half of the chapter.

Intermedia

The pioneering video artist Woody Vasulka (1990: 465) argued in his essay 'The New Epistemic Space' that 'we have moved from a relationship with technology in which we attempt to invoke the creative potential of a specific tool, to one with a technological environment invoking a new creative potential from human discourse ... new epistemic space.' In historical terms, the technological environment to which this statement refers includes the expansion of public media through tools that were emergent in the 1970s and 1980s, such as the video Portapak, cable television, and mobile projection systems. In the US in particular, these devices not only revolutionized television, but also brought the performing and literary arts directly into dialogue with the media. This occurred not only through enhanced experimentation with new media tools on the various scenes of performance but also through the expansion of the academic study of cinema and television, an expansion of which I am a product. With portability and more affordable technology came mixtures of high and low culture as well as enhanced forms of self and social expression through the media.

Late twentieth-century developments in cinema, television, video, and digital technologies have contributed to the initiation and elaboration of many discursive, embodied, and theoretical spaces important to the academic disciplines of performance, cinema, and cultural studies. The rise of cinema and media studies has called attention to differentiations between elite and mass *and* popular culture, along with an increased focus on global cinema. Developments in multimedia performance have provided a platform for experimental theatricalizations of gender, race, class, and sexuality whose fictional articulations have been vital to critical discussions of emergent social issues. Also striking is an ongoing shift away from art as commodity and artist as a singular author-genius to open networks of artistic production, collaborative performance, and conceptual articulation. The flexibility of emergent media platforms and networked systems has thus resulted in the extension of technological systems beyond prior Western media paradigms of authorship, aura, stardom, and product. Crucial to the creative potential of this new technological environment has been an increased focus on process rather than product, one sensitive to the fundamental interrelations of its media components. The term 'intermediality' refers not only to technological systems shared by divergent practices in the arts and literature but also, and foremost, to the social and conceptual networks shared by divergent communities through access to media and its various forms of cultural mediation.

What critical resources might intermediality provide for understanding global Bollywood and SRK? For understanding the critical potential *and* limits of popular culture? For renewing or renovating critical paradigms developed at different historical junctures? For translating or specifying spaces of culture, whether local, regional, national, digital, post-industrial, and so on? And for understanding the cinematic forms and tropes that organize these paradigms? Understood as a shift in emphasis from communication 'devices' (media narrowly understood) to an inquiry into the broader domain of media practices and materialities, intermedia might designate a mode of understanding transformation itself. In the wake of the three major social transformations of the decade of the 1990s in India, that is, the opening up or the liberalization of the Indian economy, the rise of Hindu right-wing nationalism, and the growth of a transnational media universe, film scholar Anustup Basu (2010: 6) reformulates the project of national cinema as an examination of 'how planetary flows of information, the spread of cottage piracy, and various cybernetic and digital intermedia ecologies besiege notions of the same—in other words, the idea of cinema as part of an endogamous national culture protected by classic vertical institutions of modernity, such as protected economies, state-owned television, censorship, distribution quotas, and import/export laws.' This new mediascape confounds previous understandings of political processes and attendant aesthetic or cinematic effects: deployments of 'traditional' patriarchal notions such as dharma (duty), for example, can bolster rather than impede techno-managerial-financial regimes of globalization in India and their movement into other postnational circuits. Basu is one of an ascendant generation of media scholars who thus place Indian cinema and media (television, calendar art, photography, advertising, and so on) at the centre of debates indexed under the rubric of globalization, debates about secularism, capitalist expansion, sovereignty, popular religiosity, and technology. Their work challenges previous models of film history, not by collapsing the history of Indian cinema, or particularly of Hindi cinema, into the category of 'Bollywood', but by attending to the formal/aesthetic and ideological *changes* in popular cinema in relation to a changing world. It is towards that end that Prasad (2003) suggests:

> Bollywood would be interesting to investigate as the symptom of such a formal transformation, understanding form not only as a dimension of textuality, but also in a larger sense as the set of relations between the elements internal to the text as well as those which constitute its habitat: its audiences, its economic structure, its ideological matrix, etc.

Approached from this angle, Bollywood may well provide insights not simply into the changing modalities of Indian national identity in a globalizing world, but also into the transformations certain forms of so-called Indian culture have wrought globally, provided that we can generate and calibrate the critical tools necessary to diagnose them.

Such an investigation promises to bear fruit in a rigorously *comparative* context, and it is precisely this context I seek to sketch briefly here. Bollywood, after all, signifies some connection between the Bombay film industry and that of Hollywood, in addition at least to Tollywood, Nollywood, and other unevenly emergent 'woods', but its mediated and widespread application as a term raises insistently comparative questions beyond the linking of industrial practices (studios, stardom, genre, and so on) or new international schemes of co-production. Does it deride Hindi popular cinema as derivative; or does it, conversely, mark its particularity within the context of these socio-political phenomena that have dominated the past decade in India? For whom does it name: for the NRI (Non-Resident Indian) in search of roots, for the European/American audience in search of cheap content tinged with the exotic, or for the indigenous industry's new generation producing work in an increasingly reflexive mode? Rosie Thomas (1985) and Gayatri Chatterjee (2005) furthermore stress in separate contexts the inherently intermedial and intertextual nature of meaning-making in popular Hindi cinema, noting that audiences have long understood elaborate schemes of citation and reference organized through the temple, calendar art, popular prints, movie posters, photo deities, other films and stars, and so on, and this field is increasingly inclusive of worldwide commercial and commodity culture, from Puma to McDonald's to *Who Wants to Be a Millionaire*? As has become clear, SRK's hyper- or mega-stardom may be the product of such a financial portfolio as to eclipse cinema's relative importance in relation to other commercial ventures he has undertaken, from real estate to product endorsements to cricket teams. How, the question becomes, do we begin to understand the changing role of popular culture in a socio-political landscape marked indelibly by the sensorium of postindustrial capitalism and its changing modes of commodification, affect, and image?

In my view, an intermedial inquiry would try to *avoid* the twin banalities, then, of treating cinema as 'one medium among others' (by changing emphasis from cinema as thing to the cinematic as a relational field) and, on the other hand, alleging in equally clichéd terms that 'cinema has always been global' (by treating specific vectors of exchange and relation between media practices). Putting previous intertextual modes for understanding popular Hindi cinema (Parsi theatre, debates about realism and the parallel cinema, mythology, national ideology, allegory) alongside new vectors of relation (not restricted to digitality but encompassing modes of adaptation, migration, piracy, censorship), I might anticipate contributing to Prasad's hope I mentioned a moment ago that through 'Bollywood', we gain insight into the phenomenon of national identity in a globalizing world. In fact, Keya Ganguly's (2010) recent book on Satyajit Ray emphasizes precisely how *concepts* are produced through combined and uneven development. 'Ideologies of the modern,' she says, 'take hold in a jumbled and disorderly manner, exposing sociohistorical contradictions peculiar to the location, and, in doing so, succeed in posing original problems in art and culture that surpass the conceptions that produced them in the first place' (Ganguly 2010: 15). In the remainder of this chapter I want to consider SRK as the name for one such 'original problem' in intermedia.

One more caveat: I do not see 'intermedia' or any other term as a one-size-fits-all critical solution. I am instead trying to make it, even against its will, energize some of the most pressing questions presented through the rubric of global Bollywood. At the very least, I think it keeps our eyes on a set of interrelationships that gave rise to its coinage, of which I will remind you now: technological innovation in media platforms, participation, and productive energies; conceptual innovation attendant upon institutionalization (of film and media studies, cultural studies, performance studies, radical sociology, feminist and gender studies, queer theory, communication studies, and so on), as well as fuelled by social movements, political horizons, and ethical engagements that sometimes challenge that very institutional legitimacy; embodied practice and performance as a vital source of theoretical imagination; and, finally, an emphasis on networks and mobilities, again not as given but as forged through persistent alliance. In Antonio Gramsci's (1971: 175) terms, 'pessimism of the intellect, optimism of the will'.

In the remainder of this chapter, then, I want to pay more specific attention to the *form* of intermedia, proliferating some questions before turning to an example in order to provide some answers. The new media landscape's emphasis on the juxtaposed pair of archive and ephemerality, perhaps epitomized in YouTube and social networking, renews our attention to segments, fragments, short forms, condensed grammars, quick references, stereotypes, and, of course, musical numbers. In the previous vocabulary of film studies that was indebted almost exclusively to Hollywood models, the musical number in particular was thought in modernist terms to interrupt a classical diegesis, thereby to emphasize elements of spectacle and excess that could not be contained by causal narrative logic, and ultimately to reveal the reflexive potentialities of the medium. Such, for example, is Jane Feuer's (1982) thesis in her book on the Hollywood musical.

Against this model, what I mean to notice in the modes of appearance associated with global SRK are instead their appropriative mobility, a mobility that calls for further thinking about media and cinematic temporality and spatialization. First, I raise the question of historicism. How do we measure and pinpoint changes in filmmaking practices attendant upon social and technological transformations? How do we write film and media histories? On the one hand, there is a clear kind of articulation of global Bollywood as emerging from the 1990s, and many have identified SRK's stardom as most spectacularly ascendant in the period, say, from *Dil Se..* (Dir. Mani Ratnam, 1998) and *Kuch Kuch Hota Hai* (Dir. Karan Johar, 1998) to that of *Kal Ho Naa Ho* (Dirs Nikhil Advani and Ron Reid Jr., 2003), that is, just around the turn of this century. I would like to know more about changes in post-production in the Indian film industry in this window (that is, about CGI and back end expenses), as well as more about the reorganization of production financing packages (since these are major things taking place in the industry all over the globe at this moment) to know whether this periodizing for the Indian context is helpfully shedding light on changes to the image writ large in global Bollywood. Changes in visual style, too, emerge from collaborations among production personnel too complex to articulate through something like 'star image' or persona alone. To put it slightly differently, we need to be able to articulate a convincing picture of what media anthropologist Brian Larkin (2008) would emphasize as 'infrastructure' alongside our sense of transformations in the nature or scale of stardom.

But there is, alongside the issue of historicizing, the issue of historicity, or theories of time and history embedded in cultural practice. Here I would diagnose a difficult dialectic of repetition and innovation in the cinema we are calling global Bollywood and in its attendant discourse. It's difficult because capitalist cultural production depends upon this dialectic; in fact, the definition of genre itself might be 'sameness with a difference', and so there is little room for disruption in the star image, little alteration to the already known, little variation in normative worldviews or happy endings. Here we have a set of questions not only about generic repetition but about auto-referentiality, remakes, adaptations, and cycles, not only looking backward but anticipating forward movement too, in franchises, sequels, and so on. These entail not only production practices and activities of reception and fandom but, in fact, embed conceptions of time and change within them. What seems necessary is a way to attend to multiple, if competing or immiscible, temporalities coexisting at the same moment.

The current cinema, finally, both expands and contracts in duration. Quotidian practices of cutting, pasting, recycling, and posting clips, whether in the more than 13 million SRK entries on YouTube, involve the segmentation of both texts and contexts in new configurations and often with unanticipated consequences. There would be much to say about industrial practices of segmentation, that is, more on the relationship of narrative to number, more on the circulation of music via soundtracks, and especially their repurposing. Even a film like *Chak De! India*, however, is segmented through the field hockey matches, providing a kind of grammar of ascension familiar to most sports competition genres. I turn to it now in some detail in order to begin to investigate these questions more concretely.

Chak De! India

Chak De! India is a fictional film about the Indian women's field hockey team winning the Women's Hockey World Cup; its story loosely modelled after the actual 2002 Indian women's victory in the Commonwealth Games. It opens seven years earlier with a game that opposes the Indian men's team to Pakistan's, in which the Indian team's captain, Kabir Khan (SRK), elects to take the penalty shot that will decide the game. He misses, is declared a national traitor, and, in faux television footage that recalls reportage of communal riots, is essentially burnt in effigy and excised from the public sphere. Seven years later, he returns as the only figure willing to coach a ragtag assemblage of regional women hockey players, a team largely shunned by its own governing association. In their journey towards the World Cup, they will have to overcome regionalism, sexism, petty arguments, competition, and individualism in order to become a team that can play for, that indeed *is* India. And in a recapitulation of Kabir Khan's fateful losing shot, the women's team will find its own fate decided by a crucial penalty shot in the final competition with Australia. Needless to say (spoiler alert), our team wins. *Chak de* India.

I want to take seriously the challenge of attending to the organization of the film as a regional-religious assemblage driven by feminism. The assemblage includes SRK's star image; the domain of cultural nationalism, including mediations among regionalism, religion, and caste; the corporate/culture industry within which 'global' success is located (hotels, McDonald's, international sports organizations, stadia, shoe and equipment brands, and so on); and discourses of gender equality and queer identity. These elements not only articulate with one another as interior to the system of *Chak De! India*, but can detach and enter into new, exterior assemblages of media and politics. Let me take them in turn.

As Kabir Khan, SRK explicitly collates multiple facets of Muslim identity. In the opening sequence, as I have mentioned, his character (named Khan rather than taking the name of the actual Muslim men's team captain, Zaftir Iqbal's the first Muslim to serve in this capacity since Partition, after whom the character is modelled), not only causes India to lose to Pakistan but further humiliates India in his post-game embrace of the Pakistani player Zamir. While SRK has himself cultivated a hybrid religious persona—as is widely known, he married a Hindu and his children apparently follow both religions at home—he nonetheless was popularly seen as crucially melded with the character of Kabir Khan even while critics praised the character as a departure from SRK's screen image in an acting job that earned him Filmfare's Best Acting Award for 2007. Retrospectively, Kabir Khan also paves the way for SRK's portrayal of another Khan, in the odd film *My Name Is Khan* (*MNIK*, Dir. Karan Johar, 2010): odd because SRK's acting talents are put to a Muslim character, Rizwan Khan, who also has Asperger's Syndrome, a condition on the autism spectrum, who travels across post-9/11 America to clear his name (from associations with terrorism) with the president himself. Co-star

Kajol plays Mandira, a Hindu woman who falls in love with Khan, and the couple endures prejudice following the 9/11 attacks (amidst much melodrama I won't describe, except to reveal that the key closing line from a fictional President Obama is 'Your name is Khan, and you are not a terrorist'). In a twist that further conflated SRK himself with these Muslim 'Khans' he portrayed, SRK was detained at Newark Airport upon entering the United States for the publicity tour for MNIK.[1]

In *Chak De! India*, Kabir Khan's traitorous loss—variously and all at once implied as throwing the game to Pakistan, embracing the enemy, and transgressing symbolic boundaries—becomes visually associated with communal violence and outright ostracism. As I suggested, images meant to mimic television news coverage witness crowds stoking suspicion, urging retribution, massing against Khan in a visual vocabulary familiar to the entire nation. As the public hysteria intensifies, the effects of ostracism are recoded in familial terms, so that Kabir Khan must leave the paternal home with his mother as a child scrawls 'traitor' on its outside wall and Khan retreats into exile.

When he returns seven years later, it is to a women's hockey team assembled according to every conceivable stereotype of regionalism, reaffirming typology as the film also sets out to construct a cultural nationalist conception of belonging. By 'cultural nationalist' I mean to refer to the abundantly documented cultural turn of the 1990s, which, in Ashish Rajadhyaksha's (2003: 32) words, proposed 'a rather freer form of civilizational belonging explicitly delinked from the political rights of citizenship, indeed delinked even from the State itself, replaced by the rampant proliferation of phrases like "*Phi Bhi Dil Hai Hindustani*" and "*Yeh mera India*/I love my India"'. Or, for that matter, *Chak De! India*. The Punjabi hothead, the Haryana tomboy, the Jharkand tribals assemble a team meant to acknowledge and gently chip away at the Hindi heartland's condescension and misconceptions, generating a culturalist unity and national pride.

The genre of the sports competition film is a fitting container for cultural nationalist aspirations, as the generic goal is both *integrative*—making a team out of many individuals, or a nation out of regional and religious difference—and *competitive*, establishing the superiority of the nation thus integrated over others, especially more privileged and powerful ones. In many ways, the integrative function key to the assemblage is a function of star charisma: it is SRK who alone can help the girls transcend their state affiliations, racial and regional assumptions, and linguistic barriers (along with some deeply gendered and sexualized trouble I discuss below) to achieve success. 'This team needs only those players who first play for India, then for their teammates, and then, if they have anything left, for themselves,' Kabir Khan tells them early on, and significantly, that they play *for* him in quite a literal way as the very team he wished to have led to victory. Insofar as this team achieves success, it is by entering smoothly into a circuit of global value where each team can fully represent its nation-state on the stage of international competition, a field to which the team finally can also fully belong.

A not-so-smooth initial encounter with global brands, in fact, shows us a team in crisis, a team fragmented and without faith in their leader, Kabir Khan. In one of my favourite and one of the film's most outrageous segments, as Khan despairs over the internal tensions that threaten to dissolve the team, the group dines out at McDonald's. Aloof in his Ray Bans, Khan watches as a group of boys taunt the girls at the restaurant. Slowly, the girls join forces to resist them, resulting in an uncontrolled frenzy in which the girls physically attack the guys, upend the restaurant's tables and chairs, spew McDonald's branded food and drink across the screen space, and ultimately end up in breathless satisfaction. Chak De. This is in fact the last scene before intermission, and the one that is meant to signal a shift towards the unity and triumph to come in the film's second act. It is irresistible in its contradictions: one must film at McDonald's (whether for product placement or for the allure of a global brand, or both), yet McDonald's can symbolically only produce anger, mayhem, conflict, and violence! As I will suggest in my conclusion, maintaining this contradiction between the material necessity of the global brand for the media system and the symbolic violence it wreaks is a crucial aspect of global Bollywood.

The film evolves, however, into an unconflicted, even full-on embrace of global brands. Visually, the film paints a stark contrast between the infrastructure of Indian field hockey (its fading but functional facilities, the parochial members of its governing body, its ill-groomed fields) and the glitz of international competition in well-lit stadia with electronic scoreboards and new uniforms and equipment. Within the final long segment of the film in which the team travels to Australia to compete in the championships, we are treated to a showcase of commodity culture, from a hotel tour of the elevator, fitness room, swimming pool, and buffet table, to global athletic brands such as Puma and Adidas (as well as TAG Heuer watches, which SRK actually endorses), to equipment such as Vijayanthi and Rakshak hockey sticks to Ultra Tech shirts. Moving through these spaces of global tourism and competition (and running through the streets of Melbourne for their workouts), the girls display a 'gee whiz' wonder at the Western glitz. The film further literalizes uneven development in framing the Indian team as younger, smaller, and inferior to their competition in the first match against Australia. Strapping, big, blond forwards with powerful drives (the term for hitting the ball on the ground over a long distance) overwhelm the dazed Indian team, unable to cooperate (and coordinate) with one another. Shown to surpass India and Kabir Khan in technology and in strategy, Australia's multiple coaches analyse plays via computer and communicate changes in plan to the team, while Khan watches a devastating 7–0 loss in quiet desperation.

As the team begins to work together in subsequent matches, they increasingly come to inhabit the world of international competition more appropriately, dressing for the banquet dinner in saris (even if Komal Chautala [played by Chitrashi Rawat], our tomboy, hates it) and functioning as teammates both on and off the field. 'More appropriately' means, in other words, in more normative gender roles, and it is at this point that I need to address the film's gender politics in more detail. In the coinage preferred by SRK himself in talking about the film, Chak De! India is a film about 'women empowerment', itself a common-sense assemblage that involves an incredible array of experience and aspiration including gender equality, respect for women, rooting for the underdog, appreciating the feeling of marginality or discrimination, being on the fringes of accepted gender, confused sexuality, assertive heterosexual womanhood, and a sense of power and agency. It is important to parse these various facets of the film's portrait of gendered success, not least because many of them are in contradistinction to one another, fracturing any sense of a unified 'message'.

Even at a narrative level, the film's feminism is complicated. The governing agency's members offer traditional notions of femininity, wishing to consign women to domesticity and modesty; the film's critique here is an ideological one, insisting on the capacities of women for strength, excellence, competitive grit in public arenas. Through the subplot involving Preety Sabarwal (Sagarika Ghatge), the talented Chandigarh player who is engaged to marry Abhimanyu Singh, the vice captain of the Indian cricket team, we watch a young woman insist upon her right to success and independence on her own terms, against her fiancé's ironic dismissal of her 'silly stick and ball game'. Here, too, while the film urges a reconfiguration of social relationships, it condemns Abhi's sexism and selfishness in fairly broad ideological strokes. In Kabir Khan's inspirational speech to his team, he stitches this critique very explicitly to maternity, to Mother India: 'You are fighting everyone: this country who believes that girls cannot hold up to men, cannot hold a job as well as a man, cannot make decisions like men. You are fighting each fool who has forgotten that if a girl has given life to him, she can do anything. Anything.'

Allegorically, of course, it is this Indian team that can do anything, these daughters of India will triumph over adversity too.

Some critics have seen in this aspect of triumph a queer allegory, whereby Kabir Khan (who, after all, is in a relationship only with his mother) is open to a queer interpretation. Here is a rather long version of the case for this reading from Charlie Henniker (2010: 35):

Shah Rukh Khan as Kabir in *Chak De! India* is clearly seen championing a confused, diverse minority group—with overtones of sexual confusion and repression, even depiction of a lesbian relationship. Further to this parallel experience represented in the film is the successful intervention Shah Rukh's character has in the sporting world and, more immediately, in the patriarchal values of India. Specifically, we see Kabir battling the bureaucratic indifference of the committee that wants to withdraw funding from his team. In doing so, Kabir proves that the women's team—previously underfunded and poorly supported within the tradition of the film—is just as good as the more publicly acceptable and endorsed male team. This notion of gendered equality is an important issue for gay rights campaigners in India, where acknowledged groups like hijras are recognized, but remain consigned to liminal spaces... Kabir uses his experience of unfair rejection and discrimination to educate a team of diverse players, who initially cannot get along linguistically or socially, perhaps even sexually, but are eventually united by their cause. This clearly opens up all kinds of agenda.

I am largely in sympathy with the goals of queer reading, even with the most radical contention that 'no film is safe', as Alexander Doty (2000: 15) puts it, from queering. But this reading runs the risk of mischaracterizing how the film's politics function *affectively*, so let me stay with it for a moment longer.

Kabir Khan does, of course, fight for resources for his team. He fights not just indifference but actual sexism by offering to pitch his team against the Indian men's team: if the women win, he gets to take them to the championship, and, if they lose, they stay home. The result is that the women aren't as good as the male team: in fact, they lose. But, as they recognize the consequences of their loss and begin to walk off the field, dejected, the *men* raise their sticks to the women in salute. Chak de. It is crucial here that affirmation for the women is routed through men's respect. The women are *not* objectively as good as the men or better; admiration is conferred by men in a subjective appreciation of their talent. It is not so much that the film doesn't advocate 'gender equality' as it is quite clear that politics are routed through men's subjective recognition of women's strengths, symbolized through their respectful raising of the sticks in a moment that actually gave me chills despite my political distaste for it. The film works affectively, then, to locate and allocate the judgement of women's roles to men, despite the various powerful nods it gives to women's strengths.

Moving from the narrative level to the film's signification then, the film certainly shifts the terms of representation in Indian cinema, hewing to a more faithfully Western generic vision. It has no female star, although some of the young women's roles in the film launched film careers for them (including Rawat and Ghatge). Consistent with the sports team genre, the film often leaves its coach/star off-screen in order to focus on relationships among the girls, although I think they are superficially drawn, and SRK is almost always visually separated from them on the sidelines and outside of the girls' locker room and dorm. Creating a visual collectivity among its supporting cast members, the film does allow them screen presence that is not always defined in relation to its star. It furthermore has no mandatory song-and-dance sequences to codify gendered and sexualized star images, although the score importantly cues affective response and functions to segment the film. Instead, it disperses femininity among the team players, and it is here, finally, that I would register a final disagreement with the kind of queer reading that diagnoses a 'lesbian relationship' and sexual confusion as a proto-queer representation.

For there are very few *actual* moments of relationship at all among the girls, and as the film comes to represent their success, it is increasingly in normative terms (they are feminized), as well as visual strategies that insert 'India' into the circuits of global commercial culture as hegemonic, as I've tried to suggest. Ultimately, this is a film about SRK and 'his 16 girls', as he calls them in the supplemental short called *Chak De Hockey*, not a film about women on a team in relation with one another, so that it would be terribly *difficult* to find a 'lesbian relationship' in the cursorily referenced glances of dorm life, or in the locker room antics that generally characterize the girls' exchanges with one another. This is a part of the assemblage that resists such deterritorialization because the structure of the assemblage must prioritize the centering of SRK, the proliferation of commodity-attachment, a victorious cultural nationalism, and a return to the paternal home, mother in tow, no longer a traitor but a patriot.

———

If the category of intermedia can help us partially to understand this ensemble of retrograde nationalist ideology with aspirational feminism, the role of the star within a culture industry that exceeds cinema, and the capacity of an assemblage to hold these contradictions together, it would make a contribution to the study of SRK and global Bollywood. It remains for me now to stitch this reading of the film back to the questions with which I began.

I have wanted to make explicit the degree to which 'global Bollywood' implicates me in its flows, multiply and insistently as a spectator for films marketed globally and available easily in the US on DVD; as a (former!) athlete aspiring towards the realm of international hockey competition the film chronicles; as a scholar bred for the study of something like 'world cinema' (that's the course for which I served as a teaching assistant in graduate school); and as someone invited into the intellectual challenges posed by the shape-shifting aesthetics and politics of the contemporary Hindi cinema. I am not a 'South Asianist' and so I am more helped by the discourses of cinema and media studies as they veer towards the creative epistemologies with which I began.

Through those epistemologies, such as those that Basu's book (2010) tracks, we confront a dizzying and pliable phenomenon not limited to the world of cinema, but a cinema enmeshed in the global capitalist sensorium of transnational advertising, product endorsements, consumer goods, global brands, computers, technicized sports and equipment, fashion, popular myths of the nation, normative gender roles, star images and icons, and transgressive sexuality, to name but a few of its aspects. This is a changing sensorium, 'fungible' as Basu (2010: 7) puts it, and it can absorb disparate, even contradictory, elements in its asssemblages.

Chake De! India, I have wanted to show, gives us a particular instance of such absorption of feminism and discourses about women's empowerment as these discourses navigate the counter-force of paternalist mythologies of national unity. Gayatri Spivak (2010) has complicated language for such an encounter, language that I will cite, and then I will gloss the citation as best I can. 'For behind this rearrangement of desires—the desire to win in the name of a nation—is the work of de-transcendentalizing the ruse of analogizing from the most private sense of unquestioning comfort to the most ferocious loyalty to named land, a ruse that uses and utilizes the axioms of reproductive heteronormativity' (Spivak 2010: 56). What does this complicated sentence mean, especially since she is not exactly talking about field hockey?

By assembling its team of girls formed *prior* to the team's national articulation, *Chak De! India* shows us private forms of belonging: to regions, to languages (mother tongues), to habits, to bodily dispositions, even to different kinds of weather. This is a kind of bottom-line comfort, an unquestioned emergence and belonging, that does not yet belong to an opposition between the private and the public: it is, in fact, a private that Spivak would call 'underived' (Spivak 2010: 17), because it does define itself *in* the opposition between the public and the private. Not yet, not in its felt and lived immediacy. That transformation or shift is the work of a nationalist imaginary, the very motor of *Chak De! India*, seeking to forge a mighty desire to win *in the name of India*, 'the most ferocious loyalty to named land' (Spivak 2010: 17). Maybe my metaphors are too old-fashioned, though: the motor and the forge belong to an older grammar of the Hindi cinema and its oppositions between tradition and modernity, whereas the imaginative vectors along which *Chak De! India* must work are strewn with McDonald's wrappers and advertisements for TAG Heuer watches, even as the film enacts a fantasy of the resolution of persistent forms of communal violence. This is the ruse of analogizing. Patient humanities work, patient arts work, can start to 'de-transcendentalize' by reading these ruses in the past as well as in the present domain of culture. What, however, of the 'axioms of reproductive heteronormativity'?

It will not baffle most of us to think that nationalism is legitimated through reproductive heteronormativity: the chain involving mother–soil–birth–family–nation performs that legitimation, as does all sorts of gender and sexuality training along the line, working the assumption—just to define 'reproductive heteronormativity' explicitly—that having children through male–female coupling gives meaning to a life. In my reading, *Chak De! India* is interested in precisely the contested domain of gender and sexuality training. At once advocating some careful attention to what women's bodies can do in the name of the nation (that is, what SRK calls 'women empowerment') and simultaneously smoothing over and soothing the differences that might erupt if 'women empowerment' really got going (got regional, got unmoored from the scripts of analogy), *Chak De! India* can be read as an assemblage that tries, in colloquial terms, to hold it together. In the same way, it both showcases global brands and reveals the havoc they provoke, unleashing violence, desire, competition, and rivalry. It is this complicated, contradictory mix of feelings, images, affects, commodities, and stories that might be said to be global Bollywood, with SRK at its centre. Far away from Mumbai, I am nonetheless drawn into its circuits and I hope to have revealed something about their inner workings through the category of intermedia.

Note

1. In a further twist, the Shiv Sena protested the opening of *MNIK* after SRK made remarks, in his capacity as the owner of the Kolkata Knight Riders cricket team, that were critical of the decision to not bring members of the Pakistani cricket team by clubs competing in the 2010 Indian Premier League. What a reprise of the character Kabir Khan's excessive proximity to Pakistan!

References

Basu, Anustup. 2010. *Bollywood in the Age of New Media: The Geo-televisual Aesthetic*. Edinburgh: Edinburgh University Press.

Chatterjee, Gayatri. 2005. 'Icons and Events: Reinventing Visual Construction in Cinema in India', in Raminder Kaur and Ajay J. Sinha (eds), *Bollywood: Indian Cinema through a Transnational Lens*, pp. 90–117. New Delhi: SAGE Publications.

Doty, Alexander. 2000. *Flaming Classics: Queering the Film Canon*. New York: Routledge.

Feuer, Jane. 1982. *The Hollywood Musical*. London: British Film Institute Publishing.

Ganguly, Keya. 2010. *Cinema, Emergence, and the Films of Satyajit Ray*. Minneapolis: University of Minnesota Press.

Gramsci, Antonio. 1971. *Selections from the Prison Notebooks*, eds and trs Quintin Hoare and Geoffrey Nowell-Smith. New York: International Publishers.

Henniker, Charlie. 2010. 'Pink Rupees or Gay Icons?', *South Asia Research*, 30 (1): 25–41.

Larkin, Brian. 2008. *Signal and Noise: Media, Infrastructure, and Urban Culture in Nigeria*. Durham: Duke University Press.

Prasad, Madhava M. 2003. 'This Thing Called Bollywood', *Seminar*, no. 525, available at http://www.india-seminar.com/2003/525/ 525%20 madhava%20prasad.htm (accessed on 9 November 2013).

Rajadhyaksha, Ashish. 2003. 'The "Bollywoodization" of the Indian Cinema: Cultural Nationalism in a Global Arena', *Inter-Asia Cultural Studies*, 4 (1): 25–39.

Sarkar, Bhaskar. 2008. 'The Melodramas of Globalization', *Cultural Dynamics*, 20 (1): 31–51.

Spivak, Gayatri Chavravorty. 2010. *Nationalism and the Imagination*. London, New York and Calcutta: Seagull Books.

Thomas, Rosie. 1985. 'Indian Cinema: Pleasures and Popularity', *Screen*, 26 (3–4): 116–32.

Vasulka, Woody. 1990. 'The New Epistemic Space', in Doug Hall and Sally Jo Fifer (eds), *Illuminating Video: An Essential Guide to Video Art*, pp. 465–70. New York: Aperture Press and BAVC.

Filmography

Chak De! India. Dir. Shimit Amin. Yash Raj Films, 2007.

Dil Se… Dir. Mani Ratnam. India Talkies and Madras Talkies, 1998.

Kal Ho Naa Ho. Dirs Nikhil Advani and Ron Reid Jr. Dharma Productions, 2003.

Kuch Kuch Hota Hai. Dir. Karan Johar. Dharma Productions, 1998.

My Name Is Khan. Dir. Karan Johar. Fox Searchlight Pictures, 2010.

Fandom: Local Receptions and Digital Culture

A Shah Rukh Khan Remix

Contemporary Negotiations of Indo-Trinidadian Masculinity

HANNA KLIEN

With the recent release of *Jab Tak Hai Jaan* (*JTHJ*, Dir. Yash Chopra, 2012), Trinidad and Tobago once again saw evidence of Shah Rukh Khan's (henceforth SRK) great popularity in the country: there were queues outside local cinemas, multiplexes had to reschedule and show the film on two screens simultaneously, passersby turned and shook heads in astonishment over the excited crowds of cinema-goers. Since their introduction in the 1930s, Hindi films have enjoyed great popularity in the multicultural Caribbean island state and have become an integral part of its mediascapes. Thus, Bollywood has influenced local performance traditions as well as media practices. However, the success of *JTJH* was surprising as most local one-screen cinemas have closed down in recent years and Hindi films have been marginalized, usually being shown on one screen only in multiplexes and only for a limited time. Undoubtedly, many devoted fans paid homage to legendary film-maker Yash Chopra, who passed away before the film's release. An equally important attraction of the film, according to viewers, was seeing SRK in a romantic film once again. Khan's enormous impact on Trinidadian cinema audiences can only be understood in the light of local constructions of the actor's star text as well as related media practices. This chapter investigates how elements of SRK's star text have been incorporated into identity formations and performative practices in Trinidad's popular culture. My focus lies on contemporary negotiations of Indo-Trinidadian masculinity drawing on two case studies of local artists.

In the context of the Indian diasporic community in Trinidad, which came into existence through the British indentureship system, Hindi cinema has been a crucial signifier of ethnic identity. Thus, many cultural markers have been derived from Hindi films as well as the Bollywood culture industry and have been used to demarcate Indo-Trinidadians from other groups, especially Afro-Trinidadians. It is remarkable how SRK's star image does not only emerge in demarcation processes, but is also very prominent in cultural hybridization processes. This becomes particularly clear when looking at the media practice of remix widespread in the Caribbean region. While the concept of remix has been applied in various contexts of globalization and media, the vibrant field of Trinidad's popular culture displaying longstanding traditions of remix, such as music forms of the African diaspora, can offer new insights into its role in Bollywood's transnational and cultural circuits. Moreover, SRK's position as global star might be understood better in the light of the eligibility of his star text to remix practices. My analysis focuses on two case studies and through these it becomes apparent that the actor's star image unmistakably signifies ethnic belonging in the local context while at the same time it is accessible for identity negotiations in a hybridized space, transcending ethnic boundaries. This dualistic characteristic quality of SRK's star text as well as its accessibility for remix practices contribute significantly to his unchallenged predominance in the reception context of Trinidad.

SRK's Star Text in a Trinidadian Context

As a global star, SRK's star image differs according to audiences and local contexts. One of the reasons for his global success that has been identified by Rajinder Dudrah (2006: 92) is also of great significance in the Trinidadian reception context: in the 1990s and early 2000s, Khan became a 'global ambassador of Bollywood cinema through his dress and performance that mediate homeland, diasporic and transnational sensibilities'. At a time when ties to the homeland had all but severed and an ambitious Indo-Trinidadian middle class strived to discard marginalization and establish itself in mainstream society, Bollywood films of that period helped to redefine what it meant to be an East Indian in the West Indies (to an extent where Bollywood might even have replaced India as reference point of diasporic identity). Films such as *Dilwale Dulhania Le Jayenge* (*DDLJ*, Dir. Aditya Chopra, 1995), *Kuch Kuch Hota Hai* (*KKHH*, Dir. Karan Johar, 1998), or *Kabhi Khushi Kabhie Gham...* (*K3G*, Dir. Karan Johar, 2006) still enjoy great popularity amongst all Hindi film fans I have encountered during field research.[1] It is, however, important to note that local response to Hindi films has always been characterized by ambiguity. One reason being that the homeland and its representations in films, which are often conflated, have been perceived as westernized by many representatives of the Indo-Trinidadian community. Westernization in this context was defined as opposition to the culturally 'pure' and preserved forms of 'Indian' culture in the Trinidadian diaspora (Manuel 1997: 22; Niranjana 2006: 174). Due to the increasing integration into mainstream society of Indo-Trinidadians in the 1990s and 2000s, SRK's 'trajectory as a mediating signifier' (Dudrah 2006: 90) played an important role for large parts of audiences. Thus, SRK has emerged as a symbol of global 'Indianness'.[2] As he embodied the bridging of differences, the negotiation of national identity and ethnic identity seems to have become engraved in his star text.

Furthermore, gender has been of essential importance to ethnic identity negotiations in Trinidad. In fact, Indian womanhood is located at the centre of discourses in the contestation of national, ethnic, and class identity of Indo-Trinidadians (Reddock 1998: 435). Simultaneously, in Hindi films of the 1990s and 2000s female characters and bodies are used as symbols of the nation (India), cultural purity, and tradition (Dudrah 2006: 80). This correlation reinforced the star image of SRK as the marker of 'Indian' values and traditions. In terms of male gender roles, another aspect of the respective films is significant. As Rachel Dwyer (2000: 100) points out, family is at the centre of the 1990s, romantic films, displaying markers of Hinduism and reflecting patriarchal values. Most of the films that have strongly influenced the local construction of SRK's star image in Trinidad adhere to this norm to a great extent. Thus, the actor has become intrinsically connected to the ideal of a family man, a phenomenon which is possibly reinforced by the off-screen star text that often portrays SRK as a devoted husband and father. Although the heroes of the 1990s display modern and cosmopolitan attitudes, essential values such as responsibility for the family, respect for parents, and a strong sense of duty, especially when it comes to encounters with the other sex, distinguish them. In the local context of Trinidad, this ideal has been renegotiated dynamically as family lies at the core of ethnic identity and masculinity. While Afro-Trinidadian men have been stereotypically represented as irresponsible and promiscuous in public discourse, the Indo-Trinidadian male has primarily been defined by his patriarchal position in the household (Mohammed 2004: 45). Responsibility towards the family could be seen as one of the core elements of SRK's star text and, at the same time, male Indo-Trinidadian gender roles. On the other hand, negative sides are also associated with the stereotype, as abusive and violent behaviour is ascribed to men of Indian descent in Trinidad (Reddock 1998: 427). Moreover, expectations connected to the male gender role can be perceived as limiting and repressive by many young men. In the field of creative cultural production, where the following case studies are located, a demarcation from as well as renegotiation of this stereotype can be observed.

In this context, another aspect of SRK's star text is significant: the artist as a successful entrepreneur. This is more closely connected to his off-screen persona, as he can be seen as a self-made man on top of the Bollywood film industry. The image is reinforced by various film texts that show him in the role of a wealthy character, as is the case in the examples mentioned above, which makes it easy for the aspiring Indo-Trinidadian middle class to identify with him. Moreover, representing a star similar to the actor in real life, as in *Om Shanti Om* (Dir. Farah Khan, 2007) or *Billu* (Dir. Priyadarshan, 2009), contributes to local constructions of the star as entrepreneur. The boundaries of on-screen and off-screen images are usually rather blurry in reception contexts, such that numerous fans in Trinidad place emphasis on the global stardom of SRK as well as his success as a businessman. While the on-screen persona generally prevails in the constitution of the star text amongst local audiences, this off-screen element seems to be of particular significance in the extremely competitive and capitalist society of Trinidad and Tobago. Accordingly, entrepreneurialism is highly valued, as Daniel Miller and Don Slater (2006) mention. They relate it to the ideal of economic and personal freedom that is deeply rooted in the historical experience of oppression (Miller and Slater: 2006: 38). However, it often relies on ethnicized oppositions, too: 'the contrast is often made between the entrepreneurship of the Indian and the lack thereof of the African' (Reddock 1998: 427). Generally, entrepreneurialism can thus be seen as an ideal located in nationalist discourses, but also within ethnic and gendered identity formations.

Consequently, SRK's star image is renegotiated in the context of local conceptions of entrepreneurialism and success. For young Indo-Trinidadian artists, as presented in the case studies, this can offer alternative identity formations along gender and ethnic lines. Generally, the pursuit of a professional career in the field of creative arts and popular culture is not only difficult due to competition and the restrictions of a small country, but for Indo-Trinidadian young talents it is also often disapproved of by their families. While this is not uncommon in other parts of the world, it is important to note that the resentment is particularly strong in the Indo-Trinidadian middle class. This can be seen in restrictions imposed on children in terms of education and choices of future professions. When conducting interviews in the Indo-Trinidadian community, I encountered a remarkable number of young people rhapsodizing wistfully on their respective creative interests without expressing any obvious reproach towards their parents: an economics student who originally desired to be a fashion designer, a passionate photographer fulfilling her duty studying medicine, or a beauty queen who would prefer modelling to achieving computer skills.[3] Those who nevertheless choose to pursue a career in the creative arts are faced with a wide range of difficulties. While many people all over the world who are active in these fields face struggle due to lack of governmental support, precarious working conditions as well as uncertain prospects for their future (the situation in Trinidad and Tobago being no exception), a particular challenge arises from the negotiations of ethnic identity and belonging in this context. At the same time it can be perceived that among the same middle-class Indo-Trinidadians entrepreneurship is highly appreciated. As I will show, the renegotiation of SRK's star text in the context of entrepreneurialism enables artists to redefine success and to re-evaluate achievements in the field of performing arts and popular culture. How these renegotiations of star text as well as identities and gender roles take place, shall be explained by using the concept of remix.

Remix as Global and Local Media Practice

The concept of remix can be applied to a variety of media practices. However, it first emerged as a term to describe the creation of an additional version of a song. Especially in hip hop and electronic music, songs used to be adjusted, for example, to a club setting by mixing them with beats or changing other elements. This moment of adjustment, that can entail processes of appropriation, re-contextualization, and hybridization, is of great interest to research concerned with global circuits of media. Thus, it has also been applied to the global reception of Bollywood and reworking of its media texts in local contexts, as, for example, in connection with song-and-dance sequences (Gopal and Moorti 2008: 36, 47). It can be observed that Bollywood, probably more than any other film industry, shows affinities to remix. Hindi cinema has always been characterized by a high density of intertextual references and repetitive patterns (Mishra 2008: 32) as well as an established tradition of remakes, many of them cross-cultural. Moreover, remix plays an essential role in the film music industry, which can be seen in various film music compilations sold in India, more often than not including remixes. With regard to the Caribbean region, a vivid remix culture can be identified. Music forms, especially of the African diaspora, and related media as well as performative practices have been discussed in this context (Hebdige 1994: 12; Rose 1994: 90; Guilbault 2005: 57). It becomes clear that various intersecting remix practices have to be taken into account in this field. Moreover, remix is by no means limited to music. As can be seen in hip hop, an American subculture that has spread globally, and its components such as graffiti as well as breakdance, remix can also be found in multimedia and performative practices. Thus, remix might be best defined as 'any reuse of an original text, as a repurposing of that text, or sometimes as any recombination of elements from many sources in the creation of a new text of any kind' (Banks 2011: 87).[4] However, to understand remix in Trinidad, let us take a closer look into its conceptualization in the context of music of the African diaspora.

Due to very early forms of institutionalization of the media practice in the Caribbean as well as its prominence in hip hop, remix has been conceptualized elaborately in this context and it is useful to relate these approaches to cultural practices in Trinidad in general. As pointed out by Dick Hebdige (1994), remix or, as it is also called, versioning is an essential characteristic of Afro-American and Afro-Caribbean music, including soca and calypso. In the Jamaican music industry, dub versions of reggae songs were firmly established as a common version by the 1960s. This phenomenon can only be understood in the context of sound systems, where, as Hebdige describes, the DJ has pre-eminence over the singer-songwriter. The concept of the DJ and how it can be applied to media reception as well as performance shall be discussed in greater detail in the context of remix and stardom. This 'DJ culture' found its continuity in American hip hop.[5] In her seminal work on hip hop, Tricia Rose (1994) introduces the distinction between remix and sample. She states that remix is the 'reworking of an entire composition' (Rose 1994: 90) and the related practice of sampling is another form where elements such as guitar or bass lines as well as lines of soul and funk songs are mixed within rap songs. Drawing on a quote by Dick Hebdige, she formulates the common form of communication entailed in both practices as follows: 'The *referenced* version takes on *alternative lives and alternative meanings* in a fresh context' (Hebdige 1994, italics for emphasis by Rose 1994). Thus, Rose and Hebdige emphasize that these media practices involve creativity and point out that through reconfiguration and re-contextualization the notions of authorship and ownership are renegotiated (Hebdige 1994: 15; Rose 1994: 68). In the context of renegotiating Indian diasporic identities, the notion of originality and creativity is of major importance. Remix is not only a form of appropriating a text, but opens up space for the transformation of an original text creating alternative meaning.

Although remix is very common in Indo-Trinidadian dominated forms of expression, the engagement with Hindi film texts and sounds in established forms of Trinidad's popular culture has been marked by restrictive attitudes.[6] To get further insight into this phenomenon, it is important to outline what Dudrah (2012: 80) has termed the 'performativity of set Bollywood routines'—not with regard to Indian actors and singers in stage shows visiting Trinidad, but local performers and artists. While remixes of popular Hindi film songs on beats of locally predominating music styles such as dancehall, soca, or hip hop are unofficially sold in DVD shops and played at events such as weddings, performances in public settings have often been marked by imitation. A very common form of performance, for instance, has been orchestras of 10 to 15 musicians playing Bollywood tunes at various occasions with the goal of imitating the original version as best as possible (Niranjana 2006: 177). Thus, media practices that could be seen as remix are often evaluated according to their degree of conformity with the original. The prime example is *Mastana Bahar*, an amateur performance contest broadcast on national television since the 1970s. Participants from all over the country compete in regional, preliminary rounds until at last the winners perform in the live show. The show's proclaimed goal is to promote Indian culture. It goes without saying that throughout the years this claim on cultural representation has been questioned many times. Although Trinidadian compositions that, for example, belong to the local folk music of chutney have also been supported in competitions, most participants imitate Hindi film songs or dances. Naturally, each of these performances could be seen as remix, as they vary from the original and include local elements. However, the most successful performers at the show have often been praised for being the best imitators (Manuel 1997: 24). Thus, while remix is a widespread practice in Indo-Trinidadian cultural forms, it does not seem to be appreciated as such. As Tejaswini Niranjana (2006: 38) points out in the context of *Mastana Bahar*, the conception of an 'Indianness' characterized by cultural purity often stifles diasporic identity negotiations. In contrast to the discourse on cultural purity stand, the actual cultural practices showing vivid dynamics of merging, mixing, and creating alternative meanings.

A highly dynamic field in the public space for negotiations of ethnic as well as gender identities has been constituted by soca and chutney soca. The music genre of soca originated in the late

1970s and combined Trinidad's national music Calypso[7] with Indo-Trinidadian and American musical forms. As discussed by Tina Ramnarine (2011: 149), Ras Shorty I, one of the central protagonists in this development, advocated the combination of '"African" and "Indian" musical characteristics as a way of promoting social unity.' Today, soca music is mainstream music and enjoys great popularity among listeners of all ethnic groups. Furthermore, various remixes drawing on Calypso and Indo-Trinidadian folk music indicate the significance of Bollywood for diasporic relations; for instance, with musicians from India reinterpreting Trinidadian songs in the style of Hindi film music (Niranjana 2006: 96). Another instance of remix described by Ramnarine (2011: 148) is the resonance of Ras Shorty I's soca song *Om Shanti Om* in the Bollywood film of the same title, starring SRK. Interestingly, this particular film displays multiple remix practices in terms of narrative as well as the frequent extra-textual references. Hindi film music has also played an important role in the genre of chutney soca, which is a mixing of the folk music style chutney and the popular carnival music soca with lyrics in English and sometimes Hindi. It primarily addresses the Indo-Trinidadian community, as can be observed by events such as the annual *Chutney Soca Monarch*. Like the *Soca Monarch* competition, this event is a firmly established part of carnival season and attracts artists of different ethnic backgrounds with prize money of roughly USD 156,000. With the space of performativity in Trinidad strongly shaped by competitions, as described by Jocelyne Guilbault (2005: 47), the *Chutney Soca Monarch* similar to *Mastana Bahar* from the 1970s enables Trinidadians of Indian descent to show their presence after formerly suffering social and economic marginalization. However, recent developments in chutney soca have led to much criticism inside the diasporic community, not least due to a seemingly unacceptable form of remix deployed.

A current phenomenon in the genre that is closely related to remix practices is the so-called rum song. For the last couple of years, a trend has emerged where chutney soca artists use (mostly older) Hindi film songs, mixing them with lyrics that refer to alcohol consumption. Well-known examples are Ravi B's *Ah drinka*, a remix of the film song *O saathi re*, and Hunter's *Puncheon* using *Geet gaata chal*. Sharda Patasar (2011), a musician and scholar, argues that Hindi film songs mainly serve to create an air of familiarity, as most artists do not even know the respective films. However, this innovation also expresses a search for sounds that reflect an Indo-Trinidadian state of being. She concludes that the phenomenon is part of a remix culture which rejects obsession with one point of origin and enables participation through repetitive patterns. I would like to add to Patasar's analysis that the rum songs, which are so heavily criticized by many voices in the Indo-Trinidadian community as they promote alcohol consumption and supposedly lack originality, offer a remarkable inwards perspective onto Indo-Trinidadian masculinity. The successful male artists, who often reach audiences beyond ethnic boundaries, seem to signify with the help of remix the opposition between the values associated with cherished Hindi film songs and the actual lived experience of many Indo-Trinidadians, also evoking the negative sides of the stereotype of the patriarchal family man as 'rum-drinker' and 'wife-beater'.

As we will see in the analysis of the case studies, remix can be found in other media and performative practices such as breakdance or theatre productions. Trinidad's popular culture displays dynamic engagement with remix practices originating in a variety of performance traditions. It is important to transcend notions of cultural origin and essentialism in this context. Following Patasar's argument, remix can be seen as a way to reflect a state of being and the diasporic self. In the context of hip hop, Rose (1994: 39) argues that repetition does not only constitute continuity, but together with the notorious 'cuts' highlights a particular historical experience and its practices can be seen as 'affirmative ways in which profound social dislocation and rupture can be managed and perhaps contested in the cultural arena'. The question arises how these concepts of remix, that are locally relevant, be applied to star texts and more specifically to SRK in Trinidad.

Remixing SRK

First of all, it is important to point out the high density of remix in SRK's on-screen star persona, which contributes to the mediating and hybrid character of the star image in general. Many songs of his blockbuster movies contain remixes of globally widespread songs such as *Pretty woman* or *Stand by me*. Furthermore, SRK's choice of films indicates his dedication to hybrid cultural forms as well as representation of intercultural encounters. As mentioned earlier, films such as *Om Shanti Om* include many signs of remix in narrative, film music, and extra-textual references. In *Ra.One* (Dir. Anubhav Sinha, 2011), the Senegalese hip-hop and R&B artist Akon appeared in a song-and-dance sequence, which was yet another important step towards globalization and cultural hybridity in Bollywood. The appearance of Akon in the film makes this aspect of Bollywood visible, in contrast to remix practices (in Bollywood and other culture industries) that obliterate sources. Thus, remix contributes to SRK as a symbol of global Bollywood.

The encounter and engagement of audiences with this star text in differing local contexts can best be understood by drawing on the concept of assemblage. Rajinder Dudrah and Amit S. Rai have introduced the term 'assemblage' to this field of study to describe the interaction of cinema with the audience and its social and cultural worlds: 'The actual body of the cinematic audience is a physical and biological as well as a social and cultural construction that interacts with the body of cinema in terms of affects and sensations that produce particular kinds of desires' (Dudrah 2006: 43). This notion of the body is of great importance to understand SRK as a global superstar whose performance on screen embodies global Bollywood's assemblage (Dudrah 2006: 95). Thus, it is continuously negotiated in the context of recipients' desires and sensations all over the world. Furthermore, this can be applied to popular culture in reception countries, where artists remix elements of the star text in a local context.

Intriguingly, Rai (2009: 169), in his analysis of India's and Bollywood's new media assemblage, points out the significance of the DJ and his/her mixing. As has been discussed earlier, music remixes are based on the DJ figure who holds more power than the writer or singer. In global media circuits this figure is of great importance. What the hip-hop DJ does with sound can be seen on a larger scale in the context of media assemblage: 'DJs layer sounds literally one on top of the other creating a dialogue between sampled sounds and words' (Rose 1994: 39). The dialogue between various elements of remixes forms the main focus of analysis in the case studies that follow. The dimensions this takes on in the context of media and cultural practices is expressed in Bank's concept of the digital griot. Griots are West-African storytellers, musicians, and canon-makers who keep up the oral tradition by moving about in communities. Accordingly, Banks (2011: 3) refers to the DJ as 'a current manifestation of the griot', who is 'standing between tradition and future, holding the power to shape how both are seen/heard/felt/known'. The DJ can thus also be seen at the intersection of local identity negotiations and global media, giving directions and offering symbols for identification. Reminding irresistibly of Banks' digital griot, Rai refers to the DJ as 'the guru of the media assemblage' (Rai 2009: 11). The DJ as guru does not only emphasize the power of this figure, but also situates it in the concept of media assemblage: 'The DJ's navigable data, both digital and constantly reassembled along new lines of movement and always hybridizing styles, unfolds interactively with the collective movement of bodies, their flows and desires' (Rai 2009: 11). Both the global star as well as artists of local popular culture can thus be conceptualized in the context of remix practices. By embodying the assemblage of a certain time and place, their performances interact with audiences, continuously reconfiguring and renegotiating identity constructions.

Case Studies

We introduce two male protagonists in the field of creative arts in Trinidad, whose work shows an affiliation to remix in their negotiation of Indo-Trinidadian masculinity: Rajin Ramroop as the founder of a dance group called Xtreme Breakers and Joel Joseph as actor, director, and founder of a drama group called Brave Heart Productions. The analysis is concerned with the elements of SRK's star text and related remix practices in their activities. The dance group Xtreme Breakers is well-known in Trinidad and is an established part of the local culture industry with booked performances on events such as the *Chutney Soca Monarch*. Rajin, in his mid-twenties, is able to live of the revenues of such performances as well as regular dance classes for different age groups that he offers in various parts of the island. Furthermore, he has represented the country in international competitions of breakdance in the US and released a

A SHAH RUKH KHAN REMIX

chutney soca song in 2013 carnival season. In his performances he frequently uses songs of films starring SRK, although he does not watch many Bollywood films in general. In contrast, Joel Joseph was a fan of the films of the 1990s and 2000s, especially those starring Kajol and SRK. Some of his greatest successes as actor and later as director were grounded in his stage performances of SRK's roles in films such as *DDLJ* and *KKHH*. Theatre adaptations of Hindi films are not unusual in Trinidad and there are various theatre companies offering them regularly. These stage shows should not be confused with global tours of stars performing scenes, songs, and dances, as the ones being referred to here are local initiatives with Trinidadian performers.[8] Thus, the film texts are adapted to the local audience and context. Joel Joseph founded his own theatre production company with co-star Shunnel Roopchand in 2006 and strongly focused on Bollywood productions as well as other India-related plays. However, his activities have never been limited to this field. He has been part of various dance groups, practiced martial arts, and lately has dedicated himself to film projects, such as the Trinidadian production of an action film.

The activities of the two artists are in many ways alternative forms of expression differing from mainstream cultural production. Although both of them engage in more established activities like, for example, filmmaking according to Western norms or chutney soca songs, they take pride in creating innovative and often hybridized cultural forms. Interestingly, elements of SRK's star text seem to emerge especially within these activities. As mentioned earlier, Bollywood-related performance traditions in Trinidad are often perceived as restrictive, many of them aiming to imitate the original and thus depreciating the creative aspect of practices such as remix. In contrast, Joel Joseph and Rajin Ramroop not only emphasize the originality of their work, but also their ambition to create and represent Trinidadian culture. Two aspects of SRK's star text seem to be relevant in this context: first, SRK is used as a symbol of 'Indianness' in the negotiation of ethnic identity in the Trinidadian context. Both artists started their careers as breakdancers, which does not necessarily imply an affinity to Afro-American culture, but certainly speaks of familiarity with associated cultural practices as well as openness for transcultural influences, in this case the globalized subculture hip hop. Their engagement in a hybridized space requires practices that allow identification with 'Indianness', for which purpose elements of SRK's star text seem to be appealing. Second, in discursive practices, the two artists' identity negotiations reflect SRK's significance as a global Indian superstar to represent alternative meanings of success. In various redefinitions of what success and professionalism can mean in a (Indo-)Trinidadian context, elements of the star text subsumed above as entrepreneur are predominant. Thus, notions of Indo-Trinidadian masculinity in society as well as in the specific field of popular culture and performing arts are renegotiated.

Up to now, actor and director Joel Joseph has been best known in the local industry for his stage productions of *DDLJ* and *KKHH*, with the last performance in May 2009 at the Queen's Hall, which is one of the main performance theatres in Port of Spain with 754 seats. Jospeh's performances had such an impact on audiences that the contact person who introduced me to him referred to him as 'Raj'—the name of the character that SRK played in *DDLJ* and the character that Joel impersonated. Moreover, his girlfriend at the time had starred with him in the female lead as Simran. In Joel's own perception too, SRK has played a very important role in his life. As he describes in an interview, this goes even further back.[9] Growing up with little positive reference to an ethnic identity and developing a prejudice against 'all things Indian', the films of the 1990s and 2000s allowed him to see 'Indianness' in a positive light. SRK played a crucial role in this rapprochement to Indian culture and finally allowed Joel a renegotiation and re-evaluation of Indo-Trinidadian masculinity. The impact of this becomes clear in his development as a dancer. First, Joel joined a breakdance group, which, as he states, offered young Indo-Trinidadian men the possibility to dance without being suspected of homosexuality. While numerous Afro-Trinidadians are associated with the performing arts (without being a target of homophobia), Joel speaks of a general reluctance of male Indo-Trinidadians to engage in this field as dancers. Breakdance and the captivating SRK films paved his way to a Bollywood dance group as well as to his career as an actor in the stage productions.

The Trinidadian theatre productions of Bollywood films generally adhere closely to the original texts in terms of dialogue and characters. However, they are remixes and thus create alternative meaning by adapting to the local context. For example, Joel Joseph emphasizes that Brave Heart Productions aimed at incorporating melodramatic elements as well as sound effects of the films in their productions, while other groups tended to present them primarily as comedy. In addition, the director also included occasional jokes about current issues in the country or Trini slang to entertain the audience. In terms of acting as well, the performances can be seen as remix. Although Joel himself states, 'Shah Rukh was the goal', he points out that by no means did that mean to copy, imitate, or mimic the star. More than interpreting the role of 'Raj', it was about finding his own version of SRK. Thus, he tenderly romances the sari-clad Simran in the notorious leather jacket that signifies Raj's Western lifestyle in the film, but in the Trinidadian theatre production rather highlights Joel's athletic physique complying with the local ideal of masculinity. At the same time, his dance style unmistakably refers to SRK's performance style, incorporating or, we could say, sampling certain gestures. In a discussion about the Bollywood star, Joel Joseph expresses his opinion that Hrithik Roshan might technically be the better dancer, but SRK conveys meaning and emotions with his style of dancing. Similarly, it is the successful conveyance of emotions and the resulting form of successful entertainment that he considers to be the essential element of SRK's acting style for his own work. What matters to Joel is to reach out to audiences by evoking strong emotions. By adapting SRK's star text in a local context and, thus, negotiating the performance of 'Indianness', the Trinidadian actor gives the audience what they want: their very own SRK. Thus, the Bollywood actor does not only serve in this context as a role model, but his star image appears in a local remix.

After the first stage show of *DDLJ*, Joel Joseph founded his own drama group and the remixed elements of the star text are reflected in his further development as artist as well as teacher, when the organization started to offer drama workshops on a regular basis. As a teacher he emphasizes on an exploration of emotions. As researcher and participant in the workshops, I experienced how members shared intimate fears, desires, and thoughts with the group in the course of this self-exploration. Many members pointed out the liberating effect it had on their lives. This corresponds with Joel Joseph's general perception that creative arts and self-expression are of central importance to personal happiness. In an interview in May 2010 in Chaguanas, he mentions that in the Indo-Trinidadian community parents rarely show appreciation for this, which in his opinion, 'keeps Indian people down'. Thus, for example, fathers make their daughters withdraw from dancing and acting groups in order to make them attend university or husbands forbid their young wives to continue dancing or acting. In this context, he refers to the stereotypical conception of Indo-Trinidadian masculinity too. As head of the family, the Indo-Trinidadian man mainly works for money, hardly spending any time with the family. Therefore, he does not see any purpose in activities that do not result in material profit, such as acting, for example. By contrasting this conventional notion of success in life with self-fulfilment through artistic expression, performativity and entertainment in the style of SRK emerge as criteria. Thereby, success as well as profit is redefined, and an alternative version of Indo-Trinidadian masculinity promoted. Reference to the ideal of the entrepreneur, in this context, shows in Joel's continual remarks on his independent achievements in the field as well as his endeavour to obtain professionalism. Thus, the disregard for creative arts is countered with the concept of entrepreneurialism. Its aspects of freedom and liberation, however, are redefined in terms of self-fulfilment leading to progress and creativity.

The second artist, Rajin Ramroop, is well established in the local culture industry with his dance group named the Xtreme Breakers, who mainly perform breakdance but also incorporate elements of chutney and soca as well as what he calls 'Indian classical' and Bollywood steps. Rajin Ramroop himself points out that the attraction of breakdance primarily lies in the entertainment factor and its flexible structure (in contrast to classical dancing). This indicates his affinity to remix practices. In this highly hybridized field of popular culture, however, it can be challenging to express belonging to the Indo-Trinidadian community and thus to affirm 'Indianness' depending on the context or setting of a performance. Bollywood and, in particular, SRK are used as signifiers of Indianness in this context. This is probably less due to a personal preference of SRK than to the local popularity of the actor. Accordingly, in Xtreme Breakers' performance at *Mastana Bahar* in 2010, two of the four songs were from SRK films, namely, *Om Shanti Om* and *Kabhi Alvida Naa Kehna*

(Dir. Karan Johar, 2006). It is of particular significance that these were remixed versions of the songs harmonized with breakdance steps, which also integrated cultural markers such as the *namaskara* gesture and other typical hand movements. As explained earlier, *Mastana Bahar* is an important site for the representation of Indo-Trinidadian culture. Consequently, it was particularly important for Xtreme Breakers to win the contest, in which they only succeeded after participating several times. The winning performance included other markers of Bollywood by staging a spectacle including props, supporting female dancers, and a total number of 15 people on stage. The artist comments on this as follows:

> We brought back the life into the show ... You have to have things that people wanna see. All the classical songs, movies ... we had many different things and we won. We broke a chain, the first time a hip hop group won *Mastana Bahar* in 40 years! Now that people see that we do it, they don't limit themselves anymore. I don't limit myself. You have never seen a guy come and do a Bollywood Remix at *Mastana Bahar*! We brought change! (from a personal interview with Hanna Klien)

The quest for the *Mastana Bahar* victory seemed to be of enormous importance for Rajin Ramroop at the time. By finally winning the competition he could firmly locate his globalized style that appeals to such a wide range of audiences, at the core of Indo-Trinidadian culture, too. Moreover, it marked a great success in terms of innovation: the Xtreme Breakers introduced a cut and remixed the local concept of Bollywood with globalized hip-hop culture. Thus, the creative potential of remix is strongly emphasized by the artist. In the context of breakdance, Rajin points out that his dancers are able to pick up different styles without any difficulties, which distinguishes them from other groups in the local culture industry and appeals to a great variety of audiences. Furthermore, his affinity to remix also reflects ambitions to embody and bridge differences, similar to SRK's role as mediating signifier. This is reflected in Rajin's discussion of stardom. The analogy between his perception of SRK and the idea of a successful entertainer becomes clear in his comment on SRK: 'He is famous already, whatever he does, people like it.' In the context of Indo-Trinidadian identity negotiations, fame can also be understood here as a position that clearly signifies Indianness and is thus unchallenged when introducing innovative, alternative elements.

This demand for free choices of cultural expression and unlimited possibilities also reflects the ideal of freedom expressed in the Trinidadian concept of entrepreneur. Generally, Rajin Ramroop's own description of his career and activities in the culture industry indicate a strong identification with this male gender role. He puts an emphasis on his organizational skills in the dance group as well as his professionalism and discipline that had a role in his success as he (has) built up a dance school and makes a living solely with dancing. However, success is not only defined by him in terms of financial independence and profit, but also by the ability to 'mash up' a crowd. This locally significant concept of 'mash up' is also used to renegotiate SRK's star image. When asked what he thinks of the star's style of dancing, Rajin replies that the best dancer is the one everyone wants to see. Similar to Joel Joseph, he does not refer to technique in this context, but relates the appeal to the ability to entertain and address diverse audiences. In the light of the triumph at *Mastana Bahar*, a resonance of SRK's star text as mediating signifier in a local context can be identified. Rajin is quick to add that although SRK is a global star, if they performed together in Trinidad, the audience's response would not differ much, as they can both dance and are well known. In this statement as well as the reluctance to acknowledge SRK's influence on his work, the artist seems keen to stress the equality of the original version to the alternative one in the local context. Clearly, the Bollywood star is seen here as a necessary element that is sampled and remixed to support the redefinition of success as an Indo-Trinidadian performer and artist. However, Rajin's identification as Trinidadian beyond ethnic boundaries seems to be in the foreground, which is reinforced by the recurrent remark that Rajin can 'mash up the place', which is a concept used by performers of all different backgrounds in Trinidad.

———

The performative practices of Joel Joseph and Rajin Ramroop give insights into how elements of SRK's star text are remixed in the context of identity negotiations. Both artists navigate fragments of the star text by recontextualizing them in a local context and relating them to the concept of entrepreneurialism. The resulting alternative version helps to renegotiate and, very importantly, represent Indo-Trinidadian masculinity in the context of performing arts and popular culture. In opposition to the family man whose economic success serves the household and leads to respectability, status and success is redefined in various ways. In demarcation to the predominating gender role which would be crippling in this realm, respectability is presented as the result of originality, innovation, and successful performance. Nevertheless, elements of SRK's star text, which are often used to reinforce the Indo-Trinidadian notion of the family man, are also relevant here. As they signify this integral image of 'Indianness' in the local context, a SRK remix is always firmly rooted in the realm of ethnicity. Thus, remixes of SRK's star text enable the artist as a cultural DJ to navigate between past and present. For the Indo-Trinidadian community that is struggling to maintain or rather create continuity while at the same time establishing a position in the midst of the multicultural island state, the impulses of such cultural entrepreneurs can be of fundamental importance. With their skilled remix practices they show that the state of being Indo-Trinidadian or the diasporic self does not have to entail restrictions and creative limitations. Instead, by remixing SRK, alternative versions of self and the embodiment of performative practices that are marked by difference (as ethnic 'other') can be enjoyed. Thus, it might be possible to experience vibrant Trinidadian remixes without resentment based on claims of ownership or anxiety of identity loss— remixes such as a breakdance performance to *Deewangi* resonating Ras Shorty I's anthem for multicultural Trinidad, or a version of *Ah drinka* resounding the film song *O saathi re* played on the national instrument, the steel pan.

Thus, Bollywood's role in Trinidad, too, is renegotiated. In opposition to its hybrid nature displaying remix or related practices, Indo-Trinidadians have tended to stress imitation more than innovation in cultural production drawing on Bollywood. Both artists discussed here display a positive attitude towards remix and the implicit *hybridization* processes, much in contrast to purist claims of cultural representation. Rajin Ramroop emphasizes its similarities with hip hop: 'Hip-hop is Bollywood in a way.' Certainly, both cultural forms acknowledge and even highlight hybridization as well as repetitive patterns in cultural production. By facilitating adaptation, recontextualization, and transformation, Bollywood and hip hop have forwarded their globalization and enjoy extremely wide circulation in today's global mediascapes. Similar to Bollywood, SRK's star text has often been used amongst Indo-Trinidadians to reinforce values and gender roles that hinder creative expression. By rejecting these restrictions, global Bollywood signified by SRK can offer a dynamic, hybridized space for artists.

The question remains why SRK's star text is particularly accessible for remix practices. In an intriguing way, the star simultaneously signifies 'Indianness' and hybridity, which has made him a primary ambassador of global Bollywood. Joel Joseph emphasizes this by putting the star into the context of other global stars: 'Sometimes there are people who come and bring it to a next level. Like Bruce Lee in Martial Arts, Bob Marley in Reggae, Michael Jackson in the performance and entertainment industry. Shah Rukh is like Michael Jackson.' Khan can thus be seen as a key figure (griot or guru) at the crossroads of cultural hybridity negotiating between the local and the global, the old and the new, the self and the other. This position might not only be due to the fact that he embodies a media assemblage, but to how he embodies it. The appeal of SRK's star text in a region so actively engaging with remix and with various diasporic communities that have faced the challenge to mediate between continuity and change over decades, implies that 'cuts' and other means of interruption are an integral part of it. Thus, the dialogue between samples and remixed elements is favoured rather than stifled by the fragmentation a star text undergoes in the context of global circulation. The space that opens up invites DJs of all origin to create new and alternative versions of the self.

Notes

1. During my dissertation on Hindi film reception in the Caribbean, I conducted field research in Trinidad in 2010, 2011, and 2012. Methods that were used included interviews, participant observation, film screenings and group discussions, and online communication among others.
2. By using the term Indianness, I refer to a multiplicity of concepts of Indian culture in diasporic communities in the Caribbean that are

manifold, but it also signifies the problematic conception of cultural purity and essentialism that various interest groups insist on so vehemently.

3. Here, another important factor is gender, as many interview partners were female. Young women are generally even more affected by negative associations of exhibitionism and indecency in creative spheres. Interestingly, many men as well as women ascribed free creative expression to Afro-Trinidadians whom they see as dominating music, acting, and other forms of popular culture.

4. Adam J. Banks (2011: 2) also points at the relevance of remix for new media, as a considerable amount of digital media practices are referred to by terminology common in hip hop, such as remix, sampling, or mash-up.

5. Many of the early hip-hop DJs who developed their sound systems on the streets of the Bronx were immigrants from the Caribbean, such as Kool Herc from Jamaica or Grandmaster Flash, whose parents were from Barbados (Hebdige 1994: 137).

6. An exception is probably dance, as local dance styles have strongly influenced Trinidadian Bollywood performances. In the public discourse, this is a fiercely debated issue which cannot be discussed here due to limited space.

7. For a discussion of Calypso's role in nation-building after independence, see Guilbault (2005: 50). The indpendence movement as well as the PNM (People's National Movement) government in the following years nationalized carnival and promoted Calypso as an expression of national culture.

8. A number of Bollywood stars, and especially singers, have performed in Trinidad and Tobago. However, since 2010, no major actor or actress has visited the island state to my knowledge.

9. The data presented here was collected in 2010 and 2011 during various interviews and personal communications during participant observation.

References

Banks, Adam J. 2011. *Digital Griots: African American Rhetoric in a Multimedia Age*. Carbondale and Edwardsville: Southern Illinois University Press.

Dudrah, Rajinder. 2006. *Bollywood: Sociology Goes to the Movies*. New Delhi: SAGE Publications.

Dudrah, Rajinder. 2012. *Bollywood Travels: Culture, Diaspora and Border Crossings in Popular Hindi Cinema*. London and New York: Routledge.

Dwyer, Rachel. 2000. *All You Want Is Money, All You Need Is Love: Sexuality and Romance in Modern India*. London: Cassell.

Gopal, Sangita and Sujata Moorti (eds). 2008. 'Introduction: Travels of Hindi Song and Dance', in Sangita Gopal and Sujata Moorti (eds), *Global Bollywood: Travels of Hindi Song and Dance*, pp. 1–61. Minneapolis: University of Minnesota Press.

Guilbault, Jocelyne. 2005. 'Audible Entanglements: Nation and Diasporas in Trinidad's Calypso Music Scene', *Small Axe*, 9 (1): 40–63.

Hebdige, Dick. 1994. *Cut 'n' Mix: Culture, Identity and Caribbean Music*. London: Routledge.

Manuel, Peter. 1997. 'Music, Identity, and Images of India in the Indo-Caribbean Diaspora', *Asian Music*, 29 (1): 17–35.

Miller, Daniel and Don Slater. 2006. *The Internet: An Ethnographic Approach*. Oxford: Berg Publishers.

Mishra, Vijay. 2008. 'Towards a Theoretical Critique of Bombay Cinema', in Jigna Desai and Rajinder Dudrah (eds), *The Bollywood Reader*, pp. 32–44. Maidenhead: Open University Press.

Mohammed, Patricia. 2004. 'Unmasking Masculinity and Deconstructing Patriarchy: Problems and Possibilities within Feminist Epistemology', in Rodha Reddock (ed.), *Interrogating Caribbean Masculinities: Theoertical and Empirical Analyses*, pp. 38–67. Kingston: University of the West Indies Press.

Niranjana, Tejaswini. 2006. *Mobilizing India: Women, Music, and Migration between India and Trinidad*. New York: Duke University Press.

Patasar, Sharda. 2011. 'Indo-Trinidadian Popular Music-Chutney: Contents and Discontents' (paper presented at the international conference on 'New Geographies: Studies in Postcoloniality and Globalization', University of the West Indies at St. Augustine, Trinidad and Tobago, 26 March).

Rai, Amit S. 2009. *Untimely Bollywood: Globalization and India's New Media Assemblage*. London: Duke University Press.

Ramnarine, Tina K. 2011. 'Music in Circulation between Diasporic Histories and Modern Media: Exploring Sonic Politics in Two Bollywood Films *Om Shanti Om* and *Dulha Mil Gaya*', *South Asian Diaspora*, 3 (2): 143–58.

Reddock, Rhoda. 1998. 'Contestations over National Culture in Trinidad and Tobago: Considerations of Ethnicity, Class and Gender', in Christine Barrow (ed.), *Caribbean Portraits: Essays on Gender Ideologies and Identities*, pp. 414–35. Kingston: University of the West Indies Press.

Rose, Tricia. 1994. *Black Noise: Rap Music and Black Culture in Contemporary America*. Hanover: Wesleyan University Press.

Filmography

Billu. Dir. Priyadarshan. Red Chillies Entertainment, 2009.
Dilwale Dulhania Le Jayenge. Dir. Aditya Chopra. Yash Raj Films, 1995.
Jab Tak Hai Jaan. Dir. Yash Chopra. Yash Raj Films, 2012.
Kabhi Alvida Naa Kehna. Dir. Karan Johar. Dharma Productions, 2006.
Kabhi Khushi Kabhie Gham…. Dir. Karan Johar. Dharma Productions, 2001.
Kal Ho Naa Ho. Dirs Nikhil Advani and Ron Reid Jr. Dharma Productions, 2003.
Kuch Kuch Hota Hai. Dir. Karan Johar. Dharma Productions, 1998.
Om Shanti Om. Dir. Farah Khan. Red Chillies Entertainment, 2007.
Ra.One. Dir. Anubhav Sinha. Red Chillies Entertainment, 2011.

Fandom Beyond Borders and Boundaries

Peru in Love with SRK

PETRA HIRZER

During my fieldwork on Bollywood in Peru in 2012, I followed a dinner invitation of a friend who happens to be an Indian dance instructor and the head, heart, and soul of Maha Raas, one of the many Bollywood-related dance academies and clubs in Peru. Fortunately, he had called me to spend the evening with him and his group of students after their weekly rehearsal. We met at a *chifa*, a Chinese–Peruvian restaurant at Lima's city centre. As soon as I had arrived, I was warmly introduced to a table of around 15 young Peruvians, all on their way to their twenties. I even recognized some of the girls from one of my previous visits to their dancing class,[1] others from their facebook profile, or other past events. As their class had gone well, they were celebrating their latest improvements in performing *Bole chudiyan* from *Kabhi Khushi Kabhie Gham…* (K3G, Dir. Karan Johar, 2001).

While I was talking to a member of the club about the latest gossip on facebook (the communication medium within Bollywood fandom both in Peru and beyond), loud screaming caught me by surprise. I turned to the girls on my left and found myself to be the cause and centre of sudden highly emotional confusion. People were talking over each other, staring at me with wide eyes, laughing, screaming, and crying all at the same time while pushing me into the limelight of everyone's attention: *You are Petra, THE Petra from facebook? You saw Shah Rukh Khan* (henceforth SRK) *for real? How was it?* They were referring to a short self-made video clip I had presented on my private facebook profile a few months earlier. Apparently, the clip had reached a wider range of audience than I was aware of. It showed nobody less than SRK attending the premiere of his blockbuster *Don 2* (Dir. Farhan Akhtar, 2011) at the Berlinale 2012, Berlin's International Film Festival and one of the most important events of the international film industry. Despite freezing winter temperatures, he spent an impressively long time in front of the cinema with the crowd of fans from Germany, Austria, and even Scandinavia, waiting, signing cards, taking pictures, and hugging some of his female fans. For the girls at the chifa in Lima, however, it was not just another scene starring SRK on a red carpet greeting his fans. He mentioned their home country Peru and signed the logo of a popular local fan club named Bada Ka Dil. This made all the difference, made them laugh and cry, made them re-view and re-post the video all over again, and in some way made them feel a little closer to their hero. 'We screamed even louder than the girls who were there. Your video made us happy. Thank you for bringing Shah Rukh Khan closer to us.'

The extensive popularity of SRK and Bollywood is not limited to India or the cultural confines of South Asia and its diasporas. All around the globe, millions of people derive pleasure and construct social meanings from Indian cinema—also in South America. The transcultural reception of SRK in Peru is part of the dynamics of media flows and mediascapes in the global cultural economy: the star and his films form the building blocks of 'imagined worlds' that have to be understood as multiple worlds which are constituted by the historically situated imaginations of persons and groups spread around the globe (Appadurai 1996: 35).

Although old and new circuits of Indian cinema have been studied extensively in connection with the South Asian diaspora and beyond (for example, Dudrah 2006 and 2012; Kaur and Sinha 2005; Larkin 2002; Mehta and Pandharipande 2011), there has been hardly any research dedicated to non-Indian audiences or diverse (fan) practices and performances in South America. Of particular interest in this area is the circulation and reception of Hindi cinema in Peru that has developed a vivid popular culture based on 'pop cosmopolitanism' in the sense of Henry Jenkins (2006). Active audiences in Peru engage in a wide range of cultural practices and forms of sociability that integrate global media flows into local settings, and establish new types of transcultural competences that link Indian and Peruvian popular culture. Peruvian Bollywood fandom today has been mainly inspired by SRK. His star and celebrity status does not only serve as a gatekeeper to India and Indian cinema but also as a marker of difference within the negotiation of fan identities. He provides a feeling of 'closeness' to his Peruvian fans—closeness that goes beyond borders and boundaries, and clearly sets him apart from other Indian or international actors.

This chapter provides an outline of the presence of Bollywood and SRK in Peru and discusses how Indian popular culture is embedded into the social worlds of young urban audiences in Lima and Arequipa. I want to demonstrate that SRK plays the leading part in this form of appropriation and hybridization of media content and media practices which reflect the 'own' as well as the 'other' in a dynamic interactive process of 'cultural mixing' (García Canclini 2003: 2). After providing a brief overview of the distribution of Indian motion pictures in Peru, this contribution will take a closer look at Bollywood fan clubs, fan discourses, and various media practices taking place both online and offline.

Bollywood in Peru

First diplomatic relations between India and Peru were established in 1963, but in 2009 the Indian community in this country amounted merely to 150 families.[2] Nevertheless, the history of Indian film-viewing as well as the popularity of Indian songs and dances date back to the late 1970s. At this time, the circulation of Hindi cinema in Latin America and the Caribbean had been influenced by cultural exchange among partners of the Non-Aligned Movement (NAM; Gopal and Moorti 2008: 27). The NAM was joined by Peru in 1973 and facilitated the distribution and availability of Indian films. Carmen, a 40-year-old Bollywood fan from Arequipa, described her first black-and-white film experiences in local cinemas, including famous productions such as *Mother India* (Dir. Mehboob Khan, 1957), *Mera Naam Joker* (Dir. Raj Kapoor, 1970), and *Haathi Mere Saathi* (Dir. M.A. Thirumugham, 1971), as 'the beginning of her great love for India and Indian culture'. The 1970s generated a first wave of fandom committed to India and Indian cinema that subsided when major international entertainment groups took over the market in the late 1990s. Since then, the distribution of films in Peru (and other parts of Latin America) was basically limited to Hollywood productions. The majority of smaller movie theatres had to shut down; these cinema halls were often sold to local catholic communities. With a few exceptions, for example, the TV broad-casting of *Mera Naam Joker* on several local channels, it became rather difficult to gain access to Indian films.

Even though this early phase popularity of Hindi cinema is still visible in my current research on Peruvian fans, the current Bollywood boom did not get under way until the turn of the millennium. The rise of DVDs did not only lead to subsequent piracy, which contributed to the circulation of cinematographic texts all around the globe, but also made countless copies of Indian films/song-and-dance-compilations available throughout Peru. Needless to say, DVDs provide not only affordable access and diversity within cinematographic culture but also better technological quality and repeated viewing possibilities. Ana, a passionate Bollywood fan from Arequipa, remembers: 'First I saw *Haathi Mere Saathi* ('*mi familia elefante*') with my family, my Mum and Dad. Then I watched it again and again and again.' As the famous Indian author Arundhati Roy pointed out in her novel *The God of Small Things*, the greatest stories are the ones you have heard and still want to hear again.

Furthermore, Dudrah (2006: 31) makes a point that the screen-ing of Bollywood films also means consuming other related cul-tural products that are mass-produced due to the popularity of the Bollywood media phenomenon. In the past decade, Indian exports to the Peruvian market became more and more evident. Nowadays, Peruvian salesmen or members of the widely spread Chinese com-munity offer everything a fan's heart may desire, ranging from Indian material culture, such as yarn, textiles, and ready-made garments to Bollywood-related products such as posters, buttons, and so on.

SRK the Dealmaker

DVD piracy and material culture are not the only reasons for the latest expansion of Bollywood fandom. Moreover, this development is shaped by changes in contemporary Hindi film, the fans' presence in various types of media, and extensive Internet coverage. As Dudrah (2006: 102) points out, the increasing international distribution of Hindi films is based on two factors: the industrial status of Indian production houses granted by the government in 1998, and the coming up of new economic models for a globalizing film industry. The recent distinction between more cosmopolitan '*hatke*' and 'KJo' (Karan Johar) movies defines certain tendencies of change that have evolved in Hindi cinema in the last decade. As Gopal (2011:16) states, '... [the] "KJo" film assembles many of the features that we associate with post 1970s popular Hindi cinema—melodrama, elaborately staged musical numbers, fairy-tale endings and a big star cast ....' KJo's two blockbusters *K3G* (2001) and *Kabhi Alvida Naa Kehna* (*KANK*, 2006) have been much more popular in diasporic contexts than in the domestic market. Gopal points out that the 'KJo' category (referring to a more traditional cinematographic narration) seems to epitomize the process of Bollywoodization (Gopal 2011: 18; also cf. Rajadhyaksha 2003). Therefore, it is hardly surprising that particularly *K3G* enjoyed groundbreaking success with Peruvian film audiences and led to contemporary Bollywood fandom. The movie presents the very first experience of Indian cinema for many of the younger fans. To this day, it has remained their all-time-favourite. DVD copies with Spanish subtitles of varied quality were rapidly distributed in the black market. Their success paved the way for many other movies to follow in the same illicit footsteps. It is quite obvious that the combination of filmic narration and the use of new technologies is one major reason for Bollywood's extensive popularity.

Urban middle-class audiences became attached not only to the portrayed image of India or Indianess but also to family values and, above all, the beat and 'danceability' of song-and-dance sequences. Still there is another, quite extraordinary reason aside from a conglomerate of plot, dance, and music—SRK. He served as the central gatekeeper of Peruvian Bollywood fandom and provided the proliferation of an actively engaged participatory spectatorship. The vast majority of fans in Peru, as in other parts of the world, literally got stuck with Bollywood after watching his movies. This enthusiasm still forms the core of fandom for large parts of Peruvian audience. It is expressed, for example, in the following reaction of a fan to the stars' performance in *My Name Is Khan* (*MNIK*, Dir. Karan Johar, 2010) in the online blog Indicine. The fan weaves English and Spanish into a hybrid, but also articulates a very explicit discourse of love and admiration:[3]

> Shahrukh Khan the only incomparable khan the best actor in the universe ... you are the only incomparable khan apoyandote [supporting you] your fans are always waiting for something new you always encounter many movies to do ... srk up high ... well you're better world ... here in Peru has many supporters including me ... I'm number one I love your acting since he first time you saw your movie until today I have 90% of your movies ... to continue the successes ... shahrukh khan's the only mundoooooooooooooo [world] ...

Community-based Fandom and the Role of the New Media

Bollywood fans may be described as consumers who build social affiliations around media texts. As Peterson (2003: 147) states, the simplest form of media sociality and media acquisition is the discursive community. The distribution of Indian popular culture in Peru generated numerous Bollywood fans and film consumers as well as the development of fan clubs all over the country that are connected with a tremendous amount of Bollywood-related web content on social media sites. The wide range of fan activities includes Bollywood dancing ('*danza hindú*') as well as the production and circulation of online *fan art* (cf. Mader, this volume). Internet entails numerous new technologies used by diverse people in diverse real-world locations (Miller and Slater 2000: 7). As the turn of the new millennium coincided with various technological changes in terms of globalization and connectivity, the World Wide Web played a vital role in the development of a Peruvian Bollywood fan base. If we take groups and chat rooms in the Microsoft Social Network (MSN) as a point of reference, this development started sometime in 2003–4. Bollywood enthusiasts began to bond online and initiated the diffusion of Indian cinema by using MSN group acquaintances from Spain and India. Seiya, founder and key player of one of the first communities in Lima named Bollywood-Perú, recalls the early days:

> We started with a few movies that friends had brought home from the United States or Spain. We spent hours translating the subtitles from English to Spanish and organized screenings of the great classic Indian films. As we tried to spread the word over the years, we became some kind of non-profit business providing Bollywood fans in Lima with the latest news and stuff from India. We also planned and conducted many local events like Holi and other dance performances or workshops related to Indian culture. Apart from movie screenings, we have never stopped working with various media in Peru and stayed in touch with the local fan-clubs. (from an interview with Seiya, from Lima, 2012)

Almost 100 well-known groups committed to Indian films and stars have mushroomed in the provinces and urban centres of Lima, Arequipa, and Trujillo since 2004. The average number of club members amounts to around 25 male and female active participants between the ages of 15 and 25. The numbers of fan clubs or participants, however, are rather vague. While conducting ethnographic research in Peru from 2008 to 2012, it became clear that there is a strong fluctuation among the various groups. The reasons are multifaceted and often based on everyday life issues such as interpersonal relationships, work, and family responsibilities. The clubs often vanish, regroup, merge, or take new names. Similarly, it is also difficult to determine the number of members of online communities who are subscribed but not actively engaged because their activity can only be traced and researched based on their web presence. Some of the most popular names are Kuch Kuch Hota Hai, Bari Dil Se, Bada Ka Dil, Comunidad India-Peru, India-Aqp Hamesha Dosti, Rada Krishna, Grupo Hindustan, Show India Dance, or Barathi Dil, the names being often connected to classic Indian movies or mythology. Liz, founder of India-Aqp Hamesha Dosti and one of the most influential fan clubs in the beginning, explains her dedication to the group:

We practically started with five people. Five people who had this dream and almost went crazy thinking about Bollywood. We started chatting and decided to meet personally to talk about our common passion. We were in love with India. A few weeks later, we started the 'taller de danza' and started practicing the songs from our favorite movies. More and more fans came to join us. We were about 60 people admiring Shah Rukh and everything that comes from India. It was like a second family. (from an interview with Liz, from Arequipa, 2008)

Peruvian fan communities demonstrate various levels of constructing closeness with media content and of enacting their admiration for SRK. One dimension of this process is related to the clubs as local forms of sociality, which represent a particular way of 'glocalizing' Bollywood and SRK. The vital role of dance in these communities fosters close in-group relations that are connected with regular meetings for learning and rehearsing steps and choreographies. The process of consuming and constructing SRK's stardom and celebrity in the sense of Nayar (2009: 146) is embedded in a wide range of transcultural practices that represent and enact proximity to India and Indian culture: the club Hamesha Dosti (mentioned earlier) greets the visitors of its website with 'namaste' and describes itself as 'Indian cultural community of Arequipa'; furthermore, some fan clubs celebrated Indian festivals (in particular Holi) time and again, and re-enacted selected elements of the ritual on the beaches of the Peruvian coast according to its colourful representation in films, for example, in *Mohabbatein* (Dir. Aditya Chopra, 2000).[4] These performances of an active audience and a hybrid fan culture are closely connected to the realm of the Internet: it is used to share and circulate activities of the diverse clubs, and forms an essential part of fandom in general.

The importance of global interconnectivity for the reception of Bollywood and SRK becomes evident in contemporary online fandom worldwide. While fans often create social relationships with other fans and share their accumulated knowledge, mass-mediated codes are negotiated within a supportive community and often relate to the acquisition of cultural artifacts and texts (for example, cf. Storey 1996). Thus, an ethnographic approach to Bollywood fans in regional contexts online and offline allows us to examine how Peruvian audiences go online and connect as fans— transforming, negotiating, and portraying their fan identities as well as constructing and consuming stardom and celebrity. In fact, the distribution of various internet technologies—and, of course, its increased extension in Peruvian middle-class homes in the past decade—plays a significant role in constructing and shaping local 'fanscapes'. Online forums, blogs, and social media sites such as facebook or Twitter have become a fashionable venue of public expression and social interaction, often without the need of text-based communication. In this context, the posting, liking, and sharing of different types of content have become popular events supported by social media technology. These signifying (media) practices are strongly embedded in social everyday worlds and, therefore, must be interpreted within the frame of everyday practices (for example, cf. Miller 2011). As Pearson (2010: 84) argues, 'the digital revolution has had a profound impact upon fandom, empowering and disempowering, blurring the lines between producers and consumers, creating symbiotic relationships between powerful corporations and individual fans, and giving rise to new forms of cultural production.' To make sense of such practices among Peruvian Bollywood fans, we use a specific set of interpretive frames following the work of Arjun Appadurai (1996): the circulation of mediated texts (aka mediascapes) is linked through imagination, which, in a globalized world, is central to all forms of agency and, therefore, a social fact itself. Thus, fanscapes in Peru can be defined as constant dynamics between online and offline spaces, fans and stars as well as processes of reading and re-reading, consuming and producing, coding and decoding, or decontextualizing and recontextualizing of (mass mediated) cultural artifacts from India and beyond.

Worshipping the Star: Shah-Rukh Mania in Peru

'I am still a fan. I keep waiting for him, he is my love' (from an interview with Soniya, from Lima, 2012). The increased popularity of SRK and his movies has both constructed and revitalized today's Peruvian fan base right from the start. All over Peru, SRK has become the omnipresent landmark of India and the personified symbol of Bollywood. To this day, the star persona of SRK has a signifying function in how local fan identities are shaped. The perception of the star always oscillates between his on-screen characters and off-screen persona, which is then mixed with various sources of fan discourse (for example, cf. Dyer 1998; Nayar 2009). Based on this mélange of image and imagination, we have to ask two main questions: How do Peruvian fan audiences relate to SRK? And what are the main activities or signifying practices of the fan culture both online and offline?

What does it mean to be a fan, I once asked a Peruvian Bollywood dancer: 'Being a fan means, that you don't change your mindset every second,' he answered. 'You don't tell people that you like something and the next moment you don't. And you don't like something just because it's in vogue. A fan has to be a fan of Shah Rukh Khan until death, and it doesn't matter if there is another rising superstar. You follow him to the end.' SRK is perceived not only as the best major actor of contemporary Indian cinema but also as the perfect Indian family man. As Evelin, a 26-year-old dancer from Arequipa, summarizes:

He is a person with a strong character. He is very energetic and sometimes appears very dominant. He is a family person, though. And he is very charismatic with his fans and everything. The moment you lay eyes on him, he catches your attention. It's something that inspires you (from an interview with Evelin from Arequipa, 2008).

The admiration of Peruvian fans for SRK is strongly embedded in their everyday lives. References to the male superstar are found everywhere, whether we are talking about communicative discourse or practices of collecting artefacts such as images, posters, wallpapers, or official merchandise. Kathi, member of a local Bollywood dance club, is still waiting for her beloved king: 'I hope you know that you have met my future husband in Berlin. He just doesn't know it yet. But the second he shows up I'm going to marry him' (from an interview with Kathi from Lima, 2012). Zoila, another passionate Peruvian fan, explains:

Of course, my love for Shah Rukh has a huge impact on my everyday life. My room is full of posters and next to my bed, I have a picture of him. I also gave my pets Indian nicknames. My cats are called Shah and Rany. Everything in my life is about India. Up to my email adress and password, everything is about Shah Rukh Khan.

When we take such statements into account, it becomes quite evident that there is a strong emotional bond between fan and star text. Peruvian fans of SRK develop a series of strategies to overcome the distance between themselves and the star. They incorporate mass-mediated texts and artefacts into their local realities, and often expend great effort to come to a feeling of 'closeness' to their object of desire. Thus, they are enacting the central paradox of the fan–star relationship: the celebrity is both intimate and distant, part of the fan audience's everyday life as well as remote from it as imaginable (Nayar 2009: 154).

Recalling the story at the beginning of this article, this process of getting closer to the star is of great importance to the fans. As SRK has never officially visited Peru, the long-distance yet desired relationship between his fans and him takes its toll. The only tool for Peruvian fandom to overcome geographical borders is the World Wide Web. In addition, the understandable lack of language skills (usually English as well as Hindi) forces fans to rely on alternative bonding strategies. It is very essential for fans to identify with their hero. Therefore, they often combine films and local realities by mixing the actual image and the imagined image with their own experiences. This also becomes evident in the everyday use of facebook. Media practices via facebook or similar internet technologies may be regarded as symbolic events where 'fan expertise' is negotiated and cultural hybridity performed within creative audiovisual or text-based contributions.

In general, images play a crucial role in mediating the relation of star to fan and vice versa. Especially on facebook, we can detect a clearly active engagement in creative activities and performances. Apart from the distribution of more or less official media content, the contribution of self-made fan art has increased in the past few years. Symbolic events do not just revolve around fan art but also around constant expressions of happiness via image, text, and sound.

Dancing and Transforming the Star: Juan Goes Shah Rukh Juan

One of the main activities of Peruvian fans of Bollywood is Bollywood dancing. Since the beginning of the recent boom of Indian cinema, fan clubs and academies dedicated to Indian dance and music have mushroomed all over the country. Ruben, for example, advertises his dance academy Maha Raas with the mantra: 'Learn to dance the choreographies of Bollywood—closer to all!'[5] Just like Ruben, however, the dance instructors learn and perform the moves and choreographies from movies or video clips. In consequence, Bollywood dancing is a participatory form of active and creative film reception. It allows the audience to experience their favourite movies firsthand. As Shresthova (2011: 4) points out in the context of the phenomenon of Bollywood dancing, all around the globe, people are beginning to discover their own local and community-based meanings for moves presented in the movies. In the case of Peru, various practices of hybridization take place. Choreographies of Indian dance are often merged with local Peruvian (respectively, Latin American) dances and traditions. This results in new cultural performances, such as 'salsa-hindú'.

When we take a closer look at the reception of stars combined with dancing practices, we detect similar processes: fans actively make use of the star persona to construct their fan identity. 'If you are dancing, you feel like the star. You are the main protagonist. And if you dance a theme of Aishwarya, you feel her and you feel like her. You feel different', a member of the fan club Barathi Dil explains. Club-affiliated fans often 'play the role' of their favourite actor. They absorb different roles and portray characteristics of the star's persona and reinterpret them by adding their own personality and dancing skills. Almost every fan club has its own SRK, always taking the lead and performing the star's parts of certain choreographies. Juan, member of a popular community in Arequipa, was nicknamed the Peruvian Shah Rukh Juan. 'To be like him, just a little bit!' he explains. SRK's facial features are imagined as familiar to an average Peruvian middle-class guy. 'Don't you agree, he just looks like Shah Rukh,' is a widespread description of male Peruvian youngsters performing Bollywood. Beto, a very talented 'hindi pop' dancer, complains about a colleague of his fan club Bada Ka Dil: 'They call him Shah Rukh. Well, it's not that he doesn't look like him. But I am more alike. I am the real Shah Rukh of the group.'

Fans incorporate and transform the star's image and recreate images of their own selves within the star. The Peruvian 'role-taking' and 'role-making' of the SRK star persona also takes place in offline events such as SRK lookalike contests or plays. The most recent event was the *Encuentro al Clon de Shah Rukh Khan* contest held in August 2013 in Lima, organized by local fan clubs in association with Cine Star Peru.[6] Since it was sponsored by the local cinema industry, the winner (name Shah Rukh Mntf on facebook) got invited to a private screening of the latest SRK movie *Chennai Express* (Dir. Rohit Shetty, 2013). Obviously, there are many different reasons for the intense response to the superstar. As we have seen, media reception is always situated between image and imagination. The same content may be read in radically different ways due to different regional or national contexts, 'with consumers reading it against the backdrop of more familiar genres and through the grid of familiar values' (Jenkins 2006: 156).

Fans also develop a strong need to express their fandom in public spaces. Individual or group-based fandom is often performed in-between online and offline spaces, Internet and 'outernet'. These constant dynamics especially become evident in the case of the 'Shah Rukh Khan FC Perú': the club is one of the most popular and comprehensive facebook fan-sites with more than 10,000 posted or archived pictures, memes, and screenshots of 'Shah Rukh, "el rey the Bollywood"'.[7] The collection ranges from official film images to live performances, commercials, fan-made drawings and collages, to pictures of local events. More than 9,000 members of the club are sometimes related to other communities or dance academies and are often engaged in local dancing or film screening events. Furthermore, they are ordering official fan merchandise such as printed T-shirts, SRK-shaped dolls, or stickers for fans for the Peruvian fan-base.

In March 2013, various online sources commented on the forthcoming International Indian Film Academy (IIFA) awards, an event of India's film industry: 'Bollywood could be soon heading to Peru. The South American nation may host the IIFA awards this year, a clear indication of India's growing screen presence in the Latin American region (Huma Siddiqui 2013).' Rumours not just about the IIFA taking place in Peru but also about SRK visiting their home country were rapidly exchanged within the highly connected fan-base. Fan gossip spread all over the country and the exchange of SRK-related media content increased these days. Fans reacted almost immediately. 'This is our chance to show our love and admiration for Shah Rukh Khan,' they posted and re-posted on their facebook wall for weeks. They mobilized online and organized a series of events to diffuse their passion for Indian cinema and especially for SRK. One of the main events was the first Bollywood flashmob in Lima,[8] organized in association with the dance academy Show India Dance. Hundreds of inspired fans participated in the performance in Lima's city centre. The flashmob was followed by a reunion of SRK's admirers from all over Peru. All these efforts resulted in a 20-minute documentary titled *My Name Is Shah Rukh Khan* about SRK, the local fan clubs, and the presence of Bollywood fandom in the country that was aired in April 2013 by a popular Peruvian TV channel.

———

As Dudrah (2006: 35) points out, Bollywood is able to provide alternative cultural and social representations that are different from dominant white and ethnocentric audio-visual possibilities. Even though the Peruvian reception of Indian cinema can hardly be seen as a guerrilla tactic against the predominant opponent Hollywood, artefacts of Indian culture (cinema as cultural text as well as material culture) have presented an additional niche for an actively engaged audience. They have gone far beyond the simple act of watching movies related to India. The experience of watching Bollywood films is transformed into a complex participatory culture where fans are turning into producers of culture themselves—constructing and performing a hybrid, 'glocal', and cosmopolitan popular culture.

In the centre of all activities is the production and enactment of proximity, closeness to Bollywood, India, Indian culture, and, above all, SRK; closeness to a community of fans; and, ultimately, closeness that goes beyond borders and boundaries, beyond the differentiation of local and global, beyond the dividing line between image and imagination. Thus, studying fan audiences allows us to explore some of the key mechanisms through which we interact with the mediated world at the heart of our social, political, and cultural realities and identities (Gray, Sandvoss, and Harrington 2007: 10).

In the context of the recent Bollywood boom in South America, SRK literally takes centre stage. On the one hand, the intense devotion of Peruvian fans to the star serves as a way to construct alternative identities from those of the mainstream society, while on the other, the star functions as the most significant marker of difference. The often unclear dividing line between his on-screen and off-screen image—a consequence of the specific star system as well as his dedication to dance and music—leads to a complete and rather unique set of images and imaginations that is different from that of other stars.

Finally, this chapter gave me the opportunity to reconnect with the Bollywood fan base in Lima. Following in the footsteps of many ethnographic researchers of the last decade, I have never actually left the so-called field because I remained present in online social spaces. I noticed that my video of SRK greeting Peru in Berlin was posted again on YouTube by a Peruvian Bollywood fan via the nickname 'Lourdes SRK 4 ever'. On this channel it has been watched again almost 5,000 times in the past couple of months. Thus, there is no end to the story yet. Bollywood fandom in Peru is a highly dynamic and complex phenomenon that has not reached its climax yet. As Shah Rukh Juan points out, 'And as long as Shah Rukh Khan is still alive, it is going to rise!'

Notes

1. Indian dance lessons (primarily Bollywood-related) are mainly conducted by local fans and organized within fan communities or dance academies. The dance instructors are not connected to the Indian film industry. They learn and perform movements they have seen in movies or video clips.

2. This information was provided by the Indian Embassy in Peru. The Indian community in Peru is mainly confined to the capital city of Lima, has a middle-class background, and is active in diverse fields of commerce.

3. The quote also reflects the strong emotive dimensions of online SRK fan communities as discussed by Rajagopalan (2011) in regard to Russian audiences.

4. Various videos document events such as a Holi celebration, a dance performance on a beach in Lima in 2009, or an open-air performance space in Lima in 2012 organized by the fan club Bollywood in Peru (see, for example, 'Holi Peru 2009', available at http://www.

youtube.com/watch?v=lyMwrTUWPgM and http://www.youtube.com/
watch?v=MaGk7LvKj30 (accessed on 19 November 2013). See also
Mader and Hirzer 2011).

5. For more on this, refer to the homepage, 'RubenDanAc', available at
http://rubendanac.blogspot.co.at/ (accessed on 19 November 2013).

6. For this, the facebook page 'Concurso "Encuentra al clon de Shah
Rukh Khan"' https://www.facebook.com/notes/star-films/concurso-
encuentra-al-clon-de-shah-rukh-khan-/574873585885137 (accessed
on 19 November 2013).

7. For this, the facebook page, 'Shah Rukh Khan FC Perú' is availble at
https://www.facebook.com/SRK.FC.Peru (accessed on 19 November
2013).

8. For more on this, refer to 'Flashmob Bollywood 2013 Lima-Perú',
available at http://www.youtube.com/watch?v=z4WObDP7b8w
(acessed on 19 November 2013).

References

Appadurai, Arjun. 1996. *Modernity at Large: Cultural Dimensions of
Globalization*. Minneapolis: University of Minnesota Press.

DEGEMS. 2009. 'Comment to "Info on SRK's My Name Is Khan"', 27 July
available at: http://www.indicine.com/movies/bollywood/infoon-srks-
my-name-is-khan/ (accessed on 15 September 2013).

Dudrah, Rajinder. 2006. *Bollywood: Sociology Goes to the Movies*. London:
SAGE Publications.

——. 2011. *Bollywood Travels: Culture, Diaspora and Border Crossings in
Popular Hindi Cinema*. London: Routledge.

Dyer, Richard. 1998. *Stars*. London: British Film Institute Publishing.

García Canclini, Néstor. 2003. '*Noticias recientes sobre la hibridación*', *Revista
Transcultural de Música/Transcultural Music Review*, no. 7, available at
http://www.sibetrans.com/trans/articulo/209/noticias-recientes-sobre-
la-hibridacion (accessed on 18 November 2013).

Gopal, Sangita. 2011. 'Sentimental Symptoms: The Films of Karan
Johar and Bombay Cinema', in Rini Bhattacharya Mehta and
Rajeshwari V. Pandharipande (eds), *Bollywood and Globalization:
Indian Popular Cinema, Nation, and Diaspora*, pp. 15–34. London:
Anthem Press.

Gopal, Sangita and Sujata Moorti (eds). 2008. 'Introduction', in *Global
Bollywood: Travels of Hindi Song and Dance*, pp. 1–60. Minneapolis:
University of Minnesota Press.

Gray, Jonathan, Cornell Sandvoss, and C. Lee Harrington. 2007. *Fandom: Identities and Communities in a Mediated World*. New York: University Press.

Jenkins, Henry. 2006. *Fans, Bloggers, and Gamers: Exploring Participatory Culture*. New York: New York University Press.

Kaur, Raminder and Ajit J. Sinha (eds). 2005. *Bollyworld: Popular Indian Cinema through a Transactional Lens*. London and New Delhi: SAGE Publications.

Larkin, Brian. 2002. 'Indian Films and Nigerian Lovers: Media and the Creation of Parallel Modernities', in Jonathan Xavier Inda and Renato Rosaldo (eds), *The Anthropology of Globalization: A Reader*, pp. 350–78. Malden: Blackwell Publishers Inc.

Mader, Elke and Petra Hirzer. 2011. '*Peruanisches Masala: Hybridisierungs-prozesse in der lateinamerikanischen Bollywood—Fankultur*', in Eva Gugenberger and Kathrin Sartingen (eds), *Hybridität, Transkulturalität und Kreolisierung: Innovation und Wandel in Kultur, Sprache und Literatur Lateinamerikas. Atención-Jahrbuch des Österreichischen Lateinamerika Instituts*, vol. 15, pp. 73–99. Münster: LIT Verlag.

Mehta, Rini B. and Rajeshwari V. Pandharipande. 2011. *Bollywood and Globalization: Indian Popular Cinema, Nation, and Diaspora*. London: Anthem Press.

Miller, Daniel. 2011. *Tales from Facebook*. Cambridge: Polity Press.

Miller, Daniel and Don Slater. 2000. *The Internet: An Ethnographic Approach*. Oxford: Berg Publishers.

Nayar, Pramod K. 2009. *Seeing Stars: Spectacle, Society and Celebrity Culture*. London: SAGE Publications.

Pearson, Roberta. 2010. 'Fandom in the Digital Era', *Popular Communication*, (8): 84–95.

Peterson, Mark Allan. 2003. *Anthropology and Mass Communication: Media and Myth in the New Millennium*. New York and Oxford: Berghahn Books.

Rajadhyaksha, Ashish. 2003. 'The "Bollywoodization" of the Indian Cinema: Cultural Nationalism in a Global Arena', *Inter-Asia Cultural Studies*, 4 (1): 25–39.

Rajagopalan, Sudha. 2011. 'Shah Rukh Khan as Media Text. Celebrity, Identity and Emotive Engagement in a Russian Online Community', *Celebrity Studies*, 2 (3): 263–76.

Roy, Arundhati. 1997. *The God of Small Things*. New York: Harper Perennial.

Shreshtova, Sangita. 2011. *Is It All About Hips? Around the World with Bollywood Dance*. New Delhi: SAGE Publications.

Siddiqui, Huma. 2013. 'Peru Looks for a Bollywood Hit', *Indian Express*, 25 March, available at http://www.indianexpress.com/news/perulooks-for-a-bollywood-hit/1092937/ (accessed on 19 November 2013).

Storey, John. 1996. *Cultural Studies and the Study of Popular Culture: Theories and Methods*. Edinburgh: Edinburgh University Press.

Filmography

Chennai Express. Dir. Rohit Shettiy. Red Chillies Entertainment and UTV Motion Pictures, 2013.

Don 2. Dir. Farhan Akhtar. Excel Entertainment, 2011.

Haathi Mere Saathi. Dir. M.A. Thirumugham. Devar Films, 1971.

Kabhi Alvida Naa Kehna. Dir. Karan Johar. Dharma Productions, 2006.

Kabhi Khushi Kabhie Gham…. Dir. Karan Johar, Dharma Productions, 2001.

Mother India. Dir. Mehboob Khan. Mehboob Productions, 1957.

Mera Naam Joker. Dir. Raj Kapoor. Raj Kapoor and K.R. Films, 1970.

Mohabbatein. Dir. Aditya Chopra. Yash Raj Films, 2000.

My Name Is Khan. Dir. Karan Johar. Dharma Productions, 2010.

Shah Rukh Khan, Participatory Audiences, and the Internet

ELKE MADER

I'm never today sometimes yesterday sometimes the next day already. I am a time challenger moving along the trail of my dreams seen eyes open.[1]
—Shah Rukh Khan on Twitter

Since the turn of the millennium, the Internet has developed into a complex global mediascape facilitating a constantly increasing flow of information and images. It interconnects people, content, and places around the globe, and accelerates communication as well as interaction. These developments exert major influence on the circulation and reception of feature films, and articulate the great significance of everyday media and visual culture for large sections of society worldwide (for example, cf., Grey 2010). In addition, the Internet provides a platform for new forms of digital popular culture made by the audience. Participatory audiences interact with media texts and images in multiple ways, and play a significant part in the construction and circulation of meaning.[2] Such media practices include a wide range of 'fan productivity' (Fiske 1992) in various cultural contexts. Furthermore, the Internet adds new dimensions to the enactment of stardom and the interface between audiences and stars. It allows new types of interactions on social networking sites, and provides a globalized space for the development of complex star-centred content worlds that can go far beyond the design and management of celebrity websites (Soukup 2006).

Such processes also take place in the realm of Bollywood. They play an important part in Bollywood's 'media assemblage' of diverse media lines (Desai et al., 2005), and embrace a myriad of web spaces created and used by diverse groups of people ranging from the Indian film industry to individual fans worldwide. According to Mitra (2008), the 'real' Bollywood is encrusted by a significant 'virtual' Bollywood on the web—the 'Bollyweb'—and comprises different kinds of web resources that are often linked together to produce a larger discursive space which is constantly changing and expanding. Mitra emphasizes the importance of the Bollyweb for the globalization of Indian cinema. Due to its high interconnectivity, it transcends regional and cultural boundaries and it is able to provide a global presence to the film industry.

The wide range of applications and users of the Bollyweb also goes hand in hand with numerous levels of diversity due to the 'the veritable explosion of audiences and sub-audiences that are distinguished by multiple and intersecting factors rather than one predictor' (Desai et al., 2005: 80). This diversity also defines Shah Rukh Khan's (henceforth SRK's) audiences that comprise a great variety of people from across the globe as well as multiple forms in which fans express their admiration for the star. One distinguishing factor among SRK's audiences today is the degree of access to information and communication technologies. Due to the digital divide, audiences with easy access to the Internet only comprise specific segments of society;[3] nevertheless, over thirteen million people had been following the star on Twitter in spring 2015.[4] Although SRK fans on the Internet are only a specific section of his varied audiences, they are of particular interest to questions concerning global Bollywood. As a distinguished media persona, SRK has a very high presence on the Internet. He is at the same time both content and agent of media practices and takes centre stage in a complex interactive and co-creative digital environment. He generates and is the source of a more or less continuous flow of texts, pictures, and videos that constitute the celebrity as a media spectacle (Nayar 2009: 22); his innumerable interviews give insight into his approach to diverse subjects (including the film industry, his work, and himself). As Nayar (2009: 69) states, a celebrity is always on, and performs continuously within the space of the spectacle. In the case of SRK, every bit of media coverage—in the sense of discursive and visual fragments of and about the star—is collected and organized on the Internet by special platforms and dedicated fans, and is available to the larger audience within hours.

SRK Content World

> That's how it all started: My first Bollywood movie was *Main Hoon Na*, and that's how I got infected. I was sitting on my computer and the TV was running in the background. Somehow the music started to catch my attention, and soon I realized that I was watching the movie instead of working on the computer. At first I was a not very enthusiastic, but then that song came—it was *Tumhe jo maine dekha*—and with it a wet Shah Rukh Khan, and emotions over emotions. Suddenly, my peace of mind was shattered. How could I have overlooked this man until now? These eyes, this body, this voice ... When I started to search the Internet, I could only find very few movies. At that time there was only *Kabhi Khushi Kabhie Gham...*, *Indian Love Story*, and *Dil Se..* (for sale in Germany). But thanks to the Internet and many Bollywood forums I got more background information; and the deeper I plunged into the world of Bollywood, the more I realized that it was not only kitsch, and that Shah Rukh Khan was much more than an actor. Now I admire him as a special person who has accomplished very much, for his country, and for all the people he reaches with his love, also here in Germany. Shukriya, Shah Rukh.[5]

This quote from a blog by a German SRK-fan describes the process of becoming an SRK-fan in Europe, and underlines the significance of the Internet in this context: digital media provide access to the digital SRK-content world that enables the fan to establish and sustain proximity with the star, and to form social relations with other fans. Thus, the slogan of a large online SRK-fan site reads: 'His world within yours'.[6] The Bollyweb also provides a space for sharing cinematic knowledge, imagination, and creativity; for the German fan quoted earlier, it has also been the beginning of extensive media practices. Today, her blog is mainly dedicated to the translation of SRK interviews, film reviews, or news items, and forms a significant landmark for German-speaking fans on the Internet.

Participatory audiences on the Internet shape contact zones for new audiences, and construct and enact connectivity between SRK, media content, individual fans, and fan communities worldwide. Together with the film industry and the press, they create and design an 'SRK-scape' based on the digitalization of media content and its circulation in interconnected fields within the larger framework of media flows in the global cultural economy (Appadurai 1996). Some fans have become mediators and culture brokers: they make Indian cinema accessible to local audiences and create a space of enculturation and hybridization. Thus, SRK online networks and sites can also be understood as a 'third space' in the sense of Homi K. Bhabha that is marked by hybridization and translation (Rutherford 1990: 211).

SRK fans who participate in this complex online content world of shared stories, visual culture, and emotions include persons living in India and South Asia, NRIs from many countries, as well as non-South-Asian audiences. Recent studies on SRK/Bollywood fans on the Internet encompass many regional cultures; for example, in Russia (Rajagopalan 2011), the German-speaking countries (Fuchs 2007; Mader and Budka 2009), France (Roudot 2008), Italy (Accari, this volume), or Peru (Hirzer, this volume). Comparable fan activities have been described by Punathambekar (2008) in regard to Bollywood film music, in particular in connection with A.R. Rahman. In all cases, fans on the Internet constitute an important dimension of the 'celebrity ecology' (Nayar 2009) of SRK; they build social and emotional affiliations around the star and the respective media content, and actively shape processes of circulation and reception. Fan sites and networks are conducted in many languages, and reflect the diversity of the global landscape of SRK fandom. Furthermore, fans from diverse countries and languages participate in international sites that link members from various corners of the globe and use mostly English for communication.[7] However, this diversified mediascape also has a lot in common: it demands access to specific technologies as well as a large array of digital competencies, and it is structured along similar formats. Specific applications such as homepages, blogs, or forums as well as various types of social media form a standardized framework for interaction and communication. Many genres of the co-creative activities (for example, artwork, videos, or fan fiction) have been developed in the context of other globalized media, and have been adapted to Bollywood later on: the first, large co-creative fan culture has developed around the American TV series *Star Trek* and its spin-off shows, and has set an example for diverse forms of 'transformative work' which includes the remixing of episodes or the writing of new or alternative seasons within the narrative framework of the series (Jenkins 1988). Today, co-creativity takes place in connection with a wide range of TV series and films worldwide, for example, Japanese anime or Bollywood films include, new forms of transformative work that have been facilitated by digital technologies (for example, digital art and remixed videos).[8]

To take a closer look at a local language of a fan site, I will be analysing the Swiss-based Bollywood forum molodezhnaja.ch that forms a gateway to Bollywood (and other South Asian cinemas) in the German-speaking countries.[9] The SRK section in this forum is by far the largest of about 50 online SRK-fan sites in German, and is the busiest place in the forum. It features 40 active threads (plus, around 80 older topics in the archive of the forum) that are connected with every aspect of the life and work of the star. The users come from different parts of Austria, Germany, and Switzerland, some of them have a South Asian, Eastern European, or Turkish background and they are mostly women in their twenties and thirties from a wide range of professional and social fields.[10]

SRK fans engage primarily with two sets of media content—his films and the extensive amount of pictures, videos, texts, and so on that are connected with his life and work, with the 'real person'. A large section of the Bollywood forum molodezhnaja.ch is dedicated to the presentation, review, and discussion of movies, and covers more than 1,500 Indian films released since 1990. SRK-starrers are by far the most popular: in 2008, *Om Shanti Om* (Dir. Farah Khan, 2007) and SRK came to Germany (to the Berlinale Film Festival), and the film, the star, and the experiences of fans during their encounters with SRK in Berlin dominated discourse and participatory practices on the forum for several months (cf. Mader and Budka 2010; Mader 2011). Since 2010, *My Name Is Khan* (*MNIK*, Dir. Karan Johar, 2010) has attracted the greatest attention: one thread is dedicated to the general discussion of the movie that was presented at the Berlinale Film Festival as well, and counts with 5,930 posts and about half a million hits giving it the most extensive discourse on a single movie in this Bollywood forum so far. Another thread on *MNIK* serves for collecting, writing, and discussing reviews. *Ra.One* (Dir. Anubhav Sinha, 2011) with 4,830 posts follows close by and *Jab Tak Hai Jaan* (Dir. Yash Chopra, 2012) has received 2,400 posts so far. Several threads cover *Don 2* (Dir. Farhan Akhtar, 2011) that was shot partly in Berlin and a total of nearly 7,000 posts are dedicated to multiple aspects of the film and its shooting. These numbers are of particular interest when compared to the reception of other Bollywood movies in the forum; movies that do not feature SRK rarely exceed a total of 200–300 posts.[11]

Among the sections of the forum dedicated to Bollywood stars, again SRK has the greatest appeal by far. Within this SRK-zone, one of the most popular threads is a link to a collection of photographs of the star. It is updated several times every day, and covers the better part of pictures of SRK available on the Internet.[12] The thread functions as a content pool: on the one hand, the respective links are supplied by the users, and on the other, it forms the base for individual collections and archives of fans that can comprise thousands of pictures. Another busy place is 'Shah Rukh's Lounge', a thread for casual conversation about the star among the users.[13] Other threads are dedicated to news and interviews (again, updated several times everyday) and contain links to a great diversity of visual and textual resources that are translated and discussed regularly; furthermore, SRK's house and family, his work as a producer, Red Chillies Entertainment, his activities regarding his cricket team Kolkata Knight Riders, and his endorsements are documented meticulously. Furthermore, a series of threads are committed to fan activities that range from participation at events (for example, premiers, concerts, and various meet-and-greet sessions), the doll Mini Khan (cf. Fuchs, this volume), to the circulation and sharing of fan art (digital artwork, videos), and fan fiction. Last but not least, a number of threads focus on the fans themselves, the (hi)stories of their fandom and their emotional engagement with the star.[14]

To participate as a fan in the content world of SRK there are many dimensions. These range from watching his films or daydreaming about him, to writing a fan fiction novel of several hundred pages. In the following sections, I will focus on two types of participation: to share in the life and work of SRK and to participate in a globalized Bollywood media culture with diverse forms of co-creativity.[15]

Interconnectivity and Intimacy: Sharing the Life of a Star

was flying across continents now in nyc ... will rest a bit and then be back with my knightwriters ... lov u all. (SRK on Twitter)[16]

On the Internet, SRK is available and consumable immediately and constantly worldwide, and there are many ways to share in the life of the star. In the SRK content world, films (narratives), star persona, and 'real' person are interconnected and merged in several ways.[17] The life of SRK can be regarded as a cluster of stories, partly told by himself in interviews, partly told in various versions in biographies, documentaries, and other videos, pictures, and texts, and last but not least retold, interpreted, discussed, and made meaningful by the audience. The documentary *The Inner and Outer World of Shah Rukh Khan* by Nasreen Munni Kabir (2005) is essential for understanding the shaping of the reception of SRK as a public and private person. Furthermore, several books—most prominently Mushtaq Shiekh's *Still Reading Khan* (2006) and Anupama Chopra's *King of Bollywood* (2007), or the TV series *Living with a Superstar* (Dir. Samar Khan, 2010) contribute to the kaleidoscope of representations of SRK's life and personality. All of these are based on extensive interviews with the star and can also be understood as part of his self-representation and of the construction of his myth. Processes of constructing and (still) reading SRK reflect the interface between representation and agency: they are related to diverse persons and groups and have been mainly conveyed by the new media during the past years.

Furthermore, networked media has been changing celebrity culture, the ways that people relate to celebrity images, how celebrities are produced, and how stardom is practised (Marwick and Boyd 2011: 139; cf. Muntean and Petersen 2009). Social networking sites (SNSs) enable fans to share the life of the star in a new way—to merge his world with their everyday life, and allow the star to reach audiences worldwide almost immediately, to be able to connect with them continuously. Baker (2013) considers

SNSs of the Bollyweb as spaces for virtual darshan, he compares the online darshan offered by many temples today with the presence of celebrities on social media.[18] In particular, he discusses the exchange of messages via Internet that facilitates the experience of a close encounter with a star and establishes a high degree of connectivity.

SRK's presence on the popular SNS Twitter has established an interactive contact zone as well as a space for self-representation. @iamsrk is one of the most prominent 'twitterati' in India: the actor joined Twitter in January 2010; since then he has used the SNS regularly (up to several tweets per day) for long periods of time, but also with extended interruptions due to hate tweets—mostly on religious issues.[19] As Marwick and Boyd (2011: 140) have pointed out, the world of celebrities on Twitter is rife with complex negotiation of multiple audiences including intimate friends, practitioners, and fans. Performers actively address and interact with fans, and this practice involves performed intimacy, authenticity, and access, and the construction of a consumable persona. Thus, a good part of SRK's tweets articulate everyday experiences. This type of communication establishes a high degree of connectivity and intimacy, and constitutes an important feature of the success of Twitter in general (Herwig 2009). On Twitter, SRK writes about his work, body/health (ranging from sleeping habits to illness and pain), or his family life, and enables the audience to follow his daily routines. He also shares his thoughts and feelings. After a shoulder surgery, for example, he tweeted: 'They say you learn from Pain. By that maxim & the nite that went by, i should be a Genius. Triple Nine Society here I come ...!!'[20] The representation of SRK's daily life on Twitter is sometimes accompanied by family pictures and other snapshots posted by him.

SRK frequently addresses his followers as his Twitter family or his 'knightwriters'—echoing the name of his cricket team Kolkata Knight Riders. He sometimes 'misuses twitter as a chat' (his own words), and answers questions from his followers during Q&A sessions: 'question time ... anyone??? only 10 ... cos i am in kids service today ...'[21] During the following 15 minutes he responded to 20 fan tweets and then said goodbye: 'have to go now. have a horror movie date with kids ... aaarrrgggghhhh!!!!' In addition to this type of everyday communication, a large number of his tweets constitute a 140-sign discourse on art, philosophy, ethics, religion, politics, human rights (for example, in regard to women in India), sports, education, and cinema. Last but not least, he uses Twitter to promote his films and his cricket team.

For the audience, Twitter offers a rich environment of interaction with SRK as well as among each other. On the one hand, people read and respond to @iamsrk's tweets: within minutes, each message from the star echoes hundreds of voices on the issue—ranging from diverse suggestions on how to treat a cold to comments on political subjects. Furthermore, fans hope (not always in vain) for an answer to their tweets—varying from birthday wishes to information about the private life of the star or his movies. On the other hand, various groups of fans have created their own followings on Twitter, where they comment and discuss SRK's tweets as well as their own private issues. @iamsrk's tweets also circulate outside of Twitter: they are quoted by journalists in other media formats, and they are collected, translated into several local languages, and discussed in fan forums. Sometimes they also become part of fan art, for example, of wallpapers on the topic of SRK tweets.

The interconnectivity between SRK and his audiences on Twitter was enacted in a particular way during the controversy that threatened the release of the film *MNIK* in Mumbai and beyond in February 2010. It was caused by the Hindu nationalist party, the Shiv Sena over some remarks of SRK in favour of Pakistani cricket players and had wide political repercussions. Debates on this subject were linked to questions of citizenship and civil society, in particular concerning the tensions between regionalism (in Mumbai and Maharashtra) on the one hand, and migration and national unity, on the other. Furthermore, freedom of speech, democracy, and nationhood were under debate. During the time of the controversy, a major shift occurred from the use of Twitter as a fan connection to media activism by the star, his audiences, and concerned citizens in general. In addition to interviews on TV and other press formats, SRK wrote about 60 tweets expressing his stand on the issue. During the high time of this Twitter campaign, 90 per cent of the tweets at the Twitter handle @iamsrk (about 25,000 tweets every day[22]) were comments on the controversy—almost entirely in support of SRK. The hashtag

#MyNameIsMumbai often went hand in hand with intertextual play and personalized transformations of 'My Name Is Khan': 'My name is Abeer and I stand by Shahrukh, from Egypt we all are by his side ...', or 'I'm not an Indian & not residing in Mumbai but I live in this world too & support democracy & @iamsrk MyNameisMeike' (from Germany). With the successful release of *MNIK* the campaign came to a happy ending, and SRK thanked his audiences on Twitter deeply for their support:

> Today i feel i will stand by with even more strength for all that stands for being indian & my country. ... thank u thank u thank u. .... i love u very very very very much. i am humbled by this show of love & kindness. so dont know what else to say. i realise today ... i am just a film hero ... u all in the theatres r the real deal ... will keep it in my heart forever. my name is fan ... & i am not a star ... u r[23]

The controversy was also part of discussions about the film and the star on many fan sites. In the Bollywood forum molodezhnaja. ch, the topic dominated the thread dedicated to general discussions about SRK for two weeks: approximately 320 posts give insight into the preoccupation of fans with the controversy, the sharing and translation of background information, and discussions with references to comparable political issues in Europe.

Sharing the life of the star on Twitter thus comprises multiple dimensions of interconnectivity and intimacy. A fan from Germany shared her reflections about communicating with @iamsrk:

> ... being on twitter with him at the same time created a feeling of virtual attachment and closeness, a special connection ... people managed to express their love for him with 140 signs, and he was touched by their love. He was also able to reach people with 140 signs ... sometimes he touched their soul, sometimes he made them thoughtful, others just listened to him and waited for more ...[24]

Design and Darshan: Co-creating the Images of SRK

> I live in a magical prism ... the world sees me thru slanted walls. I have to hold my truth within ... while knowing the prism is not a pedestal. (SRK on Twitter)[25]

Various forms of participation in the SRK content world can be designated as co-creativity, many fans are 'prosumers' of contemporary media culture who produce and consume digital images and content at the same time (cf., for example, Miller 2011). Thus, SRK figures in a multitude of visual fan art, he is the hero of hundreds of stories (and thousands of pages) of fan fiction, he stars in fan movies, and dances through a great variety of remixed and reloaded videos. Such co-creation practices relay strongly on media sociality and are closely connected to fan-sites and SNS. Ardèvol et al. (2010) emphasize the increasing relevance of audiovisual user-generated content on the Internet. This cultural phenomenon can be traced through a set of interconnected practices related to the acts of viewing, searching, producing, mixing, sharing, and distributing; it takes place in digital environments marked by interactivity, intertextuality, convergent technologies, and permanent connectivity. Such practices allow media consumption to be understood from a transformative point of view that breaks down the division between production and consumption of cultural products. Current media practices in popular culture give rise to a 'playful' relationship with audiovisual technologies leading to a more active engagement with images. Thereby, audiences are also engaged in 'intertextual play' in the sense of Peterson (2005: 130) by 'weaving elements from the media they have consumed into new narratives and artifacts that can be displayed to construct particular forms of sociality'. Fan art circulates on the Internet, functions as a digital collector's item for the respective audiences, and is part of an interactive culture of reception and interpretation of media content. Furthermore, several studies have pointed to the fact that fan art also has to be understood as a process of promoting a media product.[26]

In the following discussion, I will focus on three types of images (avatars, signatures, and wallpapers) and on their meanings for the star–audience relationship. Avatars and signatures are images used by members of SRK forums as identity markers. In the digital world, the term avatar refers to the 'reincarnation' of a person as an electronic image that represents him/her in an Internet forum, game, or virtual world (for example, second life). In the context of SRK forums, avatars are usually small square-shaped icons that appear on every post of a member and mostly display the face of SRK. Some avatars are animated, consisting of a sequence of multiple images played repeatedly. These micro-moving pictures either combine several portraits, focus on particular gestures or movements (for example, SRK dancing, running his hand through his hair, smoking, and so on), or display a miniature clip from a film. Whereas some members have been displaying the same avatar for many years, others change it time and again when they encounter a new picture that suits them particularly well.

Avatars can be understood as costumes or masks that transform the identity of the users to a certain extent and for a specific period of time: they are part of the playful media practices that establish an individual's role in an Internet community, and express and perform his/her relationship to the respective media content and star. Thus, SRK forums constitute a special kind of 'visual facebook' where the majority of users wear one of the hero's thousand faces. Putting on the face of the star to perform a role in an Internet community also echoes the practice of acting as described in this tweet: 'at the shoot ... putting on a face on my face to face another day of dream making.'[27] This line can be adapted to the use of avatars: persons from various places and backgrounds put on a digital SRK-face on their face to face the fan community on the Internet.

Most members of forums also use a signature (a block of text or an integrated digital collage of text or image) that is automatically appended at the bottom of each post. Whereas textual signatures often refer to SRK-tweets, visual signatures display the same style and content as wallpapers (that will be described later), only in smaller sizes. They are usually changed more frequently than avatars and can be understood as a personalized and customized comment to some current event in the life and work of SRK. For example, at the time of the release of a new film, many signatures will dwell on this theme. Whereas some people make their own avatars and signatures, others obtain these icons from the extensive pool of artwork in the forums by asking permission of more artsy members to use their work.[28]

Among the most popular genres of fan art are wallpapers. Originally referring to a picture or design displayed as the background of a computer screen, this format is used widely to represent a narrative or a star. In order to design a wallpaper, SRK pictures from diverse sources are transformed into new collages that generally combine images and text (for example, movie stills and quotes by the star). They reflect a great variety of styles and skills: wallpaper artists are co-creating and designing the star image and at the same time express particular aspects of the reception of the star and his films. Fans with high competence and talent in digital artwork are the elite among wallpaper artists, and many others acquire basic knowledge in this field to be able to express their relationship with and admiration for SRK.

The majority of wallpapers use visual material from public appearances, commercial advertisements, or magazines that are digitally cut out of their original contexts, reshaped, and restructured. A popular style is based on close-ups that construct proximity and intimacy between the star and spectators, and often combines multiple images of SRK. This type of assemblage allows the integration of diverse aspects of the face and/or body of the star into one frame. Facial expressions and body postures as well as the overall style of the wallpaper echo moods and emotions of fans.[29] A specific group of wallpapers are derived from screenshots or other photographic material from a movie. They focus on favourite scenes, on specific moments in a song-and-dance sequence, or on a series of facial expressions of the actor. Designing film wallpapers is a complex participatory activity and it includes multiple viewing of the respective films, engaging intensely with particular scenes or songs, breaking down scenes into pictures, and moving pictures from the film to other frames.

Gerritsen (2009) emphasizes the crucial role that images play in mediating the relation between star and fan(s): stars, in this way, not only create their fans but fans also create their stars by collecting, producing, disseminating, and consuming their images. In her study on visual practices of fan clubs devoted to the south Indian movie star Rajnikant, she shows what images do in this context, in particular how they establish a visual and affective relationship between fans and star. Similar modes of functioning apply to digital SRK fan art on the Internet: not only does it display (and play with) the many faces of SRK, it also constitutes a type of visual communication—it represents visual relationships within a 'community of sentiment'[30]—and forms part of the emotive space of SRK fans on the Internet (Rajagoplan 2011).

Baker (2013: 422) refers to the website of 'Bollywood Hungama' as a 'temple' for various aspects of virtual star-audience darshan, most notably due to the constant updated display of visual imagery of actors. Darshan—seeing a divine image and at the same time being seen—forms an essential element of visual culture in India: it is not only at the centre of many Hindu religious practices, but also part of cinema, and has recently been analysed in connection with the significance of the gaze in SRK/Karan Johar films (Klien 2013). Furthermore, the relation of the audience to the screen gods and goddesses in Indian cinema is partly based on the dynamics of darshan (Dwyer 2006: 19). Thus, the study of participatory fan cultures on the Internet also gives rise to the question of whether or in what way 'prosuming' SRK images is related to the concept of darshan.

According to Pinney (2004: 193), darshan can be understood as 'corpothetics'—a type of sensory, corporeal aesthetics: it expresses a desire to fuse the image and the beholder, a desire for closeness and contact that also forms the basis of the fan activities described earlier. The process of reproducing and designing SRK's digital image, or using it as an avatar, can be considered a playful pastime as well as a darshanic media ritual: it aims at establishing a close relationship with a star who again and again assures his audiences that he 'sees' and loves them. Fans are constantly searching the Internet for his pictures, and are producing and circulating more of them because not only must the gods keep their eyes open, but so must the practitioners 'in order to make contact with them, to reap their blessings, and to know their secrets' (Eck 1998: 1). Thus, the digital world of SRK fan-art that fosters proximity via visual interactions can also be counted into the darshanic space of Indian cinema.

———

Let the beauty we love be what we do. Onward now to do what i love doing most ... entertain. Happy darkness that surrounds the lonely spotlite. (SRK on Twitter)

SRK and his audiences on the Internet represent, enact, and perform various dimensions of global mediascapes in general and of global Bollywood in particular. Within this framework, entertainment has become a multidimensional enterprise that involves not only the cultural industries and its stars. It is increasingly influenced by media convergence, and is more and more shaped and 'prosumed' by active, digitally empowered audiences who contribute to the making of SRK's globalized polysemy. They form an extensive network dedicated to a continuous process of 'reading and re-reading Khan' from diverse personal, social, and cultural perspectives. Furthermore, they produce a globalized 'bricolage' in the sense of Claude Lévi-Strauss (1966) as they tinker with popular digital culture and a mythic universe of images, discourse, and meaning.

These processes have transformed once again the work of art in the age of mechanical reproduction. When Walter Benjamin (2007 [1936]) discussed the blurring of boundaries between authors and readers, he could hardly imagine the intensity and diversity these developments have acquired until today. Whereas many practices described in this contribution are rooted in older forms of interconnections between cinema, stars, and the public—for example, collecting star pictures and autographs, or writing a fan letter and (sometimes) sending a response—such activities have been accelerated, amplified, and transformed by new technologies and globalization.

The Internet and its SNSs constitute a globally shared space for communication and interaction that is used by cultural industries, stars, press, and audiences alike: their respective products contribute to a permanent media flow, and are available immediately worldwide. Sharing the online world of and about SRK has developed into a significant aspect of his reception; it shapes the meaning of stardom and fandom, and integrates audiences from a great diversity of cultural backgrounds. As Rajagopalan (2011) also emphasized, fans and fan forums often act as mediators and translators for local language audiences, and integrate them into a larger social and emotive space. This type of global interconnectivity also mediates between the imaginary and the everyday, between personal life worlds, feelings, media content, and SRK, who provides a variety of entertainment, and also can create closeness, relatedness, and happiness.

Notes

1. Taken from @iamsrk on Twitter, tweet 3,200 on 21 June 2012, available at https://twitter.com/iamsrk/status/215714813567963137

(accessed 19 July 2012). I want to thank 'Ujaali' from the Bollywood forum molodezhnaja.ch for her comprehensive documentation of SRK tweets.

2. On fandom and participatory audiences, cf., for example, Hills (2002); Jenkins (2006b).

3. The Digital Access Index (DAI) is measured on a scale of 0 to 1 where 1 is the higher end of the scale; the examples of countries with significant Bollywood–SRK audiences are as follows: Nigeria 0.15; India 0.32; Peru 0.44; Russia 0.50; United Arab Emirates 0.64; Germany 0.74; UK 0.77. Sweden has the highest access rate worldwide with 0.85. For more on this, see Internet World Stats, 'List of Countries by Digital Access Index—DAI', available at http://www.internetworldstats.com/list3.htm (accessed on 1 December 2013).

4. Taken from @iamsrk on Twitter on May 2013, available at https://twitter.com/iamsrk (accessed on 1 December 2013).

5. Excerpts have been taken from a post in a German-language Bollywood blog 'Dunedain-SRK', available at http://dunedain-srk.net/wp/ (accessed on 1 December 2013).

6. For more on this, refer to http://www.planetsrk.com/.

7. Good examples of long-established online international SRK-fan communities are Planet SRK (members here are from the Middle East, South Asia, diverse European countries, USA, and Latin America as well as from various NRI communities; there are sections here in Arabic, Spanish, and German as well), 'Shahrukhkhan.org', and Asian Outlook (have a German section).

8. For studies on this topic, see also the journal *Transformative Works and Cultures*, available at http://journal.transformativeworks.org/index.php/twc (accessed on 1 December 2013).

9. Bollywood-Forum is available at http://www.bollywoodforum.ch/forum/ and was established in 2003 by Marco Spieß, in German, with 6,921 threads, 1,212,121 posts, and 3,396 registered users. As the forum is widely open to non-registered users, a much larger number of persons visit the site regularly (all figures have been considered up to 1 June 2013). In an Internet forum, a 'thread' refers to an online conversation about a particular topic. Every single contribution to a particular conversation (ranging from one word or a link to several pages of text) is called a 'post'. Every time someone accesses a forum or a 'thread' (whether to read or to write a 'post'), it is counted automatically, and is called a 'hit'.

10. Due to particular cultural notions about emotions and femininity/masculinity, the better part of European fans of popular Hindi cinema

and SRK are women—in contrast to other parts of the world (India, Africa, or South America).

11. All figures have been considered up to 1 June 2013.

12. There have been approximately 2,30,000 hits per year since 2007.

13. For example, 'Shah Rukh's Lounge' featured an average of 25 posts and 920 hits every day in the spring of 2009.

14. The articulation of fan identity and the fan's emotive engagement with the star is the focus of Rajagopalan's 2011 analysis of a Russian SRK fan site available at worldsrk.borda.ru.

15. I will draw, to a large extent, on examples from the forum molodezhnaja.ch described earlier.

16. Taken from @iamsrk on Twitter, tweet 380 on 31 January 2010, available at https://twitter.com/iamsrk/status/8463271179. Twitter is a free social-networking microblogging service that allows registered members to broadcast short posts called 'tweets' which can comprise a maximum of 140 signs. Twitter members can broadcast tweets and follow other users' tweets by using multiple platforms and devices—cf. the definition of Twitter on WhatIs.com; definition of Twitter, available at http://whatis.techtarget.com/definition/Twitter (accessed on 1 December 2013). SRK uses '@iamsrk' as his Twitter name.

17. For different dimensions of the meaning of stars cf., for example, Dyer (1998), Nayar (2009), and Turner (2010); in regard to SRK, see Dwyer (2000), Rao (2009), and Rajagopalan (2011).

18. In Hinduism, the process of darshan refers to a spiritual concept of seeing (a divine image) and, at the same time, being seen (by the god or the goddess), and its beneficial effects. Darshan is also applied to diverse ritual and political contexts as well as to the media (cf. also Dwyer 2006, Klien 2013).

19. For an overview of SRK's history on Twitter, see Surti (2013).

20. Taken from @iamsrk on Twitter, tweet 4,892 on 3 June 2013, available at https://twitter.com/iamsrk/status/341474608609890304 (accessed on 13 August 2015).

21. Taken from @iamsrk on Twitter, tweet 3,325 on 3 July 2012, available at https://twitter.com/iamsrk/status/220139017612697600 (accessed on 13 August 2015).

22. These numbers are based on a sample of 1–3 hours of tweets by @iamsrk per day in the respective period of time. Later on, the tweeting frequency on the controversy decreased and gave way to other topics, often related to the film and its promotion. An exception was SRK's final statement on the issue on 11 February that caused a huge wave of response.

23. Excerpts have been taken from SRK's tweet 493–507 on 12 February 2010, available at https://twitter.com/iamsrk (accessed on 21 March 2010).
24. Excerpts have been from a longer comment in the Swiss Bollywood forum about SRK on Twitter, January 2011 (accessed on 10 February 2011).
25. Taken from @iamsrk on Twitter, tweet 2,873 on 25 January 2012, available at https://twitter.com/iamsrk/status/162126421156831232 (accessed on 11 November 2013).
26. Cf., for example, Einwächter's (2011) study on the significance of fan art for the Twilight Saga franchise.
27. The excerpt has been taken from @iamsrk's tweet 4,844 on 20 December 2012, available at https://twitter.com/iamsrk/status/281627565398040576 (accessed on 11 November 2013).
28. For comprehensive collections of SRK avatars and signatures designed mostly by members of the respective forums, see, for example, http://www.planetsrk.com/community/threads/avatars-n-signatures.151/ or http://www.bollywoodforum.ch/forum/showthread.php?t=942 (both accessed on 17 August 2014).
29. A video with wallpapers to illustrate this is available at http://www.youtube.com/watch?v=oRNxM-qHh5o (accessed on 24 May 2014).
30. A term from Arjun Appadurai used by Roudot (2008) to describe SRK's fan communities in France.
31. @iamsrk is quoting a poem from Rumi in his tweet 4,974 on 5 July 2013, available at https://twitter.com/iamsrk/status/353406605318041600 (accessed on 11 November 2011).

References

Appadurai, Arjun. 1996. *Modernity at Large: Cultural Dimensions of Globalization*. Minneapolis: University of Minnesota Press.

Ardèvol, Elisenda, Antoni Roig, Gemma San Cornelio, Ruth Pagès, and Pau Alsina. 2010. 'Playful Practices: Theorising New Media Cultural Production', in Birgit Bräuchler and John Postill (eds), *Theorising Media and Practice*. New York: Berghahn Books.

Baker, Steven. 2013. 'Virtual Darshan. Social Networking and Virtual Communities in the Hindi Film Context', in Moti Gokulsing and Wimal Dissanayake (eds), *Routledge Handbook of Indian Cinemas*. London and New York: Routledge.

Benjamin, Walter 2007 [1936]. 'The Work of Art in the Age of Mechanical Reproduction', in Sean Redmont and Su Holmes (eds), *Stardom and Celebrity: A Reader*, pp. 25–33. Thousand Oaks: SAGE Publications.

Chopra, Anupama. 2007. *King of Bollywood: Shah Rukh Khan and the Seductive World of Indian Cinema*. New York and Boston: Warner Books.

Desai, Jigna, Rajinder Dudrah, and Amit Rai. 2005. 'Bollywood Audiences Editorial', *South Asian Popular Culture*, 3 (2): 79–82.

Dwyer, Rachel. 2000. *All You Want Is Money, All You Need Is Love: Sexuality and Romance in Modern India*. London: Cassell.

————. 2006. *Filming the Gods: Religion and Indian Cinema*. London and New York: Routledge.

Dyer, Richard. 1998. *Stars*. London: British Film Institute Publishing.

Eck, Diana. 1998. *Darśan: Seeing the Divine Image in India*. New York: Columbia University Press.

Einwächter, Sophie. 2011. '"Fankulturwirtschaft" oder: Der Beitrag der Fans zum Erfolg des Twilight-Saga-Franchise', *Kultur & Geschlecht*, 8: 1–21.

Fiske, John. 1992. 'The Cultural Economy of Fandom', in Lisa Lewis (ed.), *The Adoring Audience: Fan Culture and Popular Media*, pp. 30–49. London and New York: Routledge.

Fuchs, Bernhard. 2007. 'Bollywood-Fans Meeting Online and Offline: Filmkultur im Internet, bei Stammtischen und auf Clubbings', *ZfK-Zeitschrift für Kulturwissenschaften*, 2: 69–84.

Gerritsen, Roos. 2009. 'Cine-Addictions: Image Trails Running from the Intimate Sphere to the Public Eye', *South Asian Visual Culture Series*, no. 2, available at http://archiv.ub.uni-heidelberg.de/savifadok/219/1/Roos_Gerritsen_2009._Cine_Addictions.pdf (accessed on 24 May 2015).

Grey, Gordon. 2010. *Cinema: A Visual Anthropology*. London and New York: Berg Publishers.

Herwig, Jana. 2009. 'Liminality and Communitas in Social Media: The Case of Twitter' (paper presented at the AoIR's Internet Research Conference, 8–10 October), available at http://homepage.univie.ac.at/jana.herwig/PDF/Herwig_-_Liminality_and_Communitas_in_Social_Media-_The_Case_of_Twitter.pdf (accessed on 13 August 2015)

Hills, Matt. 2002. *Fan Cultures*. London and New York: Routledge.

Jenkins, Henry. 1988. 'Star Trek Rerun, Reread, Rewritten: Fan Writing as Textual Poaching', *Critical Studies in Mass Communication*, 5 (2): 85–107.

————. 2006a. *Convergence Culture: Where Old and New Media Collide*. New York: New York University Press.

————. 2006b. *Fans, Bloggers, and Gamers: Exploring Participatory Culture*. New York: New York University Press.

Klien, Hanna. 2013. *All Eyes on Shah Rukh! An Intercultural Approach to the Gaze in Karan Johar's Films*. Münster: LIT Verlag.

Lévi-Strauss, Claude. 1966. *The Savage Mind*. Chicago and London: University of Chicago Press.

Mader, Elke. 2011. 'Stars in Your Eyes. Ritual Encounters with Shah Rukh Khan in Europe', in Axel Michaels (ed.), *Ritual Dynamics and the Science of Ritual*, vol. IV: *Reflexivity, Media, and Visuality*, pp. 463–84. Wiesbaden: Harrassowitz Verlag.

Mader, Elke and Philipp Budka. 2009. 'Shah Rukh Khan @Berlinale. Bollywood Fans *im Kontext medienanthropologischer Forschung*', in Claus Tieber (ed.), *Fokus Bollywood: Indisches Kino in Wissenschaftlichen Diskursen*, pp. 117–31. Münster: LIT Verlag.

Marwick, Alice and Danah Boyd. 2011. 'To See and Be Seen: Celebrity Practice on Twitter', *Convergence: The International Journal of Research into New Media Technologies*, 17 (2): 139–58.

Miller, Vincent. 2011. *Understanding Digital Culture*. Los Angeles: SAGE Publications.

Mitra, Ananda. 2008. 'Bollyweb: Search for Bollywood on the Web and See What Happens!' in Anandam P. Kavoori and Aswin Punathambekar (eds), *Gobal Bollywood*, pp. 268–81. New York: New York University Press.

Muntean, Nick and Anne Helen Petersen. 2009. 'Celebrity Twitter: Strategies of Intrusion and Disclosure in the Age of Technoculture', *M/C Journal*, 12 (5), available at http://journal.media-culture.org.au/index.php/mcjournal/article/viewArticle/194 (accessed on 1 December 2013).

Nayar, Pramod K. 2009. *Seeing Stars: Spectacle, Society and Celebrity Culture*. London: SAGE Publications.

Peterson, Mark Allen. 2005. 'Performing Media: Towards an Ethnography of Intertextuality', in Eric W. Rothenbuhler and Mihai Coman (eds), *Media Anthropology*, pp. 129–38. Thousand Oaks, London: SAGE Publications.

Pinney, Christopher. 2004. *Photos of the Gods: The Printed Image and Political Struggle in India*. London: Reaktion Books.

Punathambekar, Aswin. 2008. 'We're Online, Not on the Streets: Indian Cinema, New Media, and Participatory Culture', in Anandam P. Kavoori and Aswin Punathambekar (eds), *Global Bollywood*, pp. 282–99. New York: New York University Press.

Rajagopalan, Sudha. 2011. 'Shah Rukh Khan as Media Text: Celebrity, Identity and Emotive Engagement in a Russian Online Community', *Celebrity Studies*, 2 (3): 263–76.

Rao, Shakuntala. 2009. 'Shah Rukh Khan: Bollywood Superstar and Icon of the Postcolonial Nation', in Robert Clarke (ed.), *Celebrity Colonialism: Fame, Power and Representation in Colonial and Postcolonial Cultures*, pp. 173–88. Cambridge: Cambridge Scholars Publishing.

Roudot, Segolene. 2008. 'Watching Bollywood: The French Audience for Hindi Movies' (bachelor's thesis, University of Oxford, UK).

Rutherford, Jonathan (ed.). 1990. 'The Third Space: Interview with Homi Bhabha', (ed.), *Identity: Community, Culture, Difference*, pp. 207–21. London: Lawrence and Wishart.

Shiekh, Mushtaq. 2006. *Still Reading Khan*. New Delhi: Om Books International.

Soukup, Charles. 2006. 'Hitching a Ride on a Star: Celebrity, Fandom, and Identification on the World Wide Web', *Southern Communication Journal*, 71 (4): 319–37.

Surti, Aalif. 2013. 'The Silent Movie Star'. *Mumbai Mirror*, 18 February, availbale at http://mumbaimirror.com/columns/columns/The-silent-movie-star/articleshow/18554662.cms (accessed on 1 December 2013).

Turner, Graeme. 2010. 'Approaching Celebrity Studies', *Celebrity Studies*, 1(1): 11–20.

Filmography

Asoka. Dir. Santosh Sivan. Arclightz and Films, 2001.

Dil Se... Dir. Mani Ratnam. India Talkies and Madras Talkies, 1998.

Don 2. Dir. Farhan Akhtar. Excel Entertainment, 2011.

Jab Tak Hai Jaan. Dir. Yash Chopra. Yash Raj Films, 2012.

Kabhi Khushi Kabhie Gham.... Dir. Karan Johar. Dharma Productions, 2001.

Living with a Superstar: Shah Rukh Khan. Dir. Samar Khan, TV Series (10 Parts). Blue Mango Films and Red Chillies Entertainment, 2010.

Main Hoon Na. Dir. Farah Khan. Red Chillies Entertainment, 2004.

My Name Is Khan. Dir. Karan Johar. Dharma Productions, 2010.

Om Shanti Om. Dir. Farah Khan. Red Chillies Entertainment, 2007.

Ra.One. Dir. Anubhav Sinha. Red Chillies Entertainment, 2011.

Star Trek. The Original Series. Created by Gene Roddenberry, TV Series. Desilu Productions and Paramount Television, 1966–9.

The Inner and Outer World of Shah Rukh Khan. Dir. Nasreen Munni Kabir. BBC Channel 4 and Red Chillies Entertainment, 2005.

Dollywood

The Pleasures of Playing with Mini Khan

BERNHARD FUCHS

We bring the magic and sparkle of Bollywood right into the hands of its audience.
— Promotional text for the dolls Bollywood Legends, 2005[1]

The advertisement of licenced merchandizing dolls representing Bollywood actresses and actors celebrated the haptic experience as an extension of cinema; for the first time audiences could get hold of their favourite movie stars in the form of 12-inch-sized figurines. The Bollywood Legends doll series launched in September 2005 presented Kajol Devgan, Priyanka Chopra, Hrithik Roshan, and Shah Rukh Khan (henceforth SRK) as toys and was an innovative Bollywood-merchandizing experiment.[2] This product illustrates the proliferation of ancillary industries, which Ashish Rajadhyaksha (2003) describes as signs of the 'Bollywoodization of Indian cinema'. Bollywood movies inspire transnational cultural industries, which are often only loosely connected to Indian cinema. This toy was developed by British entrepreneur Shameen Jivraj (a desi with an East-African-Gujarati background). The product was designed in close cooperation with the stars, who approved all stages of its evolution right from the beginning. The global mediascape (Appadurai

1996) of Bollywood is complemented by a lesser known toy-scape: 'Dollywood'.[3]

The term 'Dollywood' has been used since 2008 in a doll photography group on the photo platform Flickr as a merging of 'Bollywood' and 'doll'. Fans developed creative practices linking cinematic experience with doll play, craft, art, and photography, operating with the material and feeding it back into visual media and social networks.[4] Textual and visual narratives are combined in fan fiction centred on doll photography; doll-based comics are designed, and videos produced from the stills are posted on the video platform YouTube adding the sonic dimension of a soundtrack.

Surprisingly, such fan activities developed only around the figure of SRK and none of the other Bollywood legends. His doll has been nicknamed Mini Khan[5] or Little King Khan. This chapter is concerned with the product and its producer, with productive consumers, and last but not least the star himself. The chapter presents ethnographic research on the Bollywood Legends as a commodity and analyses the intersection of Bollywood cinema and doll culture in the context of globalization.

Although the dolls have been marketed in the UK, the Middle East, South Africa, and India, my case studies are exclusively situated in the Western context; doll playing fans who become visible by their online performances are based in Austria, Germany, and the US.[6] The dolls have been marketed both as collectors' items for adults and as toys for children. Due to lack of visibility and methodological accessibility of child's play, I will focus on Western consumer practices of active audiences entangled in processes of culture transfer. Henry Jenkins (2006: 155) analysed a similar phenomena of Western fandom of Asian popular culture as 'pop-cosmopolitanism' stressing that 'cosmopolitans embrace cultural difference, seeking to escape the gravitational pull of their local communities in order to enter a broader sphere of cultural experience.'

From Representational Debates to *Ludism*

Theoretically, an integration of semiotics and assemblage theory is intended.[7] Assemblage theory enables an interface of the structural and the anti-structural; it highlights the tension between stable structures and the ephemeral and fluid moments of life (Marcus and Saka 2006). I combine semiotic analysis with a focus on the pleasures of media practices to avoid exhaustive representational debates framed by binary dichotomies of the Orient and the Occident. Semiotic analysis and political correctness is a prevalent scholarly approach to the toy industry (Ducille 2003). Dolls are burdened with all kinds of social and health problems. Ethnography that contextualizes their reception in child's play can hardly be found. One inspiring exemption that combines representational debates with empirical research is Elizabeth Chin's (2008) study of doll playing Afro-American girls. Fan culture and media reception cannot be reduced to semiotic processes. Media practices are not only about decoding and producing meaning; the emotional, somatic, and material dimensions are of central importance. Accordingly, the commercial presentation of these dolls is focused on emotional qualities: 'Bollywood Legends capture the total spirit and culture of Indian films, which are full of romance, colour, music, dance, fashion, and fun!'[8]

A 'philosophy of playfulness' is the ethos of contemporary media culture (Booth 2010). Especially in the context of dolls, the primary quality of engagement with media is 'ludic' (Liebes 1996). Tamar Liebes classifies four main types of involvement with media texts: a) from a *realistic* perspective media are understood as referential and discussed as true representations of the world; b) the *ideological* approach is diagnostic of the medial construction of worldviews and political subtexts; c) *aesthetic* analysis is a constructional approach that is more open and less concerned with the relation of media to the social than with the making of media texts and their aesthetic qualities; d) *ludic* readers enjoy the greatest freedom (their imagination is not restricted by reality, ideological deconstructions, or aesthetic analysis of media), these creative audiences play 'subjunctive games', engaging in role play, imagining different endings or 'abduct[ing] a character into hypothetical real-life situations' (Liebes 1996: 181).[9] Digital performativity, storytelling, re-enactment, intertextual combinations, as well as social networking and symbolic exchange are ludic engagements with the Bollywood dolls and SRK. My analysis highlights material extensions of cinema as visual, digital, and material culture. Cultural practices are embedded in a semiotic field; therefore, representational and ideological debates are relevant, but overall the 'culture of ludism' has to be emphasized in this context.[10]

Toy Stories

The Bollywood Legends dolls are a commodity situated at the intersection of toy culture, puppetry, and Bollywood cinema. The art of puppetry—where professional puppeteers use inanimate objects for storytelling, lending their voice and animating them skillfully—is an ancient tradition in India. The term for the narrator 'sutradhara'—literally 'holder of strings'—even makes it plausible that Sanskrit drama originated in marionette theatre (Sivasankaran 2010). The Rajasthani variety of this tradition—'kathputli'—is integrated into movies like the *Twinkle twinkle little star* song of *Purab aur Paschim* (Dir. Manoj Kumar, 1970); here, the protagonists watch their own parodies in a puppetry performance (a scene that dramatizes the dichotomy of the Orient and the Occident in order to show the essence of India). In the SRK movie *Paheli* (Dir. Amol Palekar, 2005) kathputlis are magically inversed in the closing section when the actors turn into dancing marionettes suggesting that the whole story is an ancient fairy tale narrated by puppeteers. Here puppetry epitomizes authentic Indian tradition. The idea to integrate the film's hero as a doll within the narrative as has been used in the movie *Jab Jab Phool Khilen* (Dir. Suraj Prakash, 1965). Here touristic souvenir dolls symbolize the nostalgic memory of a romantic holiday encounter. As 'transitional objects' representing an absent person (or entity), dolls are invested with emotions in different contexts like child's play, tourism, stardom, or religious cults.

The phantasmagoria of puppets and dolls crossing the boundary between human beings and inanimate objects, and vice versa, can be found in several myths and in films.[11] The crude horror movie *Papi Gudia* (Dir. Lawrence D'Souza, 1996)[12] is about black magic: a murderer deadly wounded in an encounter with the police enters a doll by his tantric powers, henceforth committing his crimes as an innocent-looking doll. At the climax, he tries to return to a human form and almost takes possession of the body of a small boy turning him into a limp object.[13] In *Ra.One* (Dir. Anubhav Sinha, 2011) the fantasy that the evil figure of a computer game gets out of control is presented as a modern variation of the Ramayana. SRK can be seen in the role of the other cyborg that is fighting the demonic forces. This movie is marketed as entertainment for children. Several toys—including a doll of this heroic figure, a comic book, and a video game—have been presented as merchandizing products.[14]

Do the pleasures of playing with a celebrity doll result from the experience of control over an icon?[15] The highly flexible Mini Khan doll is used in digital environments for storytelling, almost like a puppet.[16] The text on the box of the Mini Khan presents the audiences' will as the driving force behind SRK's success: 'His screen and stage presence are magnetic and what his audience want, the mega-star delivers without fail—time and time again.' Is the star imagined as the fan's marionette? Does playing with Mini Khan include the fantasy of *Being SRK*? Celebrity dolls enable a narcissistic fantasy of possessing a star, the imagination of control and manipulative power. This idea is pursued bizarrely in the surreal American movie *Being John Malkovich* (Dir. Spike Jonze, 1999) where a puppeteer discovers a secret portal to enter the brain of the famous Hollywood actor turning the living person into his vessel.

Omnipotent fantasies or the horror of transgression might be extreme forms of doll play and puppetry. Surreal narratives illustrate aspects of the relationship of cinema to materiality; cinema enables audiences to see the world through different eyes, to experience it from within the skin of an actor.[17] This point clarifies the contribution of merchandise to the 'magic' of cinema; it provides fetishized material objects—similar to practices of sympathetic magic. Dolls are the ideal touchable extensions of the skin of cinema. The puppeteer in *Being John Malkovich* talks about his fascination: 'It's the idea of being inside someone else's skin, seeing what they see, feeling what they feel' (DasGupta 2006: 445). Merchandise produces a 'proliferation of fetish surfaces—skins of an assemblage' (Rai 2008: 271).

Adults' ideas about celebrity dolls include erotic fantasies, the toy is turned into a fetish for the inapproachable star's body: 'If you can't get close enough to drool over your favourite [sic.] Bollywood heart-throb in the flesh, you might want to consider plastic replicas! [...] For the star-struck, this miniature magic surely comes very close to a dream come true.'[18]

Even the idea of black magic has ironically been raised in 2008, when German Bollywood fandom was under severe trial at a time during which the show *Temptations Reloaded* had been cancelled three days before the first screening in Berlin. This incident caused economic loss to many fans and seriously damaged the image of SRK and Bollywood in Germany (Mader and Budka 2009). The issue has also been raised among the online 'Dollywood' activists. While one doll activist reacted calmly: 'If we couldn't meet him in person at least we have the Mini Khan.' Others declared their anger, and even ill wishing could be observed; jokingly somebody suggested that the Mini Khan might be used as a vodoo doll.

Films have the ideal facilities to visualize the transgression of the boundary between inanimate objects and human beings. In scenes where magic is used, small figurines are morphed into actors as seen in *Paheli* or in *Om Shanti Om* (Dir. Farah Khan, 2007). The latter movie has a scene where tiny dancers in a snow globe are transformed into SRK and Deepika Padukone. It has been extremely inspiring for doll activists, who often recreated this scene with the SRK doll via photoshop technology. Such linkages to cinema contribute to the emotional value of Bollywood dolls as they support the fantasy that the inanimate object might be transformed into the real star.

Often doll play becomes integrated in the cinematic narrative as a mini drama mirroring the plot in a condensed form.[19] There is an 'Indian Toy Story' in the movie *Kal Ho Naa Ho* (*KHNH*, Dir. Nikhil Advani, 2003), which makes the central conflicts of the Kapur family visible in miniaturization.[20] Here doll play is used for 'clinical analysis' (in the tradition of psychoanalyst Melanie Klein), when the 'adopted' girl Gia enacts her depressing problems with the toys. When SRK enters the house like an angel, he is also represented as a doll. The movie offers a model for SRK doll play wherein dolls are used as an expressive medium.

The Bollywoodization of Barbie

The issue of cultural representation and stereotypes is at the centre of public debates and academic discourses about the globalization of Western consumerism and commodities, disputes familiar from the critique of cocacolonization and McDonaldization. The (unrealistic) dystopia of cultural isomorphization leading to a certain global uniformity is imagined in the context of Mattel's Barbie doll as well. Cultural studies and anthropological approaches identify various forms of localization of global consumer items. The neologism 'glocalization' describes mutual influences between the global and the local (Robertson 1994). Global enterprises develop strategies to penetrate local markets with new commodities; sometimes, the origin is concealed by 'culturally odourless' products (Allinson 2000; Iwabuchi 1998), but often the flavour of a local culture is purposely added (Jenkins 2006). The term 'glocommodification' describes both the localization of global commodities and the transformation of local products influenced by globalized aesthetics (Ram 2004). SRK is one of the major agents of the 'glocalization' processes. When he promotes a movie with merchandise toys at McDonald's in India, he applies to Bollywood the familiar Hollywood marketing formula (cumulating in the convergence of 'Mattel-Disney-McDonalds').

In India nowadays Bollywood (besides cricket) is seen as a proper vehicle to localize foreign products. 'Bollywoodization' has been chosen as a way to 'Indianize' several global brands. Accordingly, the toy industry also opts for a 'filmi' strategy; Mattel sought a symbiosis with the beauty, fashion, and film industries (anyway highly interwoven in India). Initially, actress Hema Malini had been selected to promote the Indian Barbie doll (Grewal 1999: 817) and more recently, top heroine Katrina Kaif became Mattel's brand ambassador, after whom a celebrity Barbie was designed. Mattel's Bollywood-Movie-Star-Barbie was launched in May 2011, almost six years after the Bollywood Legends that were produced by a small, independent company.[21] In the beautiful advertisement video the actress suggests the importance of dreams and aspirations in girls' lives:

Nearly every girl in the world has grown up playing with Barbie. I was no different. (Pause, music.) And today there's a Barbie doll inspired by me. Why not live in your dreams and make them happen? Next time they make a Barbie doll, will it be you? Barbie, I can be a Movie Star.[22]

The text on the box promises '[i]f you can dream it you can be it.' Like the Bollywood Legends before, Mattel offers a connection to a movie star via the fetish of a doll.[23] But in Mattel's message the Eurocentric ideology of universalizing Western culture ('nearly every girl in the world') characteristic for this global brand is visible. Interestingly, critics of Katrina Kaif doubt her 'Indianness' ('she doesn't really look Indian, she cannot even talk Hindi properly').[24] It is well known that she was not brought up in India. But this choice is consistent with the marketing of Mattel in India, which is focused on transnational and hybrid consumers of the middle class and elite. In India, consumerist children's culture is characteristic for the financially affluent middle classes. The first Indian Barbie has been introduced in 1991, the year of the opening of the Indian market (Grewal 1999).

In cultural studies, Mattel is criticized for its commodification of alterity reducing cultural differences to a commodity, transforming the other into static stereotypical representations by using the same doll type—with just slight alterations in colour—but equipping it with exotic costumes and pseudo-ethnographic information as an endorsement (Ducille 2003; Magee 2005).[25] The series Barbie of the World illustrates the capitalist utilization of cultural diversity, a multiculturalism that remains ignorant about social differences and power relations. Inderpal Grewal (1999) analysed the Indian Barbie as a 'traveller' (cf. with the travelling Mini Khan). As a Western woman disguised in Indian clothing, Barbie is reimagined as a tourist. The series Barbie in India is supplemented by a collector's series in the tradition of souvenir dolls highlighting regional diversity; the Expressions of India dolls bear Indian names such as the Rajasthani Roopvati. Barbie is most efficiently targeted at transnational citizens of India. At transit locations like airport shops, in five-star hotels, and metropolitan malls Barbie is sold as a souvenir to NRIs as a nostalgic memory of the homeland. The 'Bollywoodization of Barbie' is another attempt to penetrate the Indian market. Expansion to Asia is all the more important, as global sales for Barbies are actually declining.[26] Analysts of the toy industry speak of a 'post-Barbie world': in the West, Barbie has been replaced by postmodern parodies like the 'Monster High' dolls (a new brand from Mattel). Parody of Barbie and the production of anti-Barbies have become common, popular practices. Symbolic cultural conflicts are staged in the toy industry resulting in essentialist representations. Several 'Islamic' alternatives to the dominant Western brand have been created by Muslim entrepreneurs. Barbie is interpreted as a symbol of the imperialist West, of sexism and consumerism; on the contrary veiled dolls like Razanne, Fulla, Dara, and Sara, or the desi doll Aamina[27] stereotypically represent Islamic ethics, modesty, and family values (Terrebonne 2008; Yaqin 2007). But the Bollywood Legends are not presented in ideological opposition to the Barbie doll. Rather, they can rather be seen as complementary to Mattel's product.

East and West

The Bollywood Legends are an invention of ethnic entrepreneurship applying a practice of merchandizing—well established in the West—to Bollywood. They are neither parodies nor are they anti-Barbie and cannot be read as general symbols of anti-Western Occidentalism. But still a kind of Occidentalism has been included in marketing considerations calculating with diasporic nostalgia when the dolls could be used by South Asian parents to promote distinct cultural values. Shameen Jivraj has reflected on diasporic audiences:

> I talked to parents at length about this before specifically developing this product—and they missed their homelands. This is why they [are] stuck with watching Bollywood films so much because it reminded them so much of various aspects of the culture, of the dance, the moral issues, all sort of things, the fashion, all this appeals to them. I was specifically struck by the thing that their children— that they were worried because of their being away from where they originated—that their children would lose their sense of identity and knowledge *and all the good things, all the good things about Indian culture*. And I say this because some Bollywood movies go way off the mark on that front and getting a bit [doubtable]. But the parents specifically were quite keen on this. They said that they took their children to Bollywood movies because they wanted to give them a sense of who they were—and they were very excited about the idea of the doll because they said that they would buy them for their kids because that would give them a link to films and so on. (Personal interview, 19 July 2010)[28]

The Bollywood dolls definitely support the transmission of culture even in instances of cross-cultural exchange. Jivraj gave me the example of a British girl 'totally white, completely westernized' who got fascinated by Bollywood and developed a growing interest in Indian culture *after* she had been gifted the dolls. In this case, Bollywood fandom has been derived from playing with the dolls, not vice versa:

> One of the most positive things for me was this girl of a friend of mine—a white, Western tomboy you would not [suppose] to be playing with dolls. She got so enamoured with the dolls, [that] she wished from her mother the whole collection for a birthday and Christmas present; she got [interested] in Bollywood movies as she wanted to see the films [which featured] these stars. Her mother now regularly takes her to [see the Bollywood] movies. The girl goes online and [checks] when Shah Rukh's or Hrithik Roshan's next film is [due for release], and tells her mother. She learnt all the dances and her mother told [said she knew] all the words to the songs, she learnt the songs and she dances [to] them; and she's even taken the whole thing into the school—all her interest[s] and into her friends—like Bollywood theme parties. To me this is just one girl and it just happens that I know about this because she's a friend['s] daughter but she's been completely independent of any influence of me especially. To me to see what has happened is really astounding and really quite satisfying, here is a totally white, Western child who is really learning about a whole new culture as [a] result of these dolls. And that for me is quite fantastic.

In contrast to dolls that are burdened with the task of representation (like the 'Barbie of the World' or Islamic dolls), it is the task of the celebrity dolls to represent not a community but one single individual. In this regard they are relieved from the burden of representation. Especially if this individual is an actor, doors should be open for creative (and mimetic) role play inspired by movies. Still, stereotypical aspects in the original presentation of this product invite for a discussion of representational policy.

Gender Representations in the Doll's Original Outfits and Materiality

Discourses of South Asian popular culture and Indian cinema are inscribed into these dolls. At first view one might identify a typical combination of gender stereotypes and orientalism: women are presented in Indian and men in Western outfits. Such vestimentary constructions of cultural boundaries and identities are central to Bollywood. Indian values and traditions are mostly burdened on women. On the other hand, men are allowed to switch between the Orient and the Occident. The dolls of SRK and Hrithik Roshan offer a choice between desi or Western outfits; both have got their additional sherwani. In this respect, the message conveyed through the toys might be even more conservative than contemporary Bollywood, where women are presented in all kinds of outfits including Western wear and bikinis as well as saris and lehengas—without the typical anti-Western message that was common in older films. Shameen Jivraj (from a personal interview, 19 July 2010) explained to me, that as an entrepreneur, first of all she had to meet conventional expectations—Indianness would be essential for these dolls. In order to stress the Indianness of the female dolls they would have to sparkle and appear in exotic costumes. The heroes would appeal more to boys preferring action scenes, while girls were expected to stage romantic situations. Like Bollywood movies, these toys are produced for a highly diverse mass market, the South Asian diaspora being one area of focus. They are designed as toys for children and as a collector's item for adults. This reminds one of the all-inclusive concept of 'family movies' that aspire to appeal to all generations, including a global market. Broad marketing necessitates polysemy; as mainstream commodities, movies, and dolls contain ambivalences and must fulfil contradictory demands.

Practically, the doll's outfit is not confined to the original clothes. As the dolls are of the same size, as Barbie and Ken, possibilities for costume change are unlimited. Their wardrobe is enlarged by handmade clothes, complete with the costumes of dolls of competitor brands like Mattel. Merchandise provides only limited possibilities for Bollywood fans; incomplete offers create further demand and stimulate creativity. To get the costumes for the latest SRK movie, expert tailoring skills would be required. This imperative for active audiences is even stronger in Western countries such as Austria where Bollywood is 'out of place' (Mader 2011)—only a niche that is scarcely represented in mainstream media and everyday life.

Kajol's green outfit reminds one of her role in *Dilwale Dulhania Le Jayenge* (*DDLJ*, Dir. Aditya Chopra, 1995)—a milestone in Indian cinema. It is the dress that guarantees the widest recognition. But interestingly, SRK's popularity is not fixed to the earlier stage of his career. It is instead linked to his appearance in *KHNH*, which incidentally was his latest movie during the development of the doll. His orange pants are iconic for the *Pretty women* song, a celebration of hybridity and multicultural America with South Asians at the centre of it. On the contrary, Kajol's dress is the iconicity of NRI nostalgia. Even in *DDLJ* the strongest image of SRK is that of the hybrid guy with jeans, a Harley Davidson jacket, and an alpine hat. When this NRI figure has to wear desi outfits, he feels insecure and behaves in a comic way (in *DDLJ* and also in *Swades: We, the People*, Dir. Ashutosh Gowariker, 2004). Kajol in *DDLJ* is also presented in a variety of Western and Indian outfits.

The miniaturized representation of the female stars is more limited, confined to traditional roles. Even their bodies are not as flexible as those of the heroes, who are vested with the bodies of action heroes. Certainly, the design of the dolls is not only influenced by ideological considerations, but to a large extent to economic and technical necessities. A small but innovative company needs to reduce costs and risk by adhering to conventions.

But reflecting on gender issues, it is worth mentioning the childhood memories of SRK presented as text on the packaging. Here, the toys he is buying now follow the same pattern of male action versus female beauty, he buys mobile toys for his son and fashion dolls for his daughter (while his own first toy—a pink piano—certainly does not fit in this scheme). Typical, but still problematic, is the confession of the 'naughtiest thing' he 'did as a child', he 'Threw water balloons at pretty girls.' It is remarkable that the victims have not simply been girls, but pretty ones. The sentence carries erotic connotations and brings to mind associations of the festival of Holi, the divine play of Krishna and the *gopis*, eve-teasing, and the well-used trope of the wet sari used extensively in commercial Hindi cinema to convey desire. This image is certainly consistent with SRK's roles as a romantic hero. It is common in Indian cinema to romanticize 'light' forms of sexual molestation and demonize sexual violence (Ramasubramanian and Oliver 2003). Stereotypical aspects of

South Asian gender relations can be identified in mainstream cinema and in Bollywood-inspired dolls as well. Miniaturization requires reduction and exaggeration. But in spite of criticizing the conservative gender representations of the doll series, one has to admit that even these stereotypes have documented 'the spirit of Bollywood' quite well.

The Product and Its Producer

Shameen Jivraj is responsible for the concept and creative direction of the doll series Bollywood Legends. This entrepreneur with ten years of experience in the toy industry, having worked for Hasbro (one of the leading companies in this industry) on various products (among them Teletubbies, Star Wars, and the Sindy doll), experienced the British-Bollywood hype of the year 2002 with blank astonishment. Born in Kenya in 1962 and having grown up in East Africa until the age of 11, Shameen Jivraj has lively childhood memories of Hindi movies. But since her time in Africa, she had not watched any Hindi film as she was educated in a British boarding school. In 2002, when she attended a cousin's wedding in England there was plenty of waiting time, a Bollywood movie *Kabhi Khushi Kabhie Gham…* (*K3G*, Dir. Karan Johar, 2001) was running:

> Having worked on Sindy which is a very strong doll brand (the European Barbie if you like) I was struck, my God, has anyone made Bollywood dolls before because it's clearly very strong. It's a worldwide phenomenon; I can go back to my childhood. But having worked on Sindy and at Hasbro, which is among the largest toy companies in the world. I used to work on licensed products for movies. At this point of my life I thought: Has anyone done this before and if not, why not? (Shameen Jivraj, personal interview, 19 July 2010)

It was a classic case of coincidence (*ittefaq*), a combination of loitering and a magic moment as described by Amit Rai (2008; 2009) in his application of assemblage theory to Bollywood; a unique context in which different media texts and audiences meet in a specific material and architectural environment. It was one tangible incident where the 'body' of Bollywood was formed, in succession resulting in 12-inch-plastic bodies. These dolls again contribute as fetishes to specific media assemblages in many different contexts. Having just returned from Hong Kong where she had worked for BBC and looking for future options, Shameen Jivraj followed this idea as she was familiar with the intersection of toy industry and media. The social background from a trading diaspora in East Africa[29] is even more important for her professional career than her early Hindi film experience. Her education was very strict and as a girl she had to go to bed early and was not allowed to watch too many movies. Her father was a businessmen and the family often moved from one country to another. One childhood friend from Kenya, who became a businessman, provided financial support. She quickly found partners among former colleagues in the toy industry.

To establish contact with Bollywood stars turned out to be an extremely difficult and time-consuming task. Some of them denied because they found it too risky to be the first in such an innovative project. Even Ajay Devgan was worried that his wife's doll might look like a caricature, but Kajol was brave enough for this experiment. Finally these four actors and actresses, Priyanka Chopra, Kajol Devgan, Hrithik Roshan, and SRK,[30] had the confidence to take the risk to participate in the project: 'There was a lot of nervousness on their part on it as it has never been done before.' They were very serious about it and invested a lot of time and energy into the development of these dolls.

Shameen Jivraj seemed to be almost apologetic that the dolls had been manufactured in China, she had sincere plans to have it produced in India but the toy industry is not sophisticated enough in this country. The product would not have accomplished international security standards and would have become too expensive. Mattel manufactures the plastic parts in China and the textiles in India but this makes shipping necessary which would have raised the costs. Interestingly, legal conditions and tax policies in India are inconvenient for toy manufacturers. (Grewal 1999: 812)

Success and Failure

Hrithik Roshan, whose father has been a pioneer in Bollywood merchandise, was especially eager about this project, when Jivraj approached him. Immediately he recalled 'some kids in Dallas who had taken an existing doll and dressed it up like Hrithik and asked him to autograph it and he said "when they did that I was so touched and now here you are saying you're actually going to make a doll of me"' (quoted in Fuad 2006a). He felt especially honoured by the idea of his own doll being designed by a company. The final result has been described thus:

> An authentic and true representation of each actor's individual style and persona, the exquisite 12-inch figures have been designed and developed closely with them. The dolls allow for dreaming and ownership, a chance for fantasy, fashion, creative, and role play with their heroes and heroines. They present the unique opportunity for children, teens, and adults to display their icons within their homes.[31]

In September 2006 a glamorous launch of the Bollywood Legends doll series was staged at Harrods, London and at the Marriot Hotel, Mumbai. Hrithik Roshan and Kajol arrived in a horse carriage at Harrods to mark the exquisite moment. At this occasion Hrithik remarked: 'There are some moments in life that only come once like looking into the eyes of your newborn child and seeing happiness and peace personified. Another is when you look into the eyes of your own doll!' (quoted in Fuad 2006c).

The promotion of Bollywood Legends promised continuity, 'A dynamic and celebrity driven proposition, this is only just the beginning of a ground breaking new merchandizing opportunity.'[32] Shameen Jivraj had great plans to carry on further with the Bollywood Legends, to introduce new dolls of other heroes and heroines. But unfortunately, the decision was taken to stop the project within four months after the launch. Bollywood Legends have not been economically viable. For her it was heartbreaking, but she is aware of the harsh reality of the industry. Her small company could not afford to continue when the initial demand was much too low. Success, according to the toy industry, is measured in quantities: 'Barbie is sold in over 150 countries around the world, at a rate of two dolls per second' (Magee 2005: 591). Mattel can endure failure of some products and in some territories as it is operating globally based on a large diversity of toys. The Bollywood dolls failed because in the beginning, only three to four dolls were sold per day. 5,000 pieces of each doll had been produced, and after four years these dolls were still available in mint condition from online stores. (Interestingly, the SRK bias in the dolls' reception had economic consequences: greater demand for his doll resulted in higher prices.)[33] At its launch this product has been celebrated with star glitz, and one enthusiastic journalist even described it as 'nothing short of revolutionary' (Fuad 2006a). Although the brand flopped, the idea has been followed as can be seen from SRK's portrayal in the 'Bobble Head Don', a licenced product for *Don 2* (Dir. Farhan Akhtar, 2011); the G. One doll (a merchandizing product for the SRK movie *Ra.One* (Dir. Anubhav Sinha, 2011); and the Katrina-Barbie launched also in 2011. In 2009 a limited edition of Aamir Khan dolls was presented on the star's birthday as a merchandizing product for the movie *Ghajini* (Dir. A.R. Murugadoss, 2008).[34] The idea of Bollywood dolls definitely had an impact.

In the perspective of cultural studies, 'success' would be estimated differently from the toy industry, not simply by economic terms. Cultural practices, popular use-value, and even its misuse-value would be considered. Popularity is indicated and intensified by artistic adoptions and even by parodies.

Cultural Practices of Active Audiences

The creative activities of doll-playing film buffs can be observed as material-visual practices staged in the cyber space where the dolls are re-dressed, posed, and worked over, and scenes are enacted. The final products are images uploaded on the Internet, sometimes supplemented with texts, descriptions, narrations, and commentaries; only in one case the sonic dimension was added in videos on YouTube (username 'breaking free of the box' which is later discussed).[35] Some enthusiasts produce artwork with professional qualities. In other instances, photos of Bollywood Legends dolls are just side products and not the main fan activity. Interestingly, these activities seem to be restricted exclusively to SRK fans and the Mini Khan. If other actors have to be represented, usually different dolls are reworked. Other names for the doll were invented such as Little King Khan (LKK); the Flickr group LKK is a meeting point of some of the most ambitious and talented SRK doll photographers. A particular project of presenting one SRK doll photograph for every day in the year was given the poetic title: 365 Days in Dollywood.

The Travelling Mini Khan

One of the main functions of fan practices is connecting people. A symbolic link with the inaccessible star is established. At the same time, networks within the fan community are enhanced. An article from the *Times of India* illustrates the high visibility of these cyber performances:

> This passion for King Khan has united online fans of Indian cinema in a rather unique way. It made Beth Watkins, Michael Langhans, and Barbara Skoda set up bollywoodbloggers.com, one of the largest online sites for non-Indian fans of Indian cinema. Watkins and Langhans have started a project called tracking the adventures of Mini Khan. Mini Khan is a tiny Shah Rukh doll, who as some members point out, had six-packs well before the original. The doll is couriered from blogger to blogger who then uploads pictures on Mini Khan from his or her country. Along with the pictures comes a blog about their latest Bollywood escapade. The demand for Mini Khan is so great that a world map with a tracker is put up on the website to show where he currently is in the world. (Ahmed 2008)

Even a Twitter account has been registered for the Mini Khan. Beth Watkins, the American initiator of the project, explained her relation to the doll in an email:

> I bought my Mini Khan purposefully for this project, so I did not have to deal with having him for a long time and then sending him away :) But now that he is back, I do want to keep him for a while before he goes off again, even though I know people who would like to host.

When asked if she had missed Mini Khan while he was travelling, she explained:

> I did miss my Mini Khan, especially because he was gone for almost three years! I liked having a Bollywood idol, in all senses of the

word, to watch over my home and my daily activities. Even as a non-religious person, there is something about the darshan, eh? :)

This (ironic) hint towards devotional practices—darshan, the sacred gaze—is relevant (see Mader, this volume). Of course, here it is clearly a secular practice. But ritual figurines are common in different religions, not only in Hinduism.[36]

Mini Khan Goes to the Movies

The Mini Khan is taken to the premiere shows of the star's movies. On 9 November 2007 Beth's Mini Khan arrived in Vienna for the *Om Shanti Om* premiere. It was an extraordinary event: crowds of fans (some fan groups travelled from Germany as the movie had a delayed start there) and scholars with their students produced an exceptional hype for this movie, attracting even national TV which started to film inside the movie hall. The event was much over-researched to the extent that it almost seemed to implode. The dense co-presence was in clear contrast to the fans' routines of virtual performance. It was the inversion of the normal situation in Austria where Bollywood is usually absent in public space. Intensive observation and self-consciousness resulted in hyper-performativity. In Bollywood fan cultures, popularized knowledge about active Indian audience behaviour becomes translated and enacted in a Western context. Fans proudly displayed their self-created artefacts—tissue boxes and T-shirts that perfectly looked like merchandise—something that was not available at all. The desire for haptic experience became obvious as people wanted to touch the doll (only a single doll, the 'Travelling Mini Khan' was present)—and feel the six-pack abs that were an issue of gossip and was also visualized on a cardboard figure of SRK. The Mini Khan's host already felt hurt by the aggressive behaviour and lack of respect towards the tiny star. The Mini Khan figured as a centre of the touchable surface of Bollywood. Clothes were tailored according to the occasion—the doll wore the checkered jacket, much like in the premiere scene within the movie. By displaying creativity and insider knowledge, prestige is gained within fan communities. Fan cultures often show a strong tendency towards professionalism.[37]

Fans with the SRK doll at the premiere of *Om Shanti Om* in Vienna
(9 November 2007).[38]

Observing the doll's six-pack.[39]

Cinema, Dolls, and Bodies

The material aspect of the Bollywood assemblage can be exemplified
by the premiere situation, where the erotic of the fetishized body
of the star is obvious—the plastic body of the doll becomes SRK's

incorporation and the focus of attention. A similar body policy has consequently been followed by Aamir Khan in the merchandizing of his movie *Ghajini*, also with a doll and further supplemented by a computer programme for a workout session to gain the same six-pack abs as the star. In doing so, Aamir's body becomes not only an object of scopophilia, but also of branding. The media-body relates to the bodies of the audience through 'corpothetic' (Pinney 2008) experiences and practices like dance, workout, 'Bollyrobics', merchandizing, or location tourism and haptic city scapes (Dudrah 2010). Shortcomings of one's own body are contrasted with the idealized bodies of Bollywood stars.

Other Bollywood fans get annoyed when adult women bring their dolls to movie theatres; but idiosyncrasies are quite often jokingly admitted in the fan community. Doll players, women in their thirties and forties, reflect on their peculiar habits when they suddenly start with doll playing again, or even for the first time in their life. In some instances (narrated more as a kind of a joke) the touch of the doll is imagined as an erotic experience. 'Bollywood addicts' narrate self-ironic accounts of their passion, stories of outings, curious and scornful reactions, and jealous or even tolerant husbands.

Transformation into a doll is a sign of stardom; it is a contemporary form of the monument. Doll playing is an entertaining way of relating with cinema through a miniaturized, material representation of the star. It might be compared with the wax figures of celebrities in Madame Tussauds; SRK's figure was presented in London in 2007. Today his wax representation can also be found in Paris and New York City. In this situation, the figure is life-sized and similar to monumental statues, but (in bourgeois evaluation) lacks the dignity of memorials. Wax figures and statues cannot be posed like dolls; posing oneself becomes a central activity. But similar to the activities of these doll players, photographic depictions and the haptic experience are main aspects of the interaction.[40]

Breaking Free of the Box

Encounters with the real SRK are celebrated on the Internet. Paige Wilson from Los Angeles (professionally working as a teacher adviser), who is the most productive SRK-doll artist, received the star's praise for her remarkable artwork. SRK sent her a Twitter reply saying: 'saw the miniature ... fantastic. thanx.' Just a few words, but they mean a lot to her. She presents this moment as a screenshot on Flickr stating that the word 'fantastic' will never be the same again. She has even met SRK in person as she participated as an extra in a crowd scene for the movie *My Name Is Khan* (MNIK, Dir. Karan Johar, 2010) for the song *Sajda* (worship, adoration). She recreated this scene of the movie, where she can be seen close to SRK and Kajol, with dolls and produced a music video—movie stills being alternated with doll pictures.

> My 'big scene':) with Rizvan and Mandira (In real life, I'm on the right of screen shot)! Got to spend the night with SRK—well, filming with SRK that is! It's a night I'll never forget. Love to all!! Enjoy!
>
> To lighten the heart of the man himself, who has done so much to entertain us all for so long and with so much love!! (Hope you get to see it, Shahrukh) ... Enjoy!!

Scene from *My Name Is Khan* with SRK, Kajol, and Paige Wilson, recreated with dolls for a video (2010).[41]

In this context, special meaning is invested in this scene of worship; on a second layer, it becomes a document of fandom. The lyrics gain new meaning relating to the fan–star relationship: 'Since I met your sight, oh God, I have become yours' (*Jab se dekhi teri nigahen ai khuda, mein to tera ho gaya*). The many dimensions of love, adoration, and gaze collude in this moment. This is Bollywood darshan par excellence. The political context can be seen as an additional layer; in this scene the victims of 9/11 are bemoaned with an inclusion of symbols of Islamic spirituality. It is an icon of solidarity but as well a critique of anti-Islamic discrimination. (In this way MNIK jumps on the bandwagon of Islamic enterprise mentioned above.) For an American Bollywood fan like Paige Wilson, this movie is a symbol of Bollywood's arrival in the US—Bollywood's recognition of American politics.

Two main strategies can be discerned in doll photography, one is the concept of the Travelling Khan, to *contrast* the doll with reality (for example, animals, real persons, tourist sites, or the famous figurine of a dancing girl from the Indus Valley Civilization in the National Museum); and the other, which requires even more effort is the *miniaturization* of reality. Paige Wilson's style is perfectionist miniaturization. She calls her project 'Breaking Free of the Box' because initially she wanted to keep her doll in the mint condition as a collector's item.[42] But later she decided to dedicate herself to artistic photography of SRK dolls inspired by Dare Wright (1914–2001),[43] by using several SRK dolls and other non-Bollywood dolls. Any single news about SRK, not just his movies, is regarded important by her and staged with dolls; her Dollywood scenes are always ahead of the first show of new SRK movies:

> My 'Breaking Free of the Box' project pays tribute, in miniature, to Shah Rukh Khan's enormous contribution to all aspects of entertainment—film, television, concerts, advertising, and sports. With this project, I indulge my two passions: miniaturization and SRK, whose creative energy, positivity, and success give people hope that anything is possible in love, in life, and in art. Special thanks to the makers of Shah Rukh Khan's Bollywood Legends doll. Little SRK is a constant source of inspiration! From Los Angeles with lots and lots of love. Enjoy! Paige W.[44]

The sheer number of SRK images on the net produces a visual and semiotic overkill, a destruction of representation through the hyperreality of the star. Interestingly, the transformative process of miniaturization and re-enactment produces a reality on a different level, comparable to the production of myth. It is an attempt to rescue the glamour world of Bollywood from drowning in an excess of *mediolatry* (Mitchell 1986) through the materiality of the doll world, although this means a further proliferation of 'semiotic fetishism' (Mitchell 1986). The mimetic act of doll playing is explained by Paige Wilson as a tribute to the very special star which makes her a part of his specialness.

It sounds like a ritual offer to the spiritual master. By re-enactment, she participates in the qualities of the admired person. This activity gives her the feeling of becoming a part of SRK; once again global connectivity is celebrated:

> I do my project because SRK is the creative, compelling, complicated, compassionate man he is. He is special, and in this newly connected world, I'm able to share other people's similar feelings about him and be a mini part of that specialness. The possibilities for moments in doll form are endless! They're a challenge to do, but so much fun to share.[45]

Her impressive productivity is combined with the wish to give something back to SRK, to entertain him. Her rhetoric is often inspired by public statements of SRK: 'I want to create something big and new, which should make me feel that I am giving back something to the industry that has given me so much' (SRK in an interview with Afsana Ahmed).[46] For Paige Wilson the SRK dolls seem to share some of SRK's qualities:

> Even though I bought all of BL [Bollywood Legends] dolls, the others don't have the spark of genius or the likeness to the stars that Shahrukh's has! Priyanka and Kajol's dolls are actually not very photogenic either (unlike these wonderful women!). And their head and body materials don't match in colour or texture (as SRK's doll's do).

Another doll player contrasts Mini Khan's 'personality' and 'acting ability' with the 'talentless' Indian Barbie 'who just keeps her stupid smile all the time.' As an expert, Paige Wilson differentiates even among her SRK dolls and especially praises her first acquisition, which she describes as 'magic'. Contrary to the 'Travelling Mini Khan' where many people centre on just one doll, Wilson uses several dolls. She stresses that the newer doll's hand and face colour would not match and the joints would be stiff.[47] Stressing the peculiar individuality of an industrial mass product she states:

> I guess that [the] way I think of it, I have only one 'little SRK'. I bought two at first, one to take out of the box and one to stay in 'mint' condition. But that soon changed when I wanted to make my video tribute to the scene in the end of *Don*, when Don switches places with Vijay and kills him (so sad!). In fact, I think I'll upload that one again now that *Don 2* is on the horizon. Anyway, that's when I let 'little SRK 2' out of the box. Then, only recently, I bought a few more little SRKs to change the hairstyle on and to keep because I definitely wanted to keep at least one pristine and I knew I might need good parts if something on my originals needed replacing. That's when I noticed what p4d ['photos for dreams', a German photographer on flickr] always complained to me about when we compared notes on how easy or hard our dolls were to pose. She always said she was jealous of my doll's pretty hands, when her doll's hands were strangely coloured (and that hers was hard to pose—mine['s] a dream!).
>
> I've always thought that my particular doll (and his stand-in that I bought with him) is 'magic' in some way, so maybe that's actually true!! :)

Similarly, Mabel Baumgarten from Bremen (also with academic background, employed at the University of Bremen) celebrates the incredible qualities of her SRK doll: 'Sometimes it is terrific what an independent existence this figure develops. It is only a doll but one really believes that he can change his mimic.' Of course such qualities are also the effect of staging, directing, lighting, and camerawork. The experience of the doll artists comes close to filmmaking, when they struggle with the material problems of costume and set design. Sometimes they feel especially proud about their work and document the making of their art.

Mabel Baumgarten is a doll artist who produces a funny, mystery serial comics called Task Forest based on doll photography.[48] Here, the SRK doll is cast for a different character, not the star himself, but Rohan—an SRK lookalike who is a big fan of SRK and who possesses the power to transmute into a tiger. This idea is certainly inspired by SRK's perfume Tiger Eyes. On the packaging of this product the image of the star oscillates with that of a tiger.[49] The name 'Rohan' has been purposely chosen as it is the name of a fictional location from J.R.R. Tolkien's universe of Middle-earth and an Indian name too. The SRK doll is integrated into a hybrid combination of merchandizing, action, and fashion dolls related not only to Bollywood but also to other media. As an endorsement to Amit Rai's (2008, 2009) discussion of the media assemblage of Bollywood, I would like to stress on intermediality in general. This shimmering crossover ensemble of figures symbolizes contemporary hybrid media assemblages. It is especially typical for Western Bollywood consumption, but even in India, Bollywood is surrounded by multiple entertainment industries. Fusions of icons and narratives related to diverse media texts occur. This mash-up of dolls related to different genres illustrate how transmedia storytelling produces surprising extensions to Bollywood and other media. Contrary to Task Forest the 'Breaking Free' videos adhere to the original texts and are loyal adaptions to the toy medium (cf. Jenkins 2010: 945). In these comics, witty allusions to Bollywood (like bursting into movie songs) or clichés of Indian values (patriarchy, family feuds, NRIs) humorously reflect the fetishes of Bollywood (Rai 2008). Intertextuality, entertainment, play, and parody provide a special pleasure (which highly differs according to the readers special interests).[50]

In a Task Forest—wedding episode set in India—the Roopvati doll from Mattel's Expressions of India series is used, but her 'lacking acting skills' are here employed to produce the image of a silly character.[51] In this comic she is presented as incompatible, and finally has to be left alone.

Task Forest Comic by Mabel Baumgarten, 2010.[52]

How SRK Met His Doll

Shameen Jivraj (personal interview, 19 July 2010) narrated to me the situation when she presented the final product to SRK; she had documented this special moment with photos:

> Right now I am looking at these pictures. When I took the final doll to Shah Rukh—he has been to London—he has been through the whole process of approving etc. etc. and right in the end I took the doll to him (inside and outside the packaging) to show him the finished doll. And he was in London and his kids were there as well, and I showed them the pack and I showed them the doll outside of the pack, and I had a star wars doll with me for some reason—for showing him as well. And Shah Rukh and his son started putting weapons [laser swords] in his hands right they were kind of posing him as if he would do a fight [...] Now I've got these wonderful pictures with Shah Rukh with his son and with his daughter there also, and there he just took hold of this doll—and I thought—I was so much honoured watching this thing because it was like they didn't know I was there, you know, the play just took over. They were posing and playing with it. And Shah Rukh and his little daughter and I was there watching their play patterns, their plays—and it was actually Shah Rukh and his kids and I was watching. And I was—it was truly a magical moment for me and I shot pictures which I framed then in front of my board and I'm looking at them right now as I'm talking to you. [BF: I wish I could see the photos.] This was just a moment of time. I wouldn't say I was there for hours watching them, for half an hour or so.

She gave a thick description of the observational context and then started to explain the paradox of identifying somebody in a doll:

> In the mixture of his daughter's look: 'Oh this is dad but it's a doll,' his son as well—it was like part: 'This is dad: he's a doll.' It's part: 'It's a doll and I'm a child and I'm gonna play with it.' So it was fascinating. And Shah Rukh himself, he was so immersed there, so absorbed in it. And an enormous interesting thing that Shah Rukh said to me, that I found fascinating when he saw the final doll, as he looked at it and he stared at it for quite a long time and then he said: 'You know,' he said, 'the funny thing is,' he said, 'it looks like my father.' Yeah. And then he said: 'Most people tell me I look like my mother

and in this doll I see elements of my father.' And then I thought, this is interesting because it is very, very difficult to get a doll's face to look exactly like a human being, for so many technical reasons. Okay. Very, very difficult. And I, I then looked at it—and I looked at him—and I thought, how amazing? We've somehow showed a side to Shah Rukh in this doll that shows elements of his father. You know. And I think when Shah Rukh said this—I read again and again that he's sad, he's very. [BF: He was orphaned very young, yes.] Yes, and it's really sad for him that his parents are not around him anymore and for me it was very touching that he sees elements of his parents, people that mean a lot to him, in this doll. That was quite a special moment, yeah.

What made this moment so special is the narrative of authenticity, that the actor lost in doll play seems to have found himself. The commodity also becomes an expressive medium for the star. The doll's packaging informs about SRK's childhood memories: 'Wanted most in the world as a child: My parents—and I still do today.'

———

The Bollywood Legends doll series from the year 2005 is symptomatic of a rising consumerism stimulated by cinema. Transnational markets facilitate the proliferation of fetishes of Bollywood. The SRK doll has been appropriated for creative fan practices as a ludic engagement with cinema. Pop-cosmopolitans are seeking appreciation with online performances of transmedia storytelling and ritual exchange that sometimes inspire transnational cultural industries. Although this particular enterprise failed, the business idea inspired the production of similar merchandise products. The Mini Khan has become a cult object for several SRK fans and is attributed with marvellous qualities. This material object has become a touchable surface of Bollywood.

Connectivity is one pre-eminent function of the Mini Khan, reminding the star of his father, bringing fans in contact with the star or otherwise substituting a real meeting, and particularly strengthening the ties between fans. The producer established a relationship with Bollywood actors and actresses during the development of the commodity, the close contact with the movie stars in this process is stressed in the marketing policy. So the doll's magic might be not just be sympathetic (they resemble the stars)—but also contagious—the stars themselves did hold these toys in their hands and appreciated them.

Notes

1. With these words, the distribution company Spin Master Toys promoted the product of Bollywood Legends Cooperation Limited in the UK. For more, see http://www.femalefirst.co.uk/bollywood/ Hrithik+Roshan-32315.html (accessed on 5 December 2013).
2. Hrithik's father, Rakesh Roshan, already promoted his movie *Koi Mil Gaya* (2003) with a doll of the alien, Jadoo.
3. I want to thank Shameen Jivraj (entrepreneur), Beth Watkins, Paige Wilson, and Mabel Baumgarten (doll artists) for their kind cooperation and support.
4. The term 'Dollywood' has already been used in 1986 to name the theme park of American country singer, Dolly Parton. But the same notion is also applied in a different context for the intersection of cinema and puppetry; between 1952 and 1968 a productive doll-based film industry flourished in Holland that exported movies all over Europe. I want to thank Monia Acciari for information on this early 'Dollywood' from Holland; for more, see also Joop Geesink's Dollywood tribute site', available at http://www.dutch-vintage-animation.org/index.php/ en/32-home-page/36-joop-geesinks-dollywood-tribute-site-homepage-uk (accessed on 5 December 2013).
5. Here, 'Mini' derives from 'miniature' describing something tiny. Mini can be found in South Asian contexts as a real female name (short for 'Meenakshi' or 'Meena'). Film director Kabir Khan's wife, the famous actress and TV host Mini Mathur, did not change her name to Mini Khan.
6. No information could be found on the Indian reception of this product. Among the doll-playing film buffs, I could not find any South Asians.
7. Amit Rai (2008: 271) reminds us of Deleuze's 'warning about representational thought' which is constrained 'within the narrow range of analogy, contradiction, identity, and sameness. Such an idealization values consciousness as product over the intensive processes that constitute an ecology of sensation.'
8. Spin Master Toys; see Note 1.
9. These categories do not exist in isolation, several combinations can be found, and often media careers are a progression from a realistic perspective to, finally, a ludic engagement (Liebes 1996).

10. Certainly, doll play also includes the aesthetic dimension: fans praise the extraordinary aesthetic quality of the SRK doll in contrast to the other Bollywood Legend figures, or they document the making of their art and proudly present the various stages of their productions.

11. In this context, think of Pygmalion, the Golem, Pinocchio, and so on. Related to this are narratives about avatars inspired by computer games.

12. A movie inspired by a Hollywood horror picture *Child's Play* (Dir. Tom Holland, 1988) or one of its several sequels.

13. Scholars studying Indian culture via Bollywood are often confronted with the problem of multiple cultural transfers; also, this movie is a remake of a Hollywood movie. The process of adoption includes a typical style of Indianization that makes such hybrid products especially interesting. But it is important to keep in mind that *Papi Gudia* flopped in India.

14. 'Ra.One* was perhaps the first organized 360-degree campaign for an Indian film and had more than 25 brands associating themselves with the film in various capacities.' For more, see the Ernst & Young article 'Film Industry in India: New Horizons', available at http://indiainbusiness.nic.in/newdesign/upload/news/New_Horizons_Final.pdf (accessed on 5 December 2013).

15. Srinivas (2009) stresses the fact that fan groups want to exert control over their stars.

16. But because of the essential combination with photography, the digital performances analysed have more in common with picture storytelling than with puppetry.

17. It thus allows for shifting gender perspectives, thereby blurring the distinctions between male and female gaze.

18. The Bollywood Legends have been presented with these words on a Priyanka Chopra fansite; see http://www.liveindia.com/priyanka/newsf.html (accessed on 4 December 2013). Journalistic articles about the dolls get suggestive headlines such as 'Bollywood Legends in Your Bedroom'; moreover, an article published by *Oneindia*, available at http://entertainment.oneindia.in/bollywood/features/2006/spin-master-toys-280706.html (accessed on 5 December 2013) reflects a similar trend.

19. In another instance, a doll serves as the initial stimulus of the plot. In *Muqaddar ka Sikandar* (Dir. Prakash Mehra, 1978), an expensive doll symbolizes class differences.

20. The Bollywood Legends project and the movie *Kal Ho Naa Ho* were developed during the same period; the dolls were developed from 2002 until 2006. In 2003, the movie had already been released.

21. Before the launch of her personal doll, Katrina Kaif walked the ramp to present Mattel in 2009 on the occasion of the 50th anniversary of the Barbie doll at the Lakme Fashion Week.

22. For the Katrina Barbie advertisement, see http://www.youtube.com/watch?v=y4W5U56FVtU; for the making of this advertisement, see http://www.youtube.com/watch?v=_4zDjLai634 (both accessed on 5 December 2013).

23. The advertisement includes a game of luck in which children could win a chance to meet with Katrina Kaif.

24. Such comments can be found on YouTube.

25. Generally, criticism on the Barbie doll concentrates on health issues and blames the doll for the spread of bulimia. The Barbie doll is also a target of feminist campaigns which criticize it as a highly problematic role model. Even the animation movie *Toy Story 3* (Dir. Lee Unkrich, 2010) contains a parody of the gender roles of Barbie and Ken.

26. In 2012, 'Barbie's global sales declined 3 per cent to an estimated $1.3 billion worldwide. In the US she is doing even worse. Barbie's domestic sales have dropped a stunning 50 per cent since 2000 [...]. Barbie now represents 20 per cent of Mattel's $6.4 billion in revenues versus 30 per cent ten years ago' (Brown 2013).

27. The last one—Aamina—is a rag doll completely different from Barbie dolls. All these dolls are often described in the press as 'Barbies in a Burqa'. Aamina can recite essential Quranic words and sing an Islamic version of *Twinkle twinkle little star*. The Iranian doll siblings, Dara and Sara, are products of state-sponsored Islamic enterprise—like the Iranian surrogate Zam Zam Cola. Sometimes, Barbie critique is anti-Semitist, stressing that Ruth Handler (1916–2002), the inventor of the doll, was Jew.

28. I am very grateful to Shameen Jivraj for giving me an extensive and very impressive telephonic interview on 19 July 2010 and even provided helpful feedback on the chapter.

29. Edna Bonacich (1973) prominently includes East African Indians in her theory of 'middleman-minorities'. Shameen Jivraj grew up as a multilingual, learning English, Swahili, and Gujarati. Gujarati traders had old contacts with Africa that intensified at the end of the nineteenth century. The Jivraj family belongs to the Ismaili community and is related to the high-caste Lohana Hindus. Both communities originate from Sindh. For more information, see also http://jivraj.org/Life.htm (accessed on 5 December 2013). Gijsbert Oonk (2004: 17) mentions the importance of Hindi films for the third generation (born between

1960 and 2000) of East African Hindu Lohanas, who do not speak Hindi at all.

30. The selection of stars has also been influenced by *Kabhi Khushi Kabhie Gham…*, but Jivraj approached other stars as well, and Kareena Kapoor particularly was not ready to take the risk.

31. Spin Master Toys, see Note 1.

32. Spin Master Toys, see Note 1.

33. On Amazon, the SRK doll costs £14.99; whereas Kajol, Priyanka, Hrithik dolls cost only £8.99. India Store which is located in Berlin offers the SRK doll at about €70.

34. See an article published on mid-day.com in 2009, available at http://www.mid-day.com/news/2009/mar/140309-Aamir-Khan-Ghajini-dolls-Sanjay-Singhania-Birthday-boy.htm (accessed on 5 December 2013).

35. Somebody else also produces Bollywood-inspired 'doll videos'—more stills with a soundtrack, but here the Bollywood Legends are not used. This project is named Novela Bollywood Doll Story Mumbai Mambo. The producer describes it thus: 'Whereas most people are happy renting videos, I create my own stories; build my own sets; cast my own actors. Unfortunately I don't have the multi-million-dollar budgets and can't afford the big-name stars. In fact, I can't afford any actors. So I use dolls. All my fiction unfold on stages that are 1/6 scale. Some people might call these dioramas, I call them my world.' For more, see the About Us page for Jatman Productions, available at http://www.youtube.com/user/JatmanProductions/about (accessed on 5 December 2013).

36. In local Catholicism, in Vienna, a practice analogous to the Travelling Khan can be found, a so-called Migrant Madonna that is transferred from one household to the other. Even in this context, online reports from the participants are posted on a website. This modern religious ritual had a predecessor, a Migrant Little Jesus, that was accompanied by a diary. The creative possibilities with the SRK doll are certainly greater and it is not its primary task to reinforce certain values or create a devotional atmosphere, but to bring in fun and entertainment. Still these practices have a common social function, which is to strengthen social ties.

37. Bollywood blogger and doll enthusiast Beth Watkins, who has an academic background like many of the elite fans, has been acknowledged as an expert by the *Wall Street Journal* where she writes a column on Indian cinema.

38. Personal photograph taken by Elke Mader (left) and Bernhard Fuchs (right) in 2007.

39. Personal photograph taken by Bernhard Fuchs in 2007.
40. With digitization, virtual performance became a telos of popular culture. Even in the context of live performances like Bollywood flashmobs, online visibility is at the centre of the event.
41. An SRK doll tribute photograph taken by Paige Wilson @breakingfreeofbox. The image has been reproduced with the kind permission of Paige Wilson.
42. The damage of the original packaging is a sacrilege for collectors, especially when the production has been stopped. The item's value can raise enormously if it is still in mint condition.
43. This inspiration became obvious to her only later, through reflection inspired by our online conversation. Following this, she immediately depicted SRK reading a miniature Dare Wright book.
44. For more, see, 'Breaking Free of the Box (SRK doll Tributes by Paige Wilson)', on the About Us page, available at http://www.youtube.com/user/mphrw3/about (accessed on 5 December 2013).
45. Quotes have been taken from online communication via email and messages on YouTube.
46. Quote has been taken from an article published by AsianOutlook.com, available at http://www.asianoutlook.com/aoforum/showthread.php?t=6085 (accessed on 5 December 2013).
47. My own doll has the same shortcoming. But obviously there has been only one production. I am curious how these differences occurred. Here, Paige Wilson makes a comparison between the doll's quality and SRK's personality. Jokingly, she cites Gauri Khan's statement about the schizophrenic character of her husband.
48. For more, see http://ravensforest.wordpress.com/taskforest/ (accessed on 5 December 2013).
49. Also, superstar Salman Khan is associated with the tiger in fan art.
50. In this chapter, Mabel Baumgarten allowed me to include the episode 'Murderous Wedding'. She commented that she knew that 'holding hands' would not be acceptable in an Indian context, but Rohan would be totally westernized.
51. In this context, again the problematic of Mattel's representations of India becomes obvious, reminding us of Radha S. Hedge's (2001) essay in a feminist media journal, where she narrates an anecdote about her daughter's disappointment over the sari-clad Roopvati who would be useless as she could not date Ken or anybody else; she simply could not be integrated into the leisure activities of her dolls.
52. Images have been reproduced with the kind permission of Mabel Baumgarten; for more see https://ravensforest.wordpress.com/taskforest/ (accessed on 13 August 2015).

References

Ahmed, Ashwin. 2008. 'Bollywood's Phoren Fan-brigade', *Times of India*, 1 June, available at http://timesofindia.indiatimes.com/home/sunday-toi/special-report/Bollywoods-phoren-fan-brigade/articleshow/3089528.cms?referral=PM (accessed on 5 December 2008).

Allinson, Anne. 2000. 'A Challenge to Hollywood? Japanese Character Goods Hit the US', *Japanese Studies*, 20 (1): 67–88.

Appadurai, Arjun. 1996. *Modernity at Large: Cultural Dimensions of Globalization*. Minneapolis and London: Minnesota University Press.

Bonacich, Edna. 1973. 'A Theory of Middleman Minorities', *American Sociological Reviews*, 38 (5): 583–94.

Booth, Paul. 2010. *Digital Fandom: New Media Studies*. New York and London: Peter Lang.

Brown, Abram. 2013. 'Life after Barbie: Why Mattel Isn't Scared of iPads and Video Games', *Forbes India*, 6 May, available at http://www.forbes.com/sites/abrambrown/2013/04/17/mattels-life-after-barbie-inside-the-new-toys-from-the-worlds-largest-toymaker/ (accessed on 5 December 2013).

Chin, Elizabeth. 2008. 'Ethnically Correct Dolls: Toying with the Race Industry', *American Anthropologist*, 101 (2): 305–21.

DasGupta, Sayantani. 2006. 'Being John Malkovich: Truth, Imagination, and Story in Medicine', *Literature and Medicine*, 25 (2): 439–62.

Ducille, Ann. 2003. 'Black Barbie and the Deep Play of Difference', in Amelia Jones (ed.), *The Feminism and Visual Cultures Reader*, pp. 337–48. New York: Routledge, available at http://www4.ncsu.edu/~mseth2/com417s12/readings/ducille.pdf (accessed on 5 December 2013).

Dudrah, Rajinder. 2010. 'Haptic Urban Ethnoscapes: Representation, Diasporic Media and Urban Cultural Landscapes', *Journal of Media Practice*, 11 (1): 31–45.

————. 2011. *Bollywood Travels: Culture, Diaspora and Border Crossings in Popular Hindi Cinema*. London: Routledge.

Fuad, Omar. 2006a. 'Bollywood Legends in Your Bedroom', *Oneindia*, 28 July, available at http://entertainment.oneindia.in/bollywood/features/2006/spin-master-toys-280706.html (accessed on 5 December 2013).

————. 2006b. 'Bollywood Dolls for £24.99', *Oneindia*, 27 July, available at http://entertainment.oneindia.in/bollywood/news/2006/bollywood-dolls-270706.html (accessed on 5 December 2013).

————. 2006c. 'Hrithik and Kajol Launch Miniature Dolls among Great Fanfare', available at http://archive.is/shngh (accessed on 5 December 2013).

Grewal, Inderpal. 1999. 'Travelling Barbie: Indian Transnationality and New Consumer Subjects', *Positions: East Asia Cultures Critique*, 7 (3): 799–826.

Hegde, Radha S. 2001. 'Global Makeovers and Maneuvers: Barbie's Presence in India', *Feminist Media Studies*, 1 (1): 129–33.

Iwabuchi, Koichi. 1998. 'Marketing "Japan": Japanese Cultural Presence under a Global Gaze', *Japanese Studies*, 18 (2): 165–80.

Jenkins, Henry. 2006. *Fans, Bloggers and Gamers: Exploring Participatory Culture*. New York: New York University Press.

———. 2010. 'Transmedia Storytelling and Entertainment: An Annotated Syllabus', *Journal of Media & Cultural Studies*, 24 (6): 943–58.

Liebes, Tamar. 1996. 'Notes on the Struggle to Define Involvement in Television Viewing', in James Hay, Lawrence Grossberg, and Ellen Wartella (eds), *The Audience and Its Landscape*, pp. 177–86. Boulder, Colorado and Oxford: Westview Press.

Mader, Elke. 2011. 'Stars in Your Eyes: Ritual Encounters with Shah Rukh Khan in Europe', in Axel Michaels (ed.), *Ritual Dynamics and the Science of Ritual*, vol. 4, Reflexivity, Media and Visuality, pp. 463–84. Wiesbaden: Harrassowitz.

Mader, Elke and Philipp Budka. 2009. 'Shah Rukh Khan @ Berlinale. Bollywood Fans im Kontext Medienanthropologischer Forschung', in Claus Tieber (ed.), *Fokus Bollywood: Indisches Kino in Wissenschaftlichen Diskursen*, pp. 117–31. Münster: LIT Verlag.

Magee, Carol. 2005. 'Forever in Kente: Ghanian Barbie and the Fashioning of Identity', *Social Identities*, 11 (6): 589–606.

Marcus, George E. and Erkan Saka. 2006: 'Assemblage', *Theory Culture Society*, 23: 101–9.

Mitchell, W.J.T. 1986. *Iconology: Image, Text, Ideology*. Chicago: University of Chicago Press.

Oonk, Gijsbert. 2004. 'The Changing Culture of the Hindu Lohana Community in East Africa', *Contemporary South Asia*, 13 (1): 7–23.

Pinney, Christopher. 2008. *Photos of the Gods: The Printed Image and Political Struggle in India*. London: Reaktion Books.

Rai, Amit. 2008. 'On the Media Assemblage of Bollywood: Time and Sensation in Globalizing India', in Rajinder Dudrah and Jigna Desai (eds), *The Bollywood Reader*, pp. 264–75. Maidenhead and New York: Open University Press.

———. 2009. *Untimely Bollywood: Globalization and India's New Media Assemblage*. Durham and London: Duke University Press.

Rajadhyaksha, Ashish. 2003. 'The "Bollywoodization" of the Indian Cinema: Cultural Nationalism in a Global Arena', *Inter-Asia Cultural Studies*, 4 (1): 25–39.

Ram, Uri. 2004. 'Glocommodification: How the Global Consumes the Local: McDonald's in Israel', *Current Sociology*, 52 (1): 11–31.

Ramasubramanian, Srividya and Mary Beth Oliver. 2003. 'Portrayals of Sexual Violence in Popular Hindi Films, 1997–99', *Sex Roles*, 48 (7–8): 327–36.

Robertson, Roland. 1994. 'Globalisation or Glocalisation?', *Journal of International Communication*, 1 (1): 33–52.

Sivasankaran, Sreekala. 2010. 'Akhyan: Masks, Puppets & Picture Showmen Traditions of India: An Introduction', in *Akhyan: A Celebration of Masks, Puppets and Picture Showmen Traditions of India*, pp. 9–11 (brochure presented by the Indira Gandhi National Council for the Arts and Sangeet Natak Akademi, available at http://www.ignca.nic.in/PDF_data/aakhyan_brochure.pdf [accessed on 5 December 2013]).

Srinivas, S.V. 2009. *Megastar: Chiranjeevi and Tamil Cinema after N.T. Rama Rao*. New Delhi: Oxford University Press.

Terrebonne, Renée. 2008. 'Fulla, the Veiled Barbie: An Analysis of Cultural Imperialism and Agency', *MAI Review*, no. 2, available at http://www.review.mai.ac.nz (accessed on 5 December 2013).

Yaqin, Amina. 2007. 'Islamic Barbie: The Politics of Gender and Performativity', *Fashion Theory*, 11 (2–3): 173–88.

Filmography

Being John Malkovich. Dir. Spike Jonze. Astralwerks, 1999.
Child's Play. Dir. Tom Holland. United Artists, 1988.
Dilwale Dulhania Le Jayenge. Dir. Aditya Chopra. Yash Raj Films, 1995.
Don 2. Dir. Farhan Akhtar. Excel Entertainment, 2011.
Ghajini. Dir. A.R. Murugadoss. Geetha Arts, 2008.
Jab Jab Phool Khilen. Dir. Suraj Prakash. Lime Light, 1965.
Kabhi Khushi Kabhie Gham.... Dir. Karan Johar. Dharma Productions, 2001.
Kal Ho Naa Ho. Dirs Nikhil Advani and Ron Reid Jr. Dharma Productions, 2003.
Koi Mil Gaya. Dir. Rakesh Roshan. Film Kraft, 2003.
Muqaddar ka Sikandar. Dir. Prakash Mehra. Prakash Mehra Productions, 1978.
My Name Is Khan. Dir. Karan Johar. Dharma Productions, 2010.

Om Shanti Om. Dir. Farah Khan. Red Chillies Entertainment, 2007.

Paheli. Dir. Amol Palekar. Red Chillies Entertainment, 2005.

Papi Gudia. Dir. Lawrence D'Souza. Aum Films, 1996.

Purab aur Paschim. Dir. Manoj Kumar. V.I.P. Films, 1970.

Ra.One. Dir. Anubhav Sinha. Red Chillies Entertainment, 2011.

Swades: We, the People. Dir. Ashutosh Gowariker. UTV Motion Pictures, 2004.

Toy Story 3. Dir. Lee Unkrich. Pixar and Walt Disney, 2010.

Harlequining Shah Rukh Khan through Media 'Patches'

Composing the Global Image of an Indian Star in the Italian Mediascape

MONIA ACCIARI

This chapter aims to collect and stitch together information on Shah Rukh Khan (henceforth SRK) in the mediascape of Italy and to compose a coherent body of information to illustrate the global and local appeal of SRK. Homi Bhabha's theory of a 'third space', as a space of enunciation, provides an intellectual abode to accommodate media patches into a unique body of knowledge—enunciation—which articulates the perception of SRK and Bollywood in Italy. This study wishes to provide an alternative point of view, fitting in with the wider analyses of SRK as a global phenomenon, produced by international mobilization and interconnectivity.

The King of Bollywood is a comedy directed by Piyush Jha (2004), which blatantly portrays the rise and decline of a Bollywood superstar. Om Puri plays the role of the flamboyant and kitsch celebrity, Karan Kumar, also known as K.K. Interestingly and coincidently, I found myself drawn to the stories, narrated through a diverse range of shooting techniques (including the hidden camera's angle), which unveil the life of a star from behind the scene. Curiously, the nickname of the protagonist is K.K., which I read as a lucrative way to speculate on the growing, global resonance of SRK (also known as King Khan, in short, K.K.) on and off cinematic screens.

The purpose of this preamble is to put into perspective the subject of this investigation, SRK, and the pathways undertaken to access the firmament of a considerably weighty system within Bollywood—the star system. In particular, this chapter will observe the way Italy has spoken about SRK, thereby contributing to his naming as King Khan. If SRK is the king of the contemporary Bollywood, how has he constructed his kingdom? Of which territory is he now the king? To explore his global definition through an Italian point of view, I intend to provide an account of, and expand on, how the diverse media within Italy have spoken about this Indian star, and how these opinions have collectively contributed to the comprehension of SRK as harlequinesque: a visual metaphor for assorted behavioural and aesthetic traits composed together to form a meaningful entity. By charting out the presence of SRK on diverse communication platforms (here defined as 'patches') such as television, cinema, festivals, magazines, and last but not least the multitude of blogs and forums, with a specific analysis of the forum Bollywood Italia, the aim is to explain how this patchy, almost harlequinesque and inhomogeneous portrait of SRK is an important cluster within a large debate on his persona. The assemblage of the diverse voices from the different media sources are analysed as being metaphors for the colourful and meaningful patches of an evocative composition of SRK across a global panorama. The figure of Harlequin, the iconic and histrionic character of the Goldoniana *commedia dell'arte*,[1] is characterized by agility and tremendous elasticity. SRK's globetrotting and his extraordinary ubiquitous presence at numerous festivals, shooting locations, and on television programmes, magazine interviews, and journal covers, to name a few, could be regarded as tremendous Harlequinesque performances. Thus, it is essential to understand how Italy has contributed to the global signification and construction of the SRK persona; and is SRK the new Harlequin from India? This chapter will employ a textual approach to trace and collate some of the media evidence that composes SRK's global kingdom.

Framing the Kingdom

The debate in which this chapter intends to offer a contribution, regards the ways this star, the face of contemporary Bollywood in the world, is part of a large cosmopolitan popular culture which comprises a great variety of expression. The aim here is to show evidence of its presence in Italy describing how a small cluster of media attention has contributed to a greater portrayal of this star, apart from defining his kingdom and his space. As Heidegger (1969) pointed out, our experience of the world is undeniably spatial. It is throughout an experience concerning the mobilization of bodies and distances. At the same time, it also concerns the transformation of space into mental categories, which we use to organize our relationships with others; objects are touched only to be converted into signifying forms. Importantly, Homi Bhabha (2004) offers a poignant understanding of space, wherein he stresses that interdependence as well as the condition of being touched establish a system of meanings constructed into what he calls the 'third space of enunciation' (Bhabha 2006). The question here is: How is SRK's aura of global star being constructed? Would it be possible to theorize a space of enunciation for this global star within the Italian panorama?

Homi Bhabha's seminal essay 'Cultural Diversity and Cultural Differences' (2006) provides an excellent theoretical framework to investigate how all cultural systems and statements of a specific cultural happening are constructed in what he calls the 'third space of enunciation'. Through Homi Bhabha's framework, I intend to observe how the global appeal of the Indian star, SRK, is constructed within the Italian panorama. Homi Bhabha (2006) provides a cultural analysis and a key term to read the poles of cultural identity by writing about a space within which cultural identities themselves are transformed. My analysis of SRK across the Italian mediascape seeks to show and take into account the proximity of the Bollywood icon, with the distinctive personality of the Italian *commedia dell'arte* Harlequin, and to fix the lines of common recognizable traits.

Homi Bhabha's notion of the 'third space of enunciation' offers a theoretical ground to unfold on the threshold of cultural identities. Bhabha (2006) begins by considering that the revision of history, with its cultural and social baggage and critical theories, rests on the notion of cultural difference rather than on cultural diversity. Cultural diversity, he explains, is an epistemological object, an object which implies empirical knowledge, whereas cultural difference informs the process of enunciation of culture as knowledgeable, authoritative, and adequate to the construction of systems for cultural identification. While cultural diversity consists of the recognition of contents and costumes of a given culture in the era of exchange and multiculturalism, cultural difference evokes pre-given cultural forces problematizing the division of past and present, and tradition and modernity. This division of past and present undermines our common sense of homogenization as being the effect of symbols or icons, thus questioning the sense of fixed knowledge.

In this light it is necessary to re-think the common perception of identity in cultural theory. Bhabha (2004) highlights a passage from Fanon's text, who writes about the way culture involves a political and cultural struggle; the author superbly described it as 'the zone of occult intangibility where the people dwell' (Fanon 1967: 168). This idea, widely elaborated and adopted by Bhabha, perfectly encapsulates the stance to form a critique to values and aesthetics that are endorsed by the overall totality of cultures.

Cultures, as Bhabha (2006) reminds us, are never unitary in themselves, nor merely dualistic in relation of self to other; this is a dichotomy that happens in diverse cultural texts, such as literary, visual, and filmic as discussed further on. These systems of meanings cannot be satisfactory in themselves because the act of cultural enunciation—the place of utterance—is crossed by different writings or expressions. It is this 'difference' in languages that is crucial to the production of meaning and, at the same time, ensures that meanings are never simply mimetic or obvious. The difference that (in)forms any cultural action is dramatized by the disjuncture between the subject and object of a proposition—énoncé—and the subject of enunciation which is not represented or expressed straightforwardly within a text. However, its discursive embeddedness and its cultural position are acknowledged with reference to the present time and to a specific space. The production of meanings, then, is formed by a specific mobilization, which sees these two places—subject of enunciation, and subject of preposition—pass through what Bhabha (2004) calls the 'third space', which represents both the condition of any kind of language (written and visual) and the specific implication of utterance in a performative strategy.

The third space (here the imaginary kingdom of King Khan) makes the structure of meanings and references an ambivalent process. However, offering clarification on the way cultural statements and systems are contradictory and ambivalent, can allow us to question the intrinsic originality or authenticity of a given culture, even when so-called empirical evidence is used to make such claims. The third space constitutes the conditions of enunciations, guaranteeing that the meaning of the symbols of a given culture have no elemental unity or fixity, reinstating that every sign can be appropriated, translated, and re-historicized and be read anew. In this light, the image of Harlequin is pivotal. The axiom that sees Harlequin not as comparison, but as a moving metaphor to explain the complexities of SRK within the Italian mediascape defines Harlequin as a cultural statement—or rather a space of enunciation—that depicts SRK as transcending empirical and historical instances. The figure of SRK, as contextualized within a moment of liberatory cultural movement (across media), provides a wide reading of Bollywood cinema against cultural impositions. He is the negotiator and translates his cultural identities in a discontinuous and intertextual temporality and spatiality of cultural difference.

Also, as Sobchack (1994: 45), explains: Cinematic and electronic screens differently demand and shape our 'presence' to the world and our representation in it. Each differently and objectively alters our subjectivity while each invites our complicity in formulating space, time, and bodily investment as significant personal and social experience.

SRK is the very principle of 'dialectic reorganization', and the construction of his kingdom through visual texts translated into modern Western forms of information, media, and languages are the preambles of a cultural and historical dimension of a 'third space of enunciation'. The latter is a precondition for the articulation of cultural difference (Bhabha 2006), which are here analysed as media patches.

Patch One: An Overview of Bollywood in Italy

The rich text on SRK compiled by Mushtaq Shiekh (2007) is an excellent synthesis which shows the evolution of this star from his infancy to his consecration as a Bollywood star, viewed through the rich panorama of media platforms. It is worth reminding ourselves here of Menarini's observation on the crisis of cinematographic culture and its privileged screen—the silver canvas. The author writes that cinematographic culture appears to be in crisis, less people go to the cinema, critics have gained authority, cinephilia has lost its temples (cineclub, cultural associations) of aggregation, and new technologies are in constant progress (Menarini 2012). Within this changed communicational panorama, there are blogs and web portals that have now become essential tools for the divulgation of cinema and its apparatus (Menarini 2012). Menarini's affirmation provides a context to the consideration of Bollywood and its stars in Italy. These films are not yet a permanent part of the entertainment of Italy. The awareness of this industry and its culture within Italy is mostly informed through other screens. Bollywood films and SRK, despite having a vast repository in other kinds of media from Internet sites and blogs to mobile ringtones and television programming, are merely known via alternative dissemination.

A more detailed study on the arrival of Bollywood in Italy (Acciari 2011) has assessed that the Indian history of European colonization has not criss-crossed Italy, with which a wider understating of a cultural phenomenon like Bollywood could be easily associated. A screen-based investigation on the use of Indian film-culture aesthetics on the screens of Italy and specifically on television and cinema has highlighted that Italy did not take part in the Bollywood mania (Le Guellec 2006) of the 1990s which had affected the rest of Europe. Several countries in Europe were ready to welcome a new cinematographic wave from abroad, but Italy with a faltering step moved warily. Ten years after the boom of Bollywood internationally, Italy began, in 2004, to observe the effect of the internationalization of this industry, hence, it stepped out from its indolent cultural exclusivism. Web activities began mushrooming, together with television screenings of dubbed and re-edited Bollywood films for the local audience.

Patch Two: Online Reception and Discussion

Fervent online activities, particularly blogospheres and forums, provide room for thinking about how a star of a gigantic cinematographic industry has penetrated the mediascape of Italy. An early study on blogs conducted by Keren (2006: 14) points out that these online spaces are characterized by melancholy: 'The politics of blogosphere is melancholic not because it lacks joy, triumph, and exultation, but because when these emotions, like any other feelings, thoughts, or activities are present, their relation to real life is incidental … it replaces action by talk.' Keren's point of view perfectly encapsulates the emotional infrastructure of blogs dedicated to Bollywood cinema in Italy, wherein the presence of these films is scarce or re-adapted by the Italian entertainment industry through a series of cuts and amends which have entirely transformed the narrative body of these films (Acciari 2011).

These same feelings seem to be behind the formation of blogs on Bollywood stars and cinema, compensating for the scarcity of this industry in Italy. For this reason, and encouraged by Ananda Mitra's article 'Bollyweb: Search for Bollywood on the Web and See What Happens!' (2008: 268) I began a random research on the Internet, which unlocked dense online writings on Bollywood in Italy. Primarily Bollywood Italia, a forum of over 150 members, came into view. This space brings together different generations of Italians, Indian-Italians, and a growing number of non-EU or Indian fans. While interviewing the creator of this blog, seeking information on its conception, the creator mentioned: 'Currently the forum has exceeded 120 members, and there are new registrations monthly. People who come to the forum have an interest in information, advice and also ask for initiatives in Italy, including screenings, performances, magazines and more' (translated from the original conversation held in Italian between the author and Rita Sotgiu, the creator of Bollywood Italia).

The growing attention given by the mainstream media on the divulgation of Bollywood and its stars on the web raises questions regarding the cultural and global implications of forums as well as blogs in the success of this operation. Questions such as the following need to be answered: Can SRK be considered as a global icon when the vast majority of people are only exposed to selected news about him posted by 'trusted' virtual figures? Furthermore, in what way is this virtual space supporting an understanding of SRK as a global icon?

In a way similar to what happens with magazines, these kinds of spaces employ informal language and personal approaches brought in by each follower and contributor, forming a small yet significant piece of a bigger global collage on SRK. The film-viewing practices of users, as suggested by some of their comments, are scanned by the linguistic and regional milieu, with the pleasure of watching a Bollywood film integrally and without any cut; or, filtered by the knowledge or affiliation with India and Indian culture that provides a flavour to the engagement with this cinema wherein SRK is at the core of their debates.

Bollywood Italia consists of a wide selection of information divided into topics among which the following were selected for being the most discussed and were considered central to this forum: a) 'Yeh Dosti' (fans have some fun talking about Bollywood), b) 'Good Old Times' (is a discussion of films of the 1950s, 1960s, and 1970s), c) 'The Stars of Bollywood Cinema'; the folder on SRK is a rich collection of fan paraphernalia from SRK as a baby to images of the actor in the magazine Hello! to a series of collages from different films in which the star has performed.

SRK's folder consists of a series of links to his filmography, to audio files of songs from films in which he was the hero, and links to YouTube video dances from his films. In addition, a collection of various images of SRK which nostalgically began with his infancy, moving on to more contemporary images of his life as father, husband, and star are part of a large, shared album. Discussions regarding his films and his physical appearance fill the pages of this blog producing an arena of desire and becoming a 'metaphysical experience' (Dyer 1998: 45).

As corroborated by Thomas Harris (1999: 40), 'publicity methods show that the screen star is known to his or her potential audience not only through film roles but also through fan magazines, national magazines, radio, television, and newspapers.' The series of press cuttings and the assortment of images taken from film clips and pictures of the actor's personal life create within the Italian panorama an erratic picture puzzle of this star which is the result of a media collage, thus rendering SRK clearly intelligible on the cinematic canvas and other mediascapes of Italy. References to the stars, their lives, and their performances are amateur collections of pictures mostly gathered from foreign magazines and newspapers. In addition, to prolong the experience of admiring their stars, a series of downloadable images, to serve as wallpaper, are part of this online market of dreams. Mitra (2008: 277) in her analysis of Bollywood on the web suggests the following: 'This interconnection between pages, mostly personal and some institutional maintained and accessed by people across the globe, makes Bollyweb global and provides an opportunity for the real life industry to find a way of leveraging its global virtual presence.'

Together with Bollywood Italia, which is the largest online platform to discuss and approach Bollywood cinema in Italy, it is important to also mention three significant blogs. First, *Tutti Pazzi Per* Shah Rukh Khan[2] (literally translated from Italian as 'all crazy for Shah Rukh Khan') is a blog crammed with posts on diverse appearances and activities of the star. Second, the well-informed (and informing) Cine Hindi[3] with a selection of news about Bollywood and with two sub-pages that deserve attention such as Break Hindi Cinema,[4] and third, the blog Film Cine Hindi[5] hosts the latest news of Bollywood and information about its success among the Italian audience. It is coherently organized through different menus, and committed to the divulgation—almost in a journalistic and pragmatic manner—of these films and stars for the 'Bollywood-starved' audience of Italy. The content of each menu is organized through topics and links, which extensively and informatively invigorate the attention that the world projects on this industry. Filmcinehindi.blogspot.com is a well-informed and informing blog compiled in multiple languages. As stated within the blog, it is not for profit and is run by enthusiasts of Indian cinema, who comprehensively aim to connect with the rest of the globe by signalling events and appearances of films and stars globally. Although it is mentioned that this blog is not to be considered as an editorial product, it is an extensive compilation of film reviews, interviews, and videos for film buffs.

Also, facebook has a dedicated page called 'Shah Rukh Khan Italy'. Of the blogs mentioned, the first is primarily dedicated to SRK and collects an unsorted succession of images ranging from SRK's presence within Italian Bollywood magazines to his many appearances at the Rome Film Festival and includes videos as well of his commitment to promote the Bollywood industry.

The examples shown here—the forum and the blogs—are extracts of a larger global online narrative. The forum Bollywood Italia, which dedicates an entire section to debate on the SRK persona through multiple perspectives, also connects with the trend that sees this star as spokesman for an invigorated Bollywood culture. As Mitra suggests, the connotation of Bollywood as global cinema is not only due to the generous South Asian diasporic incidence worldwide, but it is also due to the mammoth presence of this industry—in different forms—on the World Wide Web, which echoes fame constantly.

A blog is an enunciation of desires and interests, and the five key reasons to blog as synthesized by Nardi et al. (2004: 43) are to provide: 'commentary and opinions; expressing deeply felt emotions; articulating ideas through writing; and forming and maintaining community forums.' Bollywood Italia perfectly provides a place to think about these five activities in which SRK is commented, discussed across links, and also enclosed and articulated within folders of images and desires. Blogospheres, apart from providing arenas for emancipation, together with nostalgic comments of users that highlight the scarce articulation of Bollywood within the Italian contexts, are indeed personal and cultural arenas in which the language of the Internet and the desire for greater visibility articulate the narrative of these online spaces. Within this global process of enunciation, SRK is the 'face of a glittering new India' as well as a 'modern day God' (Ganti 2012: 3). The popularity of SRK in Italy arrived following an already global and established success. As presented by a series of magazine articles (Malani 2010; Morgoglione 2010; Weisberg 2010),

SRK has travelled across the globe for months to promote his film *My Name Is Khan* (*MNIK*, Dir. Karan Johar, 2010), and this tireless journey has reinvigorated his popularity among a larger audience. The attention given to SRK by the media has framed the actor as the golden ring of a complex chain of global media interdependences. This position allows the star's iconicity to be viewed, known, and accepted by innumerable countries in the world. The web activity in Italy concerning the rise of this industry, stages Khan's persona as chameleonic, strong, and crucial, and also accessible by his audience internationally. Italy works and positively employs the language of new media, on the one hand, to melancholically (Acciari 2011) compensate for the lack of these films on the cinematic screen and, on the other hand, to unlock the dialogue between this industry and the entertainment circuits of Italy.

Patch Three: Bollywood Magazine

In order to further introduce Bollywood cinema within the entertainment offers of Italy, the magazine *Bollywood Magazine*, established in 2010 and edited by John Martin Thomas, has found a small niche of reception wherein the first issue was dedicated to SRK. His presence on the cover page of the journal instantly suggests that in the world, his persona is the current 'face of Bollywood'.

Mimicking the success of Indian cinema in almost every area of modern Indian life within the South Asian subcontinent and the diaspora communities abroad, the presence of *Bollywood Magazine* was necessary to construct the body of knowledge of popular Hindi cinema within the entertainment industry of Italy. *Bollywood Magazine*, mostly dedicated to the Italian audience (the magazine is written in Italian) and to a wide South Asian community, belongs to a group of magazines called 'star magazines' (Dwyer 2008) because their major preoccupation is to create a visual and textual narrative, consisting of photos and interviews with the stars of a specific industry. The narrative of this entertainment medium mostly consists of an assemblage of news about the lifestyle and appearance of stars worldwide with their luggage of families and events, together with the promotion of forthcoming films. In particular, the films *MNIK* together with *Ra.One* (Dir. Anubhav Sinha, 2011) were largely publicized through reportage and pictures of the male heroes, Rizwan and Ra.One, both played by SRK. The scope of this magazine was to highlight not only the films as new milestones among Bollywood films, but to also demonstrate that (particularly the film *MNIK* and the attention it received at the Rome Film Festival Premiere, discussed later) Italy was displaying the contemporary, evolving, and engaging face of this industry portrayed by its new icon SRK as the symbol of India being the new rising economic powerhouse (Ganti 2012).

The first issue of *Bollywood Magazine* appeared in April 2010, hosting the image of SRK, with the aim of actualizing what Ganti in an interview with Khan had suggested to be a change in attitude towards popular Hindi cinema: 'I believe this attitude will change, and I can say it with a lot of conviction, because I would also blame myself in being in that category say four or five years ago' (Ganti 2013: 2). The idea behind *Bollywood Magazine*, recently shipwrecked, was to publish a magazine that would have the features of notorious magazines like *Stardust* or *Filmfare* in order to increase awareness and to support other parallel events such as the broadcasting of Bollywood films on television; or, the landing of SRK at the Rome Film Festival and, throughout, gossiping about Bollywood stars and its industry largely neglected in Italy (Acciari 2011). The image of SRK on the cover of the first issue of *Bollywood Magazine* acts as a prophetic affirmation; popular Hindi cinema and SRK as the king of this expanding kingdom shift from being disdained to being celebrated, perfectly reflecting Bhabha's (2006) formation of a 'third space' as a 'space of enunciation'.

The magazine then, despite a trivial approach to the industry and its star, offers an important springboard to not only covering openings, and the social and cultural life of a film happening, but also weddings and parties and Hollywood stars associated with the Bollywood industry; the cover of the magazine stated: 'Hugh Jackman: *La star più contesa ai* Bollywood party' (translated from Italian as 'Hugh Jackman: The Most Contentious Star at the Bollywood Parties').

The narrative provides the reader with a glimpse of a world of luxury and glamour with events taking place in deluxe restaurants, exclusive sites, and expensive clubs. The writing style is intimate and friendly with a direct approach, often using direct speech. The interviews with Bollywood stars (such as the one with Amitabh and Abhishek Bachchan in the first issue) are written in first-person narrative, which is coherent with the rest of the narrative. Thus, the use of innuendo suggests that the direct approach is available for the reader to judge the lifestyle of the stars.

The short yet significant life of *Bollywood Magazine*, has been a resource for a small group of fans to follow the 'latest happenings' from the Bollywood industry.

Looking at this magazine allows us to reflect on the way magazines, despite being regarded as trash, reveal the creation of a space, or rather of an 'imagined community' of readers and consumers, that comes alive in the act of readership. Rather than being a trash platform (Dwyer 2008), this magazine strongly occupies an interstitial position in defining the globalization of SRK as a novel representative of Bollywood cinema; magazines are indeed part of the 'third space of enunciation' where stardom is constructed through multiple points of identification and mostly through the enunciation of fantasies. The Italian magazine is a part of what this chapter identifies as a cultural 'patch', which together with other media, particularly with online blogs and forums as discussed earlier, forms a cultural product in Italy as the main source of pleasure among larger platforms of communication. Its market of pleasure is centred on consumption, leisure, and mostly on fantasy; fantasy being the impetus for the acknowledgement and comprehension of SRK within the entertainment circuits of Italy.

Patch Four: *My Name Is Khan* at the Rome Film Festival

In 2007 the International Rome Film Festival endorsed the collaboration between Italy and India through the presence of Indian and Italian producers Yash Chopra and Riccardo Tozzi, with a co-production and co-distribution agreement that acknowledged the global uprising of the Bollywood film industry, which has since seen a series of collaborations. In 2010, the Rome Film Festival gave large space to this industry; this was partly due to the participation of SRK.

The epic story of Rizwan Khan (played by SRK) is a memorable love story, but also a story that critically condemns racial and religious discrimination in light of the events post 9/11 that hit the US and with it the rest of the world at a macrosocial and microsocial level. On 30 October 2010, the Roman Film Festival celebrated the promotion of Karan Johar's *MNIK* with a premiere of the film; SRK was the cultural broker and spokesman at this event.

Being part of the diverse crowd at this event, I could record his arrival and the atmosphere throughout was excited. Distinctive Hindi voices welcomed the Bollywood superstar with a '*Namaste Shah Rukh Khan Ji*', and a limited number of Italian fans clapped for the arrival of a hero, still new to them.

Memorably, the onset of SRK stepping onto the red carpet at the festival was introduced with a sequence of Bollywood choreographies performed by a local group of Bollywood dancers called the *Apsaras* Dance Group of Rome (name given in honour of the female spirit of the clouds and waters of Hindu and Buddhist mythology) headed by Roman dancer, Valentina Manduchi. The dances of Apsaras accompanied the Bollywood superstar during his passage to a cohort of journalists, photographers, and fans. SRK remained on the red carpet for a long time for a series of photographs, without exempting himself from the 'duties' of a star, indulging in photos of his Italian tour and signing autographs, being part of the fan memorabilia. His red carpet appearance was just the exciting beginning to his film presentation. SRK was later taken within the auditorium, at the Petrassi Room, for an interview with the Italian journalist Claudia Morgoglione, in the presence of a crowd of fans and followers. Morgoglione engaged SRK with a set of questions, which were followed by elaborate and friendly answers by the star who also drew links and showed his knowledge on Italian filmography and the entertainment industry. I was among the few fortunate people who were able to ask him a question regarding which aspect of Italian culture he was fascinated about, and if he had ever been inspired by Italian cinematography in general. The actor, who had answered the question of a journalist who had asked him to articulate the character of the film as being chameleonic in his intentions, drew back to his answer, and replied to mine with:

I am fascinated by many components of Italian culture, and apart from the rhetoric answer of food and landscape, which of course I love, I am fascinated about your cinema, and pantomime, by the exaggerated theatrical characters that have also, in some way, inspired characters of your cinema, and I am referring to pantomime masks such as Pantalone, Pulcinella, and more than everything else about Harlequine.

His answer perfectly synthesizes not only the theme of this chapter, but also provides the pretext to consider his festival appearance as part of the cultural milieu, which has seen SRK cut and collated into an Italianized, yet coherent, version of himself.

Following an apology for the absence of Karan Johar due to health problems, the actor engaged, one more time, with the crowd and with the culture by using the Italian language; he saluted and reassured his Italian fans that his Italian, made of a few simple words such as '*grazie*' and 'ciao', was improving daily.

This festival provided the film *MNIK*—and its star—with fluid and multiple interactions with diverse narratives, through the red carpet appearance, the interview, the question and answer session with the fans, and the screening of the film, forming a wide articulated space of enunciation; this third space is the one of 'interstices' (Iordanova 2010: 15), the one of transnational film festivals, which reveals how 'globalization-at-the-margin works' (Cunningham 2008: 147).

Patch Five: SRK on Italian Television

In 2007, lagging behind the rest of Europe, a series of Bollywood films titled *Amori con... Turbanti* (Loves with... Turbans) was screened on Italian television during the summer. The television format and the mixed reception of the Bollywood films (Acciari 2011) theoretically constitutes a kind of 'third space of enunciation' through hybridization in which these films undergo a narrative and stylistic adaptation for local audience. In *Amori con... Turbanti*, the films screened were borrowed from Bollywood industry and entirely dubbed in Italian. However, something was missing. These films were deprived of songs and dance sequences, thereby presenting a dramatically transformed Bollywood cinema with an *ex-novo* format. *Amori con... Turbanti* is literally translated as 'Loves with...Turbans' providing a problematic, standardized, and clichéd image of India. The word 'conturbanti' (literally meaning provocative or exciting) was divided into con... turbanti to produce a double meaning—loves with turbans and/or provocative loves. This image of Bollywood films, filtered through fallacy and misunderstanding based on conventional visions of this industry as 'exciting loves with turbans', established a hegemonic pattern of fusion which still sifts and selects notions and images of India as exotic. The title of the Italian summer season of Bollywood films has since been changed and it is now called *Le Stelle di Bollywood* (*Bollywood Stars*). The new title provides a more 'dignified' name without moving into discriminative and obsolete definitions, but the films are still randomly cut without method or logic. The films in which SRK was seen on television were *Swades: We, the People* (Dir. Ashutosh Gowariker, 2004), *Kabhi Alvida Naa Kehna* (Dir. Karan Johar, 2006), and *Chalte Chalte* (Dir. Aziz Mirza, 2003). All these films were the objects of discussion and debate among the large community that populates the aforementioned forum Bollywood Italia, wherein the fans critically and polemically accused the entertainment system of Italy of boycotting Bollywood cinema in its whole system. The following comments from the users of the forum Bollywood Italia on the film *Jodhaa Akbar* (Dir. Ashutosh Gowariker, 2008) reveal the disappointment and frustration on the way in which Bollywood films have been re-worked for the Italian national television, highlighting the above-mentioned cuttings from the original versions. The comments have been translated from Italian as follows:

1. The cuts were a shocker to me! This was not a reduced version for RAI (Italian national television), but was a ramshackle version from RAI! I still have to recover from it. Later, I will insert further comments.
2. I am happy I have seen the movie. But I believe the cuts have been so many that a new screening of the original version is a duty.[6]

Patch Six: Conclusion

The diverse types of media coverage, which have been collected throughout this chapter, are patches of a wider harlequinesque body of information which supports the view that small media clusters on SRK, populated by fans and followers across diverse platforms, interconnect with a larger framework of a cosmopolitan popular media culture inscribing SRK within the global firmament of star(dom). Throughout this chapter, the aim of mapping this icon has been to produce a form of discourse and an accurate expression of his global power based on diverse media evidence. SRK's media significance and iconicity has boosted the rise and awareness of Bollywood cinema, which Ganti (2012: 2) expressed as: 'Bollywood has been an important accoutrement of India's resignification in the global Arena.'

The image of SRK in Italy today gains the attention and fascination of his audience and the general public through a range of activities, specifically from the 'Italianized' version of Bollywood films (Acciari 2014), and also through radio chats and television appearances which makes this actor a copious and overwhelming phenomenon.

The image associable to him is the one of a modern Harlequin; his globetrotting and extensive media attention metaphorically reminds us of the acrobatic figure treasured by Italian culture. Patchy media coverage allegorically constitutes his 'official' global appeal by relating SRK to the chameleonic character of Harlequin within the global rise of Bollywood cinema.

It is significant to highlight here the productive capacities of a third space. The 'third space of enunciation', as discussed at the beginning of this chapter, is formed by an assembly of scattered media languages—the one of gossip, of blogs, of television, and festival venues—that are collated into an enunciating textuality. Bhabha (2004: 167) defines this process as 'the one of contraries' that may reveal how 'the theoretical recognition of the split-space of enunciation may open the way to a new way of conceptualizing an international culture.'

Italy, through its fragmented yet collated media viewpoints, does not struggle to be a distinctive voice of the globalization of SRK, but rather his acknowledgement is somehow Italianized and decoded through ad hoc manipulations. Metaphorically, the multiple media attentions extended to SRK, despite being formed by harlequinesque portions of media, interlock with a set of interconnected localities

(Herod 2009) providing 'local' traits to his globetrotting, and yet retaining a global feel.

Notes

1. The commedia dell'arte (translated as 'Comedy of Craft') was a sixteenth century form of theatre that originated in Italy. It was characterized by improvised scripts performed in open spaces and with masked characters. Carlo Goldoni, a Venetian writer and librettist, was among the most influential figures of this popular form of theatre.
2. The blog 'Tutti Pazzi Per Shah Rukh Khan' is available at http://tuttipazzipershahrukhkhan.iobloggo.com/ (accessed on 18 November 2013).
3. The blog 'Cine Hindi' is available at http://cinehindi.blogspot.co.uk/ (accessed on 18 November 2013).
4. The blog 'Break Cine Hindi' is available at http://breakcinehindi.blogspot.co.uk (accessed on 18 November 2013).
5. The blog 'Film Cine Hindi' is available at http://filmcinehindi.blogspot.com (accessed on 18 November 2013).
6. The mentioned comments have been made by users in Italian, these are available at http://bollywooditalia.forumfree.org/home.php (accessed on 1 September 2010).

References

Acciari, Monia. 2011. 'Indo-Italian Screens and the Aesthetic of Emotions' (PhD thesis, University of Manchester, Manchester, UK).
————. 2014. 'The Italianization of Bollywood Cinema: *Ad Hoc* Films', *Studies in European Cinema*, 11 (1): 14–25.
Bhabha, Homi K. 2004. *The Location of Culture*. New York: Routledge.
————. 2006. 'Cultural Diversity and Cultural Differences', in Bill Ashcroft, Gareth Griffiths, and Helen Tiffin (eds), *The Post-Colonial Studies Reader*. New York: Routledge.
Cunningham, Stuart. 2008. *The Vernacular: A Generation of Australian Culture and Controversy*. Brisbane: University of Queensland Press.
Dudrah, Rajinder. 2006. *Bollywood: Sociology Goes to the Movies*. London: SAGE Publications.
Dwyer, Rachel. 2008. 'The Indian Film Magazine Stardust', in Anandam K. Kavoori and Aswin Punathambekar (eds), *Global Bollywood*, pp. 240–67. New York: New York University Press.
Fanon, Frantz. 1967. *The Wretched of the Earth*. Harmondsworth: Penguin Books.

Ganti, Tajaswini. 2012. *Producing Bollywood: Inside the Contemporary Hindi Film Industry*. Durham: Duke University Press.

Harris, Thomas. 1999. 'The Building of Popular Images: Grace Kelly and Marilyn Monroe', in Christine Gledhill (ed.), *Stardom: Industry of Desire*, pp. 40–4. London: Routledge.

Heidegger, Martin. 1969. *Discourse on Thinking*, translated from German by John M. Anderson and E. Hans Freund. New York: Harper and Row Publisher.

Herod, Andrew. 2009. *Geographies of Globalization: A Critical Introduction* Oxford: Wiley Blackwell.

Iordanova, Dina and Ruby Cheung (eds). 2010. *Film Festival Yearbook 2*. Edinburgh: The University of St Andrews.

Keren, Michael. 2006. *Blogosphere: The New Political Arena*. Plymouth: Lexington Books.

Le Guellec, Gurvan. 2006. 'Paris Masala', *Zurban*, 288: 14–19.

Malani, G. 2010. 'My Name Is Khan: Movie Review', *India Times*, 1 February, available at http://movies.indiatimes.com/Reviews/Bollywood/My-Name-is-Khan-Movie-Review/articleshow/5561052.cms (accessed on 8 January 2011).

Menarini, Roy. 2012. *Le Nuove Forme della Cultura Cinematografica*. Udine: Mimesis.

Mitra, Ananda. 2008. 'Bollyweb: Search for Bollywood on the Web and See What Happens!', in Anandam K. Kavoori and Aswin Punathambekar (eds), *Global Bollywood*, pp. 268–81. New York: New York University Press.

Morgoglione, Claudia. 2010. 'La Superstar: Ecco il divo da 500 milioni di dollari: Così incarno la riscossa di Bollywood', *La Repubblica*, 31 October, available at http://www.repubblica.it/speciali/cinema/roma/2010/10/31/news/ecco_il_divo_da_500_milioni_di_dollari_cos_incarno_la_riscossa_di_bollywood-8614894 (accessed on 15 December 2010).

Nardi, Bonnie A., Diane J. Schiano, Michelle Gumbrecht, and Luke Swartz. 2004. 'Why We Blog', *Communications of the ACM*, 47 (12): 41–6.

Shiekh, Mushtaq. 2007. *Still Reading Khan*. New Delhi: Om Books International.

Sobchack, Vivian. 1994. 'The Scene of the Screen: Envisioning Cinematic and Electronic Presence', in Hans U. Gumbrecht and K. Ludwig Pfeiffer (eds), *Materialities of Communication*, pp. 83–106. Stanford: Stanford University Press.

Weisberg, Jay. 2010. 'Review: My Name Is Khan', *Variety*, 12 February, available at http://www.variety.com/review/VE1117942163.html?categoryId=31&cs=1 (accessed on 14 February 2010).

Filmography

Chalte Chalte. Dir. Aziz Mirza. Dreamz Unlimited and United Motion Pictures, 2003.

Jodhaa Akbar. Dir. Ashutosh Gowariker. UTV Motion Pictures, 2008.

Khabi Alvida Naa Kehna. Dir. Karan Johar. Dharma Productions, 2006.

My Name Is Khan. Dir. Karan Johar. Dharma Productions, 2010.

Ra.One. Dir. Anubhav Sinha. Red Chillies Entertainment, 2011.

Swades: We, the People. Dir. Ashutosh Gowariker. Ashutosh Gowariker Productions, 2004.

The King of Bollywood. Dir. Piyush Jha. Bollywood and iDream Productions, 2004.

King of Bollywood?

The Construction of a Global Image in Shah Rukh Khan's Dance Choreography

ANN R. DAVID

The camera shot takes the viewer into a luxurious bathroom, with a large circular bath centre stage. In the water is a seemingly naked Shah Rukh Khan, lying back in the foam-covered water. Two close-ups reveal him seductively caressing his bare shoulder and hand with the foamy soap bubbles. The camera pulls back and we see the water now strewn with rose petals, and as Khan lies there, showing his wet upper body and rippling arm muscles, four beautiful film heroines appear one by one, draping themselves on the edge of his bath and touching him softly. The short film is a TV advert for LUX soap to celebrate 75 years of the product's sales in India.

This chapter examines the production of global culture and the wide-ranging appeal of international film star Shah Rukh Khan (henceforth SRK) through a small sample of the Bollywood[1] films of the 1990s and the new millennium and selected media examples, such as the LUX soap advertisement (2005) discussed earlier in the chapter.[2] SRK's prolific output as an actor in Bollywood films (he starred in 33 films between 1990 and 1999 and in over 40 between 2000 and 2010), and his 'promiscuous brand' endorsing (Cayla 2008a; Chopra 2007: 156) in advertisements for products such as Pepsi, Hyundai cars, Airtel, and Dish TV have expanded his star value and sustained his dominating position and exposure, both on the large screen and on domestic television thereby playing a significant role in the development of his national and global image. I focus in particular on the presentation of SRK's bodily image and his dance moves and question how the Bollywood (dancing) body is constructed and how appeal and desire are managed and controlled for global cultural consumption. A detailed reading of selected dance sequences support this focus. The films of the 1990s, and those following after, reveal a move to engage with the growing global Indian diaspora as well as non-Asian audiences and show the rise of a new phenomenon of global Bollywood. As Vijay Mishra (2002: 269) writes, 'a study of Bombay Cinema will no longer be complete without a theory of diasporic desire because this cinema is now global in a specifically diasporic sense.' These later films demanded of their dancers and stars training in particular dance styles and a high level of movement competence in addition to a new, fit gym-styled body. Khan's place amongst the competitive world of other male Bollywood stars, Hrithik Roshan and Salman Khan, for example, is considered in this light.

Drawing additionally on ethnographic fieldwork carried out in Bollywood dance classes in urban centres in the UK, I analyse the effect of SRK's performances on both male and female audiences and dancers and seek to draw some conclusions about the mixed discourses at play in his films as well as the potential ability to cross prescribed and perceived boundaries. How is the diasporic imagination fed through his films? (see David 2010; Dudrah 2006). The chapter attempts to unpick the 'local negotiations of historically shifting relations of image production and consumption' (Desai et al. 2005: 79) in the complex context of Bollywood cinema and Khan's performances and asks whether SRK is perceived, both in India and in the global market, as the personification and king of Bollywood itself.

I have written previously in some detail about the roles taken by the song-and-dance numbers in Bollywood or Hindi film (David

2007), so I do not intend to spell out all the component factors here, nor is there space to do so, but it is important to note the very central part these sequences (filmigits) play in a three-hour-long film in both economic and entertainment terms. These songs, that feature every 20 minutes or so, are released at an earlier date than the feature film, played and endlessly replayed, thus creating an audience eager to watch and hear what have already become their favourite musical items, and establishing a ready market for the film. The songs and dances provide a 'repeat' value once the film has opened, bringing the audience back to the cinema time and time again just to watch these musical numbers. Advance sales from these audio tracks are often said to cover the whole production costs of the film (Gopalan 2002). Songs and their accompanying dance choreographies are effective on many levels within a specific film; they can provide significant moments of interruption in the narrative, or simply advance the narrative; they may interpret a hidden storyline or can allow a permissible expression of romance that may, in other ways, be inexpressible. Often they create an imagined fantasy space, intensifying the emotional content of the story and offering suggestions of eroticism. Hindi film scholar Rachel Dwyer (2000: 114) confirms that 'some types of songs, usually in conjunction with dance, present the body as a spectacle allowing for erotic display.' This element is especially noteworthy in the analysis of SRK's global appeal as I shall go on to elaborate through an investigation of his appearances in the dance sequences of films such as *Dil Se..* (Dir. Mani Ratnam, 1998), *Asoka* (Dir. Santosh Sivan, 2001), and *Om Shanti Om* (Dir. Farah Khan, 2007).

Dil Se..

I begin with the film *Dil Se..* as, despite its many critiques by film analysts and other academics (Basu 2008; Chakravarty 2000; Gehlawat 2010, and Singh 2010),[3] it is still of further interest on different levels of analysis that have so far not been the focus of other academics' work. I examine in some detail the choreographed dance moves of SRK in order to unpick the complex layering of star image, of the creation of 'fantasy space' inside and outside of the film as well as the effect of dancing in relation to the film's story and the film stars. The film's huge success in the Indian diaspora (particularly in the UK and USA), in contrast to its initial box-office failure in the subcontinent, as well as its song-and-dance scenes encourage us to examine the force of global consumption present in its repeated showings. It was the first Bollywood film to find a place in the top ten UK films in 1998, and was shown at the Cineworld Feltham Multiplex in West London five times a day to a sell-out capacity. *Chaiyya, chaiyya*, the first of the film's six songs, was voted one of the most favourite tracks in the BBC World Service poll in 2003 by people in 155 different countries worldwide. Additionally, Andrew Lloyd Weber's musical production of *Bombay Dreams* (2004) reproduced onstage the train scene and the track of *Chaiyya chaiyya*, thereby again increasing the song's popularity.

Dil Se.. is part of a trilogy of films dealing with militancy and terrorism made in the 1990s by south Indian film director Mani Ratnam and tells the story of a young news radio producer, Amarkant Varma, played by SRK who falls in love with Meghna, a girl who, unbeknown to him, is part of a revolutionary group and is training to be a suicide bomber. The film was made in the aftermath of threats to India as a nation-state from across its northern borders (primarily Pakistan) as well as from perceived dangers internally in regions such as Kashmir and, as Sujala Singh (2010: 346) notes, is 'ambivalent in [its] representation of terrorism'. A British Film Institute reviewer rather candidly stated that the 'film has to pull the subtle trick of being a star vehicle for Khan and navigating the social concerns for which Ratnam is known. This generates a certain stylistic disparity' (Sawhney 1999). The theme of love, set in tense and difficult circumstances, is portrayed through the vehicle of SRK's character as he travels to the north-east of India in his job as an investigative reporter and meets the mysterious Meghna on a train. Powerfully attracted to her, he desperately tries to pursue her as she disappears and reappears, concealing from him, until much later when her real identity as a terrorist is revealed. The six songs in the film, all composed by A.R. Rahman, show the seven stages of love as depicted in ancient Arabic literature[4]—attraction, infatuation, love, reverence, worship, obsession, and death—and emphasize not only the theme of love but aspects of Sufic wisdom that teach of the transcendence of worldly emotion and desire (Basu 2008).

The extraordinary song-and-dance number of *Chaiyya, chaiyya* by choreographer Farah Khan runs for six-and-a-half minutes and is filmed on a moving train using 80 separate cuts, as Ajay Gehlawat (2010: 37) notes. Although dancing on the top of a train racing at speed through the Indian countryside appears dramatic, on closer analysis, most of the choreography is situated on two low trucks and takes place while the train's movement is cleverly reduced to a crawling pace. A moving camera adds to the sense of rapidity. SRK's own moves on top of the carriage are mainly filmed from below with the train obscured, and could therefore have been filmed separately and cut into shot. His dancing is ingeniously framed by a group of pseudo-tribal male dancers in pristine rural costumes, their own movements emphasizing and enhancing his dance performance. Anustup Basu (2008: 161) cleverly calls this 'a utopian space for anthropological spectacle, ethnic chic, and folk bodies—all combined and set to techno rhythms.' Macho struts, jumps, head banging, pelvic thrusts, chest shimmying, and shoulder thrusts are the key components to SRK's dance all choreographed to the powerful, regular techno beat pulsating through the song. Much of the time, Khan performs to the camera, thus directing his gaze effectively at the cinematic audience, drawing us into the scene with him. His red jacket and movements are somewhat reminiscent of Michael Jackson's pop music video *Thriller* (1983), an iconic dance-song that had a profound effect on popular culture, the red jacket becoming as much of a symbol of being 'cool' as the song itself.[5]

I move from this brief analysis to discuss in more detail the third filmigit of the film *Dil Se..*, *Satrangi re* (Many colours), selecting this song as *Chaiyya, chaiyya* has already been subject to close analysis by several other scholars (for example, Basu 2008; Gehlawat 2010). *Satrangi re* is another poetic love song, clearly influenced by composer Rahman's Sufi sensibilities that combine music and notions of spirituality,[6] and the dance sequence takes place, once again, outside the storyline, creating a performative expression of SRK's character's (Amar) imagination and multiple narrative worlds. It transports the characters and the audience away from the tensions and realism of the world of terrorism and suicide bombings, placing them in an exotic, romantic, and erotic dance of love and desire. Sujala Singh (2010: 353) argues that Meghna, as a 'terrorist woman cannot participate in heterosexual desire, so the songs enact and fulfil compensatory desire through their sumptuousness and exotic locales.' This digressive mode of the song-and-dance number has been notably called a cinema 'of interruption' by film academic Lalitha Gopalan (2002: 28) who advises that these carefully created extra-diegetic moments deserve particular analysis, so essential are they to 'Indian cinema's indirectness, in-between-ness, its propensity for digression and interruptions.'

As the song *Satrangi re* begins, the viewer sees Meghna taking a bath inside an old monastery in Ladakh, where Amar has opened the door on her by mistake. This cleverly constructed opening scene signals the eroticism that is to come, linking directly with the corporeal aesthetics of the song's duets that emphasizes the would-be lovers' bodies, as well as indirectly to SRK's later LUX advertisment, discussed earlier. The camera stays for a few seconds, lingering on Meghna's wet body as SRK watches, and then cuts to the outside, panning across a mountainous desert scene in the arid hills of Ladakh, described by Gehlawat (2010: 38) as 'the crumbling clay ruins of some exotic landscape.'[7] The dry but fierce wind is whistling through the settlement of old buildings around the monastery where we now view SRK and Manisha Koirala (the female lead playing Meghna) dressed in loose, flowing, full black robes. The musical soundtrack begins as they engage in a physically demanding and passionate dance duet. The words of the song, an Urdu poem, emphasize the love Amar feels for Meghna, 'Love is an uncontrollable fire, O Ghalib (*Ishq par zor nahin hai ye vo aatish ghaalib*); You are my longing, my longing itself (*Tu hi tu tu hi tu aarzu aarzu*).'[8]

Throughout this six-minute song, Meghna moves through 11 changes of costume—outfits that range from the dramatic black robes to floating white garments, soft, green silk, and mauve chiffon, to coloured tiny bra tops and tight sarongs. At one point, she is dressed in a white, skimpy bodice made of rope and white 'harem' pants (with rope around her head, lower arms, wrists, and ankles), and both characters are shown inside some rope netting, suggesting elements of bondage, fetishism, and erotic fantasy. Here, in the song the lyrics accentuate the image of bondage, describing Meghna being 'entangled in your embrace; let me disentangle my wits' (*Teri raahon mein ulajha ulajha huun, teri baahon mein ulajha ulajha).* No doubt also the rope- and bondage-references allude to Meghna's yet-to-be discovered life of terrorism, of her role as a militant fighter trained for suicide bombings. When the lyrics repeat, stating again, 'Love is an uncontrollable fire', a burning tree appears in the desert sand, in front of which the pair now dance. It represents both the fire of love and the fire of destruction.

This same reference is underlined in Basu's work (2008: 169f), when he writes that 'in the *"Satrangi re"* sequence, the militarized grounds of Ladakh are transformed by nomadic assemblages of travel cinematography, exotic, a non-obligatory eroticism of dance movements, and urban motifs of bondage and ritualistic masochism.' The changes of the many-coloured and varied costumes allude to the description of Meghna as *'satrangi',*[9] as well as emphasizing the display of the passion of their unrequited love, suggested through Meghna's body-revealing outfits. Khan remains in black flowing robes until almost the end, when he, rather dramatically, appears in white robes, perhaps in reference to the Sufi characteristics of the song (see below). These sequences, despite Meghna's resistance to SRK's obsessive amorous advances in real story time, position the pair as intimate lovers, in what Sumita Chakravarty (2000: 233) describes as 'the liminal space of dreaming'; this is further advanced in the next sequence of the song, analysed below.

Allusions to other dance styles and iconic images populate the same song. Cutting from an open, inner courtyard, again in the monastery, we are transported to the side of lake Tso Moriri, on the Changthang Plateau in western Tibet. Both characters are now closely bound together inside a tight red robe of stretchy Lycra, dancing, of necessity, a very intimate duet. To the viewer, it is a startling transformation from watching revealing, seductive body images and movements in the preceding scenes to this unusual portrayal of restraint, disguise, and shapeless forms. Resonances of American dancer Martha Graham's famous solo piece of 1930, *Lamentation,* are created and referenced here in this part of the choreography. Graham (1991: 117) described her dance performance in the tube of material as follows, *'Lamentation,* my dance of 1930, is a solo piece in which I wear a long tube of material to indicate the tragedy that obsesses the body, the ability to stretch inside your own skin, to witness and test the perimeters and boundaries of grief, which is honourable and universal.'

Graham's piece not only deals with sorrow in a reified manner,[10] but is also particularly focused on the abstraction and reduction of the human form. The dancing body in *Lamentation* is distorted and dislocated, reduced to show only a moving shape with no specific delineation, and only the hands, feet, and part of the face are visible. It is as if her grief is actually restricting her movements (Jowitt 1988). Here, Graham rejected literal imagery in favour of the non-figurative, the covered clothed figure simply representing 'a symbol of grief' (Siegel 1985: 41). In this moving shape, the tensions within the body are highlighted as is Graham's legendary dance technique, which has as its central premise the tension and contraction of the body. *Lamentation* highlights the dynamics of the body, delineating only diagonals and asymmetrical shapes.[11]

This point is particularly of note as the use of such a similar costume to Graham's in the film *Dil Se..* creates a dramatic contrast to the expected Bollywood focus on the bodily form, with its frequent lingering and close-up shots on specific parts of the dancing bodies and on literal imagery. In this sequence, all such focus is removed and the red, stretch material appears as if part of the skin of the pair dancing inside. It emphasizes their experience of their love together and the exploration of each other's bodies, united as one. Yet, the lyrics of the song speak of the pain of unrequited love, of the grief Amar is experiencing as Meghna constantly resists and rejects him in the storyline. In the film's narrative, he is in fact unable to have and to hold the woman he thinks he loves, seeking desperately to find her after she disappears from his sights. Through the song, the narrative is interrupted and we see the dream of his romance unfolding.

As the duet in this red, stretchy robe closes, the camera returns to the mountain setting and both characters now depict—through their dance vocabulary—several very specific, devotional Sufi references. While SRK kneels on the sand, moving his body intensely and rhythmically to the music as if in trance, Koirala spins around him and in her own arc, with arms outstretched like a whirling dervish. A moving camera circles the actors, filming and emphasizing the spinning movement of the scene. Koirala then kneels in the sand and rocks her body in a similar way. For Sufi dervishes, their whirling practice (*sema*) offers a path through which the confines of the earthly bodies may be discarded and with the death of the ego, spiritual rebirth can occur. This theme of moving beyond the earthly or the physical is alluded to in several ways as I go on to argue. The scene cuts to a landscape covered in snow and the two are seen in a close embrace, then sinking slowly down to the ground. As the song closes, SRK is lying across Koirala's lap, head thrown back,[12] where she holds him and buries her face in his chest, thereby creating a dramatic religious image that is reminiscent of Michelangelo's *Pieta* in which the lifeless body of Christ is draped and cradled in Mary's arms (Basu 2008). These religious references both from Sufism and Christianity suggest notions of transcendence as well as emphasizing the emotional suffering of worldly love in contrast to the freedom of divine or transcendental love. The sculptural image of the *Pieta*, recreated in the film at this point, alludes to the suffering, pity, and compassion seen in Christ's dead body and Mary's emotional response, but we also know that in terms of Christian understanding this very image precedes that of a resurrected, reborn Christ. David Frescas (2010) writes of Michelangelo's image that 'the Pieta couples human sadness with divine destiny, juxtaposing the earthy and heavenly concerns … The Pieta intertwines divinity and humanity, employing religion as an instrument through which human emotion is expressed.'

Throughout the song—in the words, in the images, and the references invoked—there are allusions to worldly suffering (the pain of unrequited love) juxtaposed with the non-worldly (religious images) and non-physical (abstracted bodies) realms reminiscent of Sufi culture, perhaps emphasized because of composer Rahman's deep faith, and seen again in songs in the film *Asoka*, which is discussed later. I argue additionally that the way Farah Khan as choreographer plays with references to other world religions and to American popular culture[13] acknowledges and emphasizes to the audience that Hindi films are part of the global cultural economy. This is a key factor for the film's diasporic audience. The film, through its choreography, is constantly juxtaposing an invoked world of sensuous romance and joyful, free bodily expression with the darker, menacing, and more pressing aspects of global terrorism and worldly realities.

Farah Khan's creative work with the movement vocabulary for SRK's dancing allows him to stay within his parameters of competence in the dance moves, while at the same time creating a display of virility, strength, seduction, and fantasy. In his dancing, there is no doubt of Khan's physicality, his strength, his athleticism, and attack—at one point in the song *Satrangi re* he makes a high jump and dives into a forward roll[14]—and these qualities are deliberately enhanced by Farah Khan's choreography. Anupama Chopra (2007: 57) describes him as being 'a flamboyant actor' whose 'performances were gymnastic, forceful, and extravagant. He had spontaneity and physicality, not gravitas.' Yet, if the beautifully designed costumes, the exotic settings, the well-trained background dancers, and SRK's own star charisma are removed from the cinematic setting, what remains in the *actual* dancing is something simple and quite basic (static poses, running, twirling and floating fabric, shoulder and head thrusts along with grandiose gestures). In this dance number, SRK's moves are relatively simple in terms of dance performance and his partner executes most of the movement. He does, however, perform some fairly impressive lifts and partnering and there is close and provocative physical contact in these particular parts. Close-up camera shots here give an intimacy that draws the viewer in, and contrasts directly with the full-body shots of both actors as the camera draws back. These camera angles provide especially elongated shots, setting SRK amidst the vast horizon that frames his body among the rocks, the mountains, and the extensive blue sky, underlining the ruggedness and power of his performance, the martial arts moves, and stances assumed.

SRK's Charisma

As with much of the Bollywood film industry, charisma, star persona, and the creation of fantasy are the overriding premise, and this is certainly personified in SRK's dancing. Many film fans I interviewed in London stated that in their view he was not the best dancer, but they still enjoyed his performances immensely. One Bollywood devotee, Lucy, who attends a Bollywood dance class in London and who regularly watches SRK's films told me, 'He can't dance! He just gets away with it as he's so charming' (interview, August 2010). Lorena (interview, June 2010), another non-Asian Bollywood fan, spoke of his appealing eyes and his smile, but did not think he was the greatest dancer. Raminder Kaur (2005: 319) writes that young British Asians interviewed after seeing his films said, 'He's cool, he's got the balance.' At the end of his Wembley stage show *Temptations*[15] in 2004, other fans stated, 'It's his aura, his charisma,' and 'he's just perfect' (Kabir 2005, DVD notes). The global star persona developed by SRK (during the 1990s according to many commentators) and constructed by both the film industry and his fans is not of an aloof hero, but of an accessible, down-to-earth brother, son, or friend (Basu 2008: 175; Chopra 2007). Fuelled additionally by his constant presence in Indian TV advertising (as noted earlier) and by the number and range of films he has made,[16] '[h]e was the emblem of a new India, the repository of a billion fantasies' (Chopra 2007: 219). In 2005 he had the honour conferred on him by the Indian government of the status of 'Model Citizen', and was named 'King Khan' in 2006 at the Zee TV awards. Not only is he seen to be representing the new ideal Indian man, respecting family, honouring tradition, sensitive, vulnerable, and romantic, but also physically and mentally strong. His on-screen persona and star identity is understood as blending East and West in perfect harmony, a balance of modernity and tradition, affluent and trendy, while retaining integrity and restraint. SRK, states Chopra (2007: 149), 'blended in perfect proportions, Indian and Western culture' and creates a glossy 'cultural equilibrium', adored and admired by aspiring Indian yuppies and identified with Indians abroad.

The construction of a star image is well documented in film theory (see Turner 2006 [1988]; Williams 1995). Cultural and media studies academic Graeme Turner illustrates how 'a star has a signifying function which may be separate or different from the written character within the film script' (Turner 2006: 139). Through this signification, an audience knows a star both in his/her screen persona and in what appears to be an ordinary, life-like mode through the various representations in film, press, TV, fan magazines as well as social networking sites such as facebook and Twitter. SRK's personal engagement with fans through his website, through social media, and his stage shows continually allows both local and global interaction with the star, creating a seeming accessibility and maintaining his popularity. As much as the private lives of stars such as these are continually on show in the media, they also create an extensive fantasy world of characters on screen; both aspects are widely available to their audiences and add to the construction of a global image as well as global consumption. In the case of SRK, film studies academic Graeme Turner (2006: 139) notes how the casting directors do not have to work to make audiences know he is attractive, nor that he is physically strong and active.

Jigna Desai (2008: 356) writes how SRK often plays a Non-resident Indian (NRIs) or a new urban hero in his films, and that as an actor, he 'savvily performs, leverages, and has come to embody various diasporic masculine subjectivities', making him very attractive to such diasporic, global audiences. Star persona is a significant player in the global economies of Bollywood films. Indeed, English scholar Sangita Gopal and women and gender studies academic Sujata Moorti (2008: 60) confirm that 'a film with superstar Shah Rukh Khan would earn between 40 and 45 per cent of its earnings in the diaspora which together with the urban audience would comprise over 75 per cent of the film's revenues.' Additionally, ethnomusicologist Anna Morcom (2008: 79) writes in one of her interviews (with Harish Dayani) that if SRK is in the film, then the audio value is worth 30 to 35 million rupees, whereas for Akshay Kumar it might be around 10 million. The fact that the song-and-dance numbers have now migrated outside of the film genre (see David 2010; Shresthova 2011), creating a voracious interest in Bollywood dance in communities, dance schools, competitions, fitness clubs continues to fuel such global fandom for SRK. Gopal and Moorti (2008: 46) state that:

> Both in the diaspora and in India, new sets of meanings have accreted around the elaborate dances featured in the song picturizations. Choreographed sequences often migrate from the screen to the stage, to dance halls, and to community centres. These migrations not only draw on but also radically recode the meanings that the dance had in its filmic context.

Such recoded meanings and interest in the afterlife of a Bollywood dance reveals intricate nuances of desire and longing seen through the watching of and/or participation in Bollywood film dance in diasporic Asian and non-Asian audiences. It is pertinent to draw here from Arjun Appadurai's (1996: 31) theorization of global cultural processes, using his notion of 'imagination as a social practice', whereby imagination becomes 'a form of negotiation between sites of agency (individuals) and globally defined fields of possibility.' The imagined worlds of aspiring Bollywood dancers are fuelled, for example, by glamorous images of the film world and its stars, and in particular SRK, that are media-controlled (cf. Appadurai's 'mediascapes'). I question now how such appeal is managed and controlled for public consumption.

Asoka and Om Shanti Om

To begin to answer some of these pressing questions, I now turn to examine the film *Asoka* (2001), a box-office failure, but well acclaimed by film critics. The film portrays the part fictional and part historical story of Ashoka the Great who ruled southern Asia in the period of 273–232 BCE and was responsible for the rise of Buddhism in that part of the world. Chopra (2007: 191) tells how SRK, as Ashoka, 'starts out as a romantic hero, frolicking in the fields with a beautiful princess, but the bucolic idyllic is soon replaced by violence.' After much killing, his quest for power is eventually renounced and Ashoka takes on a peaceful role, embracing and spreading the message of Buddhism. SRK was co-producer, along with Juhi Chawla, and this was the first film to be produced by their new company Dreamz Unlimited. SRK does not engage in so much dancing in this film, but is notable for his physical appearance as a macho fighting warrior figure, with long hair and bare chest displaying a strong body. Some commentators made the wry observation that SRK now had to compete with another younger rising star, Hrithik Roshan, whose gym-sculpted body in *Kaho Naa... Pyaar Hai* (Dir. Rakesh Roshan, 2007) made audiences scream (Chopra 2007: 186; Deshpande 2005: 197) and created pressure for the other male stars to appear in similar fashion. One of my interviewees remarked with a smile, that as soon as SRK removes his top, as he also does in *Om Shanti Om* discussed below, all the female members of the audience around her in the cinema (in India) gasped and exclaimed out loud. Similarly, in a university class discussion about the male stars in Bollywood films, one of my dance students (Indian) remarked, 'They just have to get their pecs out, and everyone goes mad' (October 2010).[17]

Here we see a marked change in the focus of desire. Instead of the attention being specifically on the bodies of the female stars, the male leads (and their bodies) now attract as much attention. Choreographer and producer Keith Khan, speaking at Akademi's conference *Frame by Frame* on Bollywood and film dance at the Royal Opera House, London in 2009, suggested that in the last decade there has been a marked change in the Indian bodies seen on film. He described the men appearing with less chest hair and in a more sexualized manner, while women have become smaller and thinner. Certainly, the emphasis on athleticism and fitness has made a noticeable impact. During one romantic dance item in *Asoka* choreographed by Geeta Kapoor[18] to the song *Roshni se* (Filled with light; composed by Anu Malik), SRK and Kareena Kapoor are depicted in a tantilizing, sexy mode. There are not many specific dance movements in this four-minute song item that shows Kapoor in skimpy, revealing costumes—just a bandeau of material around her chest and a bare midriff, often simply posing provocatively against a tree, or lying seductively on the ground or on a tree branch. SRK's body is covered until half-way through the song, when we then see him without his kurta top. The sequences reveal close, touching embraces and some impressive lifts, filmed by cameras above the couple and whirling around them. Yet what is of particular interest is the way the dancing body is produced in this number. At one point in *Roshni se* the two stars are shown swimming and dancing underwater with chiffon costumes floating around them; then their bodies are gliding through the air as if flying; and finally, they appear performing dramatic jumps and lifts in slow motion. This creates the look of supernatural, super-heroic, physically free bodies, unbound from their human confines and with the potential to appear and to move anywhere. The ability for the dancing body on-screen to transcend the limitations of the physical dancing body, where gravity is defied and where bodies are fragmented and are seen from distorted and unconventional perspectives, challenging spatial and temporal logic, has been well documented by dance scholar Sherril Dodds (2001: 79) in her analysis of dance on-screen. Yet, while the bodies of the two characters are shown as being ethereal and unworldly, they are simultaneously charged with sexual chemistry and physical power. This apparent tension is heard in the lyrics of the song that state repeatedly, 'Touching me, they say, don't touch me' (*Chhuke bole na chhuna mujhe*), and describe being filled with light and dreams. SRK, as Ashoka, sings of seeking to find his love by searching 'above and beneath the heavens' (*Aakash upar tale*) and in the clouds and in the water. Through the use of film techniques of editing and montage, and selected camera shots, spatial and temporal elements that normally bind the physical bodies are removed, creating virtuosic and far more versatile screen bodies that can float in the clouds and dance freely under water.

SRK's dance movements, his star quality, and attractive persona is additionally enhanced in the dance scenes by being often paired with female leads who are a decade or so younger than him and by a choreography (again by Farah Khan) that emphasizes a youthful look. In *Kal Ho Naa Ho* (*KHNH*, Dirs Nikhil Advani and Ron Reid Jr., 2003) set in New York City, he works with the younger Preity Zinta (who also plays a supporting role of his potential bride in *Dil Se..*), with whom he dances exchanging cheeky smiles and jumps, executing moves packed with vitality and surrounded by young, vibrant dancers. He even appears at one stage as a hip hop b-boy. One of my respondents, a keen SRK follower, commented that much of his dance vocabulary remains the same now as when he was younger. All of these factors—the specifically designed choreography, the romantic or often ethereal settings of the dance items creating virtuosic dancing body, the younger, energetic surrounding cast—help to maintain a highly attractive screen persona and to sustain the creation of desire in his screen audiences. The spotlight on SRK's body as a locus for cinematic gaze and desire is further accentuated in the highly successful film *Om Shanti Om*[19] where in the song *Dard-e-disco*—in a very similar mode to the LUX advertisment—the physicality and sexuality of Khan's naked, oiled upper body is on full display. Here SRK plays the part of Om Prakash Makhija, reincarnated as Om Kapoor, a famous film star of the Indian film industry. In this particular scene, not only is he surrounded by half-clad dancing Western women who touch his body adoringly, but also the camera lingers in close-up over his rippling arm and chest muscles. This camera technique creates a fragmented body, immediately situating it in 'the realms of sexuality' (Dodds 2001: 41) with its foregrounding of naked flesh. It also creates the notion of a 'gym body' where fitness and workouts are privileged. At the age of 42, Khan shows a body that is toned and strong and leaner than in previous films. In the same manner as many of the leading heroines in the famous 'wet sari' scenes, SRK emerges slowly, apparently naked, from deep water, and it is only when he appears fully in the screen that we see he is in fact wearing jeans, but quite low on his hips, enough so that the pelvic bones are visible. He leans backwards from the hips, with shoulders thrust back, in an attitude of proud bodily display. Camera shots cleverly linger over his accentuated muscles and bare torso, and the whole sequence is drenched with sexuality and desire.

Neelam Sidhar Wright (2010: 89) argues in her discussion on postmodern aesthetics in Bollywood film that SRK's body offers 'a blatant commentary on the over-emphasized muscled physiques of many male film stars of the post-millennium era'. Farah Khan as director, knowingly deconstructs this and in the process creates SRK as an even greater locus of desire. The film *Om Shanti Om* parodies and reflects the nostalgia of the Indian popular film industry, SRK's character is depicted as a 'consumable hero' (Deshpande 2005: 197), his body and personality an object of longing and consumption, reinforced by the way he plays with permissive space (as described earlier) created in the song-and-dance items. Additionally, the very fact that SRK's character is a moviegoer who then becomes a film star, allows 'the spectator's dreams and desires to be realized in the diegesis' (Deshpande 2005: 94) itself.

Screen Dance to Stage Dance

Spectators' dreams and desires for the glitzy world of Bollywood are fuelled additionally by the migration of the dance form out of the film screen into local classes and staged performances. I have previously argued (David 2010) that the reproduction of Bollywood dance outside the celluloid screen enacts a complex mix of desire and longing, often fuelled by the act of film-watching itself as well as by the participation in Bollywood dance classes and performance. I argue here that SRK knowingly exploits this phenomenon in his stage tours, at film award celebrations, and often, wherever fans are present. His endearing openness and willingness to engage with fans in this way is exemplified in 2011, when performing on stage at the International Indian Film Academy (IIFA) awards, he invited one fan onto the stage and encouraged her to play the part of the leading lady in the Bollywood number he was performing. At the closing ceremony of this event, SRK taught the audience several dance steps to enable them all to participate in the last number. Other global touring shows such as *Temptations* (discussed briefly earlier) and *Temptations Reloaded* not only give fans the chance to see and interact live with SRK, but promote the songs and dances from the films, albeit somewhat adapted for a stage setting. This creates a public accessibility not only to the stars and to SRK in particular, but also to the dance moves. In November 2012, on SRK's birthday, fans in Azerbaijan choreographed a flash mob dance scene of a compilation of his dances in *Ra.One* (Dir. Anubhav Sinha, 2011), dancing to a remix of the number *Chamak challo*, which was later copied by fans in Russia, performing to onlookers in Red Square, Moscow. There are many illustrations (particularly accessible on YouTube and facebook sites) of SRK dancing with and for his fans outside of the film screen. His frequent live appearances at film festivals, conventions, and academy awards around the world produce a permeability between the screen performer and the real, live artist who cleverly 'mingles' with the fans and allows them access to himself and his dance choreography. While promoting the film *Rab Ne Bana Di Jodi* (Dir. Aditya Chopra, 2008), SRK asked fans to send video entries for a dance competition, and a group of amateur dancers in Madrid won the competition.[20] The imagined worlds of aspiring or amateur Bollywood dancers are fuelled by the glamorous images of the film world and its stars that are predominantly media-controlled.

Crossing Boundaries

Discussing the 2005 LUX advertisement described at the beginning of this chapter, a journalist on the BBC news website noted that Khan had 'ventured where no male Indian film actor has before' (Chadha 2005), stressing the fact that only female actors had ever advertised the LUX brand in India. Monica Chadha (2005) cites filmmaker Prahlad Kakkar who commented that 'Shah Rukh Khan is a man with a very strong female side—he is not ashamed of not having any hair on his chest—yet he is a man's man', here emphasizing SRK's continuing appeal to both males and females.[21] Khan himself said (cited in Jha 2005) when interviewed about the advertisement, 'Some people think it's a girlie ad, that it questions my sexuality. But I love the idea of getting into the tub, just as I had seen all my lovely leading ladies do.' Nandita Chalam (cited in Cayla 2008b), senior creative director of J. Walter Thompson, India, who directed the ad, said of SRK, 'He especially liked the idea of himself being the only male star surrounded by four beautiful women,' and added, 'Yes, he was playing with his image.' During one of his dance numbers in the 2004 world tour of his show *Temptations*, he wore a body suit with developed pecs that was on show under his jacket. It is important to question whether these overt displays of body image and sexuality create a sort of dichotomy for both SRK and his audiences, as he frequently speaks about his acting being an entirely spiritual practice. 'For me,' he says in Nasreen Munni Kabir's documentary film, aptly named *The Inner and Outer World of Shah Rukh Khan* (2005), 'acting is very spiritual ... It combines praying, it combines all sorts of soulful, religious, spiritual things that people do.' The tension between his constructed public persona and the 'real' man is further highlighted in his comments, quoted in the DVD's published material, that 'There has to be now a public face very clearly. And that public face is always smiling. And I'm tired. And I'm sometimes in a bad mood. But I cannot pass that onto people....' A certain self-awareness of his star character is also acknowledged when he stated (cited in Chopra 2007: 221), 'I live in an unreal world, my persona is unreal, I myself am unreal,' and he has also been prepared to appear in pastiched or parodic versions of himself (*Kal Ho Naa Ho*; *Om Shanti Om*). I would suggest too that this quality of flexibility, of willingness to surprise his fans, and to reconcile imagined differences is demonstrated in his dance and song sequences, where despite his serious ongoing back and neck injuries, he seizes each dance and song sequence with a vitality, spontaneity, and attack that is impressive.

The ability to cross perceived and prescribed boundaries is apparent throughout Khan's on-screen and off-screen career. One example is the portrayal of violent villains in films such as *Deewana*

(Dir. Raj Kanwar, 1992), *Darr* (Dir. Yash Chopra, 1993), and *Baazigar* (Dir. Abbas Alibhai Burmawalla and Mustan Alibhai Burmawalla, 1993), roles that started his movie career. These anti-hero film parts changed the way Bollywood film heroes were perceived, as prior to that leading men tended to play gentlemen characters that depicted a high moral and social status (Chopra 2007). SRK's transition from darker, unconventional roles to romantic heroes (for example, *Dilwale Dulhania Le Jayenge*, Dir. Aditya Chopra, 1995; *Dil To Pagal Hai*, Dir. Yash Chopra, 1997; *Kuch Kuch Hota Hai*, Dir. Karan Johar, 1998) to the performance of a young autistic man in *My Name Is Khan* (*MNIK*, Dir. Karan Johar, 2010) exemplifies his broad scope and honed acting ability, as well as his desire to consistently take on challenges. In his own life off-screen, he traversed usual conventions as a Muslim by taking on Hindu marriage vows and participating in a traditional Hindu ceremony when marrying his Hindu wife Gauri, in 1991. Their home has been widely photographed showing Hindu deities and a copy of the Koran side by side (Ahmed 2005). Many of the male film stars of Hindi cinema are Muslim and yet play the Hindu heroic roles with no obvious concern. These parts epitomize traditional Hindu and cultural values—respect for religion and Hindu deities, care and devotion in familial relationships, and so on—and often require the actor to participate in Hindu religious rituals, such as the lighting of lamps, worship of Hindu deities, chanting of prayers, or the lighting of a funeral pyre. There is also an acceptance on the part of the film audiences of these actors as Hindus, despite their Muslim backgrounds.

Khan also appears unconcerned by his appeal to gay fans and his status as a gay icon. Although he has a huge female fan base (both Asian and non-Asian), SRK knowingly plays with his attraction to male viewers, as academics Rajinder Dudrah (2008) and Charlie Henniker (2010) confirm in their writing and analyses of his films. Henniker (2010: 30) notes that Khan's appearance in the film *Om Shanti Om*, as 'a muscled, bare-chested dancer' and with 'a new "item-boy" look ... projects Shah Rukh as an object of desire, subject to the voyeuristic male gaze' and reinforces his appropriation as a gay icon. Dudrah (2006: 132) recounts how when the *Chaiyya, chaiyya* song from *Dil Se..* is played at gay Asian night clubs in the UK, SRK's display of heterosexual love for his heroine in the song and dance number is reclaimed and acknowledged 'as one of their queer anthems'. The use of the dancing body is especially foregrounded, as Dudrah (2008: 298) informs us, once again underlining how dance scenes from the films are used as permissive spaces:

> The further editing of the Dil Se [..] clip with images of the naked torso of Salman Khan also deliberately queers and displaces the dominant straight aesthetics of the clip to enable new pleasures around gender, sexuality, and the dancing body. The physical use of the body in dance, here, plays with conventional and expected patterns of heteronormativity.

SRK's playing across the boundaries of heternormativity in his films (within the context of the dominant heterosexual masculine image in Bollywood) is illustrated in the film *KHNH* whose subplot suggests a gay relationship between characters played by SRK and actor Saif Ali Khan. Their scenes contain humour, camp parodying, and caricaturing of both straight and gay roles (Dudrah 2008: 302) and can be read on a variety of levels of analysis. While the film brought the subject of homosexuality into mainstream Bollywood, it perhaps serves to reinforce, in a very Indian way, the more traditional and acceptable heterosexual relationships in its treatment of this theme (for further analysis, see Dudrah 2006 and 2008; Gehlawat 2010).[22] Speculation about a kiss on the lips SRK was said to have given to another male actor caused a huge rise in rumour-mongering on Bollywood Internet sites and magazines' gossip columns about SRK being gay. It is believed that the scene was a comic moment from his film *MNIK*, with no sexual meaning intended, but because of the furore, it has now been deleted. This kiss was all the more noteworthy because of SRK's earlier decision to never kiss on-screen after his problems with the media post his appearance in *Maya Memsaab* (Dir. Ketan Mehta, 1993). In this film, he performed a somewhat sexually explicit scene (by Indian standards) with actress Deepa Sahi. Reacting angrily to press accusations later that they were having an affair (Chopra 2007), SRK insisted from that time that all his film contracts contain a no-kissing clause, although he revoked this in 2012 in *Jab Tak Hain Jaan* (Dir. Yash Chopra) where he kissed Katrina Kaif on-screen.

A Macho Turf War?

Rivalry between SRK and several other prominent male Hindi films stars such as Salman Khan and Hrithik Roshan has frequently been the subject of Bollywood gossip columns and Internet sites.[23] Bodily image and dancing prowess has necessarily been at the forefront of such competitive macho sparring. As discussed earlier, the new masculine bodily ideal of fit, toned, and sculpted muscles emerged in Bollywood films in the mid to late 1990s, led by Salman Khan who was a keen body builder and is now often shown semi-clad or in transparent, revealing shirts (see *Maine Pyar Kiya*, Dir. Sooraj R. Barjatya, 1989; *Karan Arjun*, Dir. Rakesh Roshan, 1995; *Wanted*, Dir. Prabhu Deva, 2009; *Dabangg*, Dir. Abhinav Kashyap, 2010). Like SRK, he played romantic roles, and was 'handsome, charismatic and immensely popular' (Bose 2007: 343) but he also nurtured a 'bad-boy' image, with stories of drunken behaviour, a tempestuous relationship with female star Aishwarya Rai, and arrests for drunk driving. Indian papers (*Hindustan Times* and *Times of India* amongst others) reported in 2008 that the two film stars had nearly come to blows at a birthday party as the competitiveness and enmity between them became more public.

Hrithik Roshan, a decade younger than the two Khans, emerged as a star slightly later in 2000 with the hit film *Kaho Naa... Pyaar Hai* that was directed by his filmmaker father, Rakesh Roshan. Also showing a toned and sculpted body and wearing figure-hugging shirts, Hrithik Roshan could act and had 'impressive dance moves', writes Chopra (2007: 187). Many of my interviewees stated that although they loved SRK, Roshan was definitely 'the finest dancer' (August 2010). His meteoric rise to stardom came at a time when SRK was out of action after a knee surgery, thus threatening SRK's position as king of the Bollywood industry. Bose (2007: 344) notes that as a Bollywood hero, SRK's 'only conceivable rival is Hrithik Roshan, but then, he has a father who can always make films for him....' SRK's response, however, was to fight back. He made a rather mischievous and defiant new Pepsi advertisement (2000) that parodied Roshan's character, at the time that Roshan had just signed up to be the new face of Coca-Cola.[24] Then the following year, SRK appeared in the film *Asoka*, sporting a highly chiselled, gym-fit body (as discussed earlier), trained in martial arts and creating a strong, heroic look, and once more, constructing and controlling appeal and desire through his performing body—a reminder once again of the 'consumable hero' described by Deshpande (2005: 186).

I have argued that SRK's performativity, especially in the film dance and movement sequences, reveals a constructed Bollywood body, one that foregrounds athleticism, strength, and consumption of desire. Through the use of film and camera techniques, this mediated dancing body transcends the conventions for stage dance, producing an effect that is virtuosic and aesthetically pleasing. SRK's dancing, as well as his acting, establishes what Kaur and Sinha (2005: 15) have called a 'fantasy space' where diasporic and domestic desire can flourish. In the analysis of the filmigits, we find carefully constructed embodied forms—those of dancing bodies, fetish bodies, gym-toned athletic bodies as well as fashion bodies. In his work and his presentations of his embodied characters, SRK crosses previously prescribed boundaries, appealing to men and women and both urban and diasporic Indians as well as to a very significant sized audience of non-Indian fans. This produces a multilayered and multivalent gaze upon the dancing body, a complex mix of poignant longing, myriad identities, imagined fantasies, and diasporic dreams and memories. As Dudrah (2006: 88) has carefully noted, 'it is often through the use and performance of the body in its actual and symbolic forms that constructions of cultural identities are rendered socially visible.' SRK's personified role as the Indian male hero at home and worldwide has allowed him to become the 'esteemed global ambassador of Bollywood cinema through his dress and performance that mediate homeland, diasporic and transnational sensibilities' (Dudrah 2006: 92). Perhaps SRK is really a personification of Bollywood.

Notes

1. I deliberately use the term Bollywood, not Hindi or Bombay films, or even popular Indian cinema, as this is the term that is more widely used

in the global circuit, despite controversies over its usage. See Dudrah (2001) and Gehlawat (2010: xii) for further discussion.

2. The advertisement featured famous Bollywood actresses Hema Malini, Juhi Chawla, Kareena Kapoor, and Sridevi. See also Cayla (2008b).

3. Chakravarty and Singh focus on the film's images of terror; Basu (2008: 156) examines the musicality of *Dil Se..* as well as aesthetic 'geotele-visuality', and Gehlawat (2010) discusses, briefly, the song-and-dance numbers and levels of narrative worlds in the film.

4. The description of the seven stages was heavily promoted on the film's original website as well as on other sites related to the film (Kabir 2003: 157), but in some branches of Sufism, such as the Chistia, the stages of the path of love are divided into ten. For Sufis, the relationship between the cosmos and the divine is signified through the human connection of the lover and the beloved.

5. I am grateful to my third-year undergraduate students who, during this discussion, reminded me of this dance number in a class on popular culture. Farah Khan is also on record in the press as stating 'whatever I learnt was from watching Michael Jackson ... especially *Thriller* over and over again. I consider him my guru' (*Indian Express*, 2009).

6. A.R. Rahman, born Hindu, converted to Islam at the age of 23 and changed his name to Allah Rakha Rahman. He is a great believer in the relationship that exists between music and spirituality.

7. Gehlawat (2010: 38) also remarks that this song has 74 cuts and 10 scene changes in its 6-minute time span, with backdrops ranging from mountains to lakes, snow, and desert.

8. The lyrics have been taken from Masti, available at http://www.lyricsmasti.com (accessed on 13 March 2012).

9. *Tu hi tu tu hi tu satarangi re* ('You, only you, of the many colours').

10. Graham (1991: 117) later told the story of a woman in the audience who had cried throughout the performance over the death of her son. She told Graham that she had never been able to mourn his death until that point, but the dance piece showed her that grief was honourable and universal; and the tears then flowed.

11. Other references to famous dance pieces of the past can be found in *Devdas* (Dir. Sanjay Leela Bhansali, 2002), where the signature hip move of both Aishwarya Rai and Madhuri Dixit in the song *Dola re dola* to the word *dola* mimics that of the role of the Hostess in Nijinska's ballet *Les Biches* (1924).

12. The same image has also been used earlier in the song.

13. It is a well-known fact that Bollywood films commonly borrow from and refer to other Hollywood films, thus emphasizing their global awareness and scope.

14. For many years, SRK has dealt with a high level of pain, while acting and dancing, because of a back injury (a prolapsed disc) for which he had undergone a major surgery; he continues to take frequent physiotherapy treatment.

15. *Temptations* was a two-month live-performance tour staged to sell-out audiences in 16 cities across Europe, UK, USA, and Canada, featuring SRK and other Bollywood stars (Chopra 2007: 2). An American fan, writing on a blog called 'Bollywood Talk', made the following comment about this:

   > I was not disappointed in any way. Everything that is said about SRK is true. He has enormous energy and is very personable. The show ran for over three hours and SRK was on stage a lot. Towards the end the stars did a medley of songs from SRK's movies and I was dancing in the aisle. I was so comfortable with the music, I knew all the songs. SRK interacts with the audience. He invited people on stage and danced with them.

   For further work on Bollywood shows such as these, see Dudrah (2012) and Mazumdar (2013).

16. In the 1990s, SRK made over 30 films, and in the decade of the new millennium, over 40.

17. These discussions were part of a final-year undergraduate module I teach at the University of Roehampton, UK, titled 'Popular and Urban Dance: From Bollywood to Breakdance and Beyond'.

18. Kapoor was originally a Bollywood film dancer, who then went on to become an assistant choreographer to Farah Khan, and now choreographs her own films. She was a judge on India's TV dance show *Dance India Dance* between 2009 and 2011.

19. This film was directed and choreographed by Farah Khan and produced by SRK. Inspiration came from Rishi Kapoor's 1980 Bollywood film *Karz*, and many aspects from the original film are recreated here, including the title, which came from one of the original songs. It acknowledges and parodies the Indian film industry of the 1970s and 1980s.

20. This mimicked one of the storylines in the film, where the two main characters (played by SRK and Anushka Sharma) partner each other in a dance competition.

21. Chalam comments that neither Salman nor Hrithik have chest hair and suggests that many of the male Bollywood stars use laser treatment for its removal (Cayla 2008b).

22. There is fairly extensive writing on the topic of homosexuality and sexuality in Hindi films. See, for example, Desai (2003), Gopinath (2007), and Kavi (2000).

23. Bollywoodlife.com, for example, recently held a poll amongst its readers asking who was the favourite Khan. SRK polled 1,916 votes against Salman's 1,393.

24. The advertisement caused quite a controversy and Coca-Cola demanded an apology and immediately stop its airing.

References

Ahmed, Zbair. 2005. 'Who's the Real Shah Rukh Khan?', *BBC News*, 23 September, available at http://news.bbc.co.uk/2/hi/4274774.stm (accessed on 15 November 2013).

Appadurai, Arjun. 1996. *Modernity at Large: Cultural Dimensions of Globalization*. Minneapolis: University of Minnesota Press.

Basu, Anustup. 2008. 'The Music of Intolerable Love: Political Conjugality in Mani Ratnam's *Dil Se*', in Sangita Gopal and Sujata Moorti (eds), *Global Bollywood: Travels of Hindi Song and Dance*, pp. 153–78. Minneapolis: University of Minnesota Press.

Bose, Mihir. 2007. *Bollywood: A History*. Stroud, Gloucestershire: Tempus Publishing Ltd.

Cayla, Julien. 2008a. 'Following the Endorser's Shadow: Shah Rukh Khan and the Creation of the Cosmopolitan Indian Male', *Advertising and Society Review*, 9 (2), available at http://muse.jhu.edu/journals/advertising_and_society_review/v009/9.2.cayla01.html (accessed on 13 December 2012).

————. 2008b. 'Julien Cayla Interviews Nandita Chalam, Senior Creative Director, J. Walter Thompson, India', *Advertising and Society Review*, 9 (2), available at http://muse.jhu.edu/login?auth=0&type=summary&url=/journals/advertising_and_society_review/v009/9.2.cayla.html (accessed on 13 December 2012).

Chadha, Monica. 2005. 'Bollywood's Beau Smells of Roses', *BBC News*, 11 September, available at http://news.bbc.co.uk/1/hi/world/south_asia/4235600.stm (accessed on 14 March 2012).

Chakravarty, Sumita. 2000. 'Fragmenting the Nation: Images of Terrorism in Indian Popular Culture', in Mette Hjort and Scott MacKenzie (eds), *Cinema and Nation*, pp. 222–37. London and New York: Routledge.

Chopra, Anupama. 2007. *King of Bollywood: Shah Rukh Khan and the Seductive World of Indian Cinema*. New York and Boston: Warner Books.

David, Ann R. 2007. 'Beyond the Silver Screen: Bollywood and "Filmi" Dance in the UK', *South Asia Research*, 27 (1): 5–24.

——. 2010. 'Dancing the Diasporic Dream? Embodied Desires and the Changing Audience for Bollywood Film Dance', *Participations: Journal of Audience and Reception Studies*, 7 (2): 215–35, available at http://www.participations.org/Volume%207/Issue%202/special/david.htm (accessed on 12 November 2013).

Desai, Jigna. 2003. 'Bombay Boys and Girls: The Gender and Sexual Politics of Transnationality in the New Indian Cinema in English', *South Asian Popular Culture*, 1 (1): 45–61.

——. 2008. 'Bollywood, USA: Diasporas, Nations, and the State of Cinema', in Susan Koshy and S. Radhakrishnan (eds), *Transnational South Asians: The Making of a Neo-Diaspora*, pp. 345–67. New Delhi and Oxford: Oxford University Press.

Desai, Jigna, Rajinder Dudrah, and Amit Rai. 2005. 'Bollywood Audiences Editorial', *South Asian Popular Culture*, 3 (2): 79–82.

Deshpande, Sudhanva. 2005. 'The Consumable Hero of Globalised India', in Raminder Kaur and Ajay J. Sinha (eds), *Bollyworld: Popular Indian Cinema through a Transnational Lens*, pp. 186–206. New Delhi and London: SAGE Publications.

Dodds, Sherril. 2001. *Dance on Screen: Genres and Media from Hollywood to Experimental Art*. Basingstoke: Palgrave.

Dudrah, Rajinder. 2001. 'Vilayati Bollywood: Popular Hindu Cinemagoing and Diasporic South Asian Identity in Birmingham', *The Public*, 9 (1): 19–36.

——. 2006. *Sociology Goes to the Movies*. New Delhi and London: SAGE Publications.

——. 2008. 'Queer as Desis: Secret Politics of Gender and Sexuality in Bollywood Films in Diasporic Urban Ethnoscapes', in Sangita Gopal and Sujata Moorti (eds), *Global Bollywood: Travels of Hindi Song and Dance*, pp. 288–307. Minneapolis: University of Minnesota Press.

——. 2012. *Bollywood Travels: Culture, Diaspora and Border Crossings in Popular Hindi Cinema*. London: Routledge.

Dwyer, Rachel. 2000. *All You Want Is Money, All You Need Is Love: Sex and Romance in Modern India*. London: Cassell.

Frescas, David. 2010. 'Relating Divinity through Humanity', available at http://www.davidfrescas.com/home/Pieta.html (accessed on 22 April 2012).

Gehlawat, Ajay. 2010. *Reframing Bollywood: Theories of Popular Hindi Cinema*. London and New Delhi: SAGE Publications.

Gopal, Sangita and Sujata Moorti (eds). 2008. 'Introduction', in *Global Bollywood: Travels of Hindi Song and Dance*, pp. 1–60. Minneapolis and London: University of Minnesota Press.

Gopalan, Lalitha. 2002. *Cinema of Interruptions: Action Genres in Contemporary Indian Cinema*. London: British Film Institute Publishing.

Gopinath, Gayatri. 2000. 'Queering Bollywood: Alternative Sexualities in Popular Indian Cinema', *Journal of Homosexuality* (special issue), 39 (3–4): 283–97.

Graham, Martha. 1991. *Blood Memory : An Autobiography*. New York and London: Washington Square.

Henniker, Charlie. 2010. 'Pink Rupees or Gay Icons? Accounting for the Camp Appropriation of Male Bollywood Stars', *South Asia Research*, 30 (1): 25–41.

Indian Express. 2009. 'Michael Jackson Was My Guru: Farah Khan', 26 June, available at http://archive.indianexpress.com/news/michael-jackson-was-my-guru-farah-khan/481633/ (accessed on 11 November 2013).

Jha, Subhash K. 2005. 'I Enjoyed Doing the LUX Ad Thoroughly: Shah Rukh Khan', *Indiaglitz*, available at http://www.indiaglitz.com/channels/hindi/interview/6412.htm (accessed on 13 March 2012).

Jowitt, Deborah. 1988. *Time and the Dancing Image*. Berkeley and Los Angeles: University of California Press.

Kabir, Ananya Jahanara. 2003. 'Allegories of Alienation and Politics of Bargaining: Minority Subjectivities in Mani Ratnam's *Dil Se*', *South Asian Popular Culture*, pp. 309–28, 1 (2): 141–59.

Kaur, Raminder. 2005. 'Cruising on the *Vilayeti* Bandwagon: Diasporic Representations and Reception of Popular Indian Movies', in Raminder Kaur and Ajay J. Sinha (eds), *Bollyworld: Popular Indian Cinema through a Transnational Lens*, pp. 309–28. New Delhi and London: SAGE Publications.

Kaur, Raminder and Ajay J. Sinha (eds). 2005. *Bollyworld: Popular Indian Cinema through a Transnational Lens*. New Delhi and London: SAGE Publications.

Kavi, Ashok Row. 2000. 'The Changing Image of the Hero in Hindi Films', *Journal of Homosexuality*, 39 (3–4): 307–12.

Mishra, Vijay. 2002. *Bollywood Cinema: Temple of Desire*. New York and London: Routledge.

Morcom, Anna. 2008. 'Tapping the Mass Market: The Commercial Life of Hindi Film Songs', in Sangita Gopal and Sujata Moorti (eds), *Global Bollywood: Travels of Hindi Song and Dance*, pp. 63–84. Minneapolis: University of Minnesota Press.

Sawhney, Cary Rajinder. 1999. 'Dil Se..', *Sight & Sound*, http://old.bfi.org.uk/sightandsound/review/5 (accessed on 13 March 2012).

Shresthova, Sangita. 2011. *Is It All about Hips? Around the World with Bollywood Dance*. London and New Delhi: SAGE Publications.

Siegel, Marcia B. 1985 [1979]. *The Shapes of Change: Images of American Dance*. Berkeley and Los Angeles: University of California Press.

Singh, Sujala. 2010. 'Terror, Spectacle, and the Secular State in Bombay Cinema', in Elleke Boehmer and Stephen Morton (eds), *Terror and the Postcolonial*, pp. 345–60. Oxford: Wiley-Blackwell.

Turner, Graeme. 2006 [1988]. *Film as Social Practice*. London and New York: Routledge.

Williams, Linda (ed.). 1995. *Viewing Positions: Ways of Seeing Film*. New Brunswick: Rutgers University Press.

Wright, Neelam Sidhar. 2010. 'Bollywood Eclipsed: The Postmodern Aesthetics, Scholarly Appeal, and Remaking of Contemporary Popular Indian Cinema' (PhD thesis, University of Sussex, UK).

Filmography

Asoka. Dir. Santosh Sivan. Arclightz and Films, 2001.

Baazigar. Dirs Abbas Alibhai Burmawalla and Mustan Alibhai Burmawalla. United Seven Combines, 1993.

Dabangg. Dir. Abhinav Kashyap. Arbaaz Khan Productions, 2010.

Darr. Dir. Yash Chopra. Yash Raj Films, 1993.

Deewana. Dir. Raj Kanwar. Mayank Arts, 1992.

Devdas. Dir. Sanjay Leela Bhansali. Mega Bollywood, 2002.

Dil To Pagal Hai. Dir. Yash Chopra. Yash Raj Films, 1997.

Dil Se… Dir. Mani Ratnam. India Talkies and Madras Talkies, 1998.

Dilwale Dulhania Le Jayenge. Dir. Aditya Chopra. Yash Raj Films, 1995.

Jab Tak Hain Jaan. Dir. Yash Chopra. Yash Raj Films, 2012.

Kaho Naa… Pyaar Hai. Dir. Rakesh Roshan. Film Kraft, 2000.

Kal Ho Naa Ho. Dirs Nikhil Advani and Ron Reid Jr. Yash Raj Films, 2003.

Karan Arjun. Dir. Rakesh Roshan. Film Kraft, 1995.

Karz. Dir. Rishi Kapoor. Mukta Arts, 1980.

Kuch Kuch Hota Hai. Dir. Karan Johar. Dharma Productions, 1998.

Maine Pyar Kiya. Dir. Sooraj R. Barjatya. Rajshri Productions, 1989.

Maya Memsaab. Dir. Ketan Mehta. Forum Films, 1993.

My Name Is Khan. Dir. Karan Johar. Dharma Productions, 2010.

Om Shanti Om. Dir. Farah Khan. Red Chillies Entertainment, 2007.

Rab Ne Bana Di Jodi. Dir. Aditya Chopra. Yash Raj Films, 2008.

Ra.One. Dir. Anubhav Sinha. Red Chillies Entertainment, 2011.
The Inner and Outer World of Shah Rukh Kahn. Dir. Nasreen Munni Kabir.
 BBC Channel 4 and Red Chillies Entertainment, 2005.
Wanted. Dir. Prabhu Deva. Sahara One Motion Pictures, 2009.

'I Don't Need to Do This, but You've Got to Have Passion'

Shah Rukh Khan's Manifold Economic Activities

GYÖRGYI VAJDOVICH

In an interview at the beginning of 2013, Shah Rukh Khan (henceforth SRK) was questioned about the reason of the versatility of his activities. He answered modestly: 'I don't need to do all this. I have enough money to last a lifetime. But you've got to have passion ... I'm focussed, and I know why I'm doing what I am doing.' (Assisi, Ajwani, and Mitter 2013). While he is sticking to the image that he is a simple entertainer and does not understand business, articles about him very often conclude that he is a shrewd businessman only wearing the mask of a naive actor. He has been among the top taxpayer Bollywood stars for years, but his income does not originate simply from acting, it includes several different sources. An analysis of the activities of his company, Red Chillies Entertainment reveals that in 2009 only 60 per cent of the company's income was generated through film making.[1] The same article states that SRK is probably the richest star of Bollywood and estimates the value of all his assets to INR 1,500 crores (€176,475,000). Only one-third of that sum is constituted by the value of Red Chillies Entertainment (including all branches, even Kolkata Knight Riders), his real estate properties' value is higher than that of his film investments, and his brand endorsements are also worth half of it (Chattopadhyay and Subramanian 2010). These data seem to suggest that he does understand business very well and his sphere of interest covers rather varied areas. This chapter intends to give an overview of his activities in the entertainment business (the real estate business is out of the scope of our examination) and tries to answer the question whether his versatile activities simply intend to increase his incomes or do they really constitute some kind of 'passion' for one of Bollywood's biggest stars.

This chapter concentrates on SRK's economic activities since the beginning of the 2000s. This is the period during which the Indian entertainment industry developed to a great extent and the scope of its activities increased considerably. In 1998 the Indian government granted industry status to the film industry, which meant reduction in custom duties, exemption from excise duties and tax incentives, and made the film industry eligible for infrastructural and credit support (Mehta 2005: 136; Thussu 2008: 105). This generated a boom in the entertainment and media industry. According to the reports of Pricewaterhouse Coopers, India's media and entertainment industry produced an annual growth of 16.6 per cent between 2004 and 2008 (Business of Cinema 2009), and though the expansion has slowed down it still showed the highest growth rates in the world growing at 11.2 per cent in 2010 (Business of Cinema 2011). The 3.5 billion Indian film industry produces more than 1,000 films a year in more than 20 languages, and exports its products to more than 70 countries in the world (Ernst & Young 2011). Compared to the single state-owned TV channel in 1991, in 2012 nearly 600 channels were in operation in India (Thussu 2013), and other segments of the media industry are also growing at great speed. While previously films generated incomes mostly by tickets sold in theatres, nowadays one can witness a proliferation of revenues: music rights for films, DVDs, cable TV, satellite TV, pay-per-view, Internet download sales, mobile contents, online gaming, licensing, and merchandizing (Deprez 2010; Thussu 2008 and 2013). The cinema market has changed considerably, as the number of multiplex cinemas is increasing (Deprez 2010: 89), which foster the release of small-budget niche films or films aiming at an urban or young public. As a sign of globalization, foreign media companies like Sony, Star, or Disney entered the Indian media market as producers, co-producers, and distributors (Deprez 2010: 115; Thussu 2008: 106), while Indian companies distribute their products in more and more countries in a growing number of prints and in different formats. The expansion of the media industry is manifold and includes new fields or activities almost every year. The following chapter will try to shed light on how SRK, once a simple actor, became gradually involved in this prolific industry.

The Actor and the Star

To begin with, we have to state that SRK is first of all an actor and a star, and he will always remain that. Acting is his passion, but during the 25 years of his career he also learnt how to utilize his acting skills and star power to the most. Beside his incomes from acting (that will be discussed later on), he has different sources which are strongly related to his star persona. He regularly lends his face to advertisements, performs at different shows, or figures on TV. Some of these are long-term or large-scale activities, like he has been the brand ambassador for TAG Heuer watches since 2003 (D'costa 2012), or his series of shows in 2004 called *Temptations Tour* included performances in 12 big cities in the UK and North America, sometimes in front of 25,000 viewers (Kabir 2005). He is considered as a kind of ambassador for Bollywood films in Western countries; therefore, he is regularly invited as a special guest to film festivals or award shows. But he also performs at different shows, award galas, walks the ramp for fashion shows, and he is not ashamed of performing at weddings when he needs money. However, we have to note that these relatively stable resources (according the latest news he charges INR four to eight crores [€4,706,000 to 9,412,000] for a 30-minute performance at weddings (Banerjee 2013) help him to finance other projects that sometimes end in failure, and thereby providing him with the freedom to experiment. As he himself declares, when he needs money, he prefers to shake a leg than enter a bank (Chattopadhyay and Subramanian 2010). His presence at different galas and shows also contribute to the marketing of his films and may attract sponsors for his projects.

From Acting to Film Production

When SRK started to act in films at the beginning of the 1990s, major actors worked in four to five films at the same time and they got a salary bargained in advance. SRK was among the first actors to introduce the new system nowadays popular among big stars. They take a role in exchange of a share of the incomes and sometimes also part of the author's rights. They invest their own money and/ or work, but they get higher incomes and a much bigger control of the whole process of film making, as they can choose their script and can influence the selection of the director and other members of the staff. But this strategy also involves the star taking share of the risks and sometimes can end disastrously for them.

Amitabh Bachchan had previously had an unsuccessful attempt in this field with his company named Amitabh Bachchan Corporation Limited, but SRK played a pioneering role in this form of film production when he founded his company Dreamz Unlimited with his co-star Juhi Chawla and his director-friend Aziz Mirza. Though out of the three films realized by Dreamz Umlimited only *Chalte Chalte* (Dir.Aziz Mirza, 2003) was successful, Khan introduced this kind of 'self-financing' then which proved to be successful in the long run.

Present-day Bollywood witnesses a tendency wherein more and more top stars found their own production company and become producers of their own films. One of the first stars to establish a company was Aamir Khan, who brought to life Aamir Khan Productions for the sake of *Lagaan* (Dir. Ashutosh Gowariker, 2001). He was followed by SRK, who created Red Chillies Entertainment in 2002 with a similar purpose; while Aamir Khan made the realization of a film possible that nobody believed in (Nandy 2001), SRK launched a female director inconceivable in mainstream Bollywood until then (Farah Khan, previously a choreographer, directed *Main Hoon Na* [in 2004] for SRK and with him starring in the lead role). With the help of this production method both of them have fostered the realization of films that are unconventional, controversial, or expensive (apart from *Lagaan* and *Taare Zameen Par* [Dirs Aamir Khan, Amole Gupte, and Ram Madhvani, 2007], *My Name Is Khan* [*MNIK*, Dir. Karan Johar, 2010], *Ra.One* [Dir. Anubhav Sinha, 2011], or *Talaash* [Dir. Reema Kagti, 2012]). The realization of SRK's dream project

Ra.One would not have been possible without his own investments. Before the release of the film he admitted that they went over-budget, nearly five times over the original amount (Gupta, Bhat, and Joshi 2011)—such an excess would not be tolerated by any producer unless he finances his film himself.[3]

Beside SRK and Aamir Khan, today Saif Ali Khan, Akshay Kumar, and Ajay Devgan also produce their own films and many other stars are attempting to do the same, but only a few of them proved to be successful producers. To operate this system successfully, it is not enough to have a proper financial background; the star should be able to select scripts that would please the public, as financing a film involves much higher risks than accepting a role in it. Bollywood fans can read in the news regularly about the remuneration of a certain star for a given film or TV show, but Aamir Khan and SRK are the only ones who have no 'market price', as they do not accept roles any more without taking share of the costs and the incomes (Saif Ali Khan has also been making efforts to reach that status lately).[4] Among them, only Aamir Khan and SRK use their companies for other purposes than operating as a producer or co-producer of their own films, but SRK's strategy seems to be rather unconventional.

One of the most significant elements of the globalization in Indian film industry is the so-called corporatization. This means the process during which small-range family companies grow into large-scale companies, sometimes going public or merging with other industrial companies or banks, and often operating in different fields of the entertainment industry (Deprez 2010: 75; Ganti 2004: 88f; Kushu 2008). Path-breaking companies from this point of view are Mukta Arts or Yash Raj Films, but these were family companies of success-ful director–producers with considerable antecedents. The general trend is that successful directors try to produce their own films first, then they help their family members, assistant directors, or friends to become directors by producing their films and venture to larger-scale film production gradually. This was the path taken by Yash and Aditya Chopra at Yash Raj Films, Subhash Ghai at Mukta Arts, Karan Johar at Dharma Productions, or Farhan Akthar at Excel Entertainment. We can say that these companies developed hori-zontally, they grew bigger and bigger in the same field producing more and more films, and only after some time they started to expand vertically, that is to say, they entered into other fields of the entertainment industry. This way Mukta Arts nowadays operates in film distribution, exhibition, equipment rental, and education, while Yash Raj Films has distribution offices in India and abroad, has constructed its own studio for rent, and has a music production, a TV production, a home entertainment branch, and a merchandizing branch.

We can say that SRK took an unusual path from this point of view, as with the only exception of two of his best friend, Karan Johar's movies (*Kaal* [Dir. Soham Shah, 2005] and *Student of the Year* [Dir. Karan Johar, 2012]) Red Chillies Entertainment only produced his own films, but SRK started to enlarge his field of activity vertically from very early on. The present-day Red Chillies Advertisement subsidiary started to produce TV commercials in 2001 and the special effects company, Red Chillies VFX, started its operation with the creation of special effects for *Main Hoon Na* in 2004. First they ventured into equipment rentals and then Red Chillies Entertainment entered the Indian Premier League (IPL) with the purchase of the team Kolkata Knight Riders in 2008. A new subsidiary, Red Chillies Idiot Box started to produce TV programmes in 2009. We could also say that the fields that SRK chooses are rather unconventional; instead of setting up a distribution company or a music company to generate more income from his films, he invested in the domain of special effects which was not so popular in India, but had great prospects. Then he ventured into IPL, which is not considered to be part of the entertainment industry; however, the way SRK manages his team includes many elements of show business.

Distribution of Films

If we examine the distribution and marketing activity of SRK and his company, we can say that he is adapting Western techniques well. Film distribution and exhibition has changed rapidly in India during the last 10–15 years. While previously huge single-screen cinemas with 600–2,500 seats dominated the country (Ganti 2004: 61), nowadays approximately 75 per cent of the domestic income originates from multiplexes (Srivastava 2013) bearing a much higher number of screens with a smaller number of seats. As the prints distributed outside India generate a considerable share of the incomes, the number of prints released in foreign countries has been increasing continuously as well. If we add to these the threat of piracy, it is easy to understand that distributors are encouraged to release films in higher number of prints and in realizing the highest possible revenue during the shortest period of time.

SRK realized the importance of this strategy early on, and was always ahead of competing companies from this point of view. *Om Shanti Om* (Dir. Farah Khan) was released in 2007 with 2,000 prints (Elley 2007), a number never heard of in Bollywood cinema. In comparison, in the 1990s, 200–250 prints were the usual number (Kapoor 2010); *Hum Aapke Haun Koun...!* [Dir. Sooraj R. Barjatya, 1994] was considered as an exception with its 500 prints (Kapoor 2010; Srivastava 2013). The number of prints started to increase at the middle of the 2000s, the previous highest number was that of *Dhoom: 2* (Dir. Sanjay Gadhvi, 2006) with 1,800 prints (Sheikh 2006), but even the greatest hits did not break *Om Shanti Om*'s record during the following two years (*Ghajini*: 1,500 prints; *3 Idiots*: 1,900 prints) (IANS 2008 and Bhat 2010, respectively); only *MNIK* exceeded this number with 2,500 prints (released in two phases) (Bhat 2010). We can note a similar distribution strategy at SRK's later films: *Ra.One* got an incredible release with 4,600 prints (Bhat 2011c), while the previous highest number was only 2,800 screens for *Bodyguard* (Dir. Siddique, 2011) (Lalwani 2011). *Chennai Express* (Dir. Rohit Shetty, 2013) (4,200 screens) is also high compared to the previous and expected releases and only paralleled by *Ra.One* and *Ek Tha Tiger* (Dir. Kabir Khan, 2012) for which 4,000 prints were made (Srivastava 2013).

As SRK is the most popular Indian star in the West, he pays special attention to foreign markets. He markets his films extensively in certain countries like UK, Dubai, or Germany, and is considered one of the first stars to organize the premiere of his films abroad. *Om Shanti Om* had a red carpet world premiere in London, *MNIK* premiered in Dubai and Germany, *Ra.One* in Dubai and London, and *Chennai Express* in London, Dubai, and Kolkata consecutively.

His presence at certain Western festivals is the sign of his special status in Western countries; he is considered as a kind of ambassador of Bollywood films in the West and therefore, he often gets invited to events where Bollywood films are usually not acknowledged. In 2002

Devdas (Dir. Sanjay Leela Bhansali, 2002) was the first Bollywood feature film accepted as an official selection at the Cannes Film Festival (Jha 2002); in 2008 *Om Shanti Om* was selected into the Special Section of the Berlin Film Festival (India Glitz 2008); while in 2010 *MNIK* was included in the programme of the Official Competition at Berlin Film Festival (Jha 2009). These invitations are symptomatic of his popularity and as these festivals are not the usual forums of Bollywood films, they can be considered as homage to the Bollywood film industry represented by its greatest star.

Consequently, it is not surprising that SRK's films are distributed with a higher number of prints to foreign markets than other Bollywood hits. Compared to the average number of 300–400 prints for big Bollywood hits in the overseas market in 2009–11, *MNIK* was released with more than 550 prints abroad (boxofficeindia.com 2010), and *Ra.One* with more than 900 prints (Bhat 2011). SRK is also trying to expand his market to more and more countries. *Om Shanti Om* was distributed to less than a dozen countries, and its main novelty was that it got a release with almost twice as many prints in North America than previous Bollywood hits (Pais 2007). On the contrary, *MNIK* was distributed in 66 countries and dubbed in four European languages: Spanish, German, Russian, and Italian (Ardash 2010). It showed a new path by being released in 25 countries, which are usually not considered as traditional markets of Bollywood films (Bhat 2010), like Puerto Rico, Syria, Lebanon, Jordan, Egypt, Taiwan, Italy, or Spain (Ardash 2010). We could say that in 2007, the conquest of the UK and North America was at stake while in 2010, the aim was to expand Bollywood's influence to unconquered markets. In order to realize this aim, Karan Johar and SRK chose a new distribution partner. While previously films produced by Red Chillies were distributed abroad by Eros International, the biggest Indian distributor of Bollywood films abroad, *MNIK* was released by an international company, Fox Star, which was handling the domestic market, Fox Searchlight Pictures catered to the American market, and Twentieth Century Fox was responsible for international distribution.

Though the cooperation with Fox ended after *MNIK*, the territorial expansion continued with *Ra.One* and *Chennai Express*. *Ra.One* was distributed to such non-traditional markets as South

Korea, Taiwan, and Latin American countries (Bhat 2011), and two years later, *Chennai Express* got released in new markets like Peru, Morocco, Switzerland, Austria, France, and Israel, and was dubbed in nine languages—English, French, Spanish, Arabic, German, Hebrew, Dutch, Turkish, and Malay, and subtitled in other languages as well (Malvania 2013). Therefore, SRK's distribution policy and the conscious expansion of his public image can be regarded as a symbol of the globalization of the Indian entertainment industry, always looking for new markets and new forms of partnership.[5] This distribution strategy shows that SRK is aware of his own status inside the Bollywood film industry. Salman Khan and Aamir Khan are more profitable on the domestic market because SRK's films regularly aim more at the public of multiplex cinemas than that of the single screen cinemas (particularly *MNIK* with its controversial topic and *Ra.One* stuffed with special effects and targeting a teenage public). At the same time he has been the most popular of Bollywood stars abroad for long years. According to a statistical analysis made at the beginning of 2012, out of the 10 top grossers of all time, realizing the greatest revenues on the foreign markets, seven had SRK as the lead star (boxofficeindia.com 2012).[6] Therefore, we can state that beside his interest in new techniques and his sensibility for future trends, his distribution strategy aims to compensate his disadvantages on the domestic market with revenues realized in foreign markets.

Marketing

Considering his marketing techniques, we can state that SRK's methods have changed a lot during the last few years and he is receptive to Western techniques in this field as well. SRK generally promotes his films with himself, that is to say that he increases his presence in all kinds of media before the release of the film, making use of the appeal of his star persona. The promotion of *MNIK* was a typical example of this strategy wherein he increased his presence in the print media and TV programmes, he performed in an award show after a hiatus of two years, figured on the cover of *Filmfare* magazine, and Discovery Channel started to show a 10-part documentary on him simultaneously with the release of the film (Das 2010). Though he used the Internet and other modern technologies, good examples provided by his Twitter messages or the live telecast of the Dubai premier of *MNIK* on the facebook page of *Business of Cinema*, these could not compete with the creative marketing that Aamir Khan launched previously on facebook before the premier of *3 Idiots* (Singh 2009).[7]

On the contrary, the marketing campaign of *Ra.One* opened up new perspectives of marketing in the Indian film industry. It included methods never used before in India, and analysts described *Ra.One* as the most advertised film in the history of Bollywood (Bhat 2011a). Typically, movies with a big star cast and mega-budget releases start their marketing around eight weeks before release, but in this case the marketing campaign started in January for the film which was only released in October (Bhat 2011a), thereby resembling the trend of big Hollywood blockbusters. An unusually high sum, one-third of the production costs were spent on promotion and it used any conceivable platform of advertisement. As an article described the campaign: 'He is leaping out of McDonald's happy meals, changing colour on Horlicks' magic mugs, gleaming in blue on Cinthol deodorants, and flying out on Western Union Money Transfers. He's marketing INR 150-crore [€17,647,500] film with tie-ins worth INR 50 crore [€5,882,500]. The Badshah of Blah has become the Maestro of Marketing, talking up his film, *Ra.One*....' (Bamzai and Bari 2011). *Ra.One*'s first look was unveiled by the star on his Twitter page in January 2011, and a 10-second trailer was projected during the Cricket World Cup semi-final match between India and Australia.

SRK used his traditional methods, like the film was advertised extensively in print media, on TV and on billboards, and he made a tour of 36 cities in a promotional campaign including foreign locations (Bhat 2011a). He made a tie-up with Western Union's global payment services to launch a global mass media campaign for the film focusing on Indian diaspora countries. Nokia's new smartphones supporting Near Field Communication (NFC) technology offered free movie songs or mobile screensavers and movie trailers in Nokia priority stores for users owning the device (Bhat 2011a). As the film's story was strongly related to a computer game, Red Chillies tied up with Sony to build a Playstation console for different platforms titled

Ra.One—The Game. The game allowed players to identify with G.One or Ra.One, the hero or the villain of the film, replicated the look of the film's characters, included action sequences from the movie, and had SRK's voiceover (Bhat 2011a). Another important medium to connect with young audiences whom the film particularly targeted was the use of social networks. Red Chillies contracted UTV Indiagames to design a social game based on the film (Gupta, Bhat, and Joshi 2011), which became the most downloaded game in the country within 24 hours of its release (Bamzai and Bari 2011). However, the game was independent of the film, so it had a chance to maintain its popularity even after the release of the film. The company also launched a series of free digital comics across all major mobile platforms, adding a new episode every week (Bhat 2011c). YouTube created a dedicated video channel for *Ra.One* which included behind-the-scene shots, interviews with the stars, hosted games and a contest where participants could create *Ra.One* promos from clips, music, and dialogues of the film, and competed for most views (Bhat 2011a). It was the first customized channel for a Bollywood film on YouTube, so it initiated a new platform for digital marketing in Indian cinema (PTI 2011a), and reached 10 million hits few days before the release of the movie (Bamzai and Bari 2011). Google also cooperated with SRK declaring him 'the only actor to have a "verified" Google+ page in India', and organized multiple video chat sessions for him. Google welcomed the association as it intended to attract more users through celebrity presence on the network (Joshi 2011).

The promotional campaign of *Ra.One* lifted merchandizing to a level until then unknown in India. The production of merchandise was introduced in Bollywood by Yash Raj Films in 2006 (Business of Cinema 2006), but they have always launched a few products connected to a given film and later developed a collection related to their biggest hits. Red Chillies on the contrary released 60 products related to a single film (Bhat 2011a), all of them designed by the company and produced by HM International in China, that is, the manufacturer of all Disney's products in India. Products included pencil boxes, piggy banks, lunch boxes, notebooks, limited edition toys, sippers, and so on, and were sold in more than 3,500 stores and e-commerce sites. 90 per cent of the 400,000 stationery items and toys were sold in 15 days, so the company was obliged to order more (Bamzai and Bari 2011). Red Chillies made licencing deals with different companies for manufacturing products like jars, water bottles, frisbees, apparel, caps, and electronic items like handycams, notebooks, and tablets (PTI 2011b). A jewellery line was also designed inspired by the symbol of Ra.One, comprising necklaces, bracelets, and mobile charms, bearing the blue colour that was characteristic of SRK's outfit in the film (Bhat 2011a). As Shailja Gupta, the head of the digital and merchandising department of Red Chillies during the making of Ra.One explains, the concept of using the merchandising was different from its usual use in India:

> The only issue is that the producers of a lot of Bollywood films think of merchandizing as some moneymaking thing right now. But it's still at a nascent stage in India. For example, for Ra.One, as far as Shah Rukh is concerned, he was very clear that he's not looking to make money; he's going to use that as a marketing tool. He invested a lot of money into this but just as a marketing tool. (Yount 2012)

If we examine the promotional campaign of Chennai Express in 2013, it can be noted that SRK largely resumed his traditional methods of marketing (giving interviews, figuring in TV shows, promoting in several towns even abroad, publishing advertisements in different media), but retained certain elements of the strategy elaborated for the promotion of Ra.One. SRK used social media to a great extent using Twitter frequently during the making and the promotion of Chennai Express to regularly supply news about the film. Chennai Express also had a game version developed for mobile phones. Considering that Ra.One was the most expensive Indian film at its release, it is probable that its star/producer tried to guarantee success by using new ways of marketing, until then unknown in India. Chennai Express had a more moderate budget, so a marketing campaign with smaller budget and less creativity was sufficient to promote it. It is ironical that Chennai Express could become the biggest box office success of Bollywood cinema up to that time. Can we perhaps say that SRK was a few steps ahead of the industry with the concept, the budget, and the marketing of his dream project, Ra.One?

TV Commercials

SRK's company has been producing commercials since 2001, and the branch now operating as Red Chillies TVC has brought to life more than 250 commercials. Under the banner, TV ads are realized by successful ad-film directors and well-known Bollywood directors like Farah Khan, Karan Johar, Aziz Mirza, Santosh Sivan, Rohit Shetty, and Anurag Basu and the company has its own writers, stylists, and creative producers. The list of their clients includes famous Indian and international companies and consumer brands like Hyundai, Airtel, Videocon, ICICI, Unilever, Nokia, Pepsi, PepsiCo, Hero Honda, Dish TV, Jet Airways, and so on (see a more comprehensive list on Red Chillies' website).

Red Chillies TVC is not only a production branch of Red Chillies, but also facilitates SRK's job as a brand ambassador. When he acquires brand endorsements from different companies, the realization of the commercial is often delegated to his own TVC production company. SRK is one of the most popular brand ambassadors among Indian celebrities; over the years he has endorsed hundreds of products. If we look at the list of his famous endorsements and that of the most well-known clients of Red Chillies TVC, the lists overlap to a great extent.

SRK's endorsements also facilitate him to produce his films as he often has tie-ins with the brands that he is endorsing. He initiated this strategy at the shooting of *Phir Bhi Dil Hai Hindustani* (Dir. Aziz Mirza, 2000) in 1999 with his company Dreamz Unlimited where corporate sponsorship was utilized at a level rather unusual in India (for example, SRK wooed Juhi Chawla in front of a Swatch kiosk, they drove around in a Santro car, and so on; Deshpande 2005). Most probably any fan of SRK could cite some famous product placements from his films, like the whole football team playing in Reebook sweaters in *Main Hoon Na*, bits of dialogues about Nokia phones in several films, or the famous Reebook shoes in *MNIK*, which play an important role in the story. Farah Khan even made SRK's endorsements a subject of self-reflexivity in *Om Shanti Om*, when Om Kapoor is talking with Pappu under a huge TAG Heuer ad on the bridge—the scene has a triple function: it shows the status of the young hero, Om, in the film industry indicating that he has become a big star, it is a humorous allusion to SRK's star status and endorsements, and at the same time fulfils the requirements of a good product placement. For the realization of *Ra.One*, SRK made contracts with 25 brands for tie-ins, shooting an advertisement for each product and earning Rs 50 crore [€5,882,500] to help the financing of the big-budget film (Bamzai and Bari 2011).

TV Shows

The company's TV production branch, Red Chillies Idiot Box, started its operation in 2008 and it produced 12 TV shows. SRK's idea was to bring new concepts for Indian TV, to create series of short movies instead of star interviews and soap operas, to bring cinematic value to television (Oneindia 2008). He experimented with several new types of TV programmes: *Ghar Ki Baat Hai* (2009–10) was a situational comedy about a family's everyday life; *Knights and Angels* (2009) was a reality show hunting for cheerleaders for SRK's IPL team, Kolkata Knight Riders; *Little Star Awards* was a show in which an award was decided and judged by little kids; *Ishaan* (2010) was a musical drama targeting teenage audiences produced for Disney Channel in the vein of *Hannah Montana* (2006–11) and *High School Musical* (2006–8); and *Luv Reels* (2010–11) was a series of three romantic films introducing the concept of UGC (user-generated content), for which the makers, the actors, and the content were selected by the audience online with the aim of launching new talents in the industry. Red Chillies Idiot Box produced *Living with a Superstar* (2010), a 10-part documentary on SRK's life for Discovery Travel & Living; and the show entitled *Live My Life* (2011) in which a star selected his/her craziest fan and let the fan spend a whole day with him/her taking part in all activities. The company also created talk shows of the more conventional type, trying to renew the concept by finding new type of hosts, like the well-known designers Abu Jani and Sandeep Khosla for *The First Ladies* (2009–10), or choreographer-director Farah Khan for *Tere Mere Beach Mein* (2009). SRK's contacts always guaranteed star guests who could attract the public like Shreyas Talpade, Juhi Chawla, and Irrfan Khan, and Farah Khan figuring in *Ghar Ki Baat Hai*; Purab Kohli, Lara Dutta, or Deepika Padukone in *Knights and Angels*; or Gauri Khan herself in *The First Ladies*.

In spite of the creative ideas and new concepts Red Chillies Idiot Box did not prove to be very successful. Following SRK's steps, several film industry companies or personalities like Yash Raj Films, Paresh Rawal, Anil Kapoor, Prakash Jha, and Anurag Basu decided to enter the TV business (D'souza 2010), creating strong competition and finally SRK got to the conclusion that after all, television works on other principles than the film industry and perhaps, it is not his sphere. In 2012 he decided to shut down the TV production branch of Red Chillies and concentrate on the visual effects branch instead.

Visual Effects

SRK is known to be fascinated by all kinds of electronic equipment and interested in different technologies; no wonder, he got involved in the creation of visual effects rather early. A small crew created for him the visual effects for *Main Hoon Na* and, in 2006, he founded a new subsidiary of his company Red Chillies VFX that specialized in the production of visual effects. This new enterprise—Red Chillies VFX is the most dynamically developing branch of Red Chillies. It started with eight members and currently employs more than 300 artists (Animation Xpress.com 2013), continuously recruiting new talents and occasionally hiring freelance staff for certain jobs. The company has elaborated visual effects for more than 25 Bollywood films, creating such memorable scenes as the ghost and the real husband (both played by SRK) figuring together in *Paheli* (Dir. Amol Palekar, 2005); Don carrying his look-alike, Vijay, in *Don* (Dir. Farhan Akhtar, 2006); Deepika Padukone dancing with great stars of the 1970s in *Om Shanti Om*; Priyanka Chopra as dancing and interacting with Harman Baweja in a dance sequence of *What's Your Raashee* (Dir. Ashutosh Gowariker, 2009); the flooding of the hotel in *De Dana Dan* (Dir. Priyadarshan, 2009), and hundreds of unnoticeable effects where they added fire to a scene, multiplied the crowd, exchanged the background, or created camera movements digitally (Animation Xpress.com 2013). Furthermore, Red Chillies VFX takes active part in the production of TV commercials as well adding creative visual ideas to the ads.

Their most ambitious project was *Ra.One*, which contained more than 3,300 visual effects (VFX) shots than James Cameron's *Avatar*

(2009), containing only 2,700 (Bhat 2011b). Of these shots 90 per cent were realized in India and in majority by the Red Chillies VFX team. For *Ra.One* they used the most up-to-date technologies and they hope that *Krrish 3* (Dir. Rakesh Roshan, 2013), which the company is actually working on, will again set a new benchmark in Indian cinema from the point of view of visual effects. Red Chillies VFX was one of the first visual effects studios in India to acquire an ISO (International Organization for Standardization) certification and is now 'Motion Picture Association of America' (MPAA) Compliant Studio (Animation Xpress.com 2013). With these qualifications Red Chillies VFX aims to enter the international market to cater to Hollywood or international VFX projects. SRK invests a lot in his VFX company, he wants it to be the best VFX company in India and envisions it as the main revenue generator for Red Chillies in a few years' time (Chattopadhyay and Subramanian 2010).

Activities Outside the Moving Image Industry

In 2008 Red Chillies Entertainment bought the Kolkata Knight Riders cricket franchise in the IPL.[8] Sports are generally not considered as part of the entertainment industry, but SRK's idea was to amalgamate entertainment with sports. He had theme songs composed for the team, shot videos for them, organized a TV show in search of cheerleaders, even cooperated with Manish Malhotra walking the ramp as a show stopper for Malhotra's fashion show who created a special collection inspired by the uniform and styling of Kolkata Knight Riders (Das 2009). Due to SRK's promotional activity, Kolkata Knight Riders was a profitable company even during the first years when the team could not even get close to championship. In the business of cricket SRK created a precedent: after him, other Bollywood stars such as Preity Zinta and Shilpa Shetty also purchased a team. The presence of stars helped to promote the teams and contributed to the development of cricket into a professional sport and profitable business. Recently, SRK has announced that once an IPL-like premier league will be formed in football, he intends to buy a football team as well, preferably that of Kolkata again (Ghosh 2013). The All India Football Federation (AIFF), initiating the setting up of the league, has a similar intention that was realized with the cricket premier league wherein the objective was to make football an acknowledged sport and transform it into a profitable business, and the presence of stars would facilitate that.

SRK sometimes experiments with other new ideas as well. In November 2012, he launched a new indoor theme park for kids in Mumbai that is partly owned by him. KidZania is a 75,000 square feet edutainment park for children where real-life situations can be experienced and certain skills can be developed through games and entertainment (Kirpalani 2012).

In 2013 Red Chillies ventured into event management and the company organized the opening ceremony of the Pepsi IPL 2013 at the Salt Lake Stadium, Kolkata. The grandiose show involved a huge number of dancers; guest stars such as Katrina Kaif, Deepika Padukone, the international rapper star Pitbull were present, along with flying drummers, fireworks, and several other spectacular elements. The organizers took advantage of SRK's star personality once again; he could invite great star guests due to his contacts, acted as a host to the ceremony, and presented an attractive show himself. The fact that this single event figures on Red Chillies' website as a separate field, it may indicate that the company intends to pursue this kind of activity in the future as well.

———

After having an overview of SRK's business operations, we can state that the scope of his activities is rather wide. While traditional film companies like Mukta Arts or Yash Raj Films invested in territories that are closely related to film-making and serve as a support for film production or help to generate more income for their films, SRK seems to have opted for other ways. Earlier he followed a similar pathway striving to minimize production costs and increase incomes. We can trace this principle in the investment of his own skills (and in that of Juhi Chawla and Aziz Mirza as well) that became the foundation of Dreamz Unlimited; the purchase of a stock of technical equipment, also available for rent, that later became the foundation of his special effects company; or, his earlier dream of constructing his own studio sometime in the future. Nowadays it seems that his strategy has changed. He has abandoned certain activities; he has sold the equipment-leasing division to an assistant, stopped the production of TV shows (Assisi, Ajwani, and Mitter 2013), and does not talk any more about his desire to own a studio. The website for Red Chillies Entertainment also bears the trace of an earlier intention to purchase the right of films that may have been dismissed. SRK entered the media industry in a period of its boom, and in earlier years he followed pathways taken by other small companies that were trying to corporatize themselves. Later, as he became a significant representative of this industry, he opted for individual ways.

These days SRK takes much bigger risks in film production (see the case of *Ra.One*), invests a lot in his VFX studio, and ventures into territories that are dear to him personally, but are not related to the film industry (like sports and charitable projects targeting children and teenagers). Several of his projects seem to be path-breaking ventures, like the use of Western-style marketing techniques, the production of new types of TV programmes, the realization of a VFX-loaded film for young audiences, or the fostering of a high-tech VFX studio. In certain cases (like in the case of some of the TV shows or *Ra.One*), the questions that then arise are whether the concept was not satisfactory; or, was it simply that such an introduction was ahead of its time and the industry and the public were not yet open for such experiments. It is certain that SRK has always been sensible towards future trends and has been a trendsetter, but recently he has been concentrating on more creative activities instead of those just generating incomes. The changes in his activities may suggest that besides being a shrewd businessman, nowadays SRK involves himself with projects motivated by passion which often turn out to be profitable as well.

Notes

1. It must be noted that the analysis only examines the year 2009. According to Red Chillies Entertainment, sources cited by Chattopadhyay and Subramanian (2010), that year 60.2 per cent of the company's activities was created by film production, 19.1 per cent by TV commercials, 15.8 per cent by the production of TV programmes, 4.5 per cent by

the VFX branch, and 0.4 per cent by equipment rental. Since then the ratio has definitely changed as Red Chillies VFX has greatly increased its activities, while the production of TV shows has diminished.

2. Amounts are calculated as per the exchange rate applicable on 25 November 2013.

3. In fact, *Ra.One* was co-produced by Eros International and Red Chillies Entertainment.

4. SRK only makes an exception for Yash Raj Films, bearing great respect for Aditya and the late Yash Chopra, and never forgetting that they launched his career at the beginning of the 1990s. He declared several times that he never asks them what his remuneration would be, still he has no reason to complain as he received 30 crore (€3,529,500) for his role in *Jab Tak Hai Jaan* (Dir. Yash Chopra, 2012; as per the online source Box Office Capsule, 2013). It seems that Aamir Khan only made an exception for the Chopras as well in the case of *Dhoom 3* (Dir. Vijay Krishna Acharya, 2013) since the release of *3 Idiots* (Dir. Rajkumar Hirani) in 2009.

5. According to the definition of Anwar and Catley (2007: 292):

Globalization can be viewed as a shift towards a more integrated and inter-dependent world economy. Globalization provides opportunities for factors of production such as land, labour, capital, and entrepreneurship to extend beyond domestic markets and thus, allows for a greater degree of economies of scale in production and sales potential.

6. It must be remembered that the top-grosser lists are continuously under transformation. Because of the rapidly changing distribution and marketing technics, records are broken every few months, and this statistic did not yet contain, for example, *Agneepath*'s (Dir. Karan Malhotra, 2012), *Ek Tha Tiger*'s, or *Chennai Express*'s revenues. However, if we examine the data from the beginning of 2009, the ratio was exactly the same, but SRK's films figuring in the top 10 list were partly different (boxofficeindia.com, 2009).

7. During the promotion of *3 Idiots* on 31 December 2009, Aamir Khan launched an alternate reality game open for any fan or viewer. He disguised himself in different outfits and landed in different towns of India, every time giving a clue on facebook about his whereabouts. Fans had to track down and find him, and those who won the game (discovering the highest number of places where he turned up), could spend the New Year's Eve with him and his family.

8. Actually, in Kolkata Knight Riders, Red Chillies has 50 per cent equity; the rest belongs to Juhi Chawla and her husband.

References

Animation Xpress.com. 2013. "'Redchillies VFX" Completes 7 Power-Packed Years of Delivering Outstanding VFX: Down the Memory Lane and Future ...', 22 April, available at http://www.animationxpress.com/index.php/vfx/redchillies-vfx-completes-7-power-packed-years-of-delivering-outstanding-vfx-down-the-memory-lane-and-future (accessed on 19 August 2013).

Anwar, Sajid and Bob Catley. 2007. 'Globalization and Economic Development', in Anjum Siddiqui (ed.), *India and South-Asia. Economic Developments in the Age of Globalization*, pp. 291–320. Armonk and London: M.E. Sharpe.

Assisi, Charles, Deepak Ajwani, and Sohini Mitter. 2013. 'Shah Rukh Inc.', *Forbes India*, 6 February, available at http://forbesindia.com/article/2012-celebrity-100/shah-rukh-inc/34627/1 (accessed on 17 August 2013).

Bamzai, Kaveree and Nishat Bari. 2011. 'Khan Market: Shah Rukh Khan Turns a Marketing Maestro to Promote *Ra.One*', *India Today*, 21 October, available at http://indiatoday.intoday.in/story/shah-rukh-khan-ra.one-franchise-marketing/1/157032.html (accessed on 10 August 2013).

Banerjee, Soumyadipta. 2013. 'Shah Rukh Khan Charges a Hefty Amount for Weddings', *Times of India*, 11 May, available at http://articles.timesofindia.indiatimes.com/2013-05-11/news-interviews/39185747_1_srk-shah-rukh-4-crore (accessed on 17 August 2013).

Bhat, Varada. 2010. '*My Name Is Khan* to Be Splashed Across 2,000 Screens Globally', *The Hindu Business Line*, 7 February, available at http://www.thehindubusinessline.com/todays-paper/tp-others/tp-variety/my-name-is-khan-to-be-splashed-across-2000-screens-globally/article983249.ece?ref=archive (accessed on 10 February 2010).

Business Standard 2011a. 'Bollywood's Longest Promotion', *Business Standard*, 19 September, available at http://www.business-standard.com/article/management/bollywood-s-longest-promotion-111091900038_1.html (accessed on 10 August 2013).

———. 2011b. Cross-platform Play for Shah Rukh's Superhero Flick', 3 October, available at http://www.business-standard.com/article/technology/cross-platform-play-for-shah-rukh-s-superhero-flick-111100300098_1.html (accessed on 10 August 2013).

———. 2011c. '*Ra.One*All Set to Release Today on 4,600 Screens', 26 October, available at http://www.business-standard.com/article/companies/ra-one-all-set-to-release-today-on-4-600-screens-111102600043_1.html (accessed on 10 August 2013).

Box Office Capsule. 2013. 'Lifetime Worldwide Collections and Economics of *Jab Tak Hai Jaan*', Editorial, 27 January, available at http://www.boxofficecapsule.com/boxoffice-analysis.aspx?analysis_id=1074 (accessed on 5 August 2013).

Boxofficeindia.com. 2009. 'Overseas Earnings', 20 January, available at http://www.boxofficeindia.com/npages.php?page=shownews&articleid=734&nCat=news (accessed on 20 January 2009).

———. 2010. 'My Name Is Khan in Huge Demand Overseas', 9 February, available at http://www.boxofficeindia.com/npages.php?page=shownews&articleid=1503&nCat=news (accessed on 10 February 2010).

———. 2012. 'Top Overseas Grossers All Time: Three Idiots Number One', 21 January, available at http://www.boxofficeindia.com/arounddetail.php?page=shownews&articleid=3946&nCat= (accessed on 2 February 2012).

Business of Cinema. 2006. 'Yash Raj Films Launches Merchandizing Division with Fanaa', Editorial, 3 June, available at http://businessofcinema.com/bollywood-news/yash-raj-films-launches-merchandising-division-with-fanaa/15800 (accessed on 22 August 2013).

———. 2009. 'Indian Film Industry to Grow 11.6%; Touch Rs 185 bn by 2013', Editorial, 29 July, available at http://businessofcinema.com/news.php?newsid=13881 (accesssed on 31 July 2009).

———. 2011. 'Indian Film Industry to Touch Rs 136.5 billion in 2015: PwC', Editorial, 28 July, available at http://businessofcinema.com/news.php?newsid=18778 (accessed on 2 August 2011).

Chattopadhyay, Dhiman and Anusha Subramanian. 2010. 'SRK Inc.', *Business Today*, 21 February, available at http://businesstoday.intoday.in/story/srk-inc./1/5200.html (accessed on 17 August 2013).

Das, Chuman. 2009. 'Shah Rukh Khan to Walk the Ramp for Manish Malhotra', *Business of Cinema*, 27 March, available at http://businessofcinema.com/news.php?newsid=12543 (accessed on 2 May 2009).

———. 2010. 'After Aamir Khan, It's Now SRK's Turn to Promote His Forthcoming Film', 8 January, available at http://businessofcinema.com/news.php?newsid=15262 (accessed on 13 January 2010).

D'costa, Melissa. 2012. 'Shah Rukh Khan at TAG Heuer's Event', *Times of India*, 9 August, available at http://articles.timesofindia.indiatimes.com/2012-08-09/bollywood/33101891_1_tag-heuer-srk-shah-rukh-khan (accessed on 17 August 2013).

Deprez, Camille. 2010. *Bollywood: Cinéma et mondialisation*. Villeneuve d'Ascq: Presses Universitaire du Septentrion.

Deshpande, Sudhanva. 2005. 'The Consumable Hero of Globalised India', in Raminder Kaur and Ajay J. Sinha (eds), *Bollyworld: Popular Indian Cinema through a Transnational Lens*, pp. 186–203. New Delhi, Thousand Oaks, and London: SAGE Publications.

D'souza, Dipti Nagpaul. 2010. 'The Big Switch', *Indian Express*, 6 September, available at http://www.indianexpress.com/news/the-big-switch/677743/ (accessed on 13 August 2011).

Elley, Derek. 2007. 'Review: "Om Shanti Om"', *Variety*, 8 November, available at http://variety.com/2007/film/reviews/om-shanti-om-1200554687/ (accessed on 21 August 2013).

Ernst & Young Global Group. 2011. *Spotlight on India's Entertainment Economy: Seizing New Growth Opportunities*, Annual Report, available at http;//www.ey.com (accessed on 13 August 2015).

Ganti, Tejaswini (ed.). 2004. 'The Production and Distribution of Popular Hindi Cinema', in *Bollywood: A Guidebook to Popular Hindi Cinema*, pp. 53–90. New York and London: Routledge.

Ghosh, Shubham. 2013. 'After KKR, Shah Rukh Plans to Buy a Kolkata Football Club', *Oneindia*, 6 August, available at http://news.oneindia.in/2013/08/06/after-kkr-shah-rukh-khan-plans-to-buy-a-kolkata-football-club-1277052.html (accessed on 9 August 2013).

Gupta, Surajeet D., Varada Bhat, and Priyanka Joshi. 2011. 'Will He Be King Again?', *Business Standard*, 8 October, available at http://www.business-standard.com/article/beyond-business/will-he-be-king-again-111100800082_1.html (accessed on 10 August 2013).

IANS. 2008. 'Ghajini Already a Hit at Ticket Counters', *Hindustan Times*, 23 December, available at http://www.hindustantimes.com/News-Feed/Cinema/Ghajini-already-a-hit-at-ticket-counters/Article1-360114.aspx (accessed on 20 July 2013).

IBNLive.com. 2012. 'Talaash: Is Aamir Khan's Film a Hit Even Before the Release?', IBN Live, 29 November, available at http://ibnlive.in.com/news/talaash-is-aamir-khans-film-a-hit-even-before-the-release/307969-8-66.html (accessed on 20 July 2013).

IndiaGlitz. 2008. 'Berlin Film Festival Selects "Om Shanti Om" for Berlinale Special', available at http://www.indiaglitz.com/channels/hindi/article/36037.html (accessed on 28 September 2010).

Jha, Subhash K. 2002. 'Devdas Cannes Do', *Times of India*, 11 May, available at http://timesofindia.indiatimes.com/home/opinion/Devdas-Cannes-Do/articleshow/9505471.cms (accessed on 21 July 2013).

———. 2009. 'My Name Is Khan Can't Compete at Berlin', *Times of India*, 25 December, available at http://articles.timesofindia.indiatimes.com/2009-12-25/news-interviews/28105156_1_shah-rukh-khan-karan-competition-section (accessed on 10 February 2010).

Joshi, Priyanka. 2011. 'Shah Rukh Khan Gives Google+ a Leg Up', *Business Standard*, 21 October, available at http://www.business-standard.com/article/technology/shah-rukh-khan-gives-google-a-leg-up-111102100051_1.html (accessed on 10 August 2013).

Kirpalani, Neha. 2012. 'Photos: Shah Rukh Khan's Love for Kids, Launches "KidZania"', *Business of Cinema*, 21 November, available at http://businessofcinema.com/news/photos-shah-rukh-khans-love-for-kids-launches-kidzania/54080 (accessed on 24 November 2012).

Lalwani, Vickey. 2011. 'Salman Khan's Bodyguard vs Shahrukh Khan's Ra.One', *Times of India*, 31 August, available at http://articles.timesofindia.indiatimes.com/2011-08-31/news-interviews/29945564_1_salman-s-bodyguard-release-srk (accessed on 27 September 2011).

Malvania, Urvi. 2013. '*Chennai Express* Chugs into Seven New Markets', *Business Standard*, 5 August, available at http://www.business-standard.com/article/management/chennai-express-chugs-into-seven-new-markets-113080501169_1.html (accessed on 20 August 2013).

Mehta, Monika. 2005. 'Globalizing Bombay Cinema: Reproducing the Indian State and Family', *Cultural Dynamics*, 17: 135–54.

Nandy, Pritish. 2001. 'The Ashutosh Gowariker Interview', Rediff.com, 17 July, available at http://www.rediff.com/movies/2001/jul/17ash.htm (accessed on 19 August 2013).

Oneindia. 2008. 'Shahrukh "Red Chili" Khan's Idiot Box!', 6 May, available at http://entertainment.oneindia.in/bollywood/features/2008/shahrukh-red-chili-idiot-box-060508.html (accessed on 17 August 2013).

Pais, Arthur J. 2007. 'Shah Rukh Beats Tom Cruise', Rediff.com, 12 November, available at http://www.rediff.com/movies/2007/nov/12us.htm (accessed on 13 November 2007).

PTI. 2011a. 'SRK Launches Custom-Built Movie Channel for Ra.One', *Hindustan Times*, 26 September, available at http://www.hindustantimes.com/EntertainmentSection/Bollywood/SRK-launches-custom-built-movie-channel-for-RA-One/Article1-750411.aspx (accessed on 27 September 2011).

—————. 2011b. 'Ra.One Gets Rs 52-cr Promotional Push', IBNLive, 14 October, available at http://ibnlive.in.com/generalnewsfeed/news/raone-gets-rs-52cr-promotional-push/861677.html (accessed on 10 August 2013).

Sheikh, Aminah. 2006. '*Dhoom 2* Set to Make Big Splash', Rediff.com, 24 November, available at http://www.rediff.com/money/2006/nov/24dhoom.htm (accessed on 20 July 2013).

Singh, Manisha Pradhan. 2009. "*3 Idiots*" Marketing Blitzkrieg: Aamir Khan Disappears', *Business of Cinema*, 12 December, available at http://businessofcinema.com/news.php?newsid=15125 (accessed on 21 December 2009).

Srivastava, Priyanka. 2013. 'As Chennai Express Becomes the Fastest to Touch Rs. 100 Crore Mark at the Box Office, Here Is What It Takes to Deliver a Success', *India Today*, 18 August, available at http://indiatoday.intoday.in/story/as-chennai-express-becomes-the-fastest-to-touch-rs-100-cr-mark-at-the-box-office-here-is-what-it-takes-to-deliver-a-success%C3%A2%E2%82%AC%C2%A6/1/300066.html (accessed on 20 August 2013).

Thussu, Daya Kishan. 2008. 'The Globalization of "Bollywood": The Hype and the Hope', in Anandam P. Kavoori and Aswin Punathambekar (eds), *Global Bollywood*, pp. 97–113. New York and London: New York University Press.

————. 2013. 'India in the International Media Sphere', *Media, Culture & Society*, 35: 156–62.

Yount, Stacey. 2012. 'Introducing Shailja Gupta: Head of Red Chillies USA', *BollySpice*, 20 March, available at http://bollyspice.com/39248/introducing-shailja-gupta-head-of-red-chillies-usa (accessed on 24 August 2013).

Filmography

3 Idiots. Dir. Rajkumar Hirani. Vinod Chopra Productions, 2009.

Agneepath. Dir. Karan Malhotra. Dharma Productions, 2012.

Avatar. Dir. James Cameron. Twentieth Century Fox Film Corporation, 2009.

Bodyguard. Dir. Siddique. Funky Buddha Productions, 2011.

Chalte Chalte. Dir. Aziz Mirza. Dreamz Unlimited and United Motion Pictures, 2003.

Chennai Express. Dir. Rohit Shetty. Red Chillies Entertainment, 2013.

De Dana Dan. Dir. Priyadarshan. Venus Records and Tapes, 2009.

Devdas. Dir. Sanjay Leela Bhansali. Mega Bollywood, 2002.

Dhoom: 2. Dir. Sanjay Gadhvi. Yash Raj Films, 2006.

Dhoom 3. Dir. Vijay Krishna Acharya. Yash Raj Films, 2013.

Don. Dir. Farhan Akhtar. Excel Entertainment, 2006.

Ek Tha Tiger. Dir. Kabir Khan. Fantastic Films, 2012.

Ghajini. Dir. A.R. Murugadoss. Geetha Arts, 2008.

Ghar Ki Baat Hai. Dir. Anant Mahadevan, TV Series. Red Chillies Idiot Box, 2009–10.

Knights and Angels. TV Series. Red Chillies Entertainment, 2009.

Hannah Montana. TV Series. Disney Channel, 2006–11.

High School Musical. TV Series. Disney Channel, 2006–8.

Hum Aapke Hain Koun..! Dir. Sooraj R. Barjatya. Rajshri Productions, 1994.

Ishaan. TV series. Red Chillies Idiot Box, 2010.

Jab Tak Hai Jaan. Dir. Yash Chopra. Yash Raj Films, 2012.

Kaal. Dir. Soham Shah. Dharma Productions, 2005.

Krrish 3. Dir. Rakesh Roshan. Film Kraft, 2013.

Lagaan. Ashutosh Gowariker. Aamir Khan Productions, 2001.

Live My Life. TV Show. Red Chillies Entertainment, 2011.

Living with a Superstar. TV show. Red Chillies Idiot Box, 2010.

Luv Reels. TV Show. Red Chillies Idiot Box, Milestone Movies, and Kunal Kohli Production, 2010–11.

Main Hoon Na. Dir. Farah Khan. Red Chillies Entertainment, 2004.

My Name Is Khan. Dir. Karan Johar. Dharma Productions, 2010.

Om Shanti Om. Dir. Farah Khan. Red Chillies Entertainment, 2007.

Paheli. Dir. Amol Palekar. Red Chillies Entertainment, 2005.

Phir Bhi Dil Hai Hindustani. Dir. Aziz Mirza. Dreamz Unlimited, 2000.

Ra.One. Dir. Anubhav Sinha. Red Chillies Entertainment, 2011.

Student of the Year. Dir. Karan Johar. Dharma Productions, 2012.

Taare Zameen Par. Dirs Aamir Khan and Amole Gupte. Aamir Khan Productions, 2007.

Talaash. Dir. Reema Kagti. Aamir Khan Productions, 2012.

Tere Mere Beach Mein. TV Show. Red Chillies Etertainment, 2009.

The First Ladies. Dir. Amit Anand Chauhan. TV Series. Red Chillies Idiot Box, 2009–10.

The Inner and Outer World of Shah Rukh Khan. Dir. Kabir, Nasreen Munni. Documentary film for Channel 4, BBC Channel 4 and Red Chillies Entertainment, 2005.

What's Your Raashee? Dir. Ashutosh Gowariker. Ashutosh Gowariker Productions Pvt. Ltd, 2009.

Index

Bhabha, Homi K. xxiii, xxix, 203, 259, 261–3, 270, 275. *See also* third space

Bhojpuri cinema 113. *See also* Bollywood

Bilat Pherat (N.C. Lahiri, 1921) 51

Billu/Billu Barber (Priyadarshan, 2009) xiv, xxi, xxx, 6, 13–14, 16–17, 19–21, 162; film-making processes of 19

biographies xiv, 206

blogospheres 265, 268

blogs 190, 202–3, 237, 260, 264–8, 275; formation of 265

'Bobble Head Don', product 236. *See also Don 2*

Bole chudiyan, song 182. *See also Kabhi Khushi Kabhi Gham…*; Johar, Karan

Bollyrobics 240

Bollyweb 201–2, 265, 267; Mitra on 201

Bollywood dance club 191

Bollywood Hungama, website 213

Bollywood Italia, forum 260, 265–8, 274

Bollywood Legends 222–4, 227, 229, 235–6, 243, 249; doll series of 221, 235

Bollywood/Hollywood (Deepa Mehta, 2002) 100–1

bollywood: addicts/mania 240, 264; choreographies 193, 272; dance/dancers 272 xxviii, 101, 290, 294; dolls 223, 226, 229, 233, 235–6, 242; export-oriented commercial Hindi films 99; family-film formula xvii, 99. *See also* Chopra, Aditya; fandom 182, 186, 195, 230; film industry 15, 162, 268, 270–1, 273, 299,

315–16; films of xx, xxvii, 61, 99, 114, 122, 171–2, 270, 273–4, 290–1, 314–15; formations of 52; idols of 237; Italianized version of 275; in Italy 4–6, 87, 124, 135, 160, 222, 224, 259, 263–7, 269, 275; Khans of xxx; magazines 269–70; melodrama 53, 63; national identity and 102; star xxx, 53, 173, 176, 205, 234, 240, 264–5, 270–1, 274, 316

Bollywoodization 186, 226–7; of Indian cinema xii, 221. *See also* Gopal, Sangita; Moorti Sujata; Rajadhyaksha, Ashish

Bollywood-related dance academies, Peru 182

'Bollyworld' 109–10

Bombay Dreams, musical 282. *See also* Weber, Andrew Lloyd

Bombay/Mumbai 39, 43, 45, 80, 127

Bonnie and Clyde (Arthur Penn, 1967) 29

boxofficeindia.com 315–16

brand ambassador 18, 51, 76, 82, 310, 320; for TAG Heuer 149, 154, 310, 320. *See also* Brand SRK

brand persuasions 80. *See also* Wilkinson-Weber

Brand SRK xxi, 82. *See also* brand ambassador

Brave Heart Productions 170, 173

Break Hindi Cinema, blog 267

Breaking Free of the Box, username 236, 240, 242. *See also* Dollywood

Breaking Free videos 245. *See also* Task Forest

British–Bollywood hype 233

Eriksen, Thomas H., globalization xxviii
Europe, fan reception in 113
Excel Entertainment 312
exchange of a share, SRK 311

'face of a glittering new India' 268.
  See also 'modern day God'
facebook xxv, 182–3, 190, 192, 194,
  268, 289, 317. See also Twitter
family, companies 312; melodramas
  64
Fanaa, Aamir Khan in (Kunal
  Kohli, 2006) 130
fandom xx–xxi, xxv, 123, 145,
  185, 187, 189–90, 194, 205,
  214, 242; as community-based
  187–90
fans xix–xxii, xxv–xxix, 16–17,
  112, 183–96, 201–10, 212–14,
  236–40, 271–5, 288–9, 294–7;
  with African background
  xxviii; clubs xx, xxviii, 187–9,
  193, 212; of German-speaking
  countries xxi, 202–3; on
  Internet 203, 212; Italian 273;
  as mediators and culture brokers
  203; productivity xxv, 200; in
  Russia 295
feminism 146, 153; Tieber on 112
Film Cine Hindi, blog 267. See also
  Filmcinehindi.blogspot.com
film(s), consumers 187; distribution
  185, 313; industry xix, 127,
  144, 201, 293, 309, 312, 317;
  industry status to 309; making
  15, 18–19, 80, 99, 171, 244, 324;
  production 14–15, 78–9, 311,
  324–5; promotion of 77, 235,
  269, 272, 316–17, 318–19; of
  Ra.One 318; of SRK 53–5

Filmcinehindi.blogspot.com, blog
  267. See also Film Cine Hindi
Filmfare xxix, 316.
  See also Cineblitz; Stardust
Filmfare, award 146, 270; Best
  Acting Award for 2007 146
Film-makers 59, 100
Fiza (Khalid Mohamed, 2000) 128
Flickr 222, 236, 241
Fox Searchlight Pictures 315
Fox Star 122, 315
'Frame by Frame', conference 292

G.One xxiii, 44, 236, 318
Ganesh Chaturthi 83, 88–9.
  See also Bappa moriya; Don 2
Ganguly, Keya, on Satyajit Ray 143
Gauri Khan xv, 14, 17, 21, 297,
  321; brand ambassador for
  D'décor 93n25; on Malayan
  woman's lifestyle magazine 88.
  See also Chibber, Gauri
gay audiences 58. See also
  homosexuality
gaze xiv, 9, 15, 34, 85–7, 213, 238,
  242, 283, 293, 297
Gehlawat, Ajay, on Chaiyya,
  chaiyya 283–4
gender xiv, xviii, 140, 149, 154,
  161, 163, 298
German, Bollywood fandom
  112, 226. See also Europe, fan
  reception Gerritsen, Roos 212
Ghaffar Khan, Khan Abdul,
  Sarhaddi Gandhi 'Frontier
  Gandhi' 51. See also Khudai
  Khidmatgar Party
Ghai, Subhash 53, 98, 312
Ghajini (A.R. Murugadoss, 2008)
  236, 240, 314
Ghar Ki Baat Hai (2009–10) 321

web performance xxxi
Webchutney, Gurbaksh Singh
founder of 32
Weber, Andrew Lloyd, *Bombay Dreams* 282
Western, consumerism 226; crew 18; festivals 314; techniques 313, 316
What's Your Raashee (Ashutosh Gowariker, 2009) 322. *See also* Baweja, Harman
Wilkinson-Weber, Clare M. xxi
Wilson, Paige, doll artist 240–4. *See also* Baumgarten, Mabel
women empowerment 149, 153–4
World Wide Web 187, 192, 268
Wright, Neelam Sidhar 294

www.planetsrk.com xxxi. *See also* global Bollywood cinema

Xtreme Breakers, dance group 170, 174–5

Yash Raj Films (YRF) 54, 99, 312–13, 318, 322, 324
YouTube 143, 145, 196, 222, 236, 266, 295, 318

Zanjeer (Prakash Mehra, 1975) 105. *See also* Bachchan, Amitabh
Zee Carnival, London xi
Zee TV awards 289. *See also* King Khan
Zinta, Preity xvii, xxx, 6, 12, 63, 293, 323

About the Editors and Contributors

Editors

RAJINDER DUDRAH is Senior Lecturer in Screen Studies at the University of Manchester, UK. He has researched and published widely in film, media, and cultural studies in international journals. His books include, amongst others, *Bollywood Travels: Culture, Diaspora and Border Crossings in Hindi Cinema* (2012); *Bhangra: Birmingham and Beyond* (2007); *Bollywood: Sociology Goes to the Movies* (2006); *The Bollywood Reader* (with Jigna Desai, 2008); and *Theorising World Cinema* (with Lucia Nagib and Chris Perriam, 2011).

ELKE MADER is Professor of Social and Cultural Anthropology and a member of the research group Visual Studies in Social Sciences at the University of Vienna, Austria. She is currently working on a book on myth and ritual in globalized popular cinema. In the past years her main research interest has been in popular Hindi cinema, globalization, and fandom from the perspective of media anthropology. Her publications include *Stars in Your Eyes: Ritual Encounters with Shah Rukh Khan in Europe* (2011).

BERNHARD FUCHS studied European Ethnology at the University of Vienna, Austria, where he is employed since 1997. In both his MA and PhD thesis he observed the niche economy of South Asian migrants in Vienna. His main fields of research are media, migration, and cultural transfer. His recent project-participation titled 'Embedded Industries: Cultural Entrepreneurs in Different Immigrant Communities of Vienna' was published in 2009. He is now working on a book titled *Filmi Fulmi Masti: Bollywood macht glücklich! Kulturtransfer und cineastisches Vergnügen aus Sicht der Europäischen Ethnologie* (Bollywood Makes You Happy! Cultural Transfer and Cineastic Pleasure from the Perspective of European Ethnology).

Contributors

MONIA ACCIARI received her PhD from the University of Manchester, UK. She has worked as a Teaching Assistant at the University of Manchester, and as Film and Media Lecturer at Swansea University, UK. She has been a visiting scholar at Florida International University, USA in 2013 and has guest lectured in several universities in Italy, USA, and UK. She is currently at Swansea University as an Honorary Research Associate.

ANN R. DAVID is Principal Lecturer in Dance Studies at Roehampton University, London, UK. She has trained in the classical Indian dance styles of Bharatanatyam and Kathak, as well as other more popular forms of dance including Bollywood. Her research work investigates the impact of migration, of diasporic movement, and other socio-cultural factors on the lives and dance practices of British Asians in particular. She has published in many leading journals and presented at conferences all over the world.

RACHEL DWYER is Professor of Indian Cultures and Cinema at SOAS, University of London, UK. Her main research interest is Hindi cinema on which she has published extensively. Her next book is *Bollywood's India: Hindi Cinema As Guide to Modern India* which will be published in London, Chicago, and New Delhi.

KAMALA GANESH is Professor of Sociology at the University of Mumbai, India. Besides diaspora studies, she has researched and written on gender and kinship, culture and identity, and women's history. Her book *Boundary Walls: Caste and Women in a Tamil*

Community won the silver medal of the Asiatic Society and her jointly edited volume on urban heritage *Zero Point Bombay: In and Around Horniman Circle* was listed by the *Guardian* as among the 10 best books set in Mumbai.

JASPREET GILL teaches at University of York, UK, in the Faculty of Arts and Humanities. Her article 'Subaltern No More: Sikh Redemption in Khushwant Singh's *Train to Pakistan*' was published in *Subaltern Vision: A Study in Postcolonial Indian English Text*. Her research interests include the Anglo-Sikh wars, the Partition, and contemporary South Asian literature.

PETRA HIRZER is working on her PhD in the Department of Social and Cultural Anthropology at the University of Vienna, Austria. She finished her MA in the same department with a thesis on Bollywood fans in Arequipa, Peru. Her theoretical focus lies on processes of hybridization and appropriation in this field of global popular culture. She has completed ethnographic fieldwork in Peru for her PhD thesis that will be a continuation of the MA topic on an extended regional level. Her publications include *Peruanisches Masala: Hybridisierungsprozesse in der lateinamerikanischen Bollywood* (2011).

HANNA KLIEN is Lecturer at the Department of Social and Cultural Anthropology at the University of Vienna, Austria. She is working on a PhD thesis on female audiences of Hindi films in Trinidad based on ethnographic fieldwork among the Indian diaspora and Afro-Caribbeans. Her research focuses on questions of gender, imagination, and globalization. Her publications include *All Eyes on Shah Rukh! An Intercultural Approach to the Gaze in Karan Johar's Films* (2013).

KANCHANA MAHADEVAN is Professor of Philosophy at the University of Mumbai, India. She has been researching in feminist philosophy, continental philosophy, and socio-political philosophy. She has also been working in the interdisciplinary areas of Indian diaspora and film studies. Her forthcoming book *Between Femininity and Feminism: Colonial and Postcolonial Perspectives on Care* examines the relevance of Western feminist philosophy in the Indian context.

ASHISH RAJADHYAKSHA is a film studies scholar and Senior Fellow at the Centre for Studies in Culture and Society (CSCS), Bengaluru, India. He has published extensively on cinema and contemporary art and presented papers on these topics in conferences across the world. He has taught Film Studies at the University of Iowa, USA, the Korean National University of Arts, Seoul, and Birkbeck, University of London and at the British Film Institute. His books include *Indian Cinema in the Time of Celluloid: From Bollywood to the Emergency* (2009); *Encyclopaedia of Indian Cinema*, (with Paul Willemen, 1994); *The Sad and Glad of Kishore Kumar* (1988); *Ritwik Ghatak: Arguments, Stories* (with Amrit Gangar, 1987).

ARADHANA SETH is a production designer, art director, and filmmaker, and has worked extensively in various fields of the Indian and international film industry and the world of art. Among her documentaries and shorts are *A Lotus for You, A Buddha to be*; she has been consulting producer for *A Woman's Place*; director and cinematographer for *The God of Small Things*; director and principal researcher for *Invisible hands*. As production designer her work includes *West is West, Don, One Night with the King, Leela*, and *Fire*. Her work as an art director includes *The Darjeling Limited* and *The Bourne Supemacy*.

GYÖRGYI VAJDOVICH is Assistant Professor at the Institute for Art Theory and Media Studies, Department of Film Studies at Eötvös Loránd University, Budapest, Hungary. Her fields of research are adaptation and intermediality and contemporary Bollywood cinema. She is the founding editor of *Metropolis*, a quarterly on film theory and film history. Her book *A vámpírfilm alakváltozatai* (*Variants of Vampire Films*) co-authored with Zoltán Varga was published in 2009. She has published articles on Bollywood cinema in English, French, and Hungarian in various journals and books.

AMY VILLAREJO joined Cornell University, USA in 1997, after receiving her BA from Bryn Mawr College and PhD from the University of Pittsburgh, USA. She published her first book, a monograph on the 1933 film *Queen Christina* (co-authored with Marcia Landy 1995). At Cornell, she holds a joint appointment as Professor in the Department of Performing and Media Arts (of which she is currently chair) and the Feminist, Gender, and Sexuality Studies Programme (which she directed from 2004–7). She has published widely in cinema and media studies, including a book on film and cultural studies *Keyframes* (2001), on queer documentary *Lesbian Rule* (2003), and an introduction to the discipline of cinema and media studies, *Film Studies: The Basics* (2007) is currently being revised for its second edition which is yet to be published. More recently, she is co-editor with Jordana Rosenberg for a special issue of *GLQ*, titled 'Queer Studies and the Crises of Capitalism,' and is the author of a monograph on television, *Ethereal Queer* (2014).